W9-CRG-184

Excel® 2003
VISUAL™
ENCYCLOPEDIA

by Sherry Willard Kinkoph

Excel® 2003 Visual™ Encyclopedia

Published by
Wiley Publishing, Inc.
111 River Street
Hoboken, NJ 07030-5774

Published simultaneously in Canada

Library of Congress Control Number: 2006922515

ISBN-13: 978-0-471-78346-6

ISBN-10: 0-471-78346-3

Manufactured in the United States of America

10 9 8 7 6 5 4 3 2 1

Contact Us

For general information on our other products and
services please contact our Customer Care Department
within the U.S. at (800) 762-2974, outside the U.S. at
(317) 572-3993, or fax (317) 572-4002.

For technical support please visit www.wiley.com/
techsupport.

WILEY

Wiley Publishing, Inc.

Sales
Contact Wiley at (800) 762-2974 or fax (317) 572-4002.

CREDITS

Project Editor
Sarah Hellert

Acquisitions Editor
Tom Heine

Product Development Supervisor
Courtney Allen

Copy Editor
Tricia Liebig

Technical Editor
Namir Shammas

Editorial Manager
Robyn Siesky

Business Manager
Amy Knies

Manufacturing
Allan Conley
Linda Cook
Paul Gilchrist
Jennifer Guynn

**Vice President and Executive
Group Publisher**
Richard Swadley

Vice President and Publisher
Barry Pruett

Book Design
Kathie Rickard

Production Coordinator
Adrienne Martinez
Jennifer Theriot

Layout
Jennifer Click
Carrie A. Foster
Amanda Spagnuolo

Screen Artists
Ronda David-Burroughs
Cheryl Grubbs
Jill A. Proll

Illustrators
Ronda David-Burroughs
Cheryl Grubbs

Proofreader
Lisa Stiers

Quality Control
Leeann Harney
Joe Niesen

Indexer
Joan Griffitts

Director of Composition Services
Debbie Stailey

ABOUT THE AUTHOR

Sherry Willard Kinkoph has written and edited more than 70 books over the past 10 years covering a variety of computer topics ranging from hardware to software, from Microsoft Office programs to the Internet. Her recent titles include *Master VISUALLY eBay Business Kit, Teach Yourself VISUALLY Photoshop Elements 3.0,* and *Teach Yourself VISUALLY Office 2003*. Sherry's ongoing quest is to help users of all levels master the ever-changing computer technologies. No matter how many times they — the software manufacturers and hardware conglomerates — throw out a new version or upgrade, Sherry vows to be there to make sense of it all and help computer users get the most out of their machines.

DEDICATION

To my dear friends Robin and Alan Oglesby. Thank you for all your support and encouragement, and most of all, thank you for your precious friendship.

ACKNOWLEDGMENTS

Special thanks go out to publisher Barry Pruett and to acquisitions editor Tom Heine for allowing me the opportunity to tackle this exciting project; to project editor Sarah Hellert for her dedication and patience in guiding this project from start to finish; to copy editor Tricia Liebig, for ensuring that all the i's were dotted and t's were crossed; to technical editor Namir Shammas for skillfully checking each step and offering valuable input along the way; and finally to the production team at Wiley for their able efforts in creating such a visual masterpiece.

PREFACE

Do you look at the pictures in a book or newspaper before anything else on a page? Would you rather see an image instead of read about how to do something? Search no further. This book is for you. Opening *Excel 2003 Visual Encyclopedia* allows you to read less and learn more about the application.

WHO NEEDS THIS BOOK

This book is for a reader who has never used Excel. It is also for more computer literate individuals who want to expand their knowledge of the different features that Excel has to offer.

BOOK ORGANIZATION

This book has two parts, one that shows Excel's tools, and another that shows you how to further use those tools to complete a specific task. For your convenience, the tools and techniques are listed in alphabetical order and have cross references to related tools and techniques in the book.

Each tool or technique, usually contained on one or two pages, has an introduction to the task at hand, cross references to other relevant tasks, a set of full-color screen shots and steps that walk you through the task, and, for the techniques, a set of tips. This format allows you to quickly look at a topic of interest and learn it instantly.

THE CONVENTIONS IN THIS BOOK

A number of typographic and layout styles have been used throughout *Excel 2003 Visual Encyclopedia* to distinguish different types of information.

Bold

Bold type indicates text and numbers that you must type into a dialog box or window.

Italics

Italicized words introduce a new term and are followed by a definition.

Numbered Steps

You must perform the instructions in numbered steps in order to successfully complete a section and achieve the final results.

Indented Step Text

You do not have to perform these steps; they simply give additional information about a feature. Indented step text tells you what the application does in response to a numbered step. For example, if you click a certain menu command, a dialog box may appear, or a window may open. Indented step text may also present another way to perform a step.

Notes

Notes give additional information. They may describe special conditions that may occur during an operation. They may warn you of a situation that you want to avoid, for example, the loss of data.

 You can easily identify the tips in any section by looking for the TIP icon. Tips offer additional information, including tips, hints, and tricks. You can use the TIP information to go beyond what you have learned in the steps.

Table of Contents

Credits iii

About the Author iii

Dedication iv

Acknowledgments v

Introduction xvii

Part I: Tools 1

A

Add-Ins 2

Alignment 3

Audit 4

AutoCorrect 5

AutoFill 6

AutoFilter 7

Autoformat 8

AutoShapes 9

AutoSum 10

B

Bold 11

Borders 12

C

Cells 13

Chart Toolbar 14

Chart wizard 15

Clip Art 16

Column 17

Comma Style 18

Comment 19

Copy 20

Currency Style 21

Custom View 22

Customize 23

Cut 24

D

Decimal 25

Diagram 26

Drawing Tools 27

E

E-mail 28

Embed 29

Export 30

F

Fill Color 31

Find and Replace 32

Font 33

Font Color 34

Font Size 35

Format Painter 36

Formula Auditing 37

Freeze 38

Functions 39

G

Go To 40

Goal Seek 41

H

Header and Footer 42

Help 43

Hyperlink 44

I

Import 45

Indent 46

Italic 47

L

Link 48

M

Macro 49

Merge and Center 50

N

Name Box 51
New 52

O

Open 53
Organization Chart 54

P

Page Break 55
Page Setup 56
Paste 57
Percent Style 58
Picture 59
Picture Toolbar 60
Pivottable 61
Print 62
Print Preview 63
Properties 64

R

Range 65
Research Task Pane 66
Reviewing Toolbar 67
Row 68

S

Save 69
Smart Tags 70
Sort 71
Spelling 72
Split 73
Style 74
Subtotals 75
Symbol 76

T

Task Pane 77
Template 78
Text to Speech 79
Track Changes 80

U

Underline 81

Undo and Redo 82

V

View 83

W

Watch Window 84

Web Toolbar 85

Wordart 86

Z

Zoom 87

Part II: Techniques 89

A

Add-Ins: Load Add-Ins 90

Add-Ins: Use the Data Analysis Tools 92

Add-Ins: Use the Solver Add-In 94

Alignment: Align Cell Data..96

Audit: Apply Error Checking to a Worksheet...................................98

AutoCorrect: Correct Spelling Problems 102

AutoFill: Enter Data Series 104

AutoFilter: Filter Database Data...106

AutoFormat: Apply Preset Formatting...108

AutoShapes: Draw AutoShapes 110

AutoSum: Total Data with AutoSum 112

B

Borders: Add Borders to Cells 114

Borders: Draw a Border on a Worksheet.......................................116

C

Cells: Add Cells 118

Chart: Change the Chart Axes Scale 120

Chart: Change the Chart Axes Titles...122

Chart: Change the Chart Data Series...123

Chart: Change Chart Elements..124

Chart: Change the Chart Type 125

Chart: Create a Chart 126

Chart: Format Chart Elements 130

Clip Art: Download Clip Art from the Web 132

Clip Art: Format Clip Art...134

Clip Art: Insert a Clip Art Object 136

Clip Art: View Clip Art with the Clip Organizer 138

Column: Add a Column 140

Column: Delete a Column 141

Column: Hide a Column 142

Column: Resize a Column...143

Comment: Insert a Cell Comment 144

Customize: Change the Default File Location 146

Customize: Change the Default Font..147

Customize: Create a New Menu 148

Customize: Create a New Toolbar 150

Customize: Customize a Menu..152

Customize: Customize the Program Window 154

Customize: Customize a Toolbar 156

D

Data: Control Text Wrap 158

Data: Cut, Copy, and Paste Data 160

Data: Enter Dates and Times 162

Data: Rotate Data 164

Data Validation: Set Data Validation Rules 166

Database: Add Records Using a Data Form..168

Database: Add a Subtotal 170

Database: Create an Excel Database Table 172

Database: Edit Records 176

Database: Filter Records 178

Database: Sort Records 180

Decimal: Increase or Decrease Decimal Points 182

Delete: Delete Cell Contents or Formatting 184

Diagram: Insert a Diagram 186

Draw: Draw Objects 188

Draw: Draw a Text Box...190

E

E-mail: E-mail a Worksheet 192

Embed: Embed Data in a Worksheet 194

Errors: Fix Errors 196

Errors: Trace Errors 197

F

Find: Find and Replace Worksheet Data 198

Formatting: Apply Cell Formatting 200

Formatting: Apply Conditional Formatting 204

Formatting: Bold, Italics, and Underline 206

Formatting: Format Shapes, Lines, and Arrows...208

Formulas: Absolute and Relative Cell Referencing 212

Formulas: Construct a Basic Formula 214

Formulas: Copy a Formula 216

Formulas: Reference Cells from Other Worksheets 217

Freeze/Unfreeze: Freeze and Unfreeze Cells 218
Functions: Build a Basic Function 220

G
Go To: Navigate to a Cell or Range 224
Goal Seek: Analyze Values with Goal Seek 226

H
Help: Find Help with Excel 228
Hyperlink: Insert a Hyperlink 230

I
Import and Export: Import and Export Data 232
Indent: Indent Data 234

L
Line Color: Set a Line Color 236
Line Style: Set a Line Style 238
Link: Link Excel Data 240

M
Macro: Create a Macro 242
Macro: Manage Macros 244
Macro: Run a Macro 245
Margins: Set Page Margins 246
Merge and Center: Center Data Across Cells 248

N
Number Formatting: Change the Number Format Style 250

O
Objects: Add Shadow and 3-D Effects 252
Objects: Align Objects 253
Objects: Change an Object's Position 254
Objects: Delete an Object 256
Objects: Format an Object 257
Objects: Group Objects 258
Objects: Layer Objects 259
Objects: Move an Object 260
Objects: Resize an Object 261
Objects: Rotate and Flip Objects 262
Organization Chart: Insert an Organization Chart 264

P

Paste: Copy Attributes with the Paste Special Command...266

Picture: Crop a Picture 268

Picture: Format a Picture 270

Picture: Insert a Picture File 272

PivotTable: Create a PivotTable 274

PivotTable: Remove Blank Cells and Error Messages 278

PivotTable: Turn a PivotTable into a PivotChart 279

PivotTable: Update a PivotTable 280

Print: Add Headers and Footers...282

Print: Change Page Orientation..284

Print: Define a Print Area 285

Print: Insert a Page Break...286

Print: Preview Page Breaks...287

Print: Preview a Web Page..288

Print: Preview a Worksheet 289

Print: Print a Workbook or Worksheet..290

Print: Repeat Row or Column Headings 291

Print: Set Printing Options..292

Properties: Assign File Properties...294

Protection: Assign a Workbook Password 296

Protection: Assign a Worksheet Password..298

R

Range: Name a Range 300

Research: Use the Research Task Pane...302

Row: Add a Row 304

Row: Delete a Row 305

Row: Hide a Row..306

Row: Resize a Row 307

S

Save: Save a File to a Default Location 308

Save: Save a Workbook...310

Save: Save a Worksheet as a Web Page...312

Scenario: Create a What-If Scenario 314

Search: Conduct a File Search 318

Select: Select Worksheet Cells 320

Smart Tags: Work with Smart Tags 322

Sort: Perform a Sort 324

Spelling: Spell Check a Worksheet 326

Style: Create a Style 328

Symbol: Insert a Symbol...330

T

Task Pane: Work with Task Panes...332

Template: Apply a Template..334

Template: Create a Workbook Template 336

Text to Speech: Read Back Worksheet Cells 338

Toolbars: Display and Hide Toolbars 340

Track and Review: Keep Track of Workbook Changes...........................342

Track and Review: Merge Workbooks 346

U

Undo and Redo: Use the Undo and Redo Commands 348

V

View: Change Worksheet Views..350

View: Create a Custom View 352

W

Watch Window: Add a Watch Window 354

Web Query: Run a Web Query 356

Web Toolbar: Use the Web Toolbar Tools 360

WordArt: Insert a WordArt Object 362

Workbook: Arrange Workbook Windows 364

Workbook: Compare Workbooks 366

Workbook: Create a New Workbook 367

Workbook: Delete a Workbook 368

Workbook: Open a Workbook 369

Workbook: Open a Workbook Automatically 370

Workbook: Share Workbooks 372

Worksheet: Add a Sheet...374

Worksheet: Change Sheet Tab Colors 375

Worksheet: Change the Worksheet Background....................................376

Worksheet: Copy a Sheet 377

Worksheet: Delete a Sheet 378

Worksheet: Hide a Sheet 379

Worksheet: Move a Sheet...380

Worksheet: Name a Sheet 381

Worksheet: Protect a Sheet 382

Worksheet: Show or Hide Gridlines 384

Worksheet: Split a Sheet 385

Z

Zoom: Change the View Magnification 386

Appendix A

Chart: Understanding Excel Charts 388

Appendix B

Formulas: Operator Precedence 390

Formulas: Operators 391

Formulas: Understanding Formulas 392

Functions: Common Excel Functions 394

Appendix C

Keyboard Shortcuts: Apply Keyboard Shortcuts 396

Appendix D

Workspace: Navigate the Excel Workspace 398

Index 402

INTRODUCTION

Microsoft Excel is the most popular spreadsheet program available on the market today. Excel features an easy-to-use interface and numerous tools and commands for entering, editing, and graphing data. Whether you are building complex spreadsheets to perform mathematical calculations, tracking an inventory database, or simply figuring out a loan, Excel can help you turn even the most tedious spreadsheet tasks into effortless endeavors and produce just the results you need. You can use Excel to keep track of all kinds of data and crunch numbers. The program features powerful built-in formulas and functions you can use to produce a myriad of calculation types, ranging from basic mathematical operations to complex engineering and scientific functions.

Resembling an accounting spreadsheet, Excel makes it easy to organize and manipulate data. Once you build a worksheet, you can apply formatting attributes to make the data more presentable. You can also reorganize the data using Excel's filtering and sorting tools. You can tap into Excel's charting tools to turn your data into easy-to-read charts and graphs you can present to others. With a little know-how and practice, you can soon turn your spreadsheets into powerful workbook files that make your data work for you.

Excel 2003 Visual Encyclopedia is divided into two parts.

Part I is a comprehensive A to Z reference of Excel tools. Tools can be icons found in palettes, panes, or toolbars. Tools can also be specific commands accessed from the menu bar. A named dialog box, window, or panel that is used to accomplish a specific task can also be a tool.

Part II is an alphabetical reference of Excel techniques, including basic operations as well as advanced, solutions-based effects. Techniques represent final results from an operation that may involve the use of one or more tools.

Sherry Willard Kinkoph

Fishers, Indiana, 2006

Excel 2003 Visual Encyclopedia

Part I: Tools

Microsoft Excel offers a wide variety of tools you can use to perform all kinds of worksheet tasks and mathematical calculations on your workbook data. In this part of the book, you find a thorough A to Z listing of available tools you can use to create and format spreadsheets, and manipulate your worksheet data. Using this section of the book, you can look up a tool to learn more about its function and location in the Excel program window.

You can find Excel's many tools scattered across a variety of toolbars and menus.

In many cases, tools and commands are duplicated in several places. For example, you can find basic formatting tools on Excel's Formatting toolbar as well as in the Format Cells dialog box, which is accessed through the Format menu.

You can also use the right-click method to quickly summon a menu and select from tools and commands related to the task at hand. For example, if you right-click a cell, Excel displays a shortcut menu of commands related to the data, such as formatting commands and actions like Cut, Copy, and Paste.

You can use Excel's add-in programs to add more efficiency and tools to your worksheet projects and tasks. For example, you can use the Analysis ToolPak add-in to install functions geared toward engineering and statistical calculations, or you can install the Solver add-in to use a step-by-step wizard to evaluate formulas for goal-seeking values.

By default, Excel does not install add-ins until requested. Excel prompts you to insert the Excel CD when attempting to use an add-in. You can also find more add-ins to download and install on your computer from the Microsoft Office Web site. You can even conduct a Web search for a variety of add-in programs created by third-party sources and download them for use with Excel.

After you install an add-in, you must activate it using the Add-Ins dialog box. Excel then adds the feature to the Tools or Data menus. For example, when you install and activate the Solver add-in, Excel adds the Solver command to the Tools menu. You can turn add-ins on or off using the Add-Ins dialog box.

See also>> Add-Ins

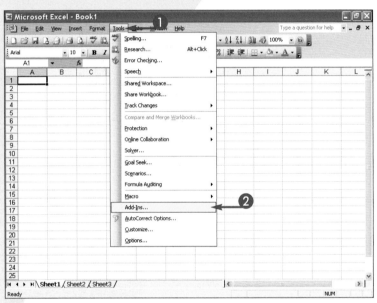

1 Click Tools.

2 Click Add-Ins.

The Add-Ins dialog box opens. You can use this dialog box to install or uninstall specific add-ins.

ALIGNMENT

Excel offers a variety of options for controlling the positioning of data and other objects you place in your worksheet cells. These positioning controls, called *alignment* commands, can help you adjust the data to best suit the appearance of your worksheet.

For example, you might want to center all the text in a column or align all number data to the left in a group of cells. You can use the Center alignment command to center text, or apply the Align Left command to make data align to the left of a cell.

By default, Excel automatically aligns text data to the left and number data to the right. You can use the alignment buttons on the Formatting toolbar

to control the horizontal alignment of data. Horizontal alignment includes left, center, and right alignments.

Data is also aligned vertically to sit at the bottom of the cell. You can change horizontal and vertical alignments to improve the appearance of your worksheet data. For example, you may prefer to center data both vertically and horizontally in a cell. For additional horizontal alignment options, you must use the Format Cells dialog box.

See also>> **Alignment**

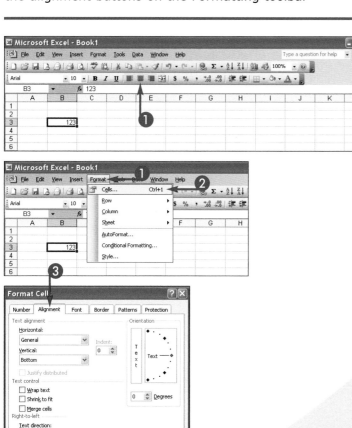

Alignment Buttons

❶ Click an alignment button on the Formatting toolbar.

Click Align Left (≣) to align data to the left.

Click Center (≣) to center align data.

Click Align Right (≣) to align data to the right.

Alignment Options

❶ Click Format.

❷ Click Cells.

The Format Cells dialog box opens.

❸ Click the Alignment tab to select alignment options.

AUDIT

You can use Excel's error checking tools to help you with errors that arise in your worksheets. When dealing with larger worksheets in Excel, it is not always easy to find the source of a formula error when scrolling through the many cells. You can utilize Excel's Formula Auditing toolbar which includes several tools for examining and correcting formula errors.

You can use the Formula Auditing toolbar to run Excel's Error Checking feature, trace errors, trace precedents and dependents, insert cell comments, evaluate formulas, check validation rules, and more. For example, when you activate the Error Checking feature, Excel scans your worksheet for errors and

helps you find solutions by graphically showing you each problem reference. You can check formula problems one at a time.

When checking a worksheet for formula problems, the Error Checking feature looks for errors such as references to empty cells, incorrect references, and inconsistent references. Error checking also evaluates the error value for incorrect arguments, numbers entered as text data, and date values entered as ambiguous text dates.

See also>> | **Audit**

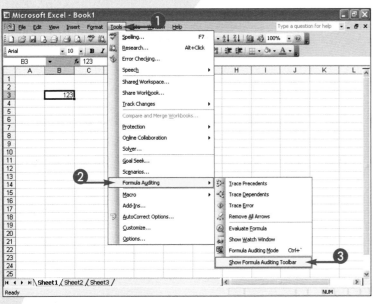

❶ Click Tools.

❷ Click Formula Auditing.

❸ Click Show Formula Auditing Toolbar.

Excel displays the Formula Auditing toolbar where you can access the various error-checking tools.

AUTOCORRECT

You can use Excel's AutoCorrect feature to quickly correct text you commonly misspell when typing in your worksheet data. AutoCorrect is turned on by default. You may have already noticed the AutoCorrect feature at work as you type in a worksheet. The corrections this feature makes are performed automatically. For example, if you type "teh" instead of "the" or "adn" instead of "and," AutoCorrect automatically fixes the mistake for you. The correction occurs as soon as you press the spacebar after typing a word.

AutoCorrect comes with a list of preset misspellings; however, the list is not comprehensive. To speed up your own text entry tasks, consider adding your own problem words to the list. For example, if you find yourself continually misspelling the same term, you can add the word to the AutoCorrect dictionary. The next time you mistype the word, AutoCorrect automatically fixes the mistake for you.

See also>> **AutoCorrect**

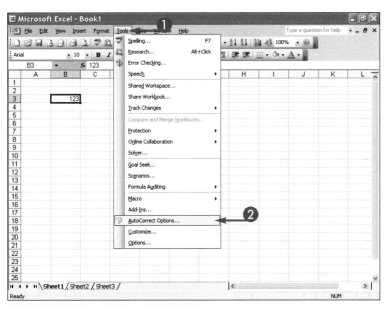

❶ Click Tools.

❷ Click AutoCorrect Options.

The AutoCorrect dialog box opens with the AutoCorrect tab displayed. You can use the options in this dialog box to view, add, and delete words to the list of entries.

AUTOFILL

You can use Excel's AutoFill feature to help you automate data entry tasks. You can use AutoFill to add duplicate entries or a data series to your worksheet cells, such as labels for Monday, Tuesday, Wednesday, and so on. For example, rather than type in column headings such as Quarter 1, Quarter 2, and so on across the top of a worksheet, you can type in the first column label and use AutoFill to fill in the rest. AutoFill automatically duplicates the label and adjusts the numbers sequentially.

You can also use AutoFill to enter duplicate data, such as the same row heading or number data across

a row or down a column. You can create your own custom data lists as well as utilize built-in lists of common entries — such as days of the week, months, and number series. You can also use AutoFill to copy formulas across cells.

When you activate a cell in a worksheet, a small fill handle appears in the lower-right corner of the selector. You can use the fill handle to create an AutoFill series.

See also>> **AutoFill**

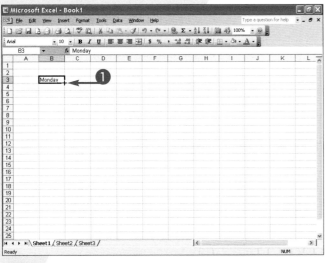

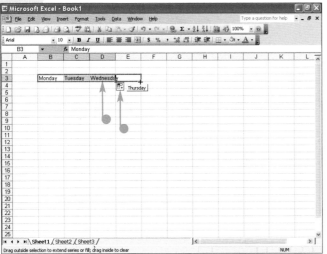

① Click and drag the cell's fill handle (+) across or down the number of cells you want to fill.

● AutoFill fills in the series in every cell you drag over.

● An AutoFill smart tag may appear offering additional options you can assign to the data.

AUTOFILTER

You can use Excel's AutoFilter feature to view only portions of your data. This feature is very useful when using Excel to create and manage database lists. For example, if you use Excel to create a list to manage sales contacts, inventory, or household valuables, for example, you can then use the AutoFilter feature to quickly view only select portions of your database list.

Unlike a sort, which sorts the entire table, a filter selects certain records to display based on your criteria, while hiding the other records that do not match the criteria. When you apply a filter, you

can specify which field to filter in the list. Excel automatically assigns drop-down filter arrows for each column heading, allowing you to apply multiple filter criteria to your list.

When applying a filter, you can choose from several filter options, including a Top 10 option for filtering database records that are a top 10 value or are in the top percent.

See also>>   **AutoFilter**

Database

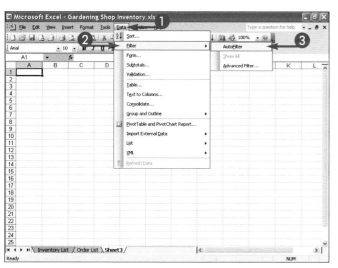

① Click Data.

② Click Filter.

③ Click AutoFilter.

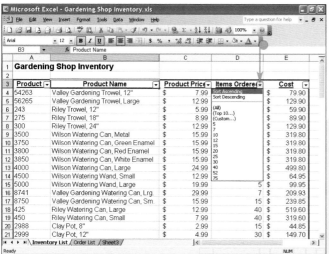

● Excel adds drop-down arrow buttons to your field labels so you can filter your data.

AUTOFORMAT

Presentation goes a long way in helping your intended audience read and interpret your spreadsheet data. Number data is especially difficult to examine, so taking time to make the data readable is an important part of creating a worksheet. If you prefer not to spend a lot of time worrying about how your data looks, AutoFormat is the tool for you.

You can use Excel's AutoFormat feature to apply preset formatting styles to your worksheet data. AutoFormat offers 16 different preset styles you can choose from, and each one creates a different look

for your worksheet. Styles include accounting styles, list styles, color styles, and 3-D styles.

The AutoFormat dialog box shows a preview of what each style looks like. The preset styles include formatting for numbers, font, font sizes, alignment, borders, and cell background colors. You can choose a preset style as-is, or fine-tune it to suit the needs of your worksheet.

See also>>

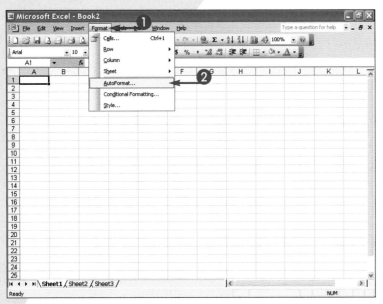

① Click Format.

② Click AutoFormat.

The AutoFormat dialog box opens. You can use this dialog box to select from a variety of preset formats.

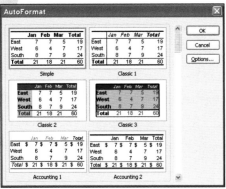

AUTOSHAPES

You can use Excel's AutoShapes feature to draw your own shapes and graphics to illustrate your worksheets. You can choose from a library of predrawn shapes in the AutoShapes palette. You can access the AutoShapes palette through Excel's Drawing toolbar. The palette includes categories for lines, arrows, basic shapes, callouts, connectors, and more. Each category includes a list of objects you can draw. For example, the Basic Shapes category lists shapes such as triangles and hexagons, while the Block Arrows category lists a variety of arrow shapes and types you can draw on your worksheet.

After you select a shape, you can control the size and position of the shape as you draw on the worksheet. After completing the shape, you can continue to move it and resize it as needed.

The Drawing toolbar also includes tools for controlling the color and thickness of the lines and shapes you draw. You can apply formatting to drawn objects after you draw the shape on the worksheet.

See also>>

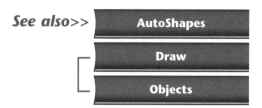

AutoShapes

Draw

Objects

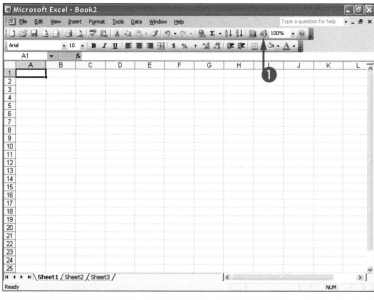

① Click the Drawing button on the Standard toolbar.

You can also click View, Toolbars, and then Drawing.

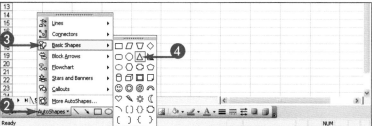

The Drawing toolbar appears at the bottom of the program window.

② Click the AutoShapes button.

③ Click an AutoShape category.

④ Click an AutoShape.

You can now draw the shape on the worksheet.

Σ AUTOSUM

You can use the AutoSum tool to speed up common mathematical tasks. AutoSum is just one of Excel's many functions. Functions are simply built-in formulas you can apply to your data.

AutoSum automatically totals the contents of cells. For example, you can quickly total a column of sales figures or a row of test scores. AutoSum works by guessing which surrounding cells you want to total, or you can specify exactly which cells to sum.

Because AutoSum is one of the most popular functions available in Excel, the AutoSum button is on the Standard toolbar for easy access.

If you prefer to apply another function instead of the Sum function, you can click the button's drop-down arrow and select another common Excel function to apply, such as AVG, COUNT, MAX, or MIN.

See also>>

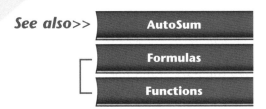

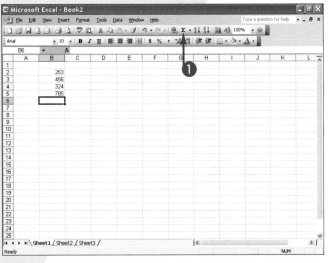

① Click the AutoSum button on the Standard toolbar.

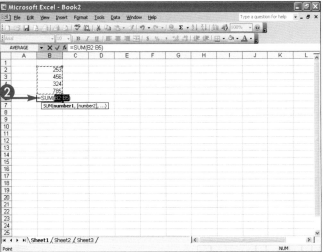

② Press Enter.

AutoSum immediately totals the adjacent cells.

B BOLD

You can apply Excel's many formatting controls to change the appearance of data in a worksheet. One of the quickest and easiest ways to add formatting to your worksheet data is to apply bold formatting. By bolding certain portions of your worksheet data, you can draw attention to a title or important numerical data. For example, you may want to apply bold to one cell in the middle of a range to make the data stand out, or you might want to bold a row of headings running across the top of your worksheet.

You can quickly assign bold formatting using the Bold button on the Formatting toolbar. Bold, italics, and underlining are common formatting characteristics found throughout most word processing, spreadsheet, graphics, and

presentation programs. Like Excel, most programs place buttons for these characteristics in an easy-to-locate toolbar.

You can also use the Format Cells dialog box to apply bold formatting to your cells. Although the Bold toolbar button is a faster method of applying bold, you may prefer to apply several formatting attributes all at once. In this case, the Format Cells dialog box offers a one-stop location for applying multiple formatting commands.

See also>> 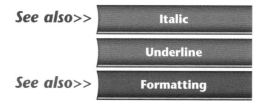 Italic

Underline

See also>> Formatting

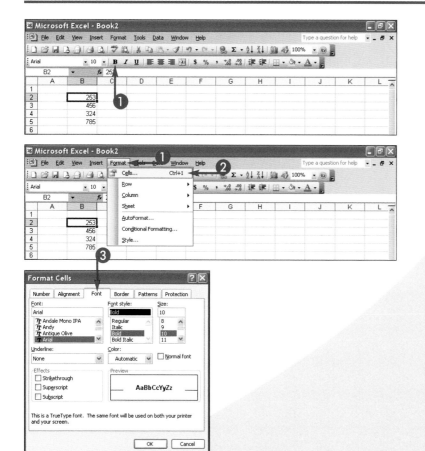

Use the Bold Button

1 Click the Bold button on the Formatting toolbar.

Excel immediately applies the formatting to the data.

Use the Format Cells Dialog Box

1 Click Format.

2 Click Cells.

The Format Cells dialog box opens.

3 Click the Font tab to view the bold formatting option.

BORDERS

You can add borders to your worksheet cells to help define the content or more clearly separate the data from surrounding cells. By default, Excel displays a grid format to help you enter data, but the borders defining the grid do not print.

You can add borders to emphasize cells. You can add borders to all four sides of a cell, or choose to add borders to just one or two sides. Any borders you add to the sheet print along with the worksheet data.

You can use the Borders button on the Formatting toolbar to quickly assign a variety of border types to a cell or range, including borders for each side of a cell and several different border styles. For example, you can choose to add a border only on the outside perimeter of a group of cells, or add borders to all the inner cells. You can also use the Format Cells dialog box to assign and customize borders.

See also>>　　　Borders

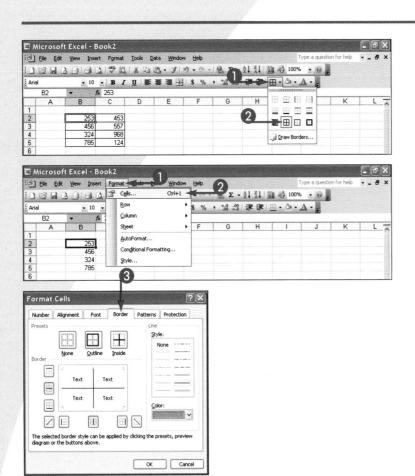

Use the Borders Button

1 Click the Borders button.

2 Click a border style.

Excel immediately assigns the border style to the cell.

Use the Format Cells Dialog Box

1 Click Format.

2 Click Cells.

The Format Cells dialog box opens.

3 Click the Border tab to view the border formatting options.

CELLS

C

Every intersection of a column and row creates a cell in an Excel worksheet. *Cells* are the receptacles for all your Excel data. Every cell has a unique name, also called an *address* or *cell reference*, in the Excel worksheet. Cell names consist of the column and row number, always listing the column first. For example, cell A1 is the first cell in the worksheet. The next cell to the right is B1.

The active cell in a worksheet is always surrounded by a highlighted border, called the *selector*. The Name box, located on the far left side of the Formula bar, always displays the name of the current cell.

You can work with groups of cells in a worksheet, called *ranges*. A range is simply a rectangular

grouping of related cells that you can connect in a column, row, or combination of columns and rows.

You can add and delete cells by inserting or removing columns and rows in your worksheet. You can also clear the contents of your cells at any time.

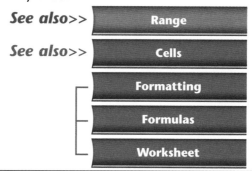

See also>> Range

See also>> Cells

Formatting

Formulas

Worksheet

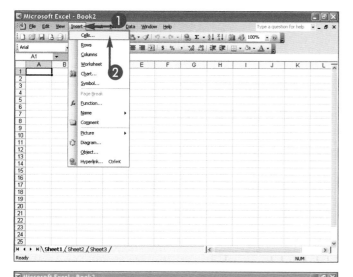

① Click Insert.

② Click Cells.

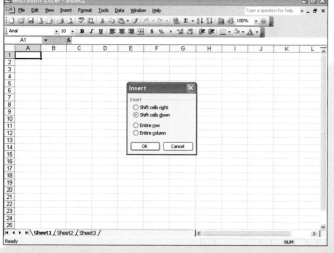

The Insert dialog box appears where you can insert cells.

CHART TOOLBAR

You can use the Chart toolbar to quickly access commands related to editing and adding to your Excel charts. Charts are a great way to give your numerical data instant visual appeal. You can use Excel's Chart Wizard tool to quickly create all types of charts, including pie charts, bar charts, and linear charts.

After you create a chart, you can make changes to the various chart elements, change the chart type, and format the chart data using tools found on the Chart toolbar. For example, you can display or hide a legend to your chart using the Legend button, or you

can change the angle of your chart text using the Angle buttons.

When you create a chart using the Chart Wizard, the Chart toolbar appears automatically. The toolbar also appears whenever you select a chart. You can close the toolbar when you are finished making your chart edits. When the toolbar is closed, you can use the View menu to access the toolbar again.

See also>>  **Chart Wizard**

See also>> **Chart**

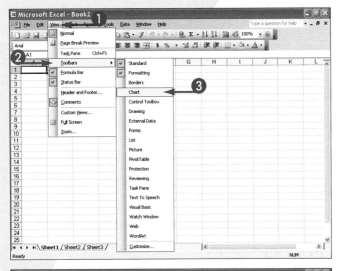

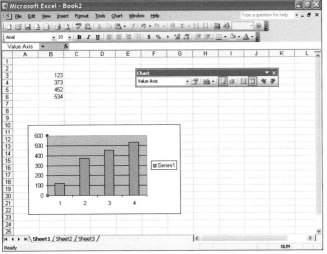

❶ Click View.

❷ Click Toolbars.

❸ Click Chart.

You can also click a chart to display the toolbar.

Excel displays the Chart toolbar.

CHART WIZARD

You can use the Chart Wizard to quickly assemble and create all kinds of charts in Excel. Charts can turn your worksheet data into a striking visual representation for others to view. Whether it is falling or rising sales, or actual costs compared to projected costs, charts make it easy for others to interpret and understand your data.

The Chart Wizard walks you through each step for creating charts, including selecting the chart type and data range, and specifying a location for the chart. You can determine exactly which type of chart works best for your data.

When creating a chart, you can choose to insert your chart on the current worksheet, or place it on a new sheet in your workbook. After you complete the Chart Wizard, Excel adds the chart to the designated location and displays a Chart toolbar you can use to fine-tune your chart.

See also>>  Chart Toolbar

See also>> Chart

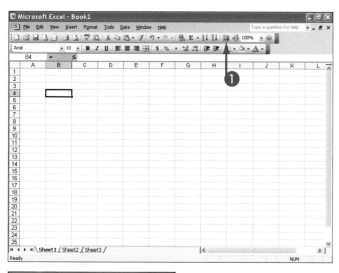

① Click the Chart Wizard button on the Standard toolbar.

You can also click Insert and then Chart.

The first Chart Wizard dialog box opens where you can step through the process for building and inserting a chart.

CLIP ART

You can add visual interest to your worksheets by inserting clip art images. *Clip art* is simply pre-drawn artwork. Excel installs with the Microsoft Office clip art collection. The collection includes a variety of categories, such as academic, business, and industry. For example, you may want to insert a graphic of currency or other monies onto your sales spreadsheet. You can look for clip art matching a specific keyword or keywords. You can peruse from any matching results and insert the clip art that best suits your spreadsheet message.

The Clip Art task pane includes tools for searching for specific types of clip art from the Office collection, including clip art graphics, photographs, movie files,

and sound files. You can also use the task pane to look through other collections installed on your computer.

If you cannot find a clip art image matching the needs of your worksheet, you can look for more clip art on the Web using the Clip Art task pane.

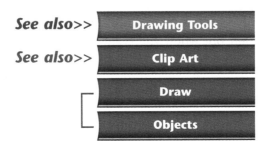

See also>> Drawing Tools

See also>> Clip Art

Draw

Objects

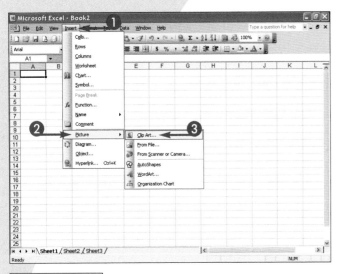

1 Click Insert.

2 Click Picture.

3 Click Clip Art.

You can also click the Insert Clip Art button on the Drawing toolbar.

The Clip Art task pane opens where you can search for and insert a clip art image.

⛛ COLUMN

C

Worksheets are formatted as a grid of columns and rows. Each worksheet is comprised of 256 columns and 65,536 rows. Every column and row has a unique identifier. Columns are labeled by alphabetical letters, while rows are numbered.

You can add columns to your worksheets to add more data. For example, you may need to add a column in the middle of several existing columns to add data you left out when you created the workbook.

You can also delete columns you no longer need in the worksheet. For example, you might remove a column of out-of-date data. When you delete an entire column, Excel also deletes any existing data within the selected cells.

You can also hide columns in your worksheets to help you with a variety of scenarios. For example, you might hide a column to prevent the data from appearing on a printout. When you hide a column, Excel simply collapses it in the worksheet so the data is no longer in view.

You can use the Insert menu to add columns to your worksheets. You can use the Format menu to access commands for adding, deleting, and hiding columns. You can also right-click over a column header to access column-related commands.

See also>>

Rows

Column

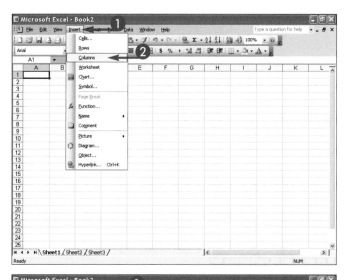

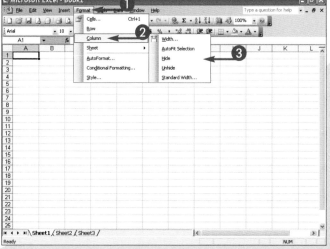

Use the Insert Menu

① Click Insert.

② Click Columns.

Excel immediately adds a column to the selected area in the worksheet.

Use the Format Menu

① Click Format.

② Click Column.

③ Click a command to apply.

Depending on the command you select, an additional dialog box may open with more options to specify.

17

COMMA STYLE

You can use number formatting to control the appearance of numerical data in your worksheet. For example, if you have a column of numbers that require commas, you can apply the Comma Style number formatting.

Excel offers 12 different number categories, or styles, from which to choose, including the Comma Style. The top three styles are available as buttons on the Formatting toolbar. You can click the Comma Style, Currency Style, or Percent Style buttons to quickly apply the designated number format to your Excel data. When you apply number formatting to data, the formatting only affects numeric values in the cell or range. Text data remains unaffected.

You can also use the Format Cells dialog box to assign any of the number styles and make adjustments to the appearance of the numeric formatting.

See also>>

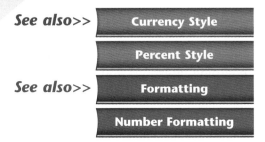

Currency Style

Percent Style

See also>>

Formatting

Number Formatting

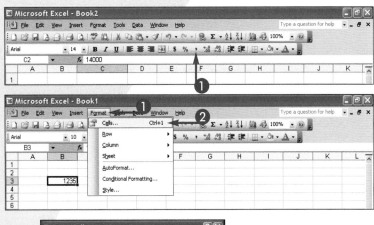

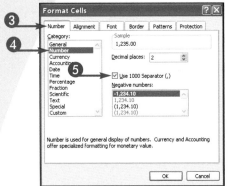

Use the Comma Style Button

1 Click the Comma Style button on the Formatting toolbar.

Excel applies commas to your number data.

Use the Format Cells Dialog Box

1 Click Format.

2 Click Cells.

The Format Cells dialog box opens.

3 Click the Number tab to view the number formatting options.

4 Click the Number category.

5 Select the option to use a comma as a thousands separator.

COMMENT

You can add comments to your worksheets to make a note to yourself about a particular cell's contents, or as a note for other users to see. For example, if you share your workbooks with other users, you can add comments to leave feedback about the data without typing directly in the worksheet.

For example, you might use a comment to leave yourself a note regarding questions you have about a formula or data, or you might insert a comment to remind yourself to check a figure at a later time.

Excel marks any cell with a comment assigned with a tiny red triangle in the corner of the cell. To view the comment, you can simply move the mouse pointer over the cell. Excel displays comments in a balloon. You can add and delete comments as needed throughout your worksheet.

See also>>

Comment

Track and Review

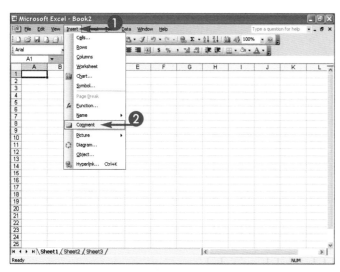

① Click Insert.

② Click Comment.

You can also right-click the cell and click Insert Comment.

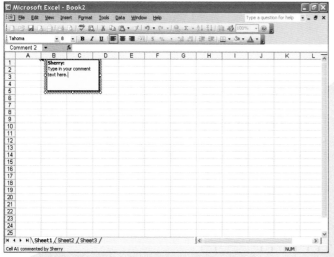

A comment balloon appears where you can type your comment text.

COPY

You can use the Cut, Copy, and Paste commands to copy data within Excel, or move and share data between other Microsoft Office programs. For example, you might cut a row of labels and paste them into another worksheet, or copy a formula from one cell to another cell in the same worksheet.

The Copy command makes a duplicate of the selected data, while the Cut command removes the data from the original file entirely. When you copy or paste data, it is placed in the Windows Clipboard until you are ready to paste it into place.

You can find quick access to the Cut, Copy, and Paste commands through the buttons on the Standard

toolbar. You can also access the Copy command through the Edit menu. In addition, you can also drag and drop data to copy it within a worksheet as long as you press and hold the Ctrl key while dragging.

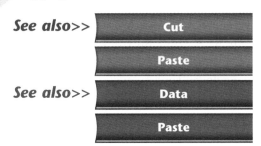

See also>> Cut

Paste

See also>> Data

Paste

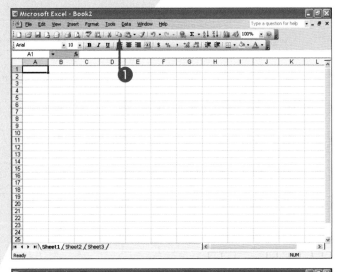

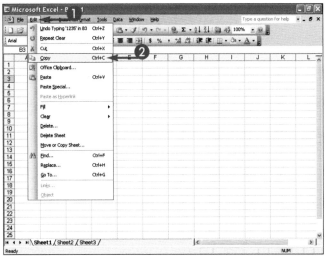

Use the Copy Button

① Click the Copy button on the Standard toolbar.

Excel copies the selected data to the Clipboard. You can then paste it to a specific area of the worksheet or workbook.

You can also press Ctrl+C to copy data.

Use the Edit Menu

① Click Edit.

② Click Copy.

Excel copies the selected data to the Clipboard. You can then paste it to a specific area of the worksheet or workbook.

CURRENCY STYLE

You can use number formatting in Excel to control the appearance of numerical data in your worksheet. For example, if you have a range of numbers that require dollar signs, you can apply the Currency Style number formatting.

Currency Style is just one of 12 different number categories, or styles, you can apply. The top three styles are available as buttons on the Formatting toolbar. You can click the Comma Style, Currency Style, or Percent Style buttons to quickly apply the designated number format to your Excel data. When you apply number formatting to data, the formatting only affects numeric values in the cell or range. Text data remains unaffected.

You can also use the Format Cells dialog box to assign any of the number styles and make adjustments to the appearance of the numeric formatting.

See also>>

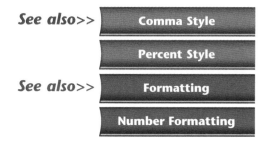

Comma Style

Percent Style

See also>>

Formatting

Number Formatting

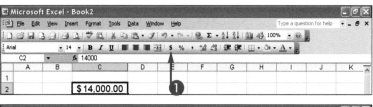

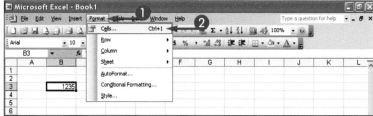

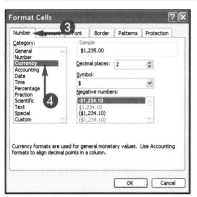

Use the Currency Style Button

1 Click the Currency Style button on the Formatting toolbar.

Excel applies dollar signs to your number data.

Use the Format Cells Dialog Box

1 Click Format.

2 Click Cells.

The Format Cells dialog box opens.

3 Click the Number tab to view the number formatting options.

4 Click the Currency category to view options for adding dollar signs to your numbers.

CUSTOM VIEW

If you have a large Excel spreadsheet and find yourself constantly searching for multiple cells, you can use Excel's Custom View feature to help you view the information you want. A custom view is similar to a style, but rather than save all the formatting you want to reuse, you save all the view attributes you want to apply into one collection. You can use a custom view to store window attributes, including split screens and hidden rows and columns.

You can use the Custom View feature to save the appearance of a worksheet, including all the view and print settings assigned to the workbook. For example, if you use AutoFilter to view portions of your Excel database list, you can save a filtered view as a custom view. If you filter the list in two or three ways, you can save each as a custom view, making it easy to return to the filtered data.

You can use the Custom View dialog box to assign a view a name and store it for future use.

See also>>   Views

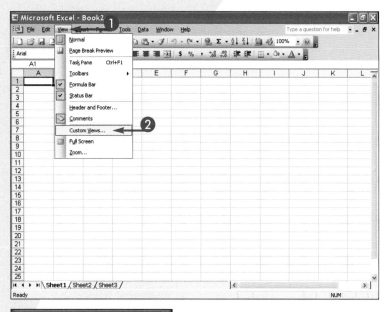

1 Click View.

2 Click Custom Views.

The Custom Views dialog box appears where you can add a new custom view.

CUSTOMIZE

You can use a variety of customizing options in Excel to customize the Excel program window to look just the way you want and to customize the way the program works. For example, you may want to turn off any toolbars or scrollbars you find unnecessary, or change the color of the worksheet gridlines.

The Options dialog box offers all kinds of options for customizing Excel. For example, you can find settings for changing the appearance of the program window, turning off the default startup task pane, hiding the Formula bar, and more.

You can use the Customize dialog box to edit Excel's toolbars and menus. When you activate the dialog box, Excel displays the program menus and toolbars in edit mode, allowing you to make changes to existing menus and toolbars as well as add new ones. You can customize existing toolbars and menus, or create new ones to suit the way you work.

See also>> **Customize**

Use the Options Dialog Box

1 Click Tools.

2 Click Options.

The Options dialog box appears where you can use the various tabs to turn Excel options on or off, or customize how the program works.

Use the Customize Dialog Box

1 Click Tools.

2 Click Customize.

The Customize dialog box appears where you can use the various tabs to customize the way in which toolbars and menus work in Excel.

CUT

You can use the Cut command in Excel to move data around a worksheet or workbook. The Cut command is one of three powerful tools you can use to copy data within Excel, or move and share data between other Microsoft Office programs. For example, you might cut a row of labels and paste them into another worksheet, or cut a formula from one cell to move it to another cell in the same worksheet.

The Cut command removes the data from the original file entirely, while the Copy command duplicates the selected data. When you copy or paste data, it is placed in the Windows Clipboard until you are ready to paste it into place.

You can find quick access to the Cut, Copy, and Paste commands through the buttons on the Standard toolbar. You can also access the Cut command through the Edit menu. In addition, you can drag and drop data to move it within a worksheet.

See also>>

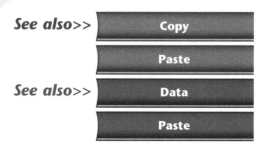

| Copy |
| Paste |

See also>>

| Data |
| Paste |

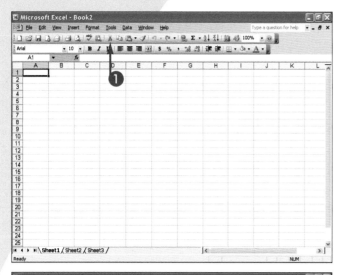

Use the Cut Button

① Click the Cut button on the Standard toolbar.

Excel cuts the data and places it in the Clipboard. You can then paste it to a specific area of the worksheet or workbook.

You can also press Ctrl+X to cut data.

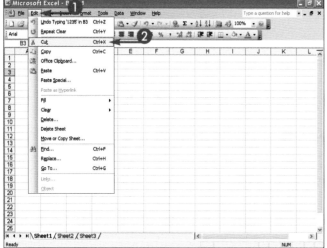

Use the Edit Menu

① Click Edit.

② Click Cut.

Excel cuts the data to the Clipboard. You can then paste it to a specific area of the worksheet or workbook, if desired.

DECIMAL

You can control the number of decimals that appear with numeric data using the Increase Decimal and Decrease Decimal commands. For example, you may want to increase the number of decimals shown in a cell, or reduce the number of decimals in a formula result.

The quickest way to add or subtract decimals is to use the Increase Decimal or Decrease Decimal buttons found on the Formatting toolbar. If you click the Increase Decimal button, Excel adds one decimal point to the selected cell or range. Click the button again to insert another decimal point. You can continue clicking the decimal buttons as many times as you need to achieve the desired results.

You can also use the Format Cells dialog box to control decimals. By applying the Number category as the format style, you can control the number of decimals, add a thousands separator, and designate how negative numbers appear in the worksheet.

See also>>

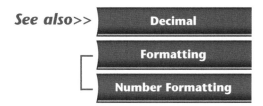

Decimal

Formatting

Number Formatting

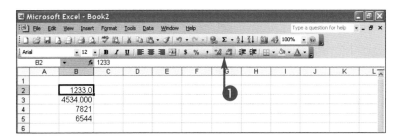

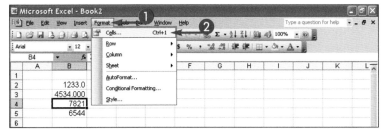

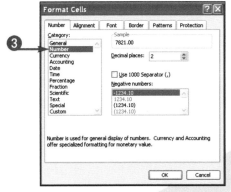

Use the Decimal Buttons

① Click a decimal button.

Click Increase Decimal (🔢) to increase the number of decimals.

Click Decrease Decimal (🔢) to decrease the number of decimals.

Excel adjusts the number of decimals showing in the cell or cells.

Use the Format Cells Dialog Box

① Click Format.

② Click Cells.

The Format Cells dialog box opens.

③ Click the Number category to set any decimal configurations.

DIAGRAM

You can use the Microsoft Office diagram feature to create all kinds of diagrams to illustrate concepts and processes on your worksheets. Diagrams are simply charts composed of individual shapes that link to form a hierarchical tree or flow diagram. For example, you might insert a hierarchical diagram in a worksheet to show the positioning of various employees in your company, or you might use a cycle diagram to show workflow in your department.

To create a diagram, you can use a drawing space, called a canvas, and add shapes to create the diagram elements. You can add as many shapes as you need to complete your diagram.

Within each shape, you can add the name or title of a person or process and format the text any way you like. You can also control the formatting of the shape itself, including the border and fill color. You can use the Organization Chart toolbar to help you format and add to your diagram.

See also>>   **Organization Chart**

See also>>   **Diagram**

Organization Chart

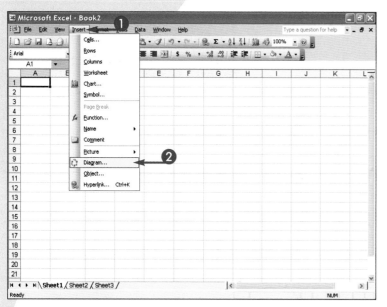

① Click Insert.

② Click Diagram.

You can also click the Insert Diagram button (⬚) on the Drawing toolbar, if that toolbar is visible.

The Diagram Gallery dialog box opens where you can choose the type of diagram you want to create.

DRAWING TOOLS

You can use Excel's many drawing tools to create your own illustrations for your worksheets. You can also use the drawing tools to control the formatting for any objects you draw or place on a worksheet, including clip art, WordArt, and more.

The Drawing toolbar contains a variety of tools you can use to create shapes, lines, and arrows, and format the objects you draw. For example, you can draw ovals, rectangles, lines, and arrows to illustrate parts of your worksheet. You can use AutoShapes to create a variety of specialty shapes. You can combine shapes with text boxes to create your own logos or other special illustrations.

After you add drawings to your worksheet, you can change the fill or line color, add 3-D or shadow effects, or change the thickness of the lines. The Drawing toolbar also offers commands for controlling positioning of any objects you draw, such as layering controls, grouping controls, alignment, and rotation controls.

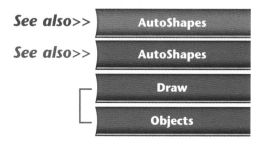

See also>> AutoShapes

See also>> AutoShapes

Draw

Objects

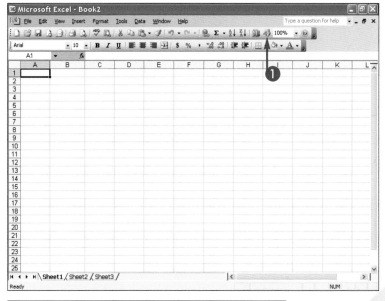

① Click the Drawing button on the Standard toolbar.

You can also click View, Toolbars, and then Drawing.

The Drawing toolbar appears at the bottom of the Excel program window.

E-MAIL

You can use the E-mail feature to e-mail a workbook without leaving the Excel program window. If you use Microsoft Outlook or Outlook Express as your e-mail editor, you can tap into the program's features to insert e-mail addresses and send your Excel data. For example, you might want to send a workbook to a colleague for review or send a sales report to your corporate headquarters.

When e-mailing Excel data, you can choose to send the entire workbook as a file attachment, or send a

selected range or worksheet as a message. If you elect to send an attachment, the data is sent as a separate workbook file the user can save and open. When you send the data as a message, the Excel data appears in the message body text.

Be sure you are logged onto your Internet account before sending an e-mail message from Excel.

See also>> E-mail

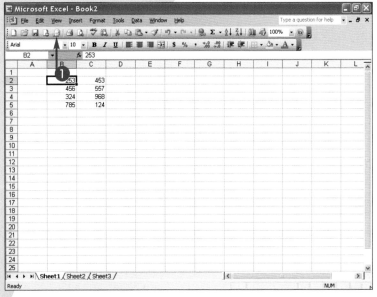

① Click the E-mail button on the Standard toolbar.

You can also click File and then click Send To and Mail Recipient.

If e-mailing as an attachment, the E-mail dialog box appears. You can choose whether you want to send the workbook as an attachment or in the message body.

EMBED

You can use the Embed command to embed objects in your worksheets. You can use embedded objects to share data between Excel files or between other programs. For example, you might embed a Word document or an Access table in your Excel worksheet. Excel's embedding feature is based on the *OLE* data-sharing protocol, which stands for Object Linking and Embedding.

With embedded data, you can edit the embedded object without leaving the destination program. Unlike linked data, which retains a direct link with the source data, embedded objects only retain a connection with the source program, not the source data. If the source object changes, the embedded object remains the same.

For example, you can embed multimedia files, such as an audio or video clip, into your worksheet to accompany a chart. Any time you need to make changes to the embedded file, you can do so without opening the source program directly. With OLE, you can access the source program's controls to make your edits from within the Excel program window.

See also>> **Link**

See also>> **Embed**

Link

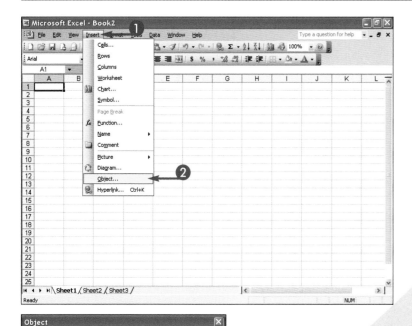

❶ Click Insert.

❷ Click Object.

The Object dialog box opens where you can specify the type of item you want to embed.

EXPORT

You can use the Save As dialog box to export your Excel data into other file formats. This option allows you to share your Excel data as different file types other users can access. For example, you might save your workbook as a text file to send to someone who does not use Excel or export your data as a 1-2-3 file for someone who uses the Lotus spreadsheet program.

The Save As dialog box offers more than 30 file formats you can export to, including older versions of Excel, Macintosh, Quattro Pro, and dBASE. If you do not see the format you want to export to, you may find a converter for the file type on the Internet. When installed, the file type is added to Excel's list.

For many of the formats, you can only convert the current sheet displayed in the workbook. In some

instances, your exported data may produce unexpected results. For example, any passwords assigned to a worksheet can cause problems in programs other than Excel, and the file may not open. Some data, such as formulas, may not convert properly into other file formats. Any features or formatting unique to the Excel program are not exported either.

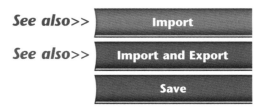

See also>> **Import**

See also>> **Import and Export**

Save

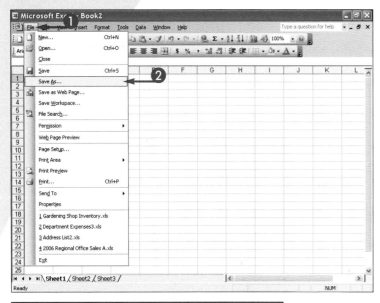

① Click File.

② Click Save As.

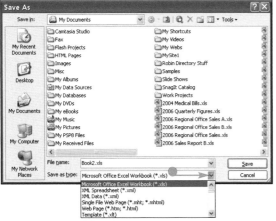

The Save As dialog box opens.

● You can use the Save as Type drop-down arrow to export the file as a specific file type.

FILL COLOR

You can change the fill color of an object or a cell using the Fill Color button. A *fill* is simply a color or pattern that fills the background of an object. For example, you can select a fill color to fill the background of a cell or fill the interior of a shape you draw using Excel's drawing tools.

By default, Excel assigns no color to a cell or shape until you specify a color choice. You can choose a fill from any of the colors available on the color palette. When applying a fill to a cell, you can choose from 40 colors. When applying a fill to an object, such as a shape, you can access additional color options through the Colors dialog

box. You can undo a fill at any time by selecting the No Fill option in the color palette menu.

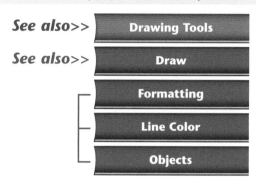

See also>> Drawing Tools

See also>> Draw

Formatting

Line Color

Objects

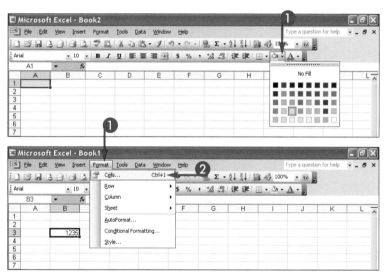

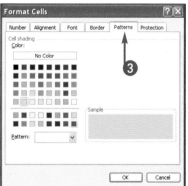

Use the Fill Color Button

1 Click the Fill Color button drop-down arrow.

You can also click the Fill button on the Drawing toolbar, if it is open.

Excel reveals a color palette.

Use the Format Cells Dialog Box

1 Click Format.

2 Click Cells.

The Format Cells dialog box opens.

3 Click the Patterns tab to view and set additional color and pattern options.

FIND AND REPLACE

You can use Excel's Find tool to search through your spreadsheets for a particular word or phrase, or to look for specific numeric data. You can use the Replace tool to replace instances of a word or data with other data. For example, you may need to look through a long spreadsheet for a particular product name and replace it with a new name. Or you may need to locate all the references to a department name.

You can use the Find and Replace dialog box to search through your spreadsheet. The dialog box features two tabs, one for conducting a search for

data, and the other for searching and replacing data. You can click the Options button in either tab to view additional search options you can apply, such as searching by rows or columns, searching for formulas or comments, or searching for case-sensitive data.

After you start a search, the Find and Replace dialog box remains open so you can continue searching or replacing data.

See also>> 　　　　**Find**

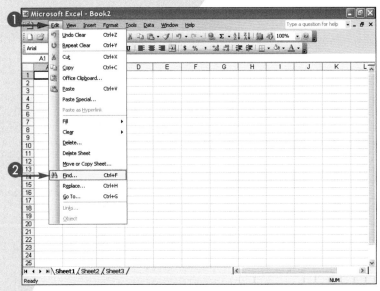

① Click Edit.

② Click Find or Replace.

The Find and Replace dialog box appears. You can use the Find and Replace tabs to look for specific data in your worksheet.

FONT

You can control the font you use for your worksheet data. A *font*, also called a typeface, is simply a set of letters, numbers, and other special characters that all share a similar look. By default, Excel assigns Arial as the font for every new workbook you create. Each time you click a cell and enter data, the Arial font is applied. You can change the font to suit your own needs. For example, you might prefer a different font for all the column headings in your spreadsheet, or a bold font for the title text of a worksheet.

The quickest way to change the font for a selected cell is to use the Font drop-down menu list on the

Formatting toolbar. The list shows all the available fonts installed on your computer.

You can also assign fonts using the Format Cells dialog box. The Font tab offers access to the full font list as well as other formatting controls, such as styles and sizes.

See also>>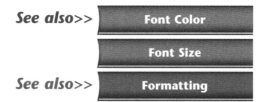

Font Color

Font Size

See also>> Formatting

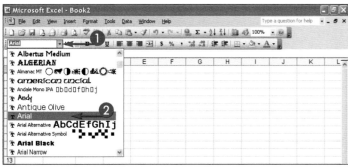

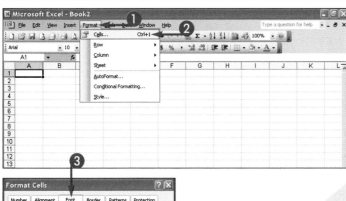

Use the Font Button

1. Click the Font drop-down arrow on the Formatting toolbar.

2. Choose a font from the list, and Excel immediately applies it to the selected data.

Use the Format Cells Dialog Box

1. Click Format.

2. Click Cells.

The Format Cells dialog box opens.

3. Click the Font tab to select from the list of available fonts.

33

FONT COLOR

You can change the color of your worksheet data using the Font Color command. For example, you may want to set the title of a worksheet in a different font color from the remaining data to give it an aesthetically pleasing appearance. Or you might change the font color for numeric data in the middle of a table to make the data stand out from the rest of the cells.

By default, Excel assigns black as the font color for every new workbook you create. You can use the Font Color button on the Formatting toolbar to quickly assign a new color to selected data in your

worksheet. When activated, a color palette of 40 color swatches appears for you to choose from.

You can also use the Format Cells dialog box to apply color to your worksheet data. In addition, you can also find the Font Color button on the Drawing toolbar.

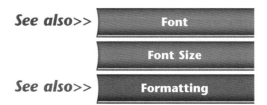

See also>> Font

See also>> Font Size

See also>> Formatting

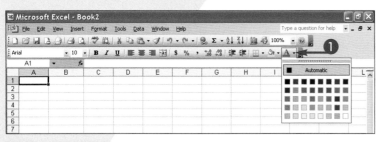

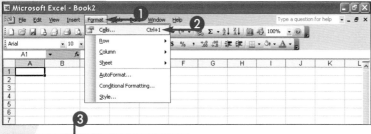

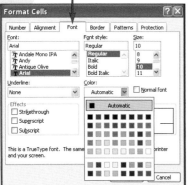

Use the Font Color Button

❶ Click the Font Color drop-down arrow on the Formatting toolbar.

You can choose a color from the color palette to apply.

Use the Format Cells Dialog Box

❶ Click Format.

❷ Click Cells.

The Format Cells dialog box opens.

❸ Click the Font tab and activate the Color drop-down arrow to assign a new color.

FONT SIZE

F

You can change the font size to change the appearance of text in a worksheet. For example, you can increase title text to appear larger than the other text in your spreadsheet. Font sizes are measured in points. By default, Excel applies a 10-point size to every new workbook you create.

The quickest way to change the font size for a selected cell is to use the Font Size drop-down menu list on the Formatting toolbar. The list shows a variety of sizes you can apply. You can also assign fonts using the Format Cells dialog box. The Font tab offers access to all the sizes as

well as other formatting controls, such as fonts and styles.

When setting different sizes for your data, always consider the legibility of the document. If you set the font size too small, the data becomes difficult to read. This is especially true for spreadsheets, which typically contain rows and rows of data.

See also>> Font

Font Color

See also>> Formatting

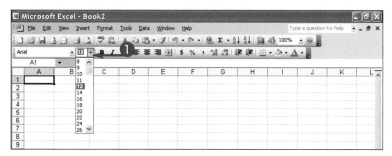

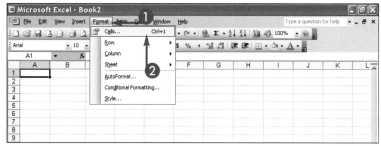

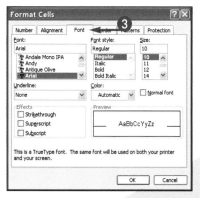

Use the Font Size Button

1 Click the Font Size drop-down arrow on the Formatting toolbar.

You can choose a font size from the list and Excel immediately applies it to the selected data.

Use the Format Cells Dialog Box

1 Click Format.

2 Click Cells.

The Format Cells dialog box opens.

3 Click the Font tab to select from the list of available sizes.

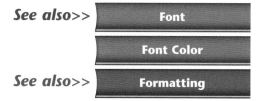

35

FORMAT PAINTER

You can use Excel's Format Painter feature to copy formatting to other data in your spreadsheet. For example, perhaps you applied a variety of formatting to a cell to create a certain look. When you want to re-create the same look elsewhere in the worksheet, you do not have to repeat the same steps you applied to assign the original formatting. Instead, you can paint the formatting to the other data in one action.

Painting with the Format Painter feature involves dragging over the data you want to format. Before applying the tool, first select the data containing the formatting you want to copy. Any data you drag over after activating the tool is immediately formatted.

If you need to keep copying formatting to several cells or ranges, you can double-click the Format Painter button to keep the tool active for as long as you need it.

See also>> **Formatting**

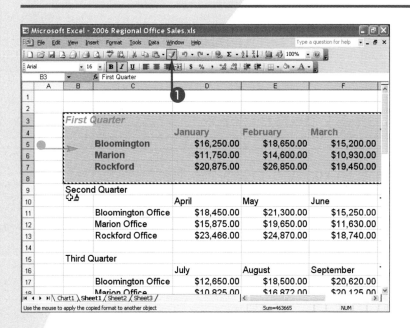

1 Click the Format Painter button on the Formatting toolbar.

● You can now drag over the data to which you want to copy formatting.

Did You Know?
To keep the Format Painter turned on for additional painting actions, simply double-click the Format Painter button. You can also use the Format Painter tool to copy column widths. To do so, click the column heading containing the width you want to copy, click the Format Painter button, and then click the column heading you want to copy the width to. Excel then copies the width.

FORMULA AUDITING

You can use Excel's Formula Auditing toolbar to help you with errors that arise in your worksheets. The toolbar includes several tools for examining and correcting formula errors. For example, you can use the toolbar to run Excel's Error Checking feature, trace errors, trace precedents and dependents, insert cell comments, evaluate formulas, check validation rules, and more.

The larger your worksheets, the harder it is to determine the source of formula errors, especially when you have to scroll through many cells. The Error Checking feature scans your worksheet for errors and helps you find solutions by graphically showing you each problem reference. You can

check formula problems one at a time using the Error Checking feature, and Excel highlights each problem in the worksheet. The Error Checking feature looks for errors such as references to empty cells, incorrect references, and inconsistent references. Error checking also evaluates the error value for incorrect arguments, numbers entered as text data, and date values entered as ambiguous text dates.

See also>>

Audit

Errors

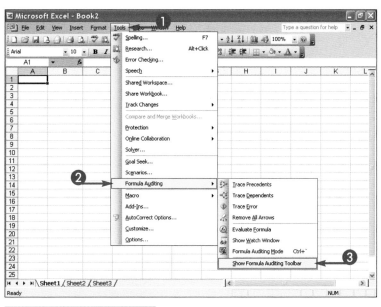

① Click Tools.

② Click Formula Auditing.

③ Click Show Formula Auditing Toolbar.

Excel displays the Formula Auditing toolbar. You can choose from the auditing tools to help with spreadsheet errors.

FREEZE

You can use Excel's Freeze command to freeze a column or row. This allows you to keep the labels in view as you scroll through larger worksheets. For example, if you are working in a long worksheet, you can freeze the column labels or titles so the information is always in view as you add more data to the cells at the bottom of the worksheet.

When you apply the Freeze command, Excel creates two panes in your worksheet, depending on where you activate the command. The area you freeze is non-scrollable, while the unfrozen areas of the worksheet are still scrollable.

To lock rows, always select the row below where you want the freeze to appear. To lock columns, select

the column to the right of where you want the freeze to appear. To lock both rows and columns, simply click the cell below and to the right of the area you want to freeze.

When you finish working with the data, you can apply the unfreeze command to make the entire worksheet scrollable again.

See also>>

See also>>	**Split**
	Freeze/Unfreeze
	Worksheet

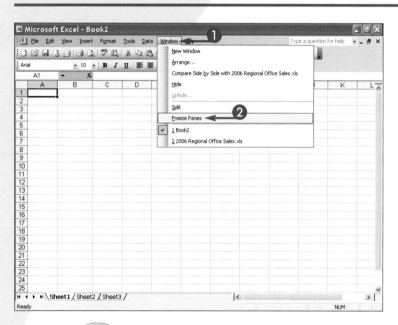

1 Click Window.

2 Click Freeze Panes.

Excel freezes the areas above the spot in the worksheet where you applied the Freeze Panes command.

TIP

Did You Know?

If you want to keep a single cell in view no matter where you scroll in the worksheet, you can use Excel's Watch Window instead of freezing panes. The Watch Window allows you to keep a cell or range in view at all times by displaying the cell in a separate window. To create a Watch Window, click the cell and then click Tools, Formula Auditing, and Show Watch Window. When the Watch Window opens, click the Add Watch button and add the cell or range to the window. To learn more about this feature, see the technique "Watch Window: Add a Watch Window."

🖋 FUNCTIONS

You can tap into a wide variety of built-in formulas, called *functions*, as a speedier way to enter formulas into your Excel spreadsheets. Functions are ready-made formulas that perform a series of operations on a specified range of values. Excel offers more than 300 functions you can use to perform mathematical calculations on your worksheet data.

You can use the Insert Function dialog box to look for a particular function from Excel's 10 function categories. Because functions are formulas, all functions must start with an equal sign (=). Functions are also distinct in that each one has a name. For example, the function that sums data

is called the SUM function, while the function for averaging values is called AVERAGE. Although you can type functions directly into your worksheet cells or use the Formula bar, you may find it easier to use the Insert Function dialog box to help construct functions. After selecting a function, you can then apply the function to a cell or range of cells in your worksheet.

See also>>

Formulas

Functions

① Click the Insert Function button on the Formula bar.

You can also click Insert and then Function.

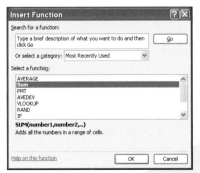

Excel displays the Insert Function dialog box where you can begin by choosing a function to apply.

GO TO

You can use the Go To command to quickly locate any cell or named range in your worksheet. The Go To tool is just one of several techniques you can use to navigate around your Excel worksheets. The longer the length of your worksheet, the more difficult it is to find the cell you are looking for — scrolling through rows and columns can be tedious. The Go To command can speed up the search. You can start your cell search at any point in the worksheet, or you can activate the Go To command from the beginning of the worksheet.

You can also use the Go To Special dialog box to locate and select cells that meet specific conditions.

For example, you can quickly locate all the cells in your worksheet that contain a specific type of data, such as all cells containing comments or formulas. You can also locate cells that meet criteria, such as the last cell in the worksheet that contains formatting or all the cells that are blank.

See also>> Range

See also>> Go To

Range

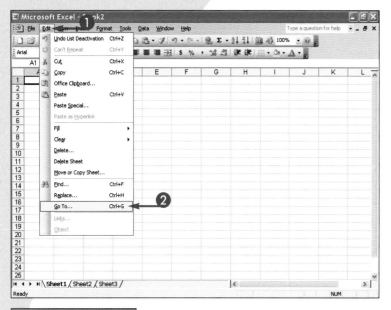

① Click Edit.

② Click Go To.

You can also press Ctrl+G or F5 at any time to summon the Go To dialog box.

The Go To dialog box opens. You can designate a cell reference or range name here.

GOAL SEEK

Excel offers several "what-if" analysis tools you can use in your worksheet data. For example, you can use Excel's Goal Seek tool to work backward to a desired result and analyze what happens when you change values along the way. If you are trying to calculate how much you can afford to spend each month on a new car purchase, Goal Seek can help you determine the loan amount for just such a goal.

You can also use Goal Seek to help you solve single variable equations of any kind. One of the

most popular uses of Goal Seek is figuring out all kinds of loan amounts and payments. You can also use Goal Seek to help figure out how much you need to sell to reach a sales goal or how many units you have to sell to break even.

See also>>   **Add-Ins**

See also>>   **Add-Ins**

Goal Seek

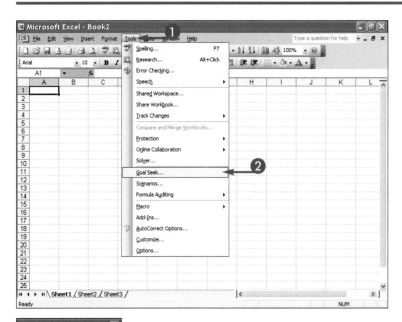

① Click Tools.

② Click Goal Seek.

The Goal Seek dialog box opens. You can assign values and references to reach the goal value.

HEADER AND FOOTER

When preparing to print a workbook, you should consider printing headers and footers on the printouts. You can use headers and footers to add text that appears at the top or bottom of every worksheet page. Headers and footers are useful for making sure every page prints with a page number, document title, author name, or date. Header text appears at the top of the page outside the text margin. Footers appear at the bottom of the page.

Headers and footers are built with *fields*, which are holding places for information that updates — such

as page numbers or dates. The Page Setup dialog box includes several preset header and footer styles you can choose from. You can also create custom headers and footers, such as a special title field. You cannot view headers or footers in the worksheet window. To view header and footer text, switch to Page Break Layout view.

See also>>   **Print**

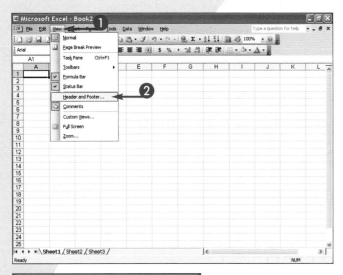

❶ Click View.

❷ Click Header and Footer.

The Page Setup dialog box opens to the Header/Footer tab where you can add your own header and footer text.

HELP

You can find help with Excel problems or questions about the program using the Help tools. The Help tools can assist you when you run into a problem or need more explanation about a particular task. The Help pane offers tools for searching topics you want to learn more about. You can choose to view the entire table of contents, or conduct a search for a particular keyword or Excel feature. With an Internet connection, you can use Microsoft's online help files to access additional articles and information about Excel features.

Excel's Help topics are arranged in a table of contents, which breaks the topics into categories — such as Printing and Workbooks and Worksheets — and numerous subtopics, such as Printer Setup. When you expand any particular category or subtopic, you can view individual Help topics. When you choose a specific topic, a separate Help window opens revealing information about the topic.

See also>>  Task Pane

See also>> Task Pane

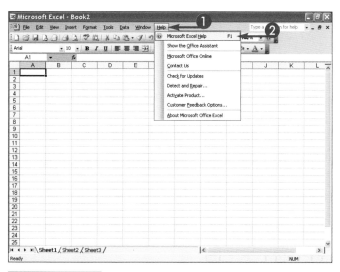

① Click Help.

② Click Microsoft Excel Help.

The Excel Help pane opens. You can use the pane to look through Help topics or search for a specific term.

HYPERLINK

You can use Excel's Insert Hyperlink command to insert hyperlinks into your worksheets that, when clicked, open a Web page. You can designate cell data as a link, or turn a graphic object into a link, such as a chart or AutoShape.

For example, you may turn a column heading into a link that, when clicked, opens a Web page detailing information about the subject. Every page on the Web has a unique address. When linking to a Web page, you must designate that address, which is the URL or Uniform Resource Locator. If you know a page's URL, you can view it on the Internet. You can also view pages using links. Hyperlinks, called links for short, connect pages through embedded URLs presented as text or images on a page. Users can jump from one page to another by clicking links.

You can also use hyperlinks to link to other files on your computer. You must designate the address or path of the page you want to link to when adding links to a worksheet.

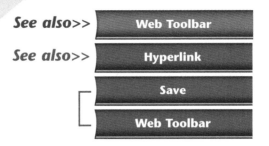

See also>> Web Toolbar

See also>> Hyperlink

Save

Web Toolbar

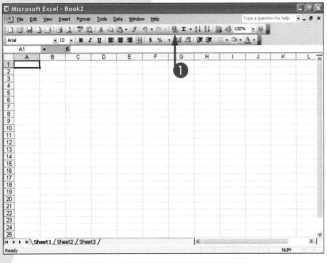

1 Click the Insert Hyperlink button on the Standard toolbar.

You can also click Insert and then Hyperlink.

The Insert Hyperlink dialog box appears where you can specify a link address.

IMPORT

You can use Excel's Import External Data command to input data from other sources into your Excel worksheet. For example, you can import text files and database and Web queries. After you import the data, you can use Excel's tools and features to perform calculations and other tasks on the data.

Excel's Import feature is particularly useful if you want to analyze data you previously typed into another file type. You can import the data into Excel rather than retyping it. Excel considers any data stored outside Excel as *external data*.

You can use the Select Data Source dialog box to specify the type of data you want to import into Excel. If you need to import data from a remote location, such as a database on a Web server, you can activate the Data Connection Wizard to step through the import procedure.

See also>> **Export**

See also>> **Import and Export**

Save

---

① Click Data.

② Click Import External Data.

③ Click Import Data.

The Select Data Source dialog box opens for you to select the file you want to import.

 INDENT

You can use Excel's Indent controls to direct the horizontal positioning of data within your worksheet cells and to help improve the appearance of your data. You can use the Increase Indent and Decrease Indent commands to quickly change the positioning of data from the left and right edges of the cell. For example, if a cell contains a paragraph of text, you can indent the entire block of text to help set it apart from surrounding cells.

You can use the Increase Indent and Decrease Indent buttons on the Formatting toolbar to quickly set an indent for a cell or range. The Increase Indent button, when clicked, inserts the width of one character to create the indent. When you activate the command more than once, you can continue to increase the amount of indent. If you click the Decrease Indent command, it decreases the indent by one character width every time the command is applied. You can also control horizontal indents using the Format Cells dialog box.

See also>>

Formatting

Margins

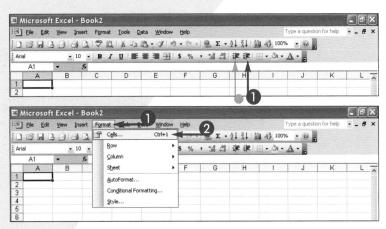

Use the Increase Indent Button

① Click the Increase Indent button on the Formatting toolbar.

● To decrease an indent, click the Decrease Indent button.

Excel indents the data.

Use the Format Cells Dialog Box

① Click Format.

② Click Cells.

The Format Cells dialog box opens.

③ Click the Alignment tab to view indent options.

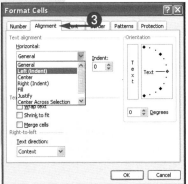

ITALIC

A quick way to add emphasis to a cell or word is to italicize the data. For example, you may want to apply italics to one cell in the middle of a worksheet to make the data stand out, or you might want to italicize a column of row headings running down the side of your worksheet to make them easier to distinguish from other columns.

The Italic command is just one of three basic formatting commands you can find throughout the Microsoft Office programs. You can assign italic formatting with a single click using the Italic button on the Formatting toolbar. Bold, italics, and underlining are common formatting characteristics found throughout most word processing, spreadsheet, graphics, and presentation programs. You can also use the Format Cells dialog box to apply italic formatting to your cells.

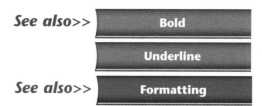

See also>>   **Bold**

See also>>   **Underline**

Formatting

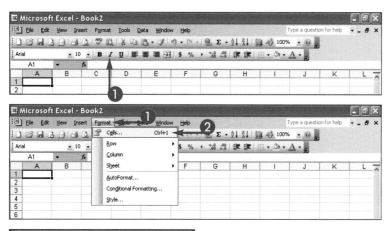

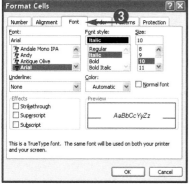

Use the Italic Button

① Click the Italic button on the Formatting toolbar.

Excel immediately applies the formatting to the data.

Use the Format Cells Dialog Box

① Click Format.

② Click Cells.

The Format Cells dialog box opens.

③ Click the Font tab to view the italic formatting options.

 # LINK

You can link data between cells, worksheets, and workbooks using Excel's OLE data-sharing protocol. OLE stands for Object Linking and Embedding. Ordinarily when you copy data, the data does not retain any connection to its source. With linking, the data retains a connection to its source, and any changes you make to the source data are immediately reflected in the linked data.

You can use linking to share data between Excel files or between other programs. You can also link data between worksheets or cells in the same worksheet or workbook. In the case of linked cells in the same worksheet, any changes you make to the source cells are immediately reflected in the destination cells.

Before applying the linking feature, first copy the data or object you want to link. Next, you can open the Paste Special dialog box and control how the linking is applied. You can also use the Insert Object dialog box to link objects in Excel; for example, you can link other files to your worksheet.

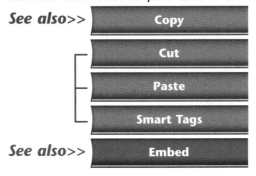

See also>> Copy

See also>> Embed

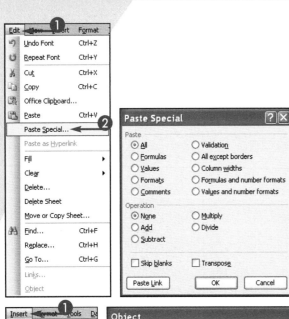

Link with the Paste Special Command

❶ Click Edit.

❷ Click Paste Special.

The Paste Special dialog box opens where you can specify options for linking your data.

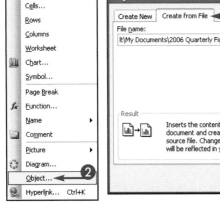
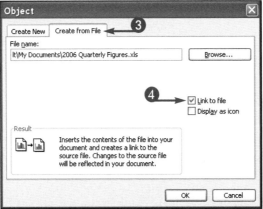

Link with the Insert Object Dialog Box

❶ Click Insert.

❷ Click Object.

The Insert Object dialog box opens.

❸ Click the Create from File tab.

❹ You can navigate to the file you want to link and activate the Link to File option to create the link.

 MACRO

You can use macros to automate the tasks you perform in Excel. A *macro* is simply a set of instructions, much like a computer program, that Excel follows in the sequence you designate. Macros are especially helpful with repetitive tasks you commonly execute. For example, you can create a macro to apply formatting, assign a formula, or print sheets. After you record a macro, Excel saves the actions so you can reuse the macro again and again.

The easiest way to create a macro in Excel is to use the macro recorder. When you use the

recorder, Excel records each action you take, including menu commands and keyboard presses. You can assign a keyboard shortcut key to your macro and activate the macro at any time using the keyboard.

You can use the Macro dialog box to manage your Excel macros. The Macro dialog box lists all the macros assigned to a workbook.

See also>> | **Macro** |

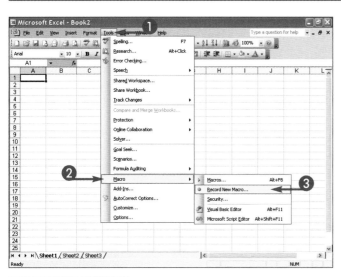

① Click Tools.

② Click Macro.

③ Click Record New Macro.

The Record Macro dialog box opens where you can specify a new macro to record.

MERGE AND CENTER

You can use the Merge and Center command to quickly create merged cells in your worksheets. Merging cells allows you to create a larger cell in the midst of the other worksheet cells. You can use the larger cell to contain labels, titles, images, and other data you want to set apart in your worksheet. For example, you can use this command to help you center a title or heading across a range of cells in your worksheet. Or you might want to merge a cell across several rows and format the text to read from top to bottom or rotate the text. You can also use

the feature to create a larger merged cell to hold a small chart in the middle of your worksheet without affecting the surrounding cells.

You can use the Merge and Center command on the Formatting toolbar, or you can activate the Merge cells option in the Format Cells dialog box.

See also>>

Merge and Center
Select

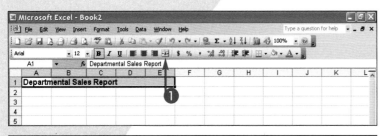

Use the Merge and Center Button

❶ Click the Merge and Center button on the Formatting toolbar.

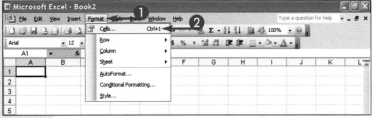

Use the Format Cells Dialog Box

❶ Click Format.

❷ Click Cells.

The Format Cells dialog box opens.

❸ Click the Alignment tab to find the Merge cells option.

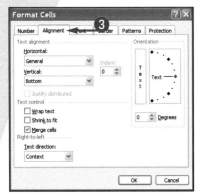

NAME BOX

You can use the Name box to navigate to specific cells or ranges in your worksheet. You can also use the Name box to assign new range names. A *range* can be a rectangular group of related cells or consist of a single cell. You can select a range to apply formatting all at once, print a selected group of cells, copy or move data as a group, or apply to formulas and functions.

The Name box stores a list of all the named ranges in your worksheet. You can quickly navigate to a range by selecting its name from the list. You can also use the Name box to move

directly to a cell anywhere in the worksheet. For example, if you type M42, Excel immediately scrolls the worksheet to cell M42 and highlights the cell.

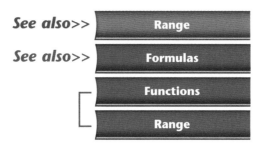

See also>> Range

See also>> Formulas

Functions

Range

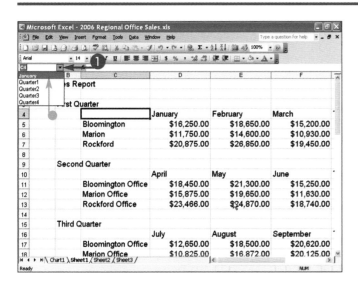

① Click the Name box drop-down arrow.

● If the worksheet includes any named ranges, you can specify a range to highlight.

TIP

Did You Know?

You can also use the Go To box to quickly locate a cell in your worksheet. You can click the Edit menu and click Go To to open the Go To dialog box, or press Ctrl+G. In the Go To dialog box, you can type the cell reference and click OK to go directly to that particular cell in the worksheet. To learn more about this feature, see the Technique "Go To: Navigate to a Cell or Range."

NEW

You can use the New command to start new Excel workbook files at any time. The quickest way to create a new file is to use the New button on the Standard toolbar. When activated, this feature instructs Excel to immediately open a new, blank workbook file. Any existing workbooks remain open as well.

If you need to start a different type of file, such as a template, you can use the New Workbook task pane. This pane lists a link for creating a new workbook as well as options for searching for and applying templates. The task pane also lists a link for creating a new workbook based on an existing workbook. For example, you may need to create several workbook files for different quarters you are tracking in your

sales department. Rather than re-create each spreadsheet, you can open the original file and click the From existing workbook link in the task pane to duplicate the workbook entirely. You can then make changes and save the data with a new filename.

See also>>

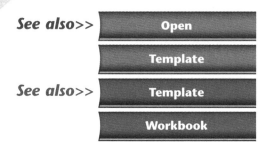

See also>>

Use the New Button

① Click the New button on the Standard toolbar.

Excel immediately opens a new workbook.

Use the New Workbook Pane

① Click File.

② Click New.

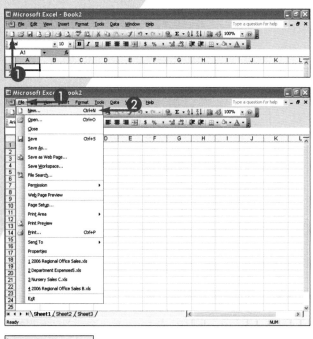

The New Workbook task pane opens where you can choose the type of file you want to create.

OPEN

You can use the New command to start new Excel workbook files at any time. The quickest way to create a new file is to use the New button on the Standard toolbar. When activated, this feature instructs Excel to immediately open a new, blank workbook file. Any existing workbooks remain open as well.

If you need to start a different type of file, such as a template, you can use the New Workbook task pane. This pane lists a link for creating a new workbook as well as options for searching for and applying templates. The task pane also lists a link for creating a new workbook based on an existing workbook. For example, you may need to create

several workbook files for different quarters you are tracking in your sales department. Rather than re-create each spreadsheet, you can open the original file and click the From existing workbook link in the task pane to duplicate the workbook entirely. You can then make changes and save the data with a new filename.

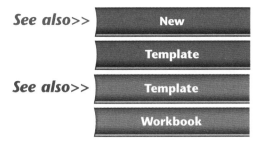

See also>> New

Template

See also>> Template

Workbook

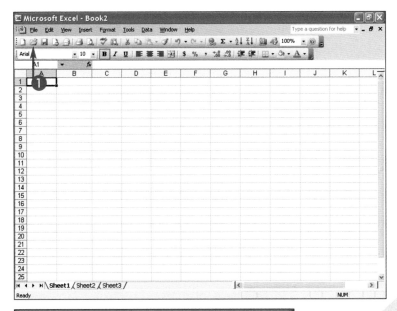

❶ Click the Open button on the Standard toolbar.

You can also click File and then Open.

The Open dialog box appears where you can select the file you want to open.

ORGANIZATION CHART

Excel offers a diagramming tool you can use to create all kinds of diagrams in your worksheets to illustrate concepts and processes. For example, you might insert an organizational chart in a worksheet to show the hierarchy in your company, or you might use a cycle diagram to show workflow in your department.

Organization charts are just one type of diagram you can create with the diagramming feature. Organization charts are composed of individual shapes that inhabit a drawing space, called a *canvas*. The shapes define the chart tree for the organization you illustrate. There are four types of shapes: superior, assistant, subordinate, and coworker. The

superior shape appears at the top of the chart. You can add as many shapes as you need to complete your chart.

Within each shape, you can add the name or title of a person or process and format the text any way you like. You can also control the formatting of the shape itself, including the border and fill color.

See also>> Diagram

See also>> Diagram

Organization Chart

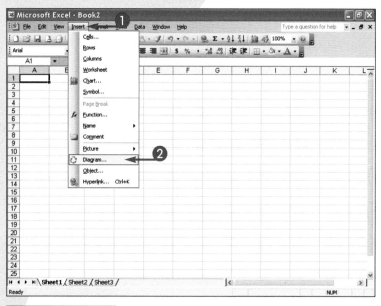

① Click Insert.

② Click Diagram.

You can also click the Insert Diagram button on the Drawing toolbar.

The Diagram Gallery dialog box opens.

③ Click the Organization Chart type to build an organization chart.

PAGE BREAK

You can add page breaks to your Excel worksheets to control how data appears on a page when you print a workbook or worksheet. Unlike other types of documents, Excel spreadsheets often cause problems during printing because the data is too long or wide to fit on a single page. You can use page breaks to designate how the data prints out.

When inserting page breaks in Excel, the page breaks appear both horizontally and vertically in a worksheet. By default, Excel determines the vertical page break based on column widths, paper size, and paper orientation. When you

make changes to any of these elements, Excel adjusts the vertical page break.

You can use Page Break Preview to see page breaks and make adjustments to the breaks. If you still have trouble printing pages, you can change the page orientation or scale the data to fit on the page using the Page Setup dialog box.

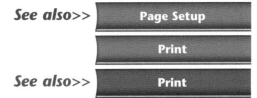

See also>>   **Page Setup**

Print

See also>>   **Print**

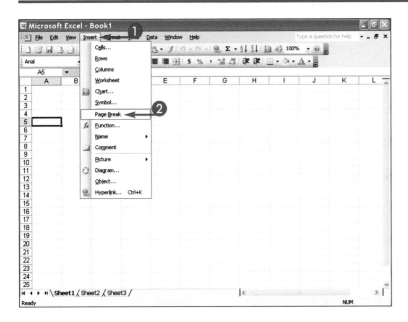

① Click Insert.

② Click Page Break.

Excel inserts a page break.

Did You Know?

You can use Excel's Page Break Preview feature to view all the manual and automatic page breaks assigned to your worksheet. To use the feature, click View and then Page Break Preview. This opens the worksheet in Page Break Preview mode. You can use this view mode to edit page breaks on the worksheet page. To learn more about this feature, see the Technique "Print: Preview Page Breaks."

PAGE SETUP

You can use the Page Setup dialog box to control any printing options you want to assign to a worksheet. For example, you can set margins, change the page orientation, and control how various elements of your worksheet prints — such as gridlines and headings.

The Page Setup dialog box offers four different tabs containing printing options. The Page tab displays controls for setting page orientation, scaling, and options for specifying paper size and print quality. The Margins tab displays controls for setting page margins. The Header/Footer tab allows you to create header and footer text to appear at the top or

bottom of every printed page. The Sheet tab displays settings for creating a print area, specifying print titles, designating a print order, and selecting which options to include with the printout, such as gridlines, and row and column headings.

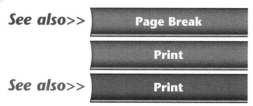

See also>>   **Page Break**

           Print

See also>>   **Print**

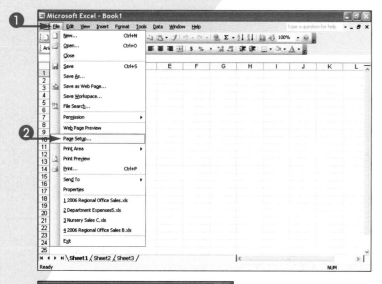

① Click File.

② Click Page Setup.

The Page Setup dialog opens where you can select from many printing options.

56

PASTE

You can use the Cut, Copy, and Paste commands to copy data within Excel, or move and share data between other Microsoft Office programs. For example, you might cut a row of labels and paste them into another worksheet, or copy a formula from one cell to another cell in the same worksheet.

The Copy command makes a duplicate of the selected data, while the Cut command removes the data from the original file entirely. When you copy or cut data, it is placed in the Windows Clipboard until you are ready to paste it using the Paste command.

You can find quick access to the Cut, Copy, and Paste commands through the buttons on the

Standard toolbar. You can also access the Paste command through the Edit menu.

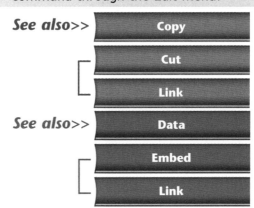

See also>> Copy

Cut

Link

See also>> Data

Embed

Link

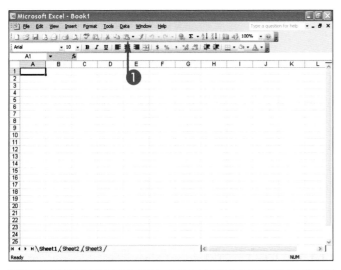

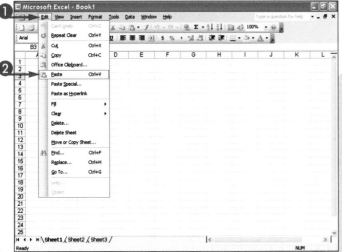

Use the Paste Button

① Click the Paste button on the Standard toolbar.

You can also click the Edit menu and click Paste.

Excel pastes the data from the Clipboard.

Use the Edit Menu

① Click Edit.

② Click Paste.

Excel pastes the cut or copied data from the Clipboard.

PERCENT STYLE

You can use Excel's number formatting styles to control the appearance of numeric data in your worksheet. For example, if you have a column of numbers that require percentage signs, you can apply the Percent Style number formatting.

You can choose from 12 different number categories, or styles, including the Percent Style. The top three styles — Comma Style, Currency Style, and Percent Style — are available as buttons on the Formatting toolbar. You can click the buttons to quickly apply the appropriate number format to your Excel data. Number formatting only affects numeric values in the cell or range, leaving text data unaffected.

You can also use the Format Cells dialog box to assign number styles and make adjustments to the appearance of the numeric formatting.

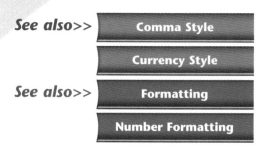

See also>>   Comma Style

            Currency Style

See also>>   Formatting

            Number Formatting

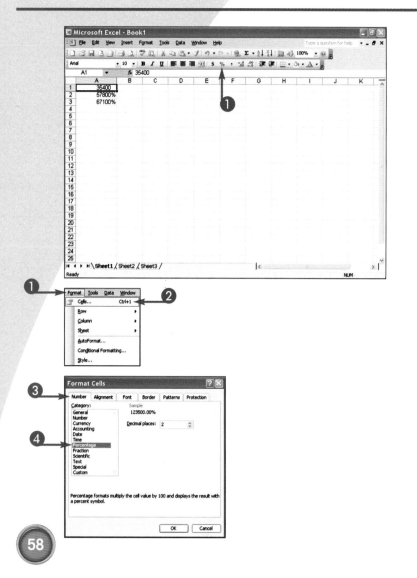

Use the Percent Style Button

1 Click the Percent Style button on the Formatting toolbar.

Excel applies percentage symbols to your number data.

Use the Format Cells Dialog Box

1 Click Format.

2 Click Cells.

The Format Cells dialog box opens.

3 Click the Number tab to view the number formatting options.

4 Click the Percentage category to view options for adding percent signs to your numbers.

PICTURE

P

You can illustrate your Excel worksheets with pictures stored on your computer. For example, if you have a photo or image file from another program that relates to your Excel data, you can insert it onto the worksheet.

Image or picture files, also called *objects* in Excel, come in a variety of file formats, such as GIF, JPEG or JPG, and PNG. After you insert a picture, you can resize and reposition it as well as perform other types of edits on the picture. In most instances, you need to resize or move the picture to fit it properly on the worksheet. You can use the same methods for moving other types of objects to move your picture. You can also apply any of

the formatting commands for editing objects in Excel, such as the positioning and alignment commands found on the Drawing toolbar.

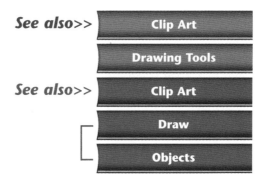

See also>>   Clip Art

Drawing Tools

See also>>   Clip Art

Draw

Objects

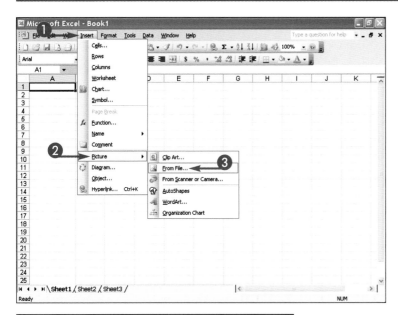

① Click Insert.

② Click Picture.

③ Click From File.

You can also click the Insert Picture button (🖼) on the Drawing toolbar, if it is open.

The Insert Picture dialog box opens where you can navigate to the picture you want to insert.

59

PICTURE TOOLBAR

You can use the Picture toolbar to format and edit any picture or image you insert into a worksheet. For example, you may need to crop the picture or make adjustments to the picture colors or contrast. The Picture toolbar contains a variety of tools you can use to fine-tune your picture to suit the needs of your worksheet.

The toolbar features several tools for improving the color, contrast, and brightness of a picture. You can use the Crop tool to crop your picture, such as deleting edges of the image you do not need to see, or cropping the picture to focus only on the subject matter. The toolbar also includes tools for rotating the picture, adding an instant border, and compressing the picture so it consumes less file space.

You can use the Set Transparent Color tool to make parts of your picture transparent, allowing you to view underlying cells and data. After you finish editing your picture, you can close the toolbar.

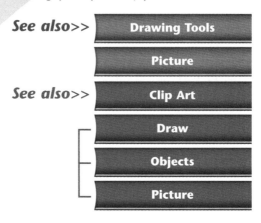

See also>> Drawing Tools

Picture

See also>> Clip Art

Draw

Objects

Picture

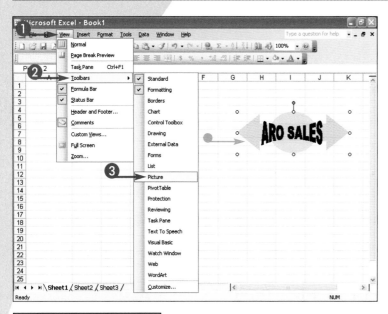

① Click View.

② Click Toolbars.

③ Click Picture.

● You can also right-click over a picture and click Show Picture Toolbar.

The Picture toolbar opens. You can use the various buttons to make changes to the picture.

PIVOTTABLE

You can use Excel's PivotTables to gauge different viewpoints of your worksheet data. A PivotTable is a reporting tool that sorts and sums your worksheet data independent of the original data layout in the spreadsheet.

For example, perhaps you have a sales order table that describes products, quantities ordered, dates, amounts, buyers, and salespersons. You can use a PivotTable to find which salesperson has the most sales, which buyer buys the most products, what items are top sellers, or who sold the most products on a given day. These are just

a few analysis points you can find out with PivotTables.

To create a PivotTable, you must start out with raw data, typically two or more criteria. Then you can use the PivotTable Wizard to help you build a PivotTable. The wizard walks you through the process, step by step. When you are ready to analyze data, you can drag fields on and off the table.

See also>>

Database

PivotTable

① Click Data.

② Click PivotTable and PivotChart Report.

The first of three Wizard dialog boxes opens to help you create a PivotTable.

PRINT

If you have a printer connected to your computer, you can print your Excel worksheets. You can send a file directly to the printer using the default printer settings, or you can open the Print dialog box and make changes to the printer settings. The Print button on the Standard toolbar sends the file to the printer automatically, without allowing you to change the settings.

The Print dialog box displays options for changing the printer, selecting a print range, and specifying the number of copies you want to print out. The dialog box also features settings for printing the active worksheet, a selected range, or the entire workbook.

If you need to fine-tune a worksheet before printing, such as changing the page margins, scaling data to fit on a page, or adding headers and footers, you can use the Page Setup dialog box.

See also>> | **Page Setup** |

| **Print Preview** |

See also>> | **Print** |

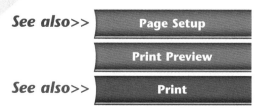

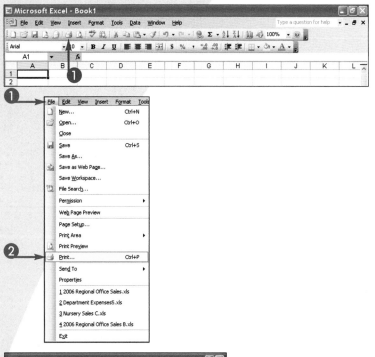

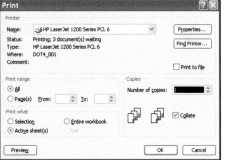

Use the Print Button

1️⃣ Click the Print button on the Standard toolbar.

Excel immediately prints the data.

Use the Print Dialog Box

1️⃣ Click File.

2️⃣ Click Print.

The Print dialog box opens where you can set any print options before printing.

PRINT PREVIEW

You can use Print Preview mode to preview workbooks and worksheets before committing them to paper. In Print Preview, you can see how your workbook looks when it is printed, including any headers, footers, and margins you have set.

Print Preview mode includes a toolbar of buttons you can use to view and check the workbook. For example, you can use the Zoom button to switch between full-page and magnified views of the worksheets. You can use the Next and Prev buttons to navigate between pages. You can use the Margins button to make changes to margins directly on the page. You can also access the Page

Setup dialog box through Print Preview to make changes to your printer settings. You can then print the workbook directly from Print Preview.

After you finish viewing and checking the pages, you can return to Normal view again by clicking the Close button.

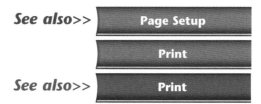

See also>> Page Setup

Print

See also>> Print

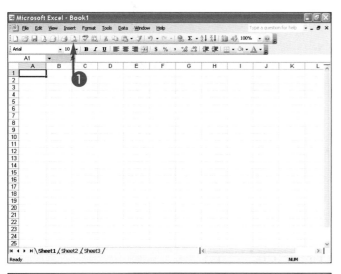

Use the Print Preview Button

① Click the Print Preview button on the Standard toolbar.

Excel displays the workbook in Print Preview mode.

Use the File Menu

① Click File.

② Click Print Preview.

Excel displays the workbook in Print Preview mode.

PROPERTIES

You can use the Properties dialog box to view and specify file properties for your workbook file. When you create a file using Excel, the program automatically saves details about the file along with the data contained within the file. Known as *file properties*, these details include information about who created the file, the name of the organization, file size, creation date, and location. To view a file's properties at any time, you can open the Properties dialog box.

The Properties dialog box includes several tabs containing details about the file. The General tab lists general information about the file, such as the file size, creation date, and file location. The Summary tab includes personal information about the file's author. You can also use this tab to add more details about a file.

The Statistics tab lists statistics about the file, including creation date and the name of the last person who saved the file. The Contents tab lists details about what the workbook contains, such as ranges, charts, and more. The Custom tab lists properties you can define for the file.

See also>> | **Properties**

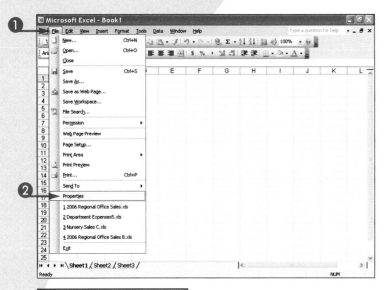

1 Click File.

2 Click Properties

The Properties dialog box opens. You can view file properties and add your own details about the file.

RANGE

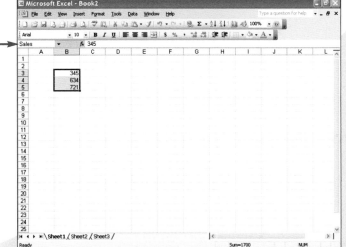

You can use ranges in your Excel worksheets to organize and work with data. A *range* can be either a rectangular group of related cells or a single cell. You can select a range to apply formatting all at once, print out a selected group of cells, copy or move data as a group, or apply to formulas and functions.

You can assign distinctive names to ranges of cells using the Name box. This makes it easier to identify the cell's contents. Normally when you select a range in Excel, the range name consists of the first cell in the group and the last cell in the group, separated by a colon — such as B24:E24. When you use the range in a formula, it is identified by the generic range name. To make formula-building easier, you can assign unique names to your ranges. For example, a range name such as Sales_Totals is much easier to recognize than a generic reference.

Range names must start with a letter or an underscore (_). After that, you can use any character, uppercase or lowercase, and any punctuation or keyboard symbols, with the exception of a hyphen or a space. In place of a hyphen or space, substitute a period or underscore.

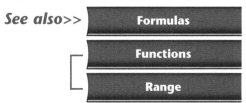

See also>>

Formulas

Functions

Range

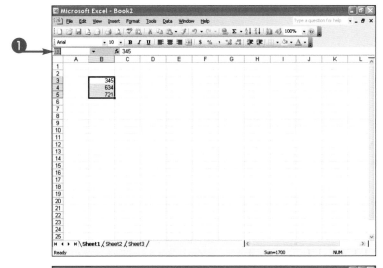

① With a range selected, click inside the Name box on the Formula bar.

② Type a name for the range and press Enter.

Excel assigns the name to the cells.

RESEARCH TASK PANE

You can use the Research task pane to access a variety of research tools. You can use the task pane to search multiple sources of information, such as the Microsoft Encarta English dictionary, a built-in thesaurus, and the Microsoft Encarta online encyclopedia. You can also use the task pane to access translation tools, search for stock quotes, and tap into other third-party services.

When using the Research task pane, you can access several reference books, as well as access research, business, and financial Web sites. The Research task

pane is just one of several task panes you can use in Excel to help with common tasks. By default, all task panes appear on the right side of the program window. You can navigate through several open task panes using the pane's navigation buttons. When finished using the Research task pane, you can close the pane to free up on-screen workspace.

See also>>

Research

Task Pane

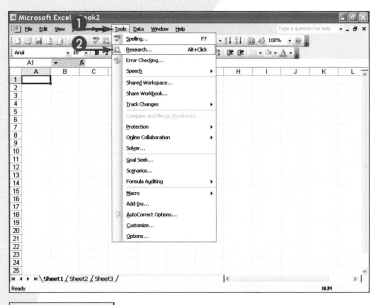

① Click Tools.

② Click Research.

The Research task pane opens. You can use this pane to look up terms, stock quotes, translate words, and more.

REVIEWING TOOLBAR

You can use Excel's Reviewing toolbar to track and view workbook changes. If you work in an environment in which you share your workbooks with others, you can use Excel's tracking and reviewing features to help you keep track of who adds changes to a file. For example, you can see what edits others have made, including formatting changes and data additions or deletions.

When you activate the reviewing process, Excel goes through each change in the worksheet and allows you to accept or reject the edit using the Accept or Reject Changes dialog box. Using the Reviewing toolbar, you can choose to accept a

single change, accept all the changes in the file, reject a change, or reject all the changes.

You can move the Reviewing toolbar to get it out of the way as you view and edit a worksheet. Like all toolbars in Excel, you can move or dock the toolbar, and close it when you no longer need to access the tools.

See also>>

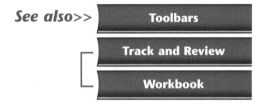

Toolbars

Track and Review

Workbook

① Click View.

② Click Toolbars.

③ Click Reviewing.

The Reviewing toolbar appears. You can use the toolbar to perform reviewing tasks.

ROW

Row and columns comprise the structure of every Excel worksheet. You can add rows to your worksheets to add more data. For example, you may need to add a row in the middle of several existing rows for data you left out when you created the workbook. Or you might add a row to create a title area for the top of your worksheet.

You can also delete rows you no longer need in the worksheet. For example, you might remove a row of out-of-date data. When you delete an entire row, Excel also deletes any existing data within the selected cells.

You can also hide rows in your worksheets to help you with a variety of scenarios. For example, you might

hide a row to prevent the data from appearing on a printout. When you hide a row, Excel simply collapses it in the worksheet so the data is no longer in view.

You can also use the Insert menu to add rows to your worksheets. You can use the Format menu to access commands for adding, deleting, and hiding rows. You can also right-click over a row header to access row-related commands.

See also>> Column

See also>> Column

Row

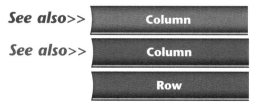

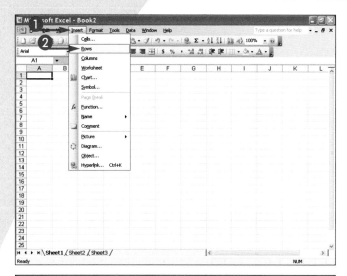

Use the Insert Menu

① Click Insert.

② Click Rows.

Excel immediately adds a row to the selected area in the worksheet.

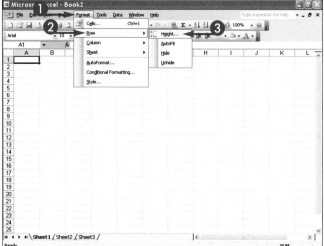

Use the Format Menu

① Click Format.

② Click Row.

③ Click a command to apply.

Depending on the command you select, an additional dialog box may open with more options to specify.

SAVE

You can save your data as a workbook file to reuse it again or share it with others. You can use the Save As dialog box to save a file. When you save a workbook, you can specify a folder or drive to save to, as well as specify a unique filename. After you save a workbook, the new filename appears in the program window's title bar.

By default, Excel workbooks are saved in the Excel file format, which uses the XLS file extension. If you want to share your workbook with a Lotus 1-2-3 user, you can save your file in the 1-2-3 format. You can also save to other file

formats, such as XML spreadsheet, text (tab delimited), CSV (Mac), DBF (dBASE), and HTML.

In addition, you can save your workbooks in file formats read by earlier versions of Excel, such as 2.1 or 4.0. You may need to do this if you want your file read by someone using an older version of Excel.

See also>> Open

See also>> Save

Workbook

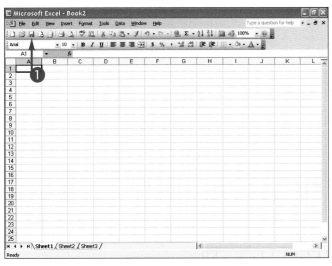

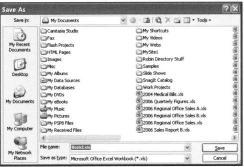

① Click the Save button on the Standard toolbar.

You can also click the File menu and click Save or Save As.

The Save As dialog box opens where you can designate a filename and folder or drive in which to store the workbook.

SMART TAGS

You can use Excel's smart tags to help you save time in your work. Smart tags are little icons that appear when Excel recognizes data and associates it with a task. Depending on the data, Excel may display smart tags for AutoCorrect options, paste options, and AutoFill options.

For example, if you copy and paste data, a smart tag appears with options for controlling how the data is copied. When you type a person's name in a worksheet cell, a smart tag might prompt you to add the name to the Microsoft Office Outlook contact folder. If you type a stock symbol in a cell, a smart tag may appear offering you instant access to the latest stock quotes.

When a smart tag icon appears, you can choose to respond to the tag or ignore it. If you proceed with other Excel tasks, the smart tag disappears. Smart tags are turned on by default in Excel.

See also>> **Smart Tags**

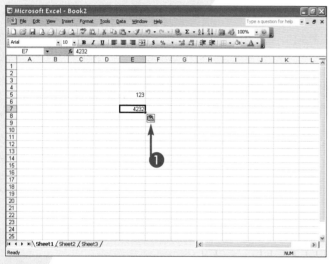

① To view a smart tag, click the smart tag icon.

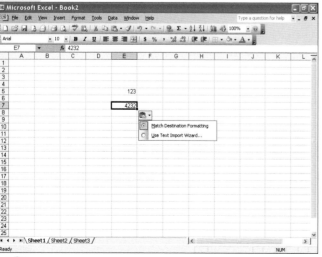

The smart tag displays a menu of actions you can perform with the data.

SORT

You can use Excel's Sort command to sort lists of data. Sorting simply rearranges the list based on the field you specify. The Sort command is especially useful when dealing with database tables in Excel. For example, you might want to sort a client table to list the names alphabetically or sort a column of prices to see which products cost the most.

You can choose from two types of simple sorts using the sort buttons on the Standard toolbar. You can perform an ascending sort to list records

from A to Z. You can perform a descending sort to list records from Z to A.

You can also use the Sort dialog box to sort your data. For example, you can sort four criteria based on your list columns. You can also sort a single column or multiple columns in your list.

See also>>

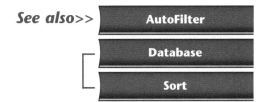

AutoFilter

Database

Sort

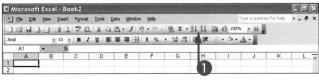

Use the Sort Buttons

① Click the Sort Ascending (AZ↓) or Sort Descending button (ZA↓) on the Formatting toolbar.

Excel sorts the records based on the field you specify.

Use the Sort Dialog Box

① Click Data.

② Click Sort.

The Sort dialog box opens where you can specify a sort.

ABC SPELLING

You can use the Spell Check tool to check your worksheets for spelling errors. This tool is especially important if you plan to share your workbook or printouts of your data with others. If you use the spell check feature in other Microsoft Office programs, such as Word, you may be used to seeing the program check your spelling as you type and underline any misspellings. Excel does not check spelling automatically, although the AutoCorrect feature is turned on by default to help with common misspellings. However, you can activate the spell check at any time to look through your worksheet for spelling mistakes.

When the spell check feature finds an error, it highlights it in the worksheet and offers suggestions for fixing the error. Depending on the word, you can replace it with a suggestion or ignore it and move on to the next error.

You can activate the Spell Check tool using the Spelling button on the Standard toolbar, or through the Tools menu.

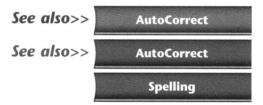

See also>> AutoCorrect

See also>> AutoCorrect

Spelling

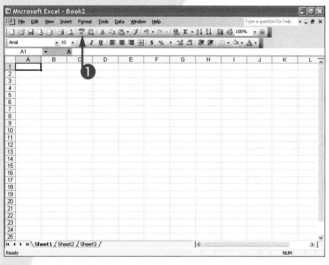

① Click the Spelling button on the Standard toolbar.

You can also click Tools and Spelling to activate the tool.

Excel searches the worksheet for mistakes, highlights any problems, and displays the Spelling dialog box if it finds an error.

SPLIT

You can use Excel's Split command to view two different areas of a worksheet on-screen at the same time. For example, you might want to view both the top and bottom of a worksheet to compare data. When you split panes in Excel, both areas of the split are scrollable.

You can split a worksheet horizontally or vertically. If you click on a row, you can split the sheet horizontally, showing two horizontal panes on-screen. If you click on a column, you can split the sheet vertically, showing two vertical panes on-screen.

Split worksheets literally split your worksheet view into two panes, with the number of viewable cells limited in each pane. To return to full worksheet view again, you can apply the Remove Split command.

See also>>   **Freeze**

See also>>   **Freeze/Unfreeze**

Worksheet

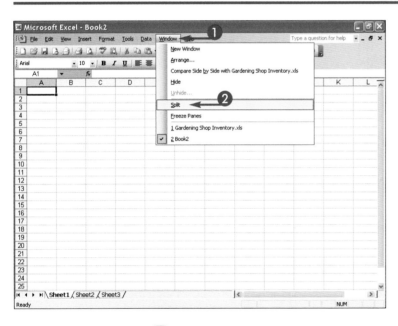

① Click Window.

② Click Split.

Excel splits the worksheet into two scrollable areas.

Did You Know?

If you want to keep one pane frozen while you scroll in the other pane, you can use Excel's Freeze Panes command instead of splitting panes. When you freeze a pane, you cannot scroll the designated area; it remains frozen in place. You might use this method to keep the cells at the top of the worksheet in view while you use the second pane to scroll around the worksheet cells. To learn more about freezing panes, see the technique "Freeze/Unfreeze."

STYLE

You can use the Style dialog box to create and assign styles to your worksheet data. A style is simply a collection of formatting, whether you define a font and size or a background color. If you use a lot of formatting in your worksheet cells, you might find that styles can save you valuable time and effort. Rather than apply various formatting commands to each cell or range separately, you can group a collection of formatting characteristics into a style and apply a single style instead.

You can create your own styles in Excel, apply existing styles, or copy styles from other workbooks.

By default, the generic Normal style is applied to every workbook you create. Other existing styles include Comma, Percent, and Currency. You can modify existing styles to create new styles, or you can create your own styles from scratch and assign them unique names.

You can use the Style dialog box to manage all the styles in a workbook, including deleting, modifying, and creating new styles.

See also>> **Formatting**

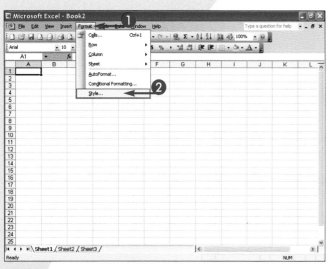

❶ Click Format.

❷ Click Style.

The Style dialog box opens. You can add new styles, apply existing styles, or delete styles you no longer need.

∑ SUBTOTALS

When using Excel to create database lists, you can use the List toolbar to quickly add a subtotal to any column in your table. For example, you can add a subtotal to a column of prices. You can use the Toggle Total Row command to automatically calculate subtotals and grand total values in any list.

When you insert automatic subtotals, Excel outlines the list, allowing you to use the Expand and Contract buttons in the outline pane to expand and contract your view of the list data.

Before attempting to add subtotals to any database list, first sort the list so all the rows you want to subtotal are grouped together in the worksheet. If your worksheet data is not organized in a list format, you can use the AutoSum function to total the data instead.

See also>> Sort

See also>> Database

Sort

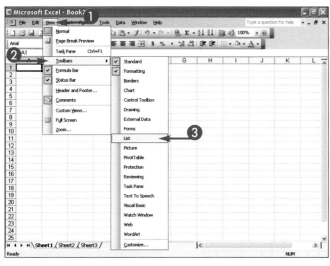

① Click View.

② Click Toolbars.

③ Click List.

④ Click the Toggle Total Row button on the List toolbar.

Excel displays a subtotal at the bottom of the column.

SYMBOL

You can use the Symbol dialog box when you need to insert a special symbol or character into an Excel worksheet that is not readily available using your keyboard, such as a registered trademark symbol, ornamental bullets, or an em dash character.

You can use the Symbol dialog box to access a wide range of special characters and symbols, including mathematical and Greek symbols, architectural symbols, and more. For example, you can access ASCII and Unicode characters using the Symbol dialog box. You can also access Wingding characters,

including smiley faces and other decorative characters.

The Symbol dialog box is divided into two tabs. The Symbols tab gives you access to your installed fonts and the various symbols. The Special Characters tab displays common characters such as proofreading symbols.

See also>> | **Symbol**

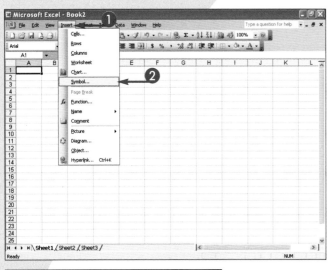

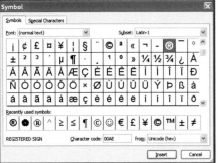

1. Click Insert.
2. Click Symbol.

The Symbol dialog box opens where you can choose a symbol to insert.

TASK PANE

Excel's task panes are a handy way to access common commands and controls. By default, any task panes you open appear on the right side of the program window. You can display more than one pane in the task pane area, and you can use the navigation buttons to view open panes. When you finish using a task pane, you can close the task pane to save on-screen workspace.

Excel offers 11 different task panes you can use, each focusing on a specific area or group of related tasks. For example, the Getting Started task pane, which appears by default when you first use Excel, gives you quick access to common

tasks such as opening existing files, starting new files, accessing the Microsoft Office Online Web site, and using search tools to look up specific information. The Clip Art task pane features tools for searching for clip art and adding artwork to your worksheets.

Some of the commands you can select in Excel open a task pane automatically. For example, when you create a new workbook, the New Workbook pane opens.

See also>> **Task Pane**

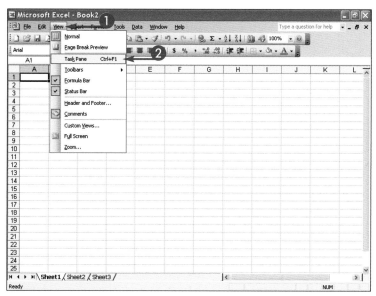

① Click View.

② Click Task Pane.

The task pane is displayed.

TEMPLATE

Templates are a useful way of speeding up workbook creation. Templates are ready-made documents you can use to quickly assemble spreadsheets. Excel includes several pre-made templates you can use containing preformatted placeholder data. All you have to do is add your own data. For example, you can apply the Balance Sheet template and add your own data to create a balance sheet for your company or department. You can use the Loan Amortization template to view loan payments over the course of a designated period of time.

You can also turn any existing worksheet into a template, or customize one of Excel's pre-made templates to suit your own needs. You might take the pre-made Sales Invoice template, for example, and

add or subtract various elements to create a workbook unique to your department's sales force activities.

Excel stores pre-made templates in the Templates folder, a subfolder of the Documents and Settings folder. You can access the templates using the Templates dialog box. Excel templates use the .xlt file extension. Any file you save in the .xlt format is a template file style.

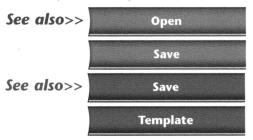

See also>> **Open**

Save

See also>> **Save**

Template

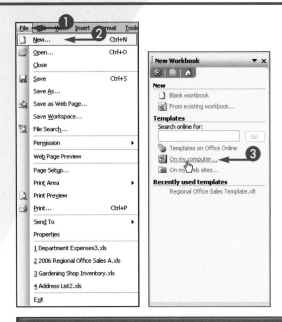

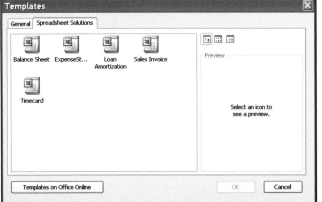

1 Click File.

2 Click New.

The New Workbook task pane opens.

3 Click the On My Computer link.

The Templates dialog box opens. You can select a template to apply.

TEXT TO SPEECH

If you need to proofread your spreadsheet or compare data between two spreadsheets, you can use the Text to Speech tool to help you with the task. The Text to Speech tool reads back the data in your worksheet cells. The tool works by reading the data in each cell. If you hear an error, you can stop the procedure and make any necessary corrections.

To use the Text to Speech tool, you must have a sound card and speakers installed with your computer. The first time you use the feature, Excel prompts you to install it first.

You can use the Text to Speech toolbar to control how the feature works. The toolbar includes several buttons for controlling how Excel reads back your data. For example, you can choose to play back the data by columns or rows. As the feature reads the data in a cell, Excel highlights that cell in the worksheet.

See also>>   **Toolbars**

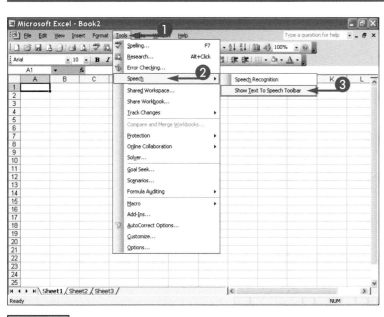

① Click Tools.

② Click Speech.

③ Click Show Text To Speech Toolbar.

The Text To Speech toolbar appears. You can use the toolbar to start the read-back feature.

TRACK CHANGES

You can use Excel's tracking and reviewing features to help you edit and manage changes made by multiple users to the same workbook file. You can use the tracking and reviewing features to see what edits others have made, including formatting changes and data additions or deletions.

The tracking feature works by changing the color for each person's edits, making it easy to see who changed what in the workbook. As each person works with the file, Excel highlights each change in the workbook by surrounding the changed cell in a colored border. You can see details about the change when you move the mouse pointer over the cell.

A comment box appears with a description of the change. When you review the workbook, you can choose to accept or reject the changes.

When you activate the tracking feature, Excel automatically enables the workbook sharing feature, allowing you to share the file over a network with other users, if needed. In a network scenario, two or more users can access the file at the same time.

See also>>

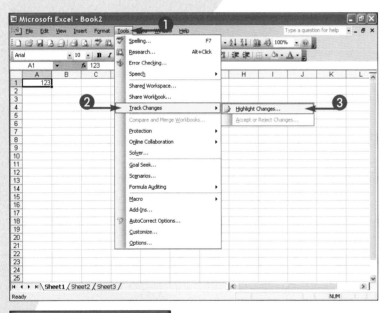

① Click Tools.

② Click Track Changes.

③ Click Highlight Changes.

The Highlight Changes dialog box opens. You can use this dialog box to turn on the feature and control other user's edit capabilities.

UNDERLINE

One of the quickest and easiest ways to change the appearance of your worksheet data is to apply any of Excel's basic formatting commands. For example, you can use the Underline command to instantly add an underscore to your data. By underlining certain portions of your worksheet data, you can draw attention to a title or important numerical data. You may want to apply underlining to one cell in the middle of a worksheet to make the data stand out, or you might want to underline a row of headings across the top of your worksheet to make them easier to distinguish.

You can assign underline formatting with a single click using the Underline button on the Formatting toolbar. Bold, italics, and underlining are common

formatting characteristics found throughout most word processing, spreadsheet, graphics, and presentation programs. Like Excel, most programs place buttons for these three common commands on the Formatting toolbar for easy access.

You can also use the Format Cells dialog box to apply underline formatting to your cells. The dialog box contains additional controls for setting a type of underscore.

See also>> **Bold**

Italic

See also>> **Formatting**

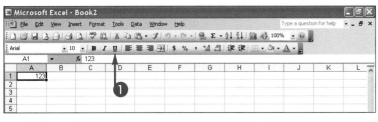

Use the Underline Button

1 Click the Underline button on the Formatting toolbar.

Excel immediately applies the formatting to the data.

Use the Format Cells Dialog Box

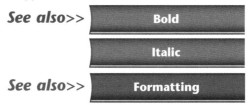

1 Click Format.

2 Click Cells.

The Format Cells dialog box opens.

3 Click the Font tab to view the underline formatting option.

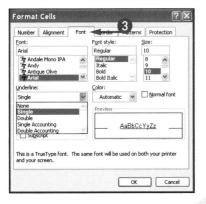

UNDO AND REDO

Two of the most useful commands found in any program, including Excel, are the Undo and Redo commands. You can use the Undo and Redo commands to make quick fixes of your edits and Excel actions. For example, if you accidentally delete a cell's content and suddenly realize you need to keep it, you can undo the deletion using the Undo command. If you decide to delete it again, you can apply the Redo command to redo the deletion action again.

Excel keeps track of the most recent actions and edits performed on your worksheet. You can undo

and redo up to 16 actions. For example, you can use the Undo command to undo the previous action, or the last 10 actions. You cannot, however, choose to undo the tenth action down the list without also undoing the other nine recent actions as well. The same is true with the Redo command.

See also>>

Research

Task Pane

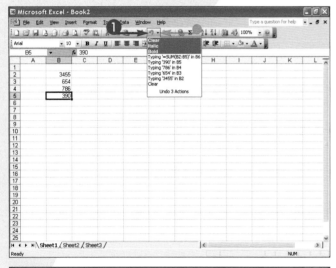

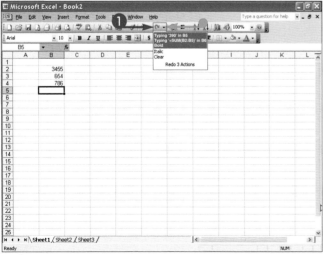

Use Undo

1 Click the Undo button.

● To undo several actions, click the drop-down arrow to display the list.

You can also click Edit and then Undo or press Ctrl+Z to undo an action.

Excel immediately undoes the previous action.

Use Redo

1 Click the Redo button.

● To redo several actions, click the drop-down arrow to display the list.

You can also click Edit and then Redo or press Ctrl+Y to redo the action.

Excel immediately reapplies the previous action.

VIEW

You can use Excel's view modes to view your worksheet in different ways. Excel offers several view modes you can use to zoom in and view your data, preview it for printing, or display the worksheet without a lot of program elements surrounding it. You can use Normal view and Full Screen view modes to toggle your overall view of a worksheet.

By default, Normal view displays your worksheet along with all the program control elements, such as the toolbars. You can switch to Full Screen

view to see the worksheet without all the toolbars and title bar. It allows you to view the worksheet with only the scroll bars and menu bar available. Full Screen view allows you to see more of your worksheet data, while Normal view includes all the tools you need to work with your worksheet.

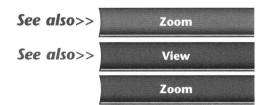

See also>> Zoom

See also>> View

Zoom

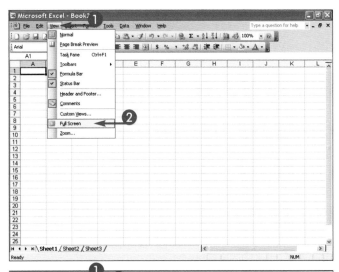

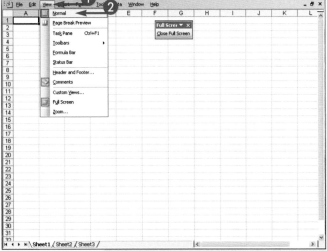

Change to Full Screen View

❶ Click View.

❷ Click Full Screen.

Excel switches to Full Screen view and displays the Full Screen toolbar.

Change to Normal View

❶ Click View.

❷ Click Normal.

Excel switches to Normal view.

WATCH WINDOW

You can use a Watch Window to keep track of data in a particular cell or range of cells even when the cells are no longer in view. This is particularly useful if you want to keep your eye on a particular formula or the cells you use to create a formula. You might also use a Watch Window to keep track of a particular cell's data as you work with the rest of your worksheet.

You can also use the Watch Window to view cells in other worksheets or sheets in a linked workbook.

The Watch Window is simply a mini-window that floats on top of the worksheet regardless of where you scroll. When you no longer need to keep a cell or

range in view, you can close the Watch Window. The Watch Window behaves much like other Excel toolbars, which means you can move it around onscreen or dock it on any side of the program window. You can resize and move the window to suit your own work needs.

See also>>

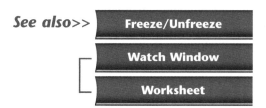

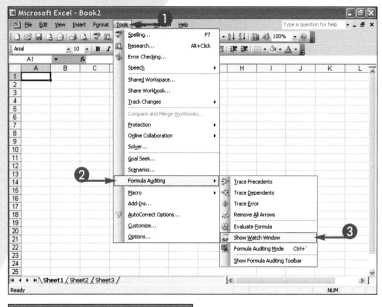

① Click Tools.

② Click Formula Auditing.

③ Click Show Watch Window.

You can also click View, Toolbars, and then Watch Window.

The Watch Window dialog box opens.

84

WEB TOOLBAR

You can use the Web toolbar and your Internet connection to access the Web directly from Excel without leaving the program window. For example, you can use the Web toolbar to open a specified URL, open your default home page, or display a page from your Favorites folder. When you activate any of the toolbar features, your default Web browser opens to display the actual Web page.

You must be connected to the Internet to use the Web toolbar features. If you are not connected to the Internet, you are prompted to do so before viewing any page.

You can use the Alt+Tab keyboard shortcut to switch between a Web page and the Excel program window.

Like the other Excel toolbars, you can move the Web toolbar or dock it along any of the sides of the program window.

See also>>   **Web Toolbar**

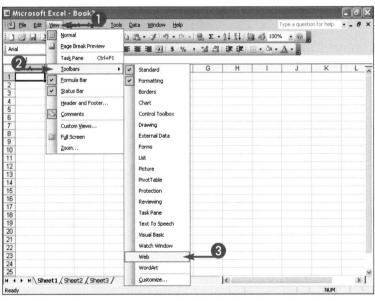

① Click View.

② Click Toolbars.

③ Click Web.

● The Web toolbar appears. You can use the buttons to access Web-related commands.

WORDART

Excel installs with several different types of graphics tools you can use to help illustrate your worksheet data. For example, you can use the WordArt feature to turn text into interesting graphic objects for use in your worksheets. You can create arched text to appear over a range of data. You can create text graphics that bend and twist, or display subtle shadings of color. You can also use WordArt text to create logos.

The WordArt tool is common among all the Microsoft Office programs. You can use it to create a wide variety of text effects. You can also adjust the

formatting of a WordArt object to create a graphic object suited for your worksheet display.

When you activate the WordArt tool, you can follow two distinct steps to create your WordArt object. The first step involves choosing a design, and the second step involves typing in your text and formatting it just the way you want. After you insert the WordArt object into your worksheet, you can move and resize it as needed, or use the commands on the WordArt toolbar to make changes to the object.

See also>>

Objects

WordArt

❶ Click Insert.

❷ Click Picture.

❸ Click WordArt.

You can also click the WordArt button on the Drawing toolbar.

The WordArt Gallery dialog box opens. You can use this dialog box to select a WordArt design.

ZOOM

You can use Excel's Zoom tool to change how you view worksheet cells and data. For example, you may prefer to zoom in for a closer look, making the data easier to read on your computer screen. For a larger worksheet, you might want to zoom out to see more of the cells.

Excel's magnification settings are based on percentages. If you zoom your view to 50%, for example, you see much less detail and view more of the worksheet cells. If you zoom your view to 200%, you see your cell data close up. The Zoom controls offer several preset magnification levels you can assign, or you can type in your own percentage to zoom. Any time you want to return

to a normal magnification setting, select the 100% percentage for the zoom.

You can also select a group of cells and apply the Selection zoom option on the Zoom drop-down menu. This zooms in on the selected cells only. You might use this technique to view a range of cells in a worksheet.

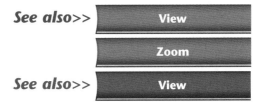

See also>> View

Zoom

See also>> View

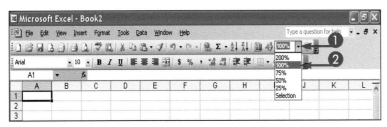

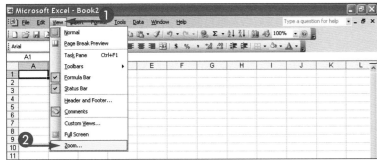

Magnify with the Zoom Button

1 Click the Zoom button drop-down arrow.

2 Click a magnification setting.

Excel immediately changes the magnification of the worksheet.

Magnify with the Zoom Dialog Box

1 Click View.

2 Click Zoom.

The Zoom dialog box appears. You can select a magnification percentage here.

Excel 2003 Visual Encyclopedia

Part II: Techniques

Microsoft Excel is a powerful program for organizing data and crunching numbers. You can perform an endless variety of tasks to manipulate the data you enter into a spreadsheet, and you can use the application for all kinds of projects at home as well as in an office environment. Whether you are preparing a worksheet to share with others, or getting ready to start creating formulas and building functions, you can use the techniques shown in this section of the book to help you with the undertaking.

This section of the book presents numerous techniques you can use to apply formatting, write formulas, create charts, draw objects, and more. Depending on the action you want to perform, a technique may use one or more Excel tools to complete the action. This section also includes basic information you need to know in order to understand how formulas and functions work in Excel. Arranged in A to Z fashion, you can easily find the technique you need to help you make the most of your worksheet data and master the Excel program.

ADD-INS:
Load Add-Ins

Excel offers a variety of add-ins you can install to extend the program's capabilities. Add-ins are simply programs included with Excel to offer additional worksheet efficiency. For example, the Analysis ToolPak add-in adds functions geared toward engineering and statistical calculations. The Solver add-in offers a step-by-step wizard for evaluating formulas for goal-seeking values.

By default, Excel does not install add-ins until requested. To install add-ins supplied with Excel, you may need to insert the Excel CD when prompted. You can also find Excel add-ins to download and install on your computer from the Microsoft Office

Web site. You can also conduct a Web search for a variety of add-ins created by third-party sources and download them for use with Excel.

After you install an add-in, you must activate it using the Add-Ins dialog box. Excel then adds the feature to the Tools or Data menus. For example, when you install and activate the Solver add-in, Excel adds the Solver command to the Tools menu. You can turn add-ins on or off using the Add-Ins dialog box.

See also>>   **Add-Ins: Data Analysis**

Add-Ins: Solver

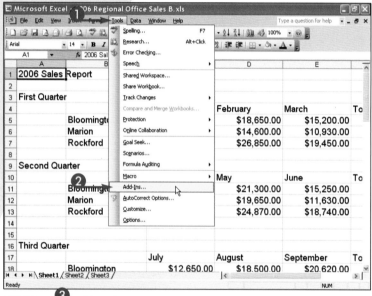

① Click Tools.

② Click Add-Ins.

The Add-Ins dialog box opens.

③ Select the option for the add-in you want to load.

④ Click OK.

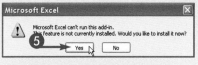

A prompt box appears.

⑤ Click Yes to install the feature.

Excel installs the add-in.

Excel adds a menu command for the feature on the Tools or Data menu.

Depending on the add-in, you may need to insert the Excel CD and complete additional setup steps to install the program.

TIPS

Remove It

You can unload any add-in you install. Unloading an add-in can free up memory as well as reduce the number of menu commands appearing on the Tools or Data menus. To unload an add-in, simply reopen the Add-In dialog box and deselect the program you no longer want to use. After unloading, the add-in program name remains on the Tools or Data menu until you restart the Excel program window.

Attention

If Excel has trouble finding the add-in you want to install, you may need to do a little investigating to find out why. Start by checking the default folder where Microsoft Office stores installed add-in files. Add-in files use the .xla file extension and are typically located in the Microsoft Office/Office folder or Library folder, or in the Documents and Settings/username/Application Data/Microsoft/AddIns path. Secondly, you can try reinstalling the add-in. If you use Excel on a network, check with the administrator to find out the availability of the program.

ADD-INS:
Use the Data Analysis Tools

If you need to perform more powerful statistical functions or engineering analysis, you can access Excel's Data Analysis tools. The Data Analysis tools include functions for random number generation, sampling, regression analysis, and more. With the Data Analysis tools, you provide the data from your worksheet and the tool provides the results. The add-in prompts you to define the input parameters and then displays the results of the function in the cell or range you specify.

The Analysis ToolPak is just one of several add-in programs you can install to enhance your work with Excel. You can use the Add-Ins dialog box to turn

add-ins on or off. You must first activate the Analysis ToolPak add-in before attempting to use the command. If you have not yet installed the Excel add-ins, the program prompts you to do so.

The Analysis ToolPak includes 15 engineering and statistical functions you can use for correlation analysis, Fourier analysis, exponential smoothing, and rank and percentile analysis.

See also>>

Add-Ins: Load

Add-Ins: Solver

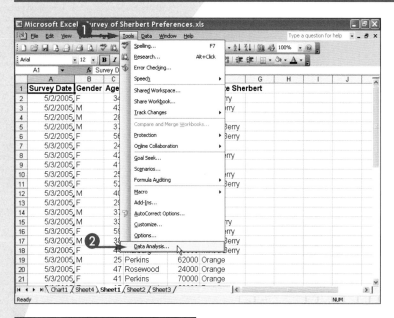

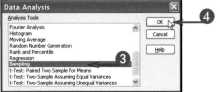

➊ Click Tools.

➋ Click Data Analysis.

> ***Note:*** *You must install and activate the Analysis ToolPak to add the Data Analysis command to the Tools menu.*

The Data Analysis dialog box opens.

➌ Click the analysis tool you want to use.

You can use the scroll bar to view all the available tools.

➍ Click OK.

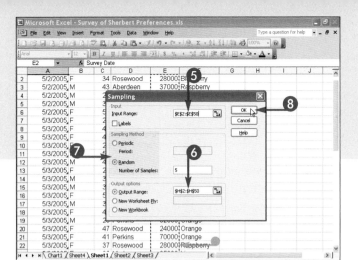

The tool's dialog box opens.

⑤ Select or type the input range to use in the analysis.

● Excel selects the range.

⑥ Select or type the output range to use in the analysis.

⑦ Select any additional options to apply to the tool, sampling methods in this example.

⑧ Click OK.

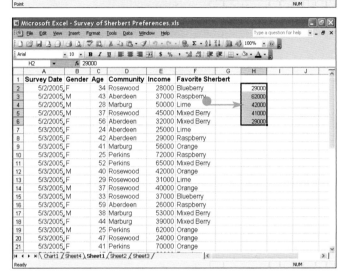

Excel executes the analysis tool.

● In this example, the Sampling tool produces a random sampling of income values.

Did You Know?

You can use Excel's Help files to learn how each tool works. In the Data Analysis dialog box, select the tool about which you want to learn more and then click the Help button. This opens the Excel Help window where you can read more about the tool and its settings. It helps to have some familiarity with statistical principles to fully utilize the Data Analysis tools. To learn more about installing add-ins, see the previous section.

Try This

To keep your original data intact, you can save the worksheet you want to analyze under a different filename. If you want to test out more Data Analysis tools, you can also create a practice sheet and add random data to create an input range. You must define an input range of data organized into columns and rows upon which you want to perform analysis, so take time to organize the data before attempting to analyze the information.

ADD-INS:
Use the Solver Add-In

Excel's Solver add-in can help you figure out a formula's optimal value using a group of related cells. To use Solver, you must first define the target cell, which is related to other cells through formulas. Solver analyzes the formulas that create the target cell's answer to try different solutions. You must also specify which changing cells Solver can modify to optimize the solution in the target cell.

When the Solver add-in completes the calculation, it displays the Solver Results dialog box and you can keep the results or change the values to produce new results. If the Solver Results dialog box displays an

error, you can adjust the referenced values and try again.

Solver works similarly to Excel's Goal Seek tool, but offers more options. Solver is just one of several add-in programs that come with Excel. To use Solver, you must first load the add-in. When the add-in is activated, the Solver feature appears as a command on the Tools menu.

See also>>  **Goal Seek**

See also>> **Add-Ins: Load**

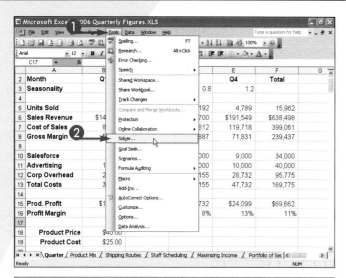

① Click Tools.

② Click Solver.

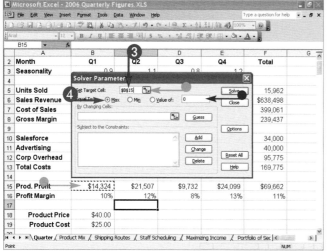

The Solver Parameters dialog box opens.

③ Click in the Set Target Cell box and type a cell reference for the target cell.

● You can also select a range directly on the worksheet.

● You can click here to collapse and expand the dialog box while clicking cells in the worksheet.

④ Select an Equal To option.

● If needed, type a value here.

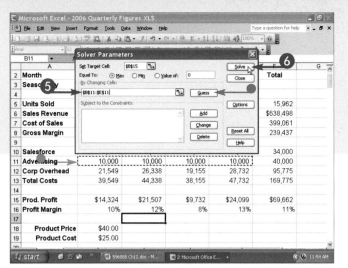

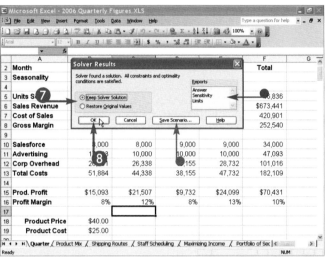

⑤ Click in the By Changing Cells box and type a cell reference to compare against the target cell.

● You can also select a range directly on the worksheet.

To enter multiple cells, separate each cell reference with a comma.

⑥ Click Solve.

● You can click Guess to make Solver automatically propose adjustable cells based on the target cell.

The Solver Results dialog box opens and Excel makes changes to the designated target cell.

⑦ Select whether you want to save the solution or restore the original values.

● If you click Keep Solver Solution to save the results as a report, click a report type.

● To save the changes as a scenario, click here.

⑧ Click OK.

Excel closes the Solver Results box.

TIPS

Did You Know?

Excel installs with a sample workbook, named solvsamp.xls, which you can use to practice Solver problems. You can find the file using the path C:\Program Files\Microsoft Office\ Office11\Samples. You can save your practice work as a new worksheet in the folder of your choice.

Attention

If Solver stops before completing a task, the cause may result from several reasons. For example, depending on the complexity of your task, Solver may take a few moments to produce a solution, and if you interrupt the solution process, Solver cannot complete the task. Also be careful not to select the Show Iteration Results check box in the Solver Options dialog box (click the Tools menu and click Solver to open the Solver dialog box, and then click the Options button to open the Solver Options dialog box) before you activate the Solve command.

ALIGNMENT:
Align Cell Data

You can control the alignment of data within your worksheet cells. For example, you might want to center all the text in a column or align all number data to the left in a group of cells. With Excel's alignment controls, you can position data to best suit the appearance of your worksheet.

By default, Excel automatically aligns text data to the left and number data to the right. Data is also aligned vertically to sit at the bottom of the cell. You can change horizontal and vertical alignments to improve the appearance of your worksheet data.

For example, you may prefer to center data both vertically and horizontally in a cell.

You can use the alignment buttons on the Formatting toolbar to control the horizontal alignment of data. Horizontal alignment includes left, center, and right alignments. For additional horizontal alignment options, you can use the Format Cells dialog box. You must use the Format Cells dialog box to control the vertical alignment of data. Vertical alignments include Top, Center, Bottom, Justify, and Distributed.

See also>> **Formatting: Apply Cell**

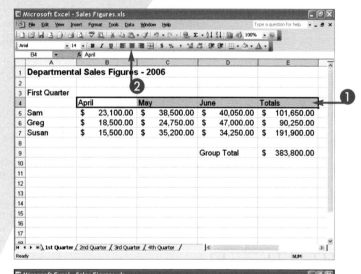

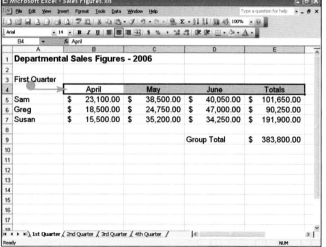

Set Horizontal Alignment

① Select the cells you want to format.

② Click an alignment button on the Formatting toolbar.

Click Align Left (▤) to align data to the left.

Click Center (▤) to center align data.

Click Align Right (▤) to align data to the right.

● Excel immediately applies the alignment to your cells.

In this example, the cell data is now centered.

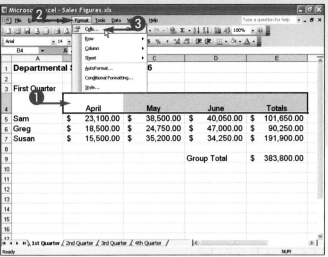

1. Select the cells you want to format.
2. Click Format.
3. Click Cells.

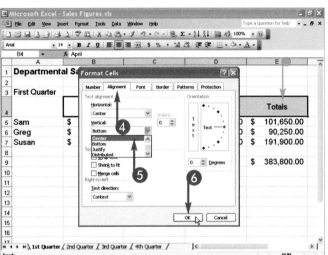

The Format Cells dialog box opens.

4. Click the Alignment tab.
5. Click ☑ and select a vertical alignment.
6. Click OK.

● Excel applies the vertical alignment to the cells.

TIPS

Did You Know?

To justify cell text, you must open the Format Cells dialog box and display the Alignment tab, as outlined in the steps in this section. Justified text creates both a left and right alignment and spreads out the text between the cell margins. After you open the Format Cells dialog box, you can click the Horizontal ☑ and click Justify to assign justification to your cell text.

Did You Know?

You can also rotate the data in a cell to change the orientation of text or numbers. For example, you may want to make column heading text appear at an angle to better fit more columns on a page. To control the orientation of data, you can use the Orientation settings in the Format Cells dialog box. Click Format, Cells, and then click the Alignment tab to view the Orientation options.

AUDIT:
Apply Error Checking to a Worksheet

To help you with errors that arise in your worksheets, you can utilize Excel's Formula Auditing toolbar, which includes several tools for examining and correcting formula errors. For example, you can use the toolbar to run Excel's Error Checking feature, trace errors, trace precedents and dependents, insert cell comments, evaluate formulas, check validation rules, and more. The Formula Auditing toolbar is just one of many ways you can check a worksheet for errors.

When dealing with larger worksheets in Excel, it is not always easy to figure out the source of a formula error when scrolling through the many cells. The Error Checking feature scans your worksheet for errors and helps you find solutions by graphically

showing you each problem reference. You can check formula problems one at a time using the Error Checking feature, and Excel highlights each problem.

When checking a worksheet for formula problems, the Error Checking feature looks for errors such as references to empty cells, incorrect references, and inconsistent references. Error checking also evaluates the error value for incorrect arguments, numbers entered as text data, and date values entered as ambiguous text dates.

See also>>

Errors

Formulas: Construct

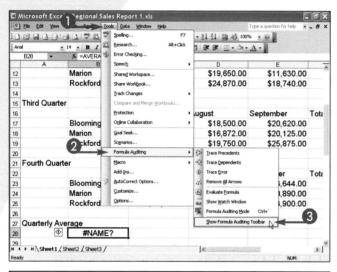

Apply Error Checking

❶ Click Tools.

❷ Click Formula Auditing.

❸ Click Show Formula Auditing Toolbar.

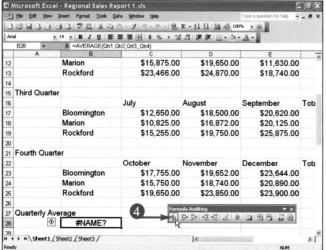

Excel displays the Formula Auditing toolbar.

❹ Click the Error Checking button.

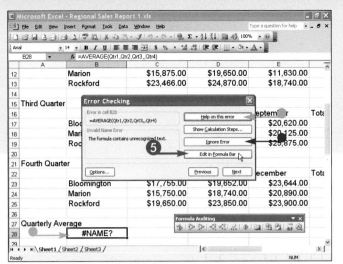

- Excel displays the Error Checking dialog box and highlights the first cell containing an error.

⑤ To fix the error, click Edit in Formula Bar.

- To find help with an error, click here to open the Help files.

- To ignore the error, click Ignore Error.

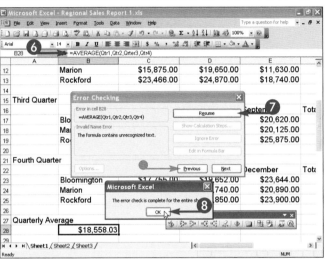

⑥ Make edits to the cell references in the Formula bar.

⑦ Click Resume.

- You can use the Previous and Next buttons to scroll through all the errors on the sheet.

⑧ When the error check is complete, click OK.

Did You Know?

The following table explains the different types of error values that can appear in cells when an error occurs.

Error Message	Problem	Solution
######	The cell is not wide enough to contain the value	Widen the column width
#DIV/0!	Dividing by zero	Edit the cell reference
#N/A	Value is not available	Check to make sure the formula references the correct value
#NAME?	Does not recognize text in a formula	Make sure the name referenced is correct
#NULL!	Specify two areas that do not intersect	Check for an incorrect range operator or correct intersection problem
#NUM!	Invalid numeric value	Check the function for an unacceptable argument
#REF!	Invalid cell reference	Correct cell references
#VALUE!	Wrong type of argument or operand	Double-check arguments and operands

AUDIT:
Apply Error Checking to a Worksheet (Continued)

Auditing tools can trace the path of your formula components and check each cell reference that contributes to the formula. This allows you to graphically see how a formula's referenced cells contribute to the formula. For example, by tracing the referenced cells, you might determine you referenced an incorrect cell in the formula or used the wrong range to build the formula.

When tracing the relationships between cells, you can display tracer lines, also called arrows. You can

choose to find *precedents*, cells referred to in a formula, or *dependents*, cells that contain the formula results. The Formula Auditing toolbar includes tools for tracing both types of relationships as well as turning off trace arrows when you no longer want to view precedents or dependents.

As all toolbars in Excel, you can display or hide the Formula Auditing toolbar as needed. When you finish tracing references, you can close the toolbar to view more of your work area.

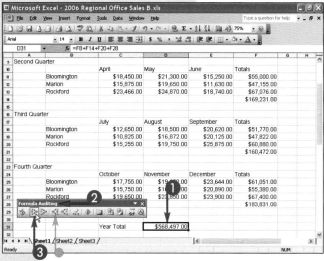

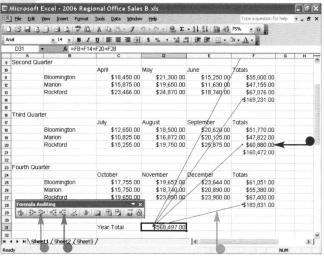

Trace Precedents

1 Click the cell containing the formula results or content you want to trace.

2 Display the Formula Auditing toolbar.

3 Click the Trace Precedents button.

● To trace dependents instead, click the Trace Dependents button.

● Excel displays trace lines from the current cell to the cells referenced in the formula.

You can make changes to the cell contents or changes to the formula to make any corrections.

● In this example, the trace lines show that the wrong total cell is referenced.

● You can click the Remove Precedent Arrows button to turn off the trace lines.

● To turn off the dependent trace lines, click the Remove Dependent Arrows button.

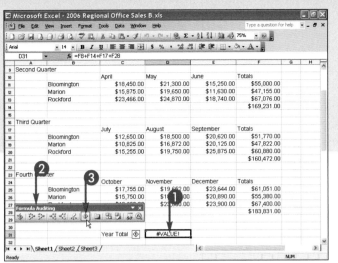

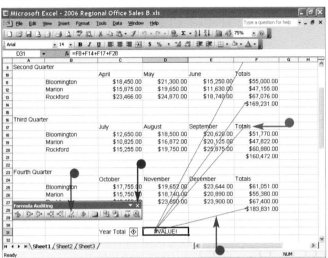

Trace Errors

1. Click the cell containing the error you want to trace.

2. Display the Formula Auditing toolbar.

3. Click the Trace Error button.

● Excel displays trace lines from the current cell to any cells referenced in the formula.

You can make changes to the cell contents or changes to the formula to correct the error.

● In this example, a text cell is referenced in the formula instead of a numeric value.

● You can click the Remove All Arrows button to turn off the trace lines.

● You can click here to hide the toolbar.

Did You Know?

Excel displays a Smart Tag icon (⊕) any time you encounter an error. You can click ⊕ to view a menu of options, including options for correcting the error. For example, you can click the Help on This Error command from the menu to find out more about the error message.

More Options

You can click the Evaluate Formula button (⊕) on the Formula Auditing toolbar to check over your formula or function step-by-step. When you click the cell containing the formula you want to evaluate, and click ⊕, Excel opens the Evaluate Formula dialog box. You can then evaluate each portion of the formula for correct references and values.

AUTOCORRECT:
Correct Spelling Problems

You can use the AutoCorrect feature to quickly correct text you commonly misspell when typing in your worksheet data. For example, if you find yourself continually misspelling the same term over and over, you can add the word to the AutoCorrect dictionary. The next time you mistype the word, AutoCorrect automatically fixes your mistake.

You may have already noticed the AutoCorrect feature kicking in as you typed in a worksheet. The corrections this feature makes are performed automatically. For example, if you type "teh" instead of "the" or "adn" instead of "and," AutoCorrect

automatically fixes the mistake for you. The correction occurs as soon as you press the Spacebar after typing the word. If you prefer to keep the original spelling, simply activate the Undo command.

AutoCorrect comes with a list of preset misspellings, however, the list is not comprehensive. To speed up your own text entry tasks, consider adding your own problem words to the list.

See also>>   **Spelling**

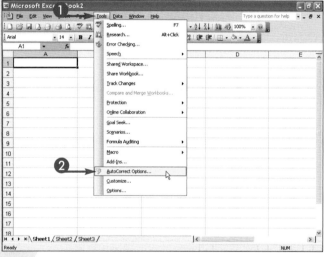

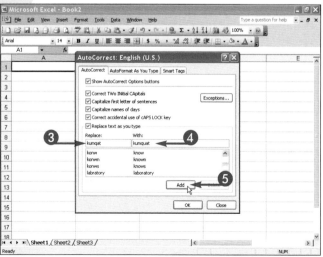

Add a Misspelling

① Click Tools.

② Click AutoCorrect Options.

The AutoCorrect dialog box opens with the AutoCorrect tab displayed.

③ Type the common misspelling in the Replace text box.

Be sure to type the word exactly as you normally misspell it.

④ Type the correct spelling in the With text box.

⑤ Click Add.

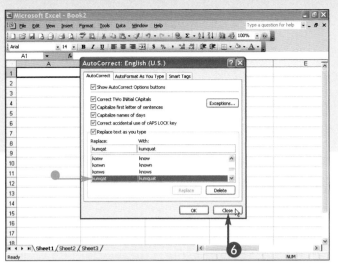

● AutoCorrect adds the word to the list.

The next time you misspell the word, AutoCorrect corrects it for you.

You can repeat Steps 3 to 5 to add more words to the list, as needed.

6 Click Close to exit the dialog box.

Use AutoCorrect

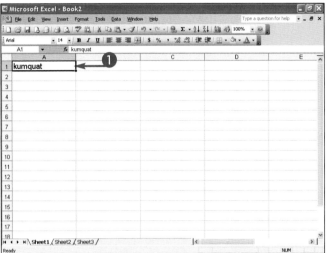

1 Click in the worksheet and type the word you commonly misspell.

Within seconds after typing the word, AutoCorrect fixes the mistake.

Note: If you type something you do not want corrected, press Ctrl+Z to undo AutoCorrect before you continue typing anything else.

TIPS

Delete It

You can remove or edit a word from the AutoCorrect list. Open the AutoCorrect dialog box to the AutoCorrect tab. Click the word you want to remove and click Delete. To edit a word, select it from the list and make your change in the Replace or With text boxes. Click OK to exit the dialog box and apply your changes.

Customize It

You can customize how the AutoCorrect feature works. You can also select or deselect options for AutoCorrect to be on the lookout for, such as typing two initial caps or capitalizing the first letter of a sentence. To control any of the AutoCorrect options, you must first open the AutoCorrect dialog box; click Tools and then AutoCorrect Options. Make any changes to the options. You can also turn the feature off. Deselect the Replace Text As You Type check box. This turns the feature off. Click OK to exit the dialog box and apply your changes.

AUTOFILL:
Enter Data Series

You can use Excel's AutoFill feature to help you automate data entry tasks. You can use AutoFill to add duplicate entries or a data series to your worksheet cells, such as labels for Monday, Tuesday, Wednesday, and so on. For example, rather than typing column headings such as Quarter 1, Quarter 2, and so on across the top of a worksheet, you can type in the first column label and use AutoFill to fill in the rest. AutoFill automatically duplicates the label and adjusts the numbers sequentially.

You can also use AutoFill to enter duplicate data, such as the same row heading or number data across

a row or down a column. You can create your own custom data lists as well as utilize built-in lists of common entries such as days of the week, months, and number series. You can also use AutoFill to copy formulas across cells.

When you make a cell active in the worksheet, a small fill handle appears in the lower-right corner of the selector. You can use the fill handle to create an AutoFill series.

See also>> **Data**

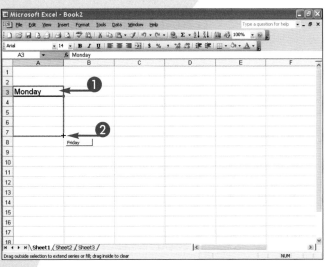

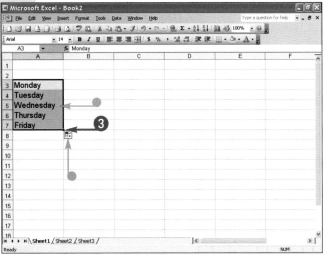

AutoFill a Text Series

① Type the first entry in the text series.

② Click and drag the cell's fill handle across or down the number of cells you want to fill.

You can also use AutoFill to copy the same text to every cell you drag over.

③ Release the mouse button.

● AutoFill fills in the text series.

● An AutoFill smart tag may appear offering additional options you can assign to the data.

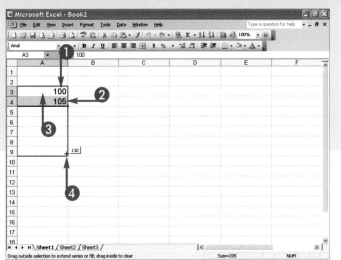

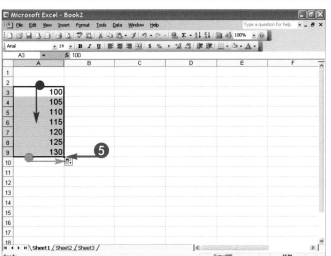

① Type the first entry in the number series.

② In an adjacent cell, type the next entry in the number series.

③ Select both cells.

④ Click and drag the fill handle across or down the number of cells you want to fill.

⑤ Release the mouse button.

● AutoFill fills in the text series.

● An AutoFill smart tag may appear offering additional options you can assign to the data.

Did You Know?

You can add your own custom list to AutoFill's list library. To do so, first create the custom list in your worksheet cells. Then select the cells containing the list you want to save and click the Tools menu and then Options. This opens the Options dialog box. Click the Custom Lists tab and click Import. Excel adds the data series to the list of custom lists. Click OK to exit the dialog box.

Did You Know?

You can double-click the AutoFill handle to automatically extend a data series to match the number of cells in an adjacent column or row. For example, if column A has a series of data extending from cell A3 to cell A6, and you want to create another series matching the same number of cells in row B, you can double-click the AutoFill handle. Simply enter the first data series in cell B3 and then double-click the AutoFill handle. Excel automatically fills the series up to cell B6 for you.

AUTOFILTER:
Filter Database Data

When using an Excel worksheet as a database, you can use a filter to view only portions of your data. You can use Excel as a database program to organize, sort, filter, and analyze lists of data. For example, you might create an Excel database list to manage sales contacts, inventory, household valuables, and more. You can then use the AutoFilter feature to quickly view only select portions of your database list.

Unlike a *sort*, which sorts the entire table, a *filter* selects certain records to display based on your criteria, while hiding the other records that do not match the criteria. When you apply a filter, you can specify which field to filter in the list. Excel automatically assigns drop-down filter arrows for each column heading, allowing you to apply multiple filter criteria to your list.

When applying a filter, you can choose from several filter options, including a Top 10 option for filtering only the top 10 values or top percent of the database records.

See also>>   **Database**

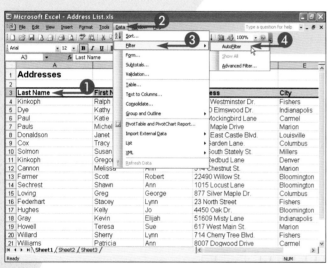

① Select the field labels for the data you want to sort.

② Click Data.

③ Click Filter.

④ Click AutoFilter.

If you used the Create List command to create a database list, your table already displays the AutoFilter buttons.

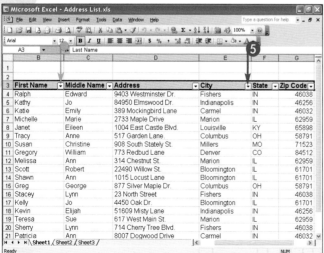

● Excel adds drop-down arrow buttons to your field labels.

⑤ Click an arrow.

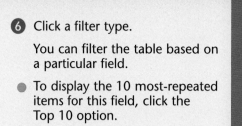

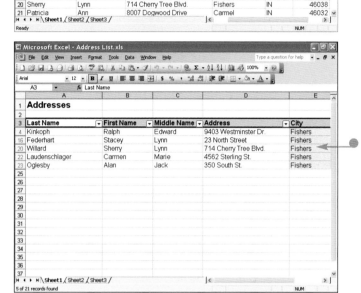

6 Click a filter type.

You can filter the table based on a particular field.

● To display the 10 most-repeated items for this field, click the Top 10 option.

● To customize your filter, you can click this option.

● Excel filters the table.

To view all the records again, display the filter list and click All.

Did You Know?

AutoFilter lists a Top 10 option for every field. You can use the option to quickly filter for the top or bottom 10 items in your table. For example, you might want to view the top 10 salespeople, or the bottom 10 sellers from your product list.

Did You Know?

You can activate the Custom command in the filter drop-down menu list to open the Custom AutoFilter dialog box. Then you can further customize the filter by selecting operators and values to apply on the filtered data. To learn more about customizing AutoFilters, see Excel's Help files.

AUTOFORMAT:
Apply Preset Formatting

You can use Excel's AutoFormat feature to apply preset formatting styles to your worksheet data. With spreadsheets, presentation goes a long way in helping the intended audience read and interpret your data. Number data is especially difficult to examine, so taking time to make the data readable is an important part of creating a worksheet. If you prefer not to spend a lot of time worrying about how your data looks, AutoFormat is the tool for you.

AutoFormat offers 16 different preset styles you can choose from, and each one creates a different look

for your worksheet. Styles include accounting styles, list styles, color styles, and 3D styles. The AutoFormat dialog box shows a preview of what each style looks like. The preset styles include formatting for numbers, font, font sizes, alignment, borders, and cell background colors. You can choose a preset style as-is, or fine-tune one to suit the needs of your worksheet.

See also>> **Formatting**

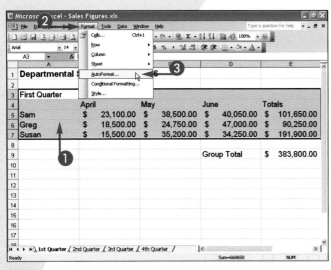

① Select the cells you want to format.

② Click Format.

③ Click AutoFormat.

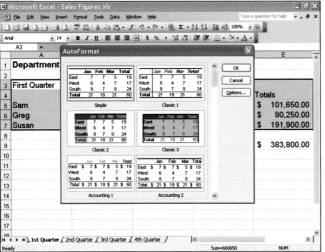

The AutoFormat dialog box opens.

You can use the scroll arrows to view all the available styles.

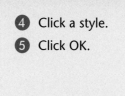

④ Click a style.

⑤ Click OK.

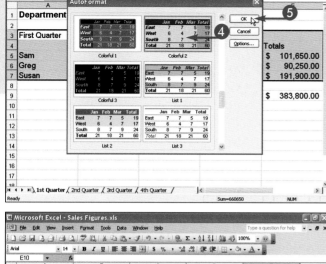

● Excel applies the formatting to the selected data.

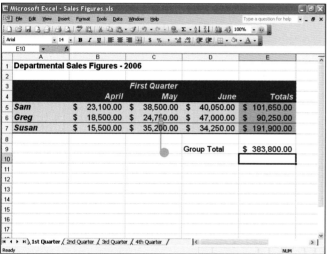

Customize It

If you like some aspects of a style, but want to change others, you can customize the style. Simply click the Options button in the AutoFormat dialog box to display the individual formatting options. For example, you can choose to turn off some formatting while leaving other formats on for the style. You can also add your own formatting to the style after it is applied to the worksheet cells.

Did You Know?

If you find yourself applying the same set of formatting over and over again in your worksheets, you can assign the formatting as a style. A *style* is simply a collection of formatting commands you can apply to your data all at once rather than applying the commands one at a time. To learn more about creating styles in Excel, see the Style technique.

AUTOSHAPES:
Draw AutoShapes

You can use Excel's drawing tools to draw your own shapes and graphics for your worksheets. One of the fastest ways to add a drawing is to create an AutoShape. You can choose from a library of predrawn shapes in the AutoShapes palette. You can access the AutoShapes palette through Excel's Drawing toolbar. The palette includes categories for lines, arrows, basic shapes, callouts, connectors, and more. Each category includes a list of objects you can draw. For example, the Block Arrows category lists a variety of arrow shapes and types you can draw on your worksheet.

After you select a shape, you can control the size and position of the shape as you draw on the

worksheet. After completing the shape, you can continue to move it and resize it as needed.

AutoShapes are just one of several features you can find on Excel's Drawing toolbar. The toolbar also includes tools for controlling the color and thickness of the lines and shapes you draw. You can apply formatting to drawn objects after you draw the shape on the worksheet.

See also>>

Draw

Objects

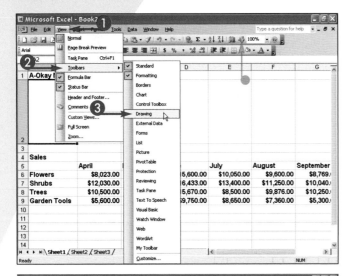

1. Click View.
2. Click Toolbars.
3. Click Drawing.
- You can also click the Drawing button on the Standard toolbar.

The Drawing toolbar appears at the bottom of the program window.

4. Click the AutoShapes button.
5. Click an AutoShape category.
6. Click an AutoShape.

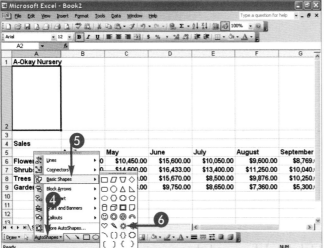

110

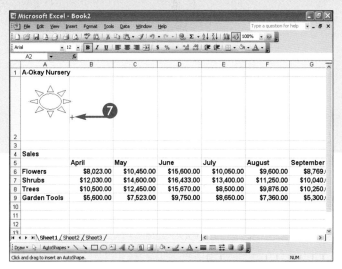

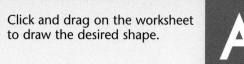

7 Click and drag on the worksheet to draw the desired shape.

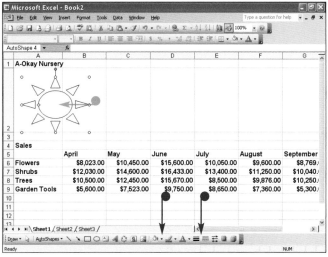

● When you release the mouse, Excel completes the shape.

Note: You can move and resize the object or edit it with the Drawing toolbar buttons.

● You can use these buttons to add a fill color or define the line thickness and color of the shape after drawing the shape.

TIPS

Customize It

You can access additional AutoShapes to draw with Excel's Clip Art task pane. To find more AutoShapes, click the AutoShapes button on the Drawing toolbar and click More AutoShapes. The Clip Art task pane opens revealing more shapes you can utilize in your worksheets. Simply select the one you want to apply, and then move or resize it to suit your needs.

Try This

You can retain an AutoShape's proportions by holding down the Shift key while dragging the shape on a worksheet. This same technique also works for any objects you draw using the Drawing toolbar tools. For example, if you click the Oval tool and hold the Shift key while drawing, Excel maintains a perfect circle shape.

AUTOSUM:
Total Data with AutoSum

Excel's functions can help you speed up common mathematical tasks. Functions are simply built-in formulas you can apply to your data. One of the most popular functions available in Excel is the AutoSum function. AutoSum is so popular that a handy button is on the Standard toolbar for easy access.

AutoSum automatically totals the contents of cells. For example, you can quickly total a column of sales figures or a row of test scores. AutoSum works by guessing which surrounding cells you want to total, or you can specify exactly which cells to sum.

If you prefer to apply another function instead of the Sum function, you can click the button's drop-down arrow and select another common Excel function to apply, such as AVG, COUNT, MAX, or MIN.

See also>> AutoSum

See also>> Functions

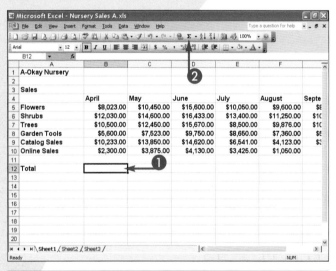

① Click in the cell where you want to insert a sum total.

② Click the AutoSum button on the Standard toolbar.

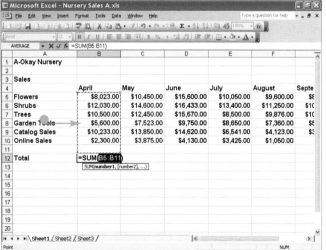

● AutoSum immediately attempts to total the adjacent cells.

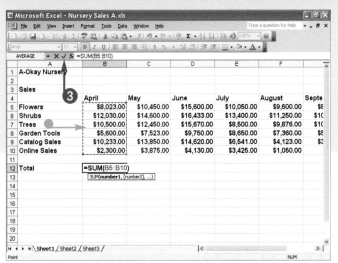

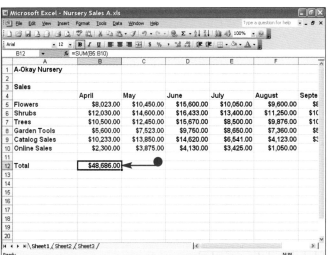

- To sum a specific range of cells, select the cells you want to include in the sum.

③ Press Enter or click the Enter button on the Formula bar.

● Excel totals the selected cells.

TIPS

Did You Know?

You can use the AutoCalculate feature to quickly sum cells or apply results from several other popular functions without having to insert a formula or function. You can select a group of cells you want to total and Excel immediately adds all the cell contents and displays a total in the status bar at the bottom of the program window. To change the calculation type, right-click over the total on the status bar and click another function. To sum noncontiguous cells, press and hold the Ctrl key while clicking cells.

Did You Know?

You can apply AutoSum to both rows and columns at the same time. Simply select both the row and column of data you want to sum, along with a blank row and column to hold the results. Apply the AutoSum function, and Excel sums the row and column and displays the results in the blank row and column.

BORDERS:
Add Borders to Cells

You can add borders to your worksheet cells to help define the content or more clearly separate the data from surrounding cells. By default, Excel displays a grid format to help you enter data, but the borders defining the grid do not print out.

You can add borders to emphasize cells. You can also add borders to all four sides of a cell, or just one or two sides. Any borders you add to the sheet are printed along with the worksheet data.

You can use the Borders button on the Formatting toolbar to quickly assign a variety of border types to

a cell or range, including borders for each side of a cell and several different border styles. For example, you can choose to add a border only on the outside perimeter of a group of cells, or add borders to all the inner cells. You can also use the Format Cells dialog box to assign and customize borders.

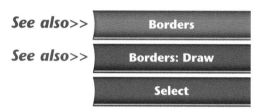

See also>> Borders

See also>> Borders: Draw

Select

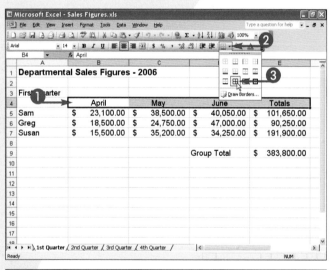

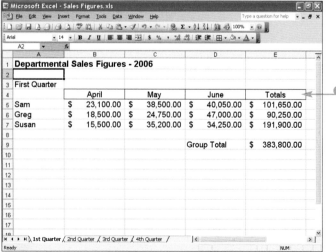

Add Quick Borders

1 Select the cells you want to format.

2 Click the Borders button.

To apply the current border selection shown, simply click the Borders button, not the arrow.

3 Click a border style.

● Excel immediately assigns the borders to the cell.

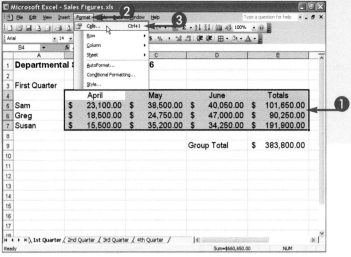

1 Select the cells you want to format.

2 Click Format.

3 Click Cells.

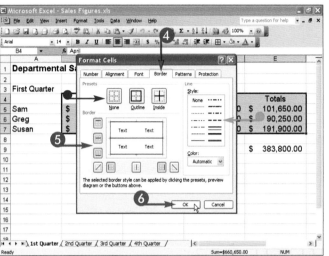

The Format Cells dialog box opens.

4 Click the Border tab.

5 Click the type of border you want to assign.

You can click multiple border buttons to create a custom border.

● To set a particular line style to the border, click a style here.

● You can also click a preset style to assign.

6 Click OK.

Excel assigns the border.

Did You Know?

You can turn the worksheet gridlines on or off. By default, Excel displays gridlines to help you differentiate between cells as you build your worksheets. You can turn gridlines off to view how your data will look when printed. Click the Tools menu and then click Options. Click the View tab and deselect the Gridlines check box (☑ changes to ☐) to turn gridlines off. Excel does not print gridlines unless you specify.

Try This

By default, all borders you add to your cells appear in the default color, black. You can add color to your cell borders using the Format Cells dialog box. Start by selecting the cells containing the borders you want to add color to, click the Format menu, and then click Cells. Click the Border tab, click the Color drop-down arrow, and then choose a color for the borders.

BORDERS:
Draw a Border on a Worksheet

You can draw your own borders to truly customize your worksheet and set off cells and data. You can use the Draw Border feature to customize exactly where you want to place a border in a cell. A border is simply a line defining the edges of a cell or range. For example, you might draw a border in the middle of a range of cells, or choose only to border the right side of a cell. You can use the Draw Border feature to create unique borders within a range of cells, such as drawing a border around all but the middle few cells in a range.

When you activate the Draw Border feature, the Borders toolbar appears. You can use the toolbar

tools to draw and erase border lines on your worksheet, as well as control the line style and color. Excel offers 13 different line styles you can apply to customize your borders, including dashed lines, thick lines, and double lines.

The Borders toolbar also offers the Draw Grid tool, which you can use to quickly draw borders around a group of cells.

See also>> **Borders**

See also>> **Borders: Add**

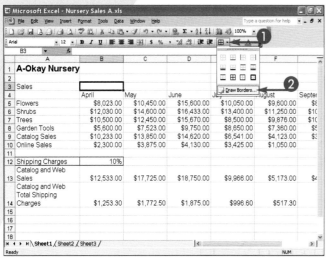

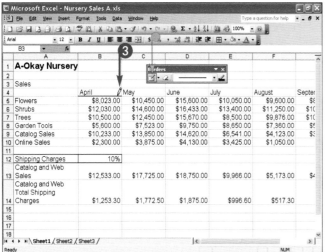

Draw a Border Line

1 Click the Borders button.

2 Click Draw Borders.

● The Borders toolbar opens with the Draw Border button activated.

3 Draw a border where you want it to appear on the worksheet.

Excel immediately adds a line.

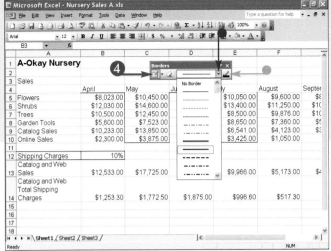

- To change the line color, click the Line Color button and then click another color.

- To change the line style, click here and then click another style.

④ When you are finished creating your borders, click the Draw Border button to turn the Draw Border command off.

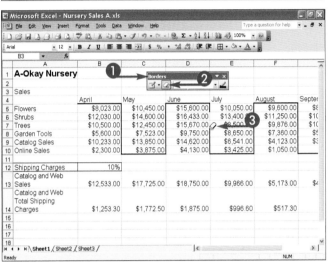

Erase a Border Line

① Display the Borders toolbar.

Note: See the previous steps to learn how to activate the Draw Borders feature.

② Click the Erase Border button.

③ Drag over the border you want to remove.

Excel removes the border.

TIPS

Change It

To draw a grid of border lines on a worksheet rather than single lines, click the drop-down arrow next to the Draw Borders button on the Borders toolbar. Then click Draw Border Grid. You can now drag across a range of cells to quickly add borders to all the cells. To customize the line style and color, assign the style and color options before dragging across the cells.

Try This

If you are having difficulty viewing the worksheet cells while trying to draw borders, try magnifying your view. Click the Zoom button on the Standard toolbar and select a larger magnification setting, such as 200 percent.

CELLS:
Add Cells

You may already know you can add columns and rows to your Excel worksheets. You can also add individual cells. For example, perhaps you have painstakingly created a multiple-column list of sales figures only to find you left out a cell in the middle of the list. You can add a cell to the list and shift the surrounding cells over to make room for the addition.

You can add blank cells to your worksheet using the Insert Cells dialog box. You can use the dialog box to insert a single cell, multiple cells, or an entire row or column. When using the Insert Cells command, you can control which direction the existing cells shift to make room for the new cell or cells.

To add a single cell, simply click the worksheet where you want to add the cell. To add multiple cells, first

select where you want to insert new cells, selecting the number of cells you want to add. If the cell or cells you select already contain formatting, the new cells also have the same formatting applied.

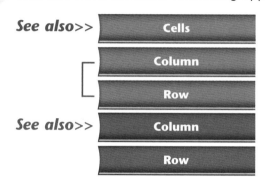

See also>> Cells

See also>> Column

Row

Column

Row

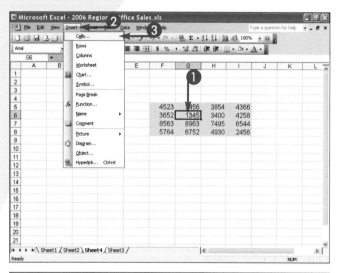

① Click a cell where you want to insert a new cell.

To add more than one cell, select the number of cells you want to add.

② Click Insert.

③ Click Cells.

You can also right-click the cell and click Insert.

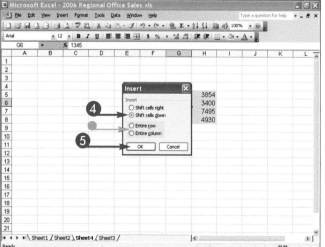

The Insert dialog box opens.

④ Click a direction in which you want the cells to shift.

● If you want to insert an entire row or column, select one of these options.

⑤ Click OK.

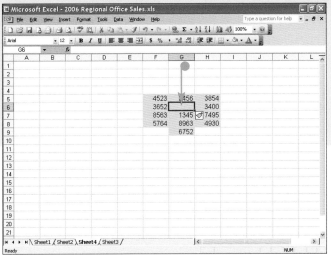

● Excel inserts a blank cell.

Note: To repeat the action again, you can press Ctrl+Y and add another blank cell in the same fashion.

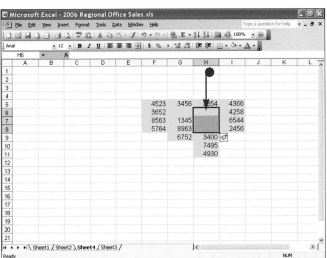

● In this example, multiple new cells are added.

TIPS

More Options

If you insert a cell into the middle of a group of cells, the new cell inherits all the formatting already assigned. If you want to control how the formatting is set in the new cell, you can click the smart icon (⌖) that appears when you insert the cell. The smart icon offers you three choices for controlling the formatting. You can choose the same formatting from the cell above the newly added cell, choose the formatting from the cell below, or clear the formatting entirely.

Did You Know?

When you add cells, any formula references to the adjusted cells that move to make room for the new cells, change accordingly. Excel does this by default, regardless of whether the cell references are relative or absolute. For example, perhaps you insert data into cells B3, B4, and B5 and create a formula elsewhere in the worksheet that references cell B5. If you insert a new cell into the group, say below cell B3, Excel makes sure the cell references change to adjust for the newly added cell.

CHART:
Change the Chart Axes Scale

You can use the Format Axis dialog box to make changes to the way in which the category (X) or value (Y) axis is displayed in a chart. For example, you may want to make the category (X) axis tick marks appear at different intervals, or change the unit measurement for the value (Y) axis. The Format Axis dialog box features several tabs for making changes to the chart axes.

You can use the Scale tab to make adjustments to the appearance of the X or Y axis in a chart. Depending on which axis you choose to edit, the Scale tab displays different options for controlling the scale of an axis. For example, if you select the category (X) axis to edit, the Scale tab displays options for controlling where you want the value (Y)

axis to cross the X axis, or specify how you want the categories spaced along the X axis.

When editing the value (Y) axis, the Scale tab displays options for changing the number in which the Y axis starts and stops, adjust the interval of tick marks, or specify the display units.

See also>>   Chart Toolbar

See also>>   Chart: Create

Chart: Format

Appendix A

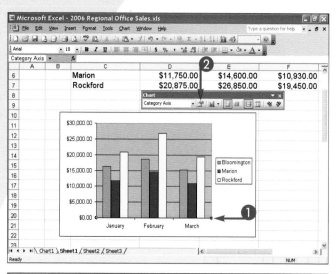

Edit the X Axis

① Click the category (X) axis.

② Click the Format Axis button on the Chart toolbar.

Note: You can also right-click the selected axis and click Format Axis or click the Format menu and click Selected Axis.

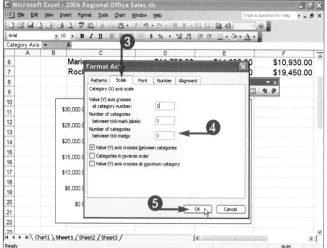

The Format Axis dialog box opens.

③ Click the Scale tab.

The tab displays options for setting the category (X) axis.

④ Click any options you want to set for the X axis.

⑤ Click OK.

Excel applies any changes to the axis.

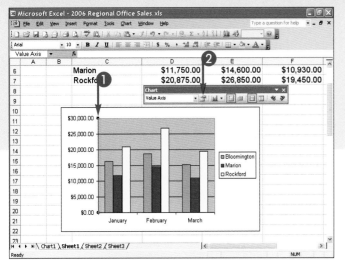

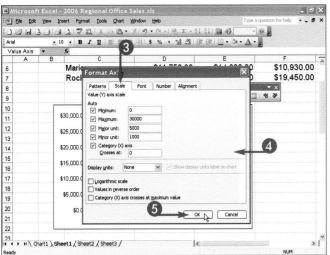

Edit the Y Axis

1 Click the value (Y) axis.

2 Click the Format Axis button on the Chart toolbar.

Note: You can also right-click the selected axis and click Format Axis or click the Format menu and click Selected Axis.

The Format Axis dialog box opens.

3 Click the Scale tab.

The tab displays options for setting the Y axis.

4 Click any options you want to set for the Y axis.

5 Click OK.

Excel applies any changes to the axis.

More Options

You can format other aspects of the X or Y axis using the Format Axis dialog box. For example, you can click the Patterns tab and make changes to the formatting of the axes lines, such as setting a new color or line thickness. You can click the Font tab to make changes to the font and size used for the category (X) axis, or click the Alignment tab to adjust the alignment of the axis text labels.

Did You Know?

If you are choosing between using a scatter chart, which displays values on both the category (X) axis and the value (Y) axis, and a line chart, which displays values only on the Y axis, it may be helpful to know that you cannot make as many adjustments to the line chart's category (X) axis as you can with a scatter chart. For this reason, you may prefer to use a scatter chart to access additional scaling options for customizing the axes.

CHART:
Change the Chart Axes Titles

You can change the titles of the X or Y axis on your chart. For example, you may prefer to give the axes more descriptive titles, or if your titles are too long, you may want to shorten the title text. You can change chart title information using the Chart Options dialog box.

With the exception of pie charts, all charts have an X axis and at least one Y axis. By default, the Chart Wizard does not add titles to the chart or axes unless you type then in while using the wizard. You can add titles at a later time using the Titles tab in the Chart Options dialog box.

When assigning axis titles, it is important to remember which axis is which in the chart. With the

example of a bar chart, the X axis typically appears across the bottom of the chart, illustrating categories, such as sales people or regions. When you add an X axis title, it appears below the X axis categories. The Y axis runs up and down the left side of the chart. When you add a Y axis title, it appears perpendicular to the Y axis.

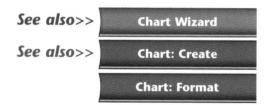

See also>> **Chart Wizard**

See also>> **Chart: Create**

Chart: Format

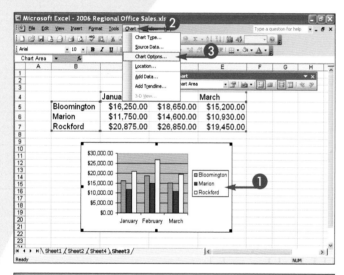

① Select the chart you want to edit.

② Click Chart.

③ Click Chart Options.

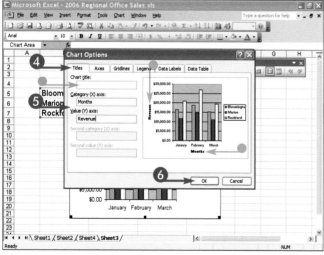

The Chart Options dialog box opens.

④ Click the Titles tab.

⑤ Type a title for the X or Y axis you want to edit.

● The new axis titles appear in the preview area.

● You can assign a title for your chart using this text box.

⑥ Click OK.

Excel applies the new titles to the chart.

Note: Any time you add elements to your chart, the existing elements may appear crowded. You can resize your chart to fit the new chart objects.

CHART:
Change the Chart Data Series

You can make changes to a chart's data series. A data series is a group of data points, such as a line in a bar chart tracking rising and falling sales figures. Each point on the line represents a change in data based on the series of cells you selected to create the chart.

For example, if your chart tracks the monthly sales of your company's sales staff, the data series is the values found in the monthly totals for each salesperson in the worksheet. If you left out a salesperson, or need to expand the monthly values to include another quarter's worth of sales, you can make your changes directly on the worksheet without leaving the selected chart.

Whenever you make changes to the data referenced in your chart, the chart data is automatically updated. For example, if you change a value, the chart updates to reflect the new value. If you need to add more data to the chart, you can easily update the source cells.

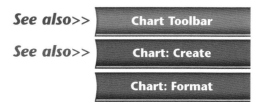

See also>> **Chart Toolbar**

See also>> **Chart: Create**

Chart: Format

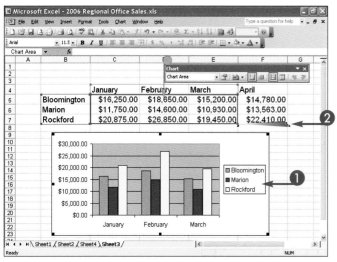

1 Select the chart you want to edit.

● Excel surrounds the chart with selection handles and marks the source data in the worksheet with a colored border.

2 Click and drag the corner handle of the source range to add or subtract cells.

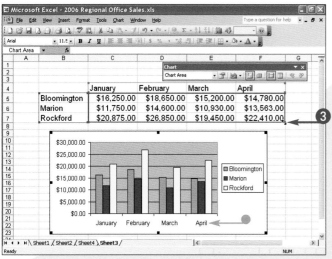

3 Release the mouse button.

● Excel updates the chart with any changes.

CHART:
Change Chart Elements

You can change existing and add additional chart elements to your Excel charts, such as including data labels, adding gridlines, or a legend. The Chart Options dialog box lists a variety of chart objects you can turn on or off in your chart.

The Titles tab offers options for adding chart or axes titles. You might add additional titles to both the axes in your chart to clarify the data you are presenting.

The Axes tab offers options for controlling the appearance of the category (X) and value (Y) axes in your chart. For example, you can hide or display the X and Y axes, if needed. The Gridlines tab includes settings for controlling the appearance of gridlines in your chart. For example, your chart might be easier

to read if you turn on minor intervals on the category (X) or value (Y) axis.

You can use the Data Labels tab to display or hide data labels in your chart, such as displaying the series name. Use the Data Table tab to show the values for each data series underneath the chart, or to show legend keys for each series.

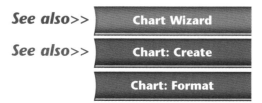

See also>>   Chart Wizard

See also>>   Chart: Create

Chart: Format

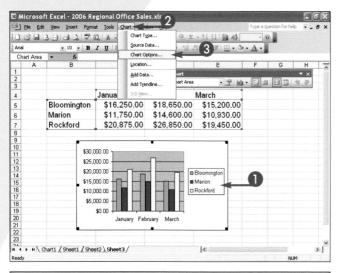

1 Select the chart you want to edit.

2 Click Chart.

3 Click Chart Options.

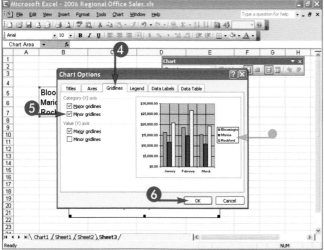

The Chart Options dialog box opens.

4 Click the tab for the type of object you want to add.

5 Designate any new elements you want to include.

● The preview area shows what the new objects will look like on the chart.

6 Click OK.

CHART:
Change the Chart Type

You can change the chart type at any time to present your data in a different way. For example, you might want to change a bar chart to a line chart, or you may find a different bar chart style more appealing than a plain bar chart.

Excel offers 11 types of charts, and each type includes a variety of styles. Line charts, column charts, and bar charts are three of the most common charts people use. A line chart illustrates your chart data as a line with markers at key points along the line. Instead of markers on a line, a bar chart shows a bar for each value. Scatter charts allow you to compare pairs of values. The cylinder, cone, and pyramid charts are 3-D column

charts that use other shapes instead of columns to illustrate the data series.

You can use the Chart toolbar to quickly change to another chart type. If you prefer to choose a different style rather than a different chart entirely, you can open the Chart Type dialog box.

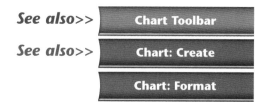

See also>> Chart Toolbar

See also>> Chart: Create

Chart: Format

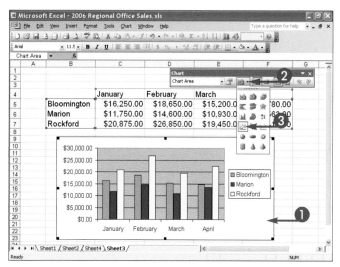

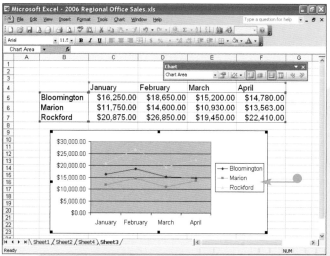

① Click an empty area of the chart to select the chart.

The Chart toolbar appears.

Note: If the Chart toolbar does not appear, click the View menu, Toolbars, and then Chart to display the toolbar.

② Click the Chart Type button on the Chart toolbar.

③ Click a new chart type.

Note: You can also reopen the Chart dialog box to change the chart type. Simply click the Chart menu and then click Chart Type.

● Excel applies the type to the existing chart.

CHART:
Create a Chart

You can use the Chart Wizard to quickly assemble and create all kinds of charts in Excel. The wizard walks you through each step for creating the chart, including selecting the chart type, data range, and specifying a location for the chart. You can determine exactly which type of chart works best for your data.

When activated, the Chart Wizard uses a series of four dialog boxes — each presents an important step along the way for creating a chart. You can use the first dialog box to choose the type of chart you want to create. You can choose from 14 chart types and numerous sub-types.

The second dialog box allows you to confirm or select the range of data you want to chart. The third dialog

box displays the various chart options you can apply, such as assigning chart and axes titles or a legend. You can use the various tabs to assign chart options such as controlling the chart's gridlines or data labels.

See also>> | Chart Toolbar

Chart Wizard

See also>> | Chart: Change Chart Axes Titles

Chart: Change Chart Data Series

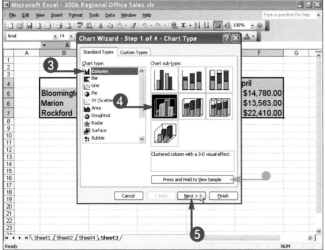

1. Select the range of data you want to chart.

   Include any headings and labels, but do not include subtotals or totals.

2. Click the Chart Wizard button on the Standard toolbar.

   Note: You can also click the Insert menu and then Chart.

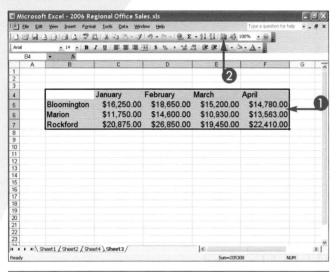

The first Chart Wizard dialog box opens.

3. Click a chart type.

4. Click a chart sub-type.

● You can click and hold this button to view a sample of your data as depicted in the chart type you select.

5. Click Next.

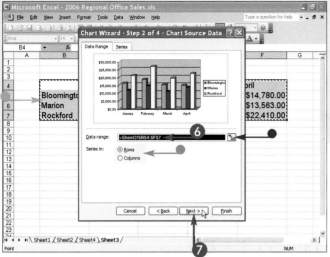

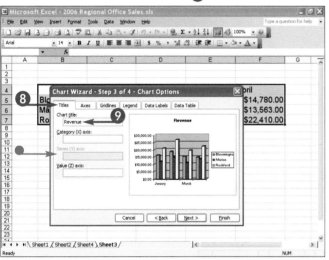

6 Verify the data range.

● If the data range is incorrect, you can select the correct range on the worksheet.

● Click the Collapse Dialog button if you want to move the wizard out of the way to select cells.

● You can change the orientation for the data series by choosing one of these options.

7 Click Next.

8 Click the Titles tab if it is not already selected.

Note: Depending on the chart type you select, the available wizard tabs may vary.

9 Type a title for your chart.

● You can also type axis titles.

Did You Know?

The data you select for a chart does not have to be adjacent to each other. To select noncontiguous cells and ranges, select the first range in the Excel worksheet and then press and hold the Ctrl key while selecting additional ranges to include. If the Chart Wizard dialog box is in the way, you can move it by dragging its title bar, or click the Collapse/Expand button (🔳) at the end of the Data Range field.

More Options

You can create a custom chart with a little help from the Chart Wizard. You can click the Custom Types tab in the first Chart Wizard dialog box that appears. The Custom Types tab offers a variety of chart backgrounds and color selections to help you create a customized chart to your liking. After selecting the one you want, you can continue creating the chart using the rest of the Wizard dialog boxes.

CHART:
Create a Chart (Continued)

You can use the last Chart Wizard dialog box to determine where you want to place the chart. You can choose to insert your chart on the current worksheet, or place it on a new sheet in your workbook. If you embed the chart on the current sheet, you can treat the chart like any other object you add to a spreadsheet — which means you can move, resize, and edit the chart as a separate element from your worksheet data. If you place the chart on a new worksheet and it takes up the entire sheet in the workbook, you cannot move and resize it like an embedded chart.

After you complete the Chart Wizard, Excel adds the chart to the designated location and displays a Chart

toolbar you can use to fine-tune your chart. For example, you may want to change the formatting of the chart elements, or try assigning another chart type. You can use the Chart toolbar to access a variety of chart tools for formatting and changing the chart.

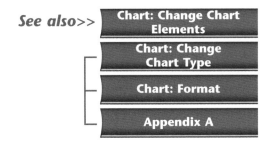

See also>>

| Chart: Change Chart Elements |
| Chart: Change Chart Type |
| Chart: Format |
| Appendix A |

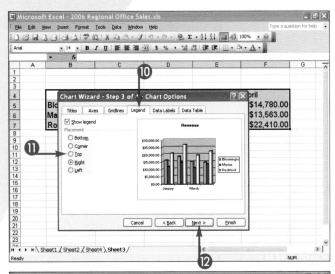

⑩ Click the Legend tab.

⑪ Specify a location for the legend.

⑫ Click Next.

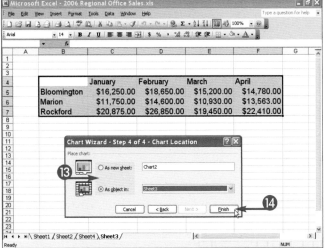

⑬ Designate a location for the chart.

To create the chart on a new sheet in your workbook file, click the As New Sheet option and give the sheet a title.

To embed the chart in the current sheet, click the As Object In option.

⑭ Click Finish.

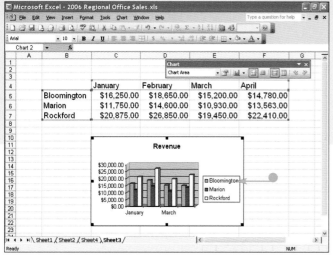

- Excel creates the chart and displays it in the designated sheet.

  In this example, the chart is embedded into the current sheet.

  When embedding a chart, you may need to make room for it in the worksheet, or you can move it to another location on the sheet.

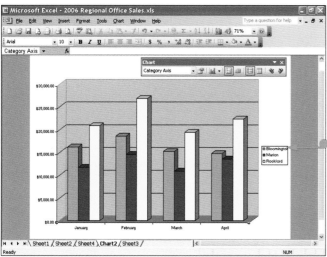

- In this example, the chart appears on its own sheet in the workbook.

TIPS

More Options

If you customize a chart, fine-tuning the chart elements and formatting, you can save the chart as a chart type in Excel. Right-click the chart and click Chart Type. In the Chart Type dialog box, click the Custom Types tab. Select the User-defined option (○ changes to ◉) and then click the Add button. The Add Custom Chart Type dialog box appears where you can enter a name and description of the chart. Excel then adds it to the list of custom charts that appear in the Custom Types tab. You can reuse the chart at any time.

Did You Know?

You can add an organizational chart to track hierarchy of an organization or method. When you insert an organization chart, Excel starts you with four shapes to which you can add your own text. You can add additional shapes and branches to the chart as needed. Click Insert, Picture, and then Organization Chart. Excel immediately adds a basic organization chart to your worksheet and displays the Drawing toolbar and the Organization Chart toolbar. You can then click a chart shape and type your text. To learn more about this feature, see the technique "Organization Chart: Insert an Organization Chart."

CHART:
Format Chart Elements

You can change the formatting for any of the elements, called *objects* in Excel, contained within a chart. For example, you can change the background color or pattern for the plot area, or change the color of a data series on the chart. You may decide you need to change the color of several chart elements to make them easier to read in a presentation.

You can click various chart elements and change the formatting using the Chart toolbar as well as use the tools found on the Formatting and Drawing toolbars. You can also move and resize different chart elements to change the visual appeal of a chart.

You can open the Format dialog box for any particular chart object and access a variety of

formatting commands and features. For example, if you select the plot area of the chart to edit and open the Format Plot Area dialog box, you can access a variety of colors and border styles you can apply to the plot area.

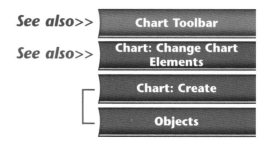

See also>> Chart Toolbar

See also>> Chart: Change Chart Elements

Chart: Create

Objects

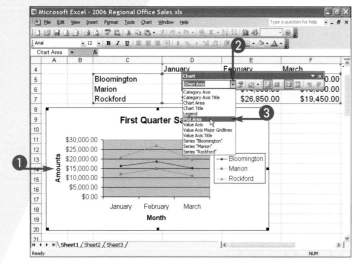

① Select the chart.

The Chart toolbar appears.

Note: If the Chart toolbar does not appear, click the View menu, Toolbars, and then Chart to display the toolbar.

② Click the Chart Objects button on the Chart toolbar.

③ Click the chart object you want to edit.

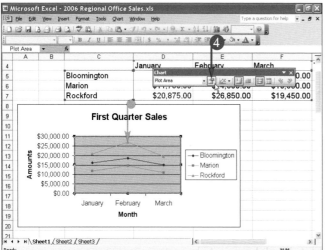

● Excel selects the object in the chart.

④ Click the Format button on the Chart toolbar.

Depending on the chart object you want to edit, the Format button may have a different name.

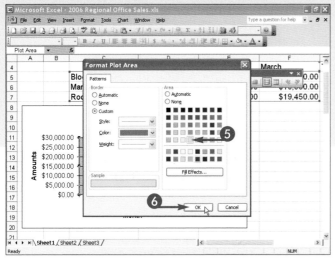

The Format dialog box for the chart object opens.

5 Make any changes to the chart object, as needed.

In this example, a new fill color is applied.

Depending on the chart object you edit, the dialog box may offer different tabs of formatting options you can apply.

6 When finished with your edits, click OK.

Excel applies any changes to the chart.

● In this example, a new fill color is added to the plot area.

TIPS

Did You Know?

You can change the font for your chart text. You can double-click any chart element to open the Format dialog box and quickly make edits. For example, if you double-click chart text, the Format dialog box for the element opens and you can click the Font tab to make changes to the font, font size, color, and style.

More Options

To print only the chart in your Excel workbook, first select the chart on the worksheet, click the File menu, and then click Print. The Print dialog box opens. Make sure the Selected Chart option is selected (○ changes to ◉), and then click OK to print the chart. If the chart is on its own sheet, you can just click the Print button () to print the sheet.

CLIP ART:
Download Clip Art from the Web

Clip art is a great way to illustrate your Excel worksheets. For example, you might use clip art to illustrate the topic of a spreadsheet. Excel installs with the Microsoft Office Clip Art gallery, a collection of clip art images you can use in your Excel spreadsheets.

If you cannot find the clip art image you are looking for, you can check the Microsoft Office Web site. You can peruse the site for additional clip art to use in your workbooks, and if you find something you want to use, you can download and import it into a clip art collection in the Microsoft Clip Organizer.

For example, you can conduct a search on the Microsoft Office Web site for the type of clip art you

need. Clip art is arranged into categories. You may find one or several clip art images to use. When you activate the Download command, the File Download dialog box opens where you can download the file or files.

You must log on to your Internet connection to view the Office Web pages and download clip art.

See also>> **Clip Art**

See also>> **Clip Art: Insert**

Clip Art: View

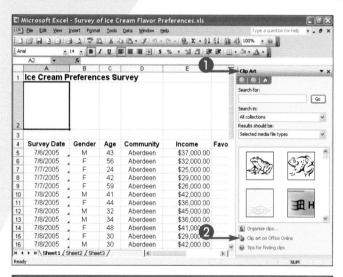

① Display the Clip Art task pane.

Note: You can click the Insert menu and then Clip Art to open the Clip Art task pane.

② Click Clip Art on Office Online.

Note: You must first log on to your Internet connection before clicking the Web site link.

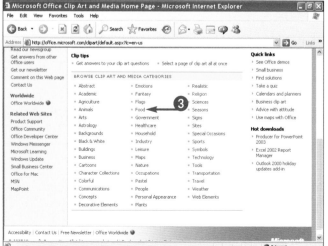

Your default Web browser opens to the Office Web site.

③ Click a clip art category link.

To look for a particular media format, you can click the Search drop-down arrow at the top of the Web page and choose a format.

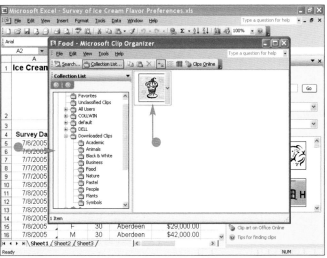

- You can use the Search tools at the top of the page to find a particular clip art image to download.

- You can use the navigation links to move through the clip art pages.

④ Select a check box to choose an image to download.

- The clip art is added to your download basket.

⑤ When you are ready to download the images, click the Download link and follow the download instructions as prompted.

- When the download is complete, the clip art is added to the Clip Organizer window where you can view it in the Downloaded Clips category.

Did You Know?

You can purchase clip art collections from computer and office supply stores, as well as find clip art collections to buy on the Internet. For example, if you need to use a lot of work-related clip art, you can look for a business collection of clip art or find collections geared toward certain industries, such as architecture or banking. You can also find clip art for free on the Web, but most sites require registration or a subscription for their services.

Caution

Although it is tempting to use any artwork you find on the Internet, be very careful about using copyrighted images. Most images on the Internet are protected by copyrights, and you cannot reuse them without permission. If you do use a copyright-protected image, be sure to cite its source. You can also ask permission of the Web site's administrator concerning the clip art you find.

CLIP ART:
Format Clip Art

You can edit the clip art objects you add to a worksheet by accessing the Format dialog box. For example, using the dialog box, you can make adjustments to the clip art's color and lines. You can use the Format dialog box to format all kinds of objects you add to Excel, including AutoShapes, WordArt, pictures, and more. Depending on the object, the Format dialog box name may vary, and the dialog box will also display different formatting options you can apply depending on the type of object you are trying to format.

You can make subtle changes to pre-drawn art by adding a border around the clip art. You can use the

Colors and Lines tab in the Format Picture dialog box to add a border, or you can use the Line Style (▤) and Line Color buttons (▨) on the Drawing toolbar to add a border. Depending on the clip art background, you can also make changes to the artwork's fill color or transparency setting.

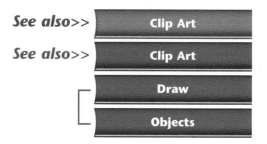

See also>> **Clip Art**

See also>> **Clip Art**

Draw

Objects

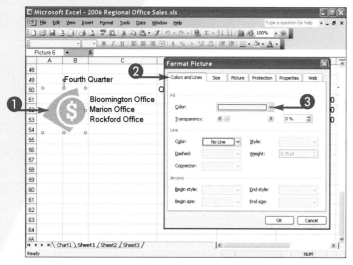

❶ Double-click the clip art you want to edit.

You can also right-click the object and activate the Format command or click the Format Picture button (▨) on the Picture toolbar.

The Format Picture dialog box opens.

❷ Click a tab.

❸ Change any formatting options you want to assign to the clip art object.

You can use the Colors and Lines tab to make changes to the fill color or line or arrow colors of the clip art.

● You can use the Size tab to make changes to the size and scale of the clip art.

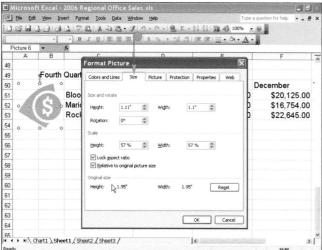

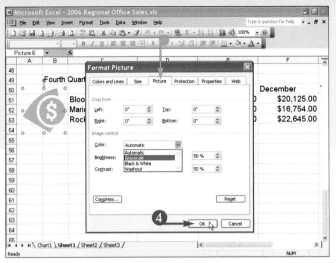

● You can use the Picture tab to make changes to cropping and the appearance of the clip art.

④ Click **OK**.

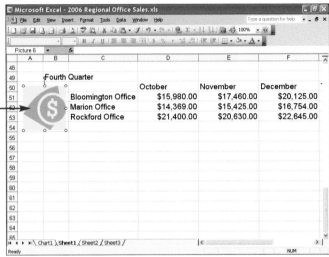

● Excel applies any new settings to the clip art.

TIPS

More Options

You can completely change the look of a clip art image using the Image Control Color options in the Picture tab of the Format Picture dialog box. For example, you can change the clip art to a grayscale image, or make the clip art semi-transparent to use as a watermark or other background image in your worksheet. Click the Picture tab, and then click the Color drop-down arrow to display a list of options.

Did You Know?

You can ungroup a clip art image and make changes to various pieces of the object to create a new look. To apply the ungroup command, first select the object and display the Drawing toolbar. Click the Draw button and click Ungroup. A prompt box appears asking if you want to convert the object to a drawn object; click Yes. You can now click individual elements of the image and make changes, such as choosing a new color.

CLIP ART:
Insert a Clip Art Object

You can add visual interest to your worksheets by inserting clip art images. Clip art is simply pre-drawn artwork. Excel installs with the Microsoft Office clip art collection. The clip art collection contains a large variety of artwork, ranging from business and government to food and travel.

You can use the Clip Art task pane to look for specific types of clip art. For example, you can insert clip art, photographs, movie, and sound clips. If you are looking for a particular image, you can type a keyword or words to search for, and then conduct a search of the Microsoft Office clip art collection. The task pane displays any matching results. You can move your mouse pointer over an image in the pane to learn more about the name and size of the clip art.

After you insert a clip art image, you can move and resize the image to suit your worksheet needs. Like other objects you add to Excel, you can edit the clip art object at any time to make changes to the way it appears in your worksheet.

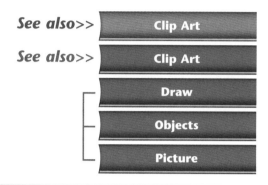

See also>>   Clip Art

See also>>   Clip Art

Draw

Objects

Picture

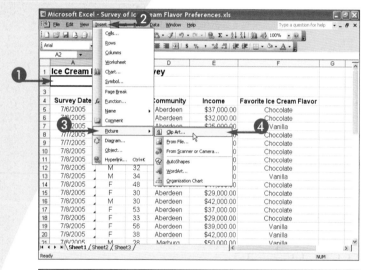

① Click the cell in which you want to add clip art.

You can also move the clip art to a particular location after inserting it onto the worksheet.

② Click Insert.

③ Click Picture.

④ Click Clip Art.

You can also click the Insert Clip Art button (🖾) on the Drawing toolbar.

The Clip Art task pane opens.

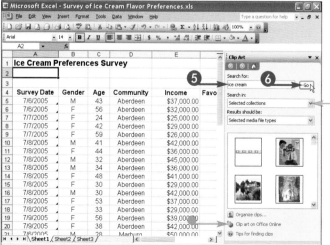

⑤ To search for a particular category of clip art, type a keyword or phrase here.

● To search a particular collection, click here and click a collection.

● You can also search for clip art on the Office Web site by clicking this link.

⑥ Click the Go button.

The Clip Art task pane displays any matches for the keyword or phrase you typed.

- To view information about a clip art image, move the mouse pointer over the image.

⑦ To add a clip art image to your worksheet, click the image.

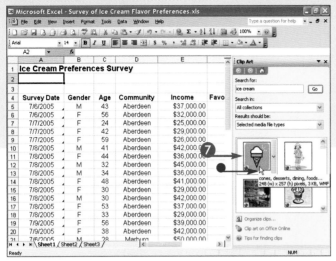

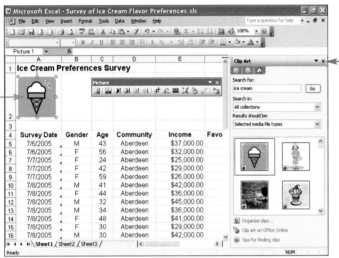

- Excel inserts the clip art and displays the Picture toolbar.

You can resize or move the clip art, if needed, or resize a cell to fit the clip art.

To deselect the clip art, click another area on the worksheet.

- You can click here to close the pane.

TIPS

More Options
To search for a particular type of media, click the Results Should Be drop-down arrow. The drop-down menu displays a list of different media types. You can select or deselect which types to include in your search. If you leave the All Media Types check box selected, Excel searches for a match among all the available media formats.

More Options
To find out more about the clip art's properties in the Clip Art task pane, move the mouse pointer over the image listed, click the drop-down arrow that appears, and then click Preview/Properties. This opens the Preview/Properties dialog box where you can learn more about the file size, filename, file type, its creation date, and more.

C

CLIP ART:
View Clip Art with the Clip Organizer

You can use the Microsoft Clip Organizer to view clip art collections on your computer. You can also insert clip art from the Organizer window and place it in your Excel worksheet. For example, when you need to insert a specific clip art image from one of your collections, you can use the Clip Organizer window to locate and insert the image.

The Microsoft Clip Organizer window organizes your clip art into several types of collections: My Collections, Office Collections, Shared Collections, and Web Collections. My Collections and Office Collections always appear listed first in the Organizer window. My Collections lists all the clip art and graphics found on your computer. Office Collections includes all the

clip art files that install with Microsoft Office. You can further organize your clip art into a Favorites collection stored within the My Collections group.

You can use the Organizer window to search for clip art, move clip art from one collection to another, copy clip art, and remove clip art you no longer want. You can also access clip art online.

See also>>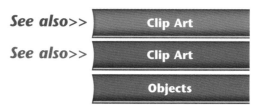

See also>>

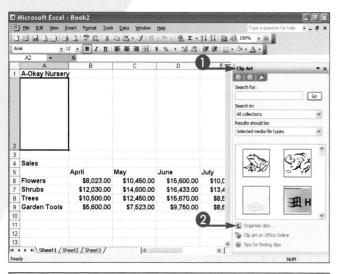

① Display the Clip Art task pane.

② Click Organize Clips.

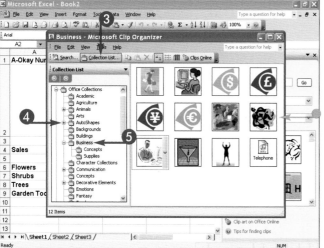

The Microsoft Clip Organizer window opens.

③ Click the Collection List button, if the list is not already viewable.

④ Click a collection expand icon to expand a collection list.

⑤ Click a category.

If some categories include subcategories, click the category expand icon to expand the list.

● The Clip Organizer displays thumbnails of available clip art.

- You can use these buttons to change how clip art is listed in the window.

- To view information about a clip art image, move the mouse pointer over the image.

  To add a clip art image to Excel, drag and drop the clip art onto your worksheet.

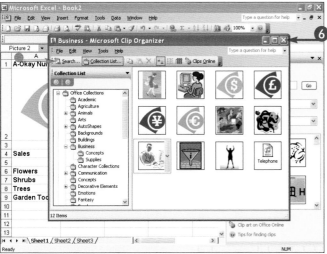

- You can click the Search button to display settings for conducting a search for clip art on your computer.

6 When finished viewing clip art, click the Close button.

  The Microsoft Clip Organizer window closes.

TIPS

More Options

Microsoft Clip Organizer assigns keywords to any clip art you import, basing the keywords from the folder and format of the clip. You can assign your own, more meaningful names to a clip art image. Click the clip in the Organizer window, click the Edit menu, and then click Keywords. This opens the Keywords dialog box. Type the keyword you want to use in the Keyword text box and click Add. To add a caption that appears when you move the mouse pointer over the image, type a caption in the Caption box. Click OK to apply your changes.

Try This

You can create a macro that inserts a clip art image, or any other image file, such as a logo, when you activate the macro keystrokes. Click Tools, Macro, and then Record New Macro. The Record Macro dialog box opens. Type a name for the macro, type a shortcut letter, and then click OK. A macro toolbar appears on the worksheet. Perform all the steps you normally perform to insert the clip art or image file. When finished, click Stop Recording (■) on the macro toolbar. To test the macro, click a blank area of your worksheet and press Ctrl+ the letter you assigned as the shortcut key. Excel automatically inserts the clip art image for you.

COLUMN:
Add a Column

You can add columns to your worksheets to add more data or add more space around existing data. For example, you may need to add a column in the middle of several existing columns to add data you left out the first time you created the workbook. Or you might add a column to create a new group of labels for your rows.

The fastest way to add a column is to use the shortcut menu. You can also use the Insert menu to add rows and columns to your worksheets. When you add a column, Excel automatically shifts the existing columns over in the worksheet to make room for the new column.

By default, Excel displays a smart tag icon any time you add a new column. You can choose to ignore the smart tag or click the smart tag icon to view additional formatting options available for the new column.

See also>>

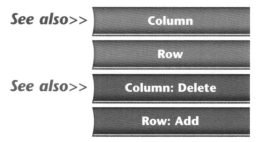

Column
Row

See also>>

Column: Delete
Row: Add

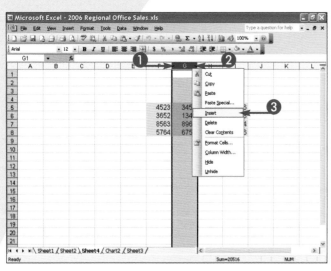

① Click the column to the right of where you want to insert a new column.

② Right-click the selected column.

③ Click Insert.

Note: *You can also click the Insert menu and then Columns.*

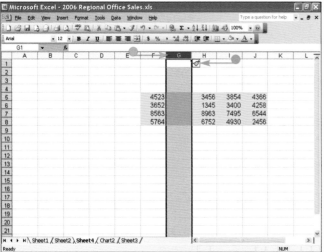

● Excel adds a column.

● A smart tag may appear when you insert a column. You can click the icon to view a list of options you can assign.

COLUMN:
Delete a Column

C

You can remove columns or rows you no longer need in a worksheet. For example, you might remove a column of out-of-date data or delete a column to cut down on extra space surrounding other data in a worksheet.

When you delete an entire column or row, Excel also deletes any existing data within the selected cells. For this reason, you need to make sure you are not deleting any important data from your worksheet before deleting a column. If you accidentally delete a column you need to keep in the worksheet, you can immediately apply the Undo command to reinsert the column.

When you delete a column, Excel moves the other columns over to fill the space left by the deletion. You can delete a single column or multiple columns in your worksheet. To remove more than one column, first select all the columns you want to delete before applying the Delete command.

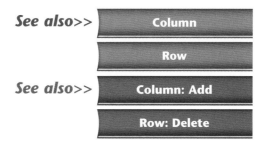

See also>> Column

Row

See also>> Column: Add

Row: Delete

---

① Click the column you want to delete.

② Right-click the selected column.

③ Click Delete.

Note: *If you press the Delete key, Excel deletes the column's content instead of the entire column.*

● Excel deletes the column, and all the columns at right shift over, to fill the void.

Note: *You can also use the Edit menu to remove a column. Click Edit and then click Delete.*

141

COLUMN:
Hide a Column

You can hide columns in your worksheets to help you with a variety of scenarios. For example, if you work in an area in which other people can view your computer screen, you can hide columns to keep confidential information out of view. You might hide a column to prevent data from appearing on a printout. You can also hide data to move it out of the way so you can concentrate on other areas of a worksheet. For example, you might hide a group of columns between the left and right side of a wide worksheet to allow you to focus on the data at either end.

When you hide a column, Excel simply collapses it in the worksheet so the data is no longer in view. When you are ready to view the data again, you can

activate the Unhide command and expand the column again. You can hide a single column or multiple columns in a worksheet. The only way you know a column is hidden is by examining the column headers along the top edge of the worksheet.

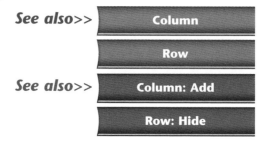

See also>> Column

Row

See also>> Column: Add

Row: Hide

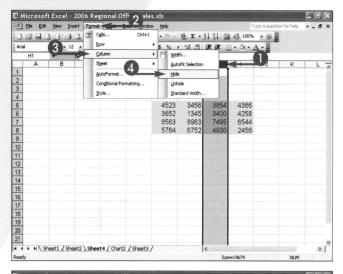

① Click the column you want to hide.

You can also select multiple columns to hide.

② Click Format.

③ Click Column.

④ Click Hide.

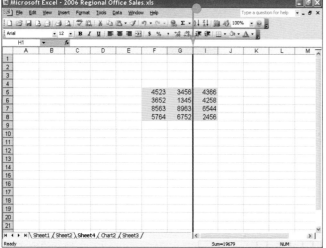

● Excel hides the column by shifting the other columns over.

Note: To unhide a column, select the columns to the right and left of the hidden column and click the Format menu, Column, and then Unhide.

Note: You can also hide an entire sheet in your workbook. Click the Format menu, Sheet, and then Hide.

COLUMN:
Resize a Column

You can resize your worksheet's columns to accommodate text or make the worksheet more aesthetically appealing. When you resize a column, you are resizing the overall width of the column. For example, you might make a column wider to fit a long line of text, or a large number.

One of the easiest methods for resizing a column is to simply drag the column edge to a new position. Using this method, you can control exactly how wide to make the column width. Excel displays a screen tip detailing the size of the column as you drag the column edge. You can also use the Format menu to control column width.

You can adjust the column width of a single column or a group of multiple columns. To apply the adjustment to multiple columns, first select the columns before performing the resizing action.

See also>>

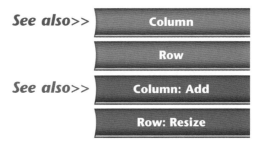

| Column |
| Row |
| Column: Add |
| Row: Resize |

See also>>

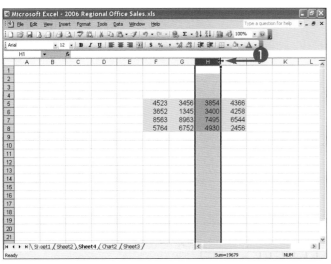

1. Move the mouse pointer over the border of the column you want to resize.

   Note: You can also click the Format menu, Column, and then Width to open the Width dialog box and set a column width value.

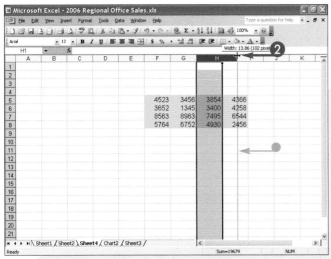

2. Click and drag the border to the desired size.

   ● A dotted line marks the new border of the column as you drag.

3. Release the mouse button and the column is resized.

COMMENT:
Insert a Cell Comment

You can add comments to your worksheets to make a note to yourself about a particular cell's content, or as a note for other users to see. For example, if you share your workbooks with other users, you can add comments to leave feedback about the data without typing directly into the worksheet. Excel displays comments in a balloon.

When you add a comment to a cell, the comment balloon contains the name of the person leaving the comment as well as the comment text. A comment can contain a single word or entire paragraphs. Excel does not display the comment balloon unless you

move your mouse over the cell containing the comment. When you are not viewing a comment, it remains hidden, out of the way. You can easily identify cells containing comments by looking for a tiny black icon in the upper-right corner.

You can add a comment using the Insert menu or using the shortcut menu.

See also>>  Comment

See also>> Track and Review

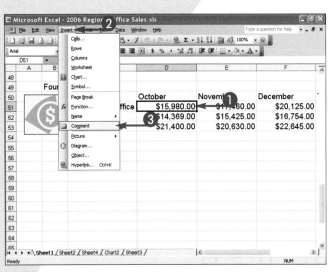

Add a Comment

1 Click the cell to which you want to add a comment.

2 Click Insert.

3 Click Comment.

You can also right-click the cell and click Insert Comment.

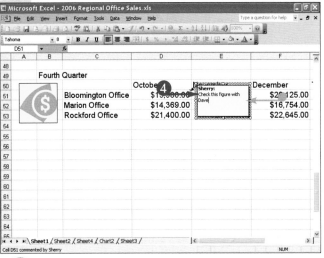

● A comment balloon appears.

4 Type your comment text.

5 Click anywhere outside the comment balloon to deselect the comment.

● Comment cells display a tiny red triangle in the corner.

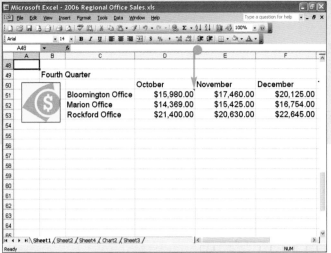

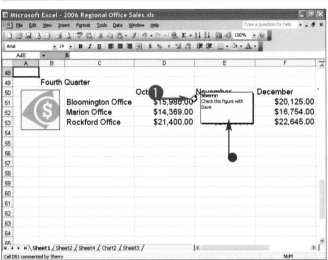

View a Comment

① Position the mouse pointer over the upper-right corner of the cell.

● The comment balloon appears displaying the comment.

Note: To remove a comment, right-click the comment and click Delete Comment.

TIPS

Customize It

To change the name a comment displays, click Tools and then Options to open the Options dialog box, click the General tab, and type a new entry in the User Name box. This changes the user name setting for all the Microsoft Office programs, however. You can also customize the comment shape and choose one of Excel's AutoShapes instead. Right-click the cell containing the comment and click Edit Comment. Click the border of the comment to select it and then click the Draw button on the Drawing toolbar. Click Change AutoShape and then click a new callout shape for the comment.

Did You Know?

If the worksheet's tracking features are turned on, you can add a comment to another user's comment. Excel's tracking features enable you to see the edits each user makes to the workbook. After all the edits are completed, you can decide which edits to accept or reject to create a final file. To turn on workbook tracking, click Tools, Track Changes, and then Highlight Changes. To learn more about Excel's tracking feature, see the technique "Track and Review: Keep Track of Workbook Changes."

CUSTOMIZE:
Change the Default File Location

By default, Excel's Open and Save As dialog boxes are automatically set up to display and store your files in the My Documents folder. The My Documents folder is a handy place to store files — it is easy to remember the folder name and easy to locate when you need it.

You may prefer to keep your workbooks in a different folder. For example, you may want to designate a special work folder for all your Excel projects and keep the files separate from other documents you create on your computer.

You can specify another folder as the default folder and save yourself time otherwise spent navigating to the folder containing your Excel files every time you display the Open or Save As dialog boxes.

You can use the Options dialog box to set up a different default file path. Then, whenever you open the Open or Save As dialog boxes, Excel displays all the files in the specified default folder.

See also>> **Alignment**

See also>> **Formatting**

---

❶ Click Tools.

❷ Click Options.

The Options dialog box opens.

❸ Click the General tab.

❹ Click inside the Default File Location box and type the new path to which you want to save your Excel files.

❺ Click OK to apply the changes.

The next time you display the Open or Save As dialog boxes, the default folder contents are displayed.

CUSTOMIZE:
Change the Default Font

By default, Excel assigns Arial, 10-point as the font and font size in every new workbook you open. Any data you type into the worksheet cells uses the default settings. If you prefer a different font and size as the default, you can designate another choice using the Options dialog box.

For example, you may want to assign a larger font size to make your worksheet data easier to read. Or your company may require a uniform font on all the documents you create, including spreadsheets.

You can assign any font available on your computer as the default workbook font. However, for best results, it is always a good idea to choose a font that is easy to read, especially for the spreadsheet structure of columns and rows of data. Legibility is a big issue when reading spreadsheet data, so be sure to choose a font and font size that are easy on the eyes.

See also>>  **Font**

See also>> **Formatting**

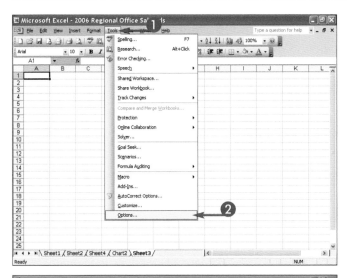

1 Click Tools.

2 Click Options.

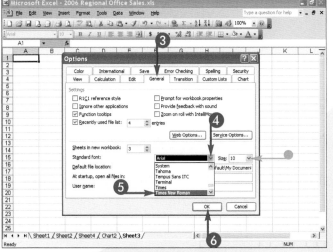

The Options dialog box opens.

3 Click the General tab.

4 Click the Standard Font drop-down arrow.

5 Click a font.

● You can change the default font size here.

6 Click OK.

Excel applies the new font the next time you start a new workbook.

CUSTOMIZE:
Create a New Menu

You can create your own menus in Excel and populate them with only the commands you use the most. For example, if you find yourself using the same command over and over again, but waste precious moments looking for and applying the command, you can place it on a custom menu for easy access.

You might create a customized menu for spreadsheet tasks unique to your workflow, or tasks you regularly use to create or format spreadsheet data. When you create a custom menu, it appears on the menu bar along with the default menus.

You can use the Customize dialog box to create and build a custom menu. When you activate the dialog box, Excel displays the program menu in edit mode, allowing you to make changes to existing menus and toolbars as well as add new ones. As soon as you exit the Customize dialog box, the program's menus and toolbars return to normal view mode.

See also>>

Customize:
Create New Toolbar

Customize:
Customize Menu

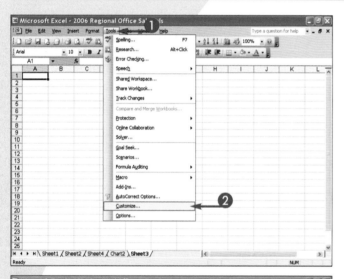

① Click Tools.

② Click Customize.

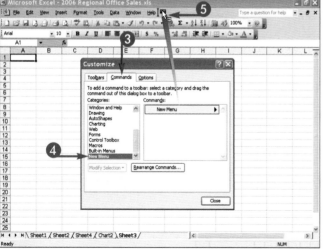

The Customize dialog box opens.

③ Click the Commands tab.

④ Click New Menu in the Categories list.

Excel displays the New Menu command.

⑤ Drag the New Menu command where you want it to appear on the menu bar.

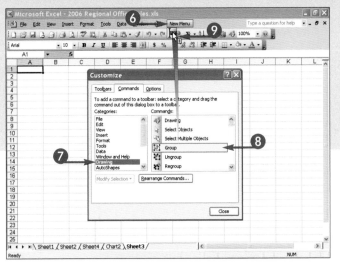

6 Click the menu.

Excel displays a blank drop-down menu, labeled New Menu.

7 Click a command category.

8 Click a command.

9 Drag the command to the menu and drop it on the menu list.

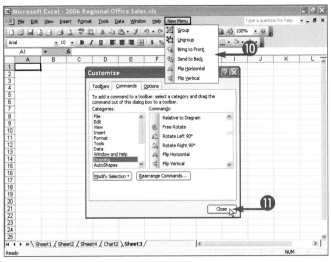

10 Continue adding more commands to the custom menu as needed.

You can drag the commands to reposition them in the menu list.

11 Click Close.

Excel closes the Customize dialog box.

TIPS

More Options

To give a new menu a distinct name, open the Customize dialog box, right-click the menu in the menu bar, and then click Name. Excel highlights the menu name. Type a new name and press Enter. Excel assigns the new name to the menu. Click Close to exit the Customize dialog box and save your changes.

Delete It

To remove a custom menu you no longer want, simply reopen the Customize dialog box and then drag the menu off the menu bar. As soon as you drag it off, the menu is deleted.

CUSTOMIZE:
Create a New Toolbar

You can create your own toolbars in Excel and populate them with buttons for commands and features you use most often. You can then keep your custom toolbar displayed for easy access.

For example, if you find yourself using Excel commands not readily available on the default toolbars, you can place them on a custom toolbar. This can save you time looking for and applying the command or feature using menus. You might create a customized toolbar for spreadsheet tasks unique to your workflow, or tasks you regularly use to create special objects on your worksheets.

You can use the Customize dialog box to create and build a custom toolbar. When you activate the dialog box, Excel displays the program menus and toolbars in edit mode, allowing you to make changes to existing menus and toolbars as well as add new ones. As soon as you exit the Customize dialog box, the program's menus and toolbars return to normal view mode again.

See also>>

Customize:
Customize Menu

Customize:
Customize Toolbar

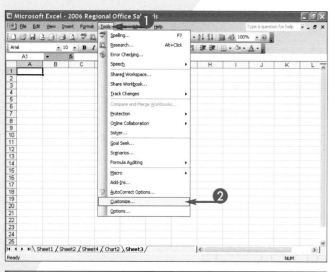

① Click Tools.

② Click Customize.

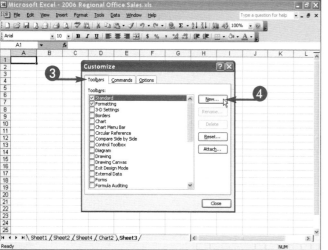

The Customize dialog box opens.

③ Click the Toolbars tab.

④ Click the New button.

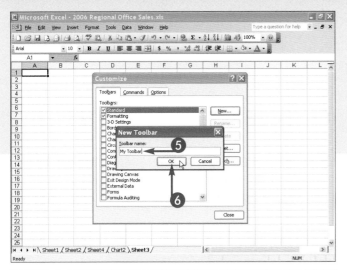

The New Toolbar dialog box opens.

5 Type a name for the new toolbar.

6 Click OK.

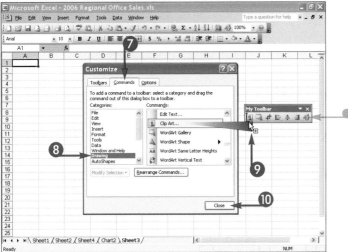

Excel displays the new toolbar.

7 Click the Commands tab.

8 Click a category.

9 Click and drag the command to the toolbar.

● You can continue adding more commands to the custom toolbar as needed.

You can also drag the buttons to reposition them in the toolbar.

10 Click Close.

Excel closes the Customize dialog box.

TIPS

More Options

You can give your toolbar buttons different names. Open the Customize dialog box, right-click the button you want to name, and then click inside the Name box. Type an ampersand (&) followed by a new button name. When you press Enter, the name is assigned. Click Close to exit the Customize dialog box.

Try This

You can create a customized toolbar button for any Excel toolbar. Open the Customize dialog box, and then right-click the button you want to edit on the toolbar. Click Edit Button Image to open the Button Editor dialog box. You can use the color palette to change the color of the existing button, or you can draw a new button image on the grid. You can use the Erase tool to remove parts of the button image, and you can use the arrow buttons to reposition the image. When you finish with your edits, click OK to apply the changes.

CUSTOMIZE:
Customize a Menu

You can customize which commands appear on the default Excel menus. For example, you may want to add commands for tasks you use the most, or remove commands for features you never use.

Although the creators of Excel do a great job of grouping related commands, you may find you need to access a few additional commands. For example, rather than open the Format Cells dialog box to set angled text, you can add the command to the Format menu for quicker access.

You can use the Customize dialog box to edit Excel menus. When you activate the dialog box, Excel displays the program menus and toolbars in edit mode, allowing you to make changes to existing

menus and toolbars as well as add new ones. As soon as you exit the Customize dialog box, the program's menus and toolbars return to normal view mode again. The Commands tab in the dialog box lists all the commands you can use in Excel, arranged by category. You can pick and choose which commands you want to add to your menus.

See also>>

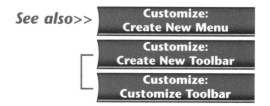

Customize:
Create New Menu

Customize:
Create New Toolbar

Customize:
Customize Toolbar

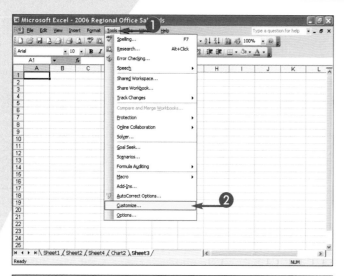

① Click Tools.

② Click Customize.

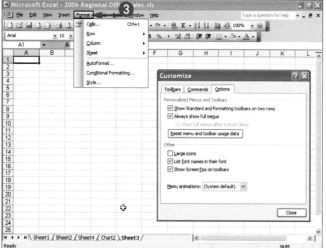

The Customize dialog box opens.

③ Click the menu you want to edit.

When the Customize dialog box is open, you can edit toolbars and menus.

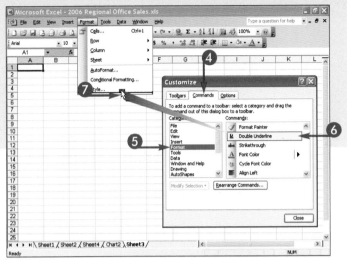

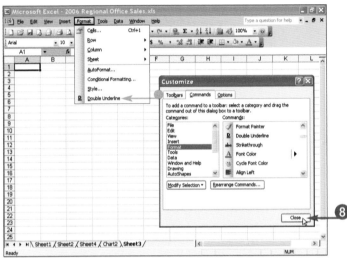

④ Click the Commands tab.

⑤ Click a command category.

⑥ Scroll to the command you want to add.

⑦ Click and drag the command from the list box and drop it on the menu where you want it to appear.

● The command is added to the menu.

You can continue adding more commands to the menu as needed.

To remove a command from the menu, drag it off the menu.

⑧ When finished, click Close.

More Options

By default, Excel is set up to show the most recently used commands on your menus. To turn off this setting and always display full menus, open the Customize dialog box and click the Options tab. Select the Always Show Full Menus check box (☐ changes to ☑) and click Close. Now the menus appear in full every time you click a menu name.

Did You Know?

If you make a lot of changes to your Excel menus and toolbars and decide you no longer want to keep the customized settings, you can restore the menus or toolbars to their default states. To do so, open the Customize dialog box, click the Options tab, and then click the Reset Menu and Toolbar Usage Data button. Click Close to exit the dialog box and apply the defaults. Excel returns the menus and toolbars to their original commands and appearances.

CUSTOMIZE:
Customize the Program Window

You can customize the Excel program window to look just the way you want. For example, you may want to turn off any toolbars or scroll bars you find unnecessary, or change the color of the worksheet gridlines.

The Options dialog box offers all kinds of options for customizing Excel. The View tab, as demonstrated in this technique, includes settings for changing the appearance of the program window. You can turn off the default startup task pane, turn off sheet tabs, hide the Formula bar, and more. Turning some of the program elements off can free up on-screen workspace, allowing you to view more of the worksheet.

The View tab groups program window elements into four areas: Show, Comments, Objects, and Window options. The Show options include the startup task pane and the Formula bar. You can control the appearance of comments in your worksheet using the Comments options. The Objects options control the appearance of graphic objects you add to a worksheet, such as clip art. The Window options control elements such as gridlines and scroll bars.

See also>>

Workbook

Worksheet

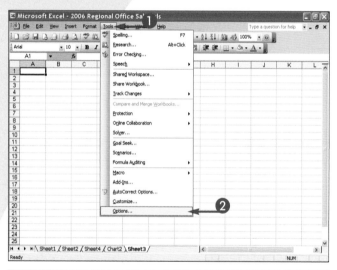

① Click Tools.

② Click Options.

The Options dialog box opens.

③ Click the View tab.

④ Set any View options you want to turn on or off.

● Click a Show check box to control the appearance of the Formula bar, Status bar, and Task Pane.

● The Comments options control the appearance of comments in a workbook.

● The Objects options control the appearance of objects in a workbook.

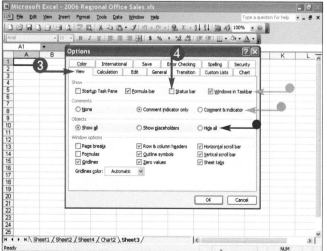

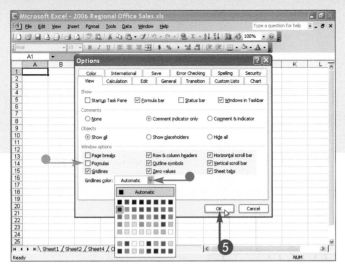

● Select from the Window options to control elements such as scroll bars, gridlines, and sheet tabs.

● To change the gridline color, click here and click a color.

⑤ Click OK.

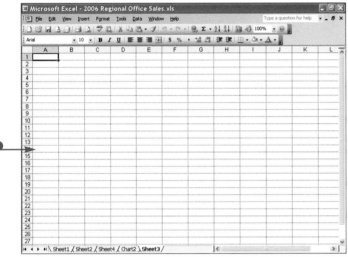

Excel applies any changes you made to the program window.

● In this example, the Formula bar and Status bar are hidden, and the gridline color is now dark red.

More Options

You can click the General tab in the Options dialog box to control how many recently opened files are listed in the File menu, how many sheets appear in a new workbook, and the default font and size. To learn more about setting a default file location, see the technique "Customize: Change the Default File Location."

Did You Know?

If Excel's default toolbar buttons appear too small on-screen, you can enlarge them. To do so, click Tools and then Customize to open the Customize dialog box. Click the Options tab, and then select the Large Icons check box (☐ changes to ☑). Excel immediately increases the size of the toolbar buttons on all toolbars you display. Click Close to exit the dialog box. To return the toolbar buttons to their default size again, simply return to the Customize dialog box and deselect the Large Icons option.

CUSTOMIZE:
Customize a Toolbar

You can customize any Excel toolbar, or even create your own toolbar containing only the buttons you use the most. Every toolbar includes a set of default buttons. You can add to the button set, or subtract buttons from the set to tailor the toolbar to work the way you want.

You can use the Customize dialog box to edit Excel's toolbars. When you activate the dialog box, Excel displays the program menus and toolbars in edit mode, allowing you to make changes to existing menus and toolbars as well as add new ones. As soon as you exit the Customize dialog box, the

program's menus and toolbars return to normal view mode again. The Toolbars tab in the dialog box lists all the toolbars available in Excel, and the Commands tab lists all the available commands you can add to your toolbars. You can pick and choose which commands you want to add to customize any menu in Excel.

See also>>

Customize:
Create New Toolbar

Customize:
Customize Menu

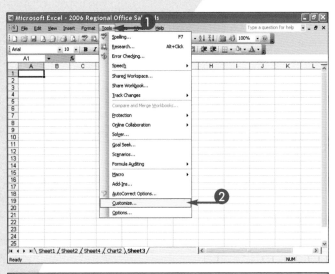

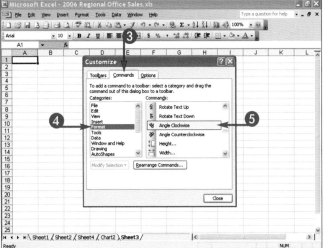

① Click Tools.

② Click Customize.

The Customize dialog box opens.

③ Click the Commands tab.

④ Click a command category.

⑤ Scroll to the command you want to add.

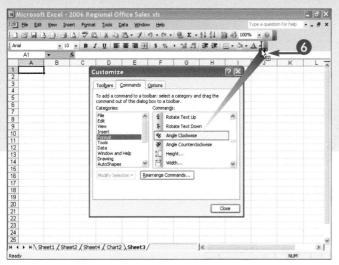

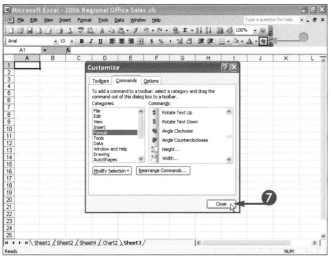

6 Click and drag a command from the list box and drop it on the toolbar where you want it to appear.

● The button is added to the toolbar.

You can continue adding more buttons to the toolbar as needed.

To remove a button from the toolbar, drag it off the toolbar.

7 When finished, click Close.

More Options

By default, Excel is set up to show only the most recently used buttons on the Standard and Formatting toolbar. To view additional default buttons at any time, click the Toolbar Options button at the far right of a toolbar and then click the button you want to use. You can also use the Toolbar Options menu to access the Customize dialog box or turn off button display. Click the Toolbar Options button and then click the Add or Remove Buttons command.

Did You Know?

You can remove and rearrange buttons on a toolbar without needing to open the Customize dialog box. To do so, first move the mouse pointer over the button and hold down the Alt key. To remove the button, drag it off the toolbar. To rearrange the button order, drag the button to a new position on the toolbar and drop it in place.

DATA:
Control Text Wrap

You can control how data fits into a worksheet cell by activating the Text Wrap command. By default, any text you type into a cell stays on one line. For longer text entries, this means the text may appear to span several columns. To make the text stay in one cell and wrap to fit the cell width, you can activate the text wrapping feature using the Format Cells dialog box.

For example, you may want to type a paragraph in a cell. You can use the Text Wrap command to ensure it all fits into the confines of a single cell.

By increasing the number of lines of text that fit into a cell, you are also increasing the height of the cell. Excel automatically adjusts the cell height for you as you type.

You can choose to activate the Text Wrap command before or after you type your cell text.

See also>> **Alignment**

See also>> **Formatting**

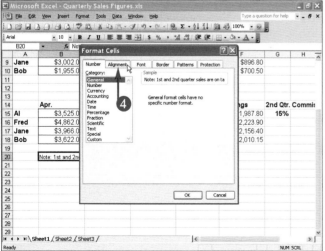

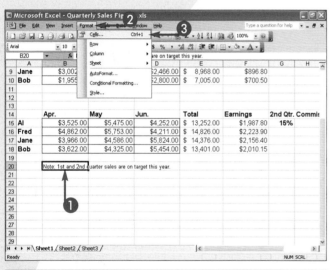

1 Select the cell or range to which you want to assign text wrapping.

2 Click Format.

3 Click Cells.

You can also right-click the cell and click Format Cells.

The Format Cells dialog box opens.

4 Click the Alignment tab.

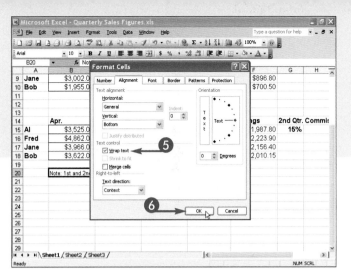

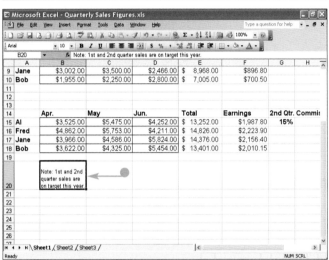

⑤ Select Wrap Text.

⑥ Click OK.

● Excel applies text wrapping to the cell or cells.

TIPS

Caution

If you adjust the row height manually, you may not be able to see the text wrapping in a cell. To resize the row for text wrapping, click the Format menu, click Row, and then click AutoFit. Excel resizes the entire row based on the contents of the cell with the most data.

Did You Know?

You can also set your own line breaks in a cell. By default, Excel breaks the text line for you as you type. You can add your own line breaks by clicking where you want to insert a break and pressing Alt+Enter. Excel breaks the line where specified.

DATA:
Cut, Copy, and Paste Data

You can use the Cut, Copy, and Paste commands to copy data within Excel, or move and share data between other Office programs. For example, you might cut a row of labels and paste them into another worksheet, or copy a formula from one cell to another cell in the same worksheet. You can also drag and drop data to move and copy it within a worksheet.

The Copy command makes a duplicate of the selected data, while the Cut command removes the data from the original file entirely. When you copy or cut data, it is placed in the Windows Clipboard until you are ready to paste it into place.

You can also use the Cut, Copy, and Paste commands to move and copy charts, clip art, WordArt objects, pictures, shapes, and other objects.

You can use the Cut, Copy, and Paste buttons on the Standard toolbar to move and copy data. You can also find the same commands on the Edit menu. You can right-click selected data and activate the commands from the shortcut menu that appears.

See also>>

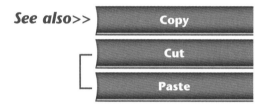

Copy

Cut

Paste

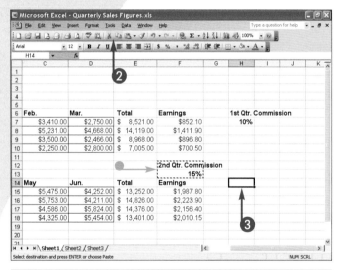

Cut or Copy Data

1. Select the cell or data you want to move or copy, F12 and F13 in this example.

2. Click the Cut button (![cut]) to move data, or click the Copy button (![copy]) to copy the data.

   Note: You can also use the Cut, Copy, and Paste commands to move and copy entire rows or columns.

   ● Excel surrounds the cell or cells with a dashed line, and the data is placed in the Windows Clipboard.

3. Click where you want to insert the data.

   You can also open another workbook or worksheet to paste the data.

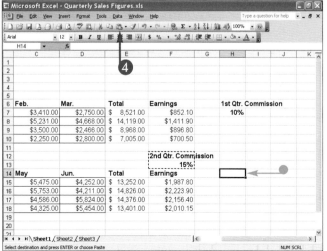

4. Click the Paste button.

   ● The data appears in the new location.

   Note: A smart tag may appear when you paste the data. You can click the icon to view a list of options you can apply to the pasted data.

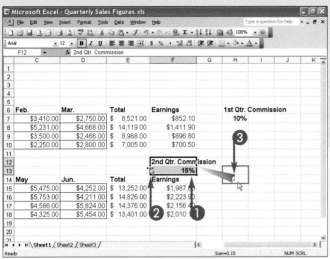

Drag and Drop Data

1 Select the data you want to move or copy.

2 Move the mouse pointer over the selected cell's border.

3 Click and drag the data to a new location in the worksheet.

To copy the data, press and hold the Ctrl key while dragging.

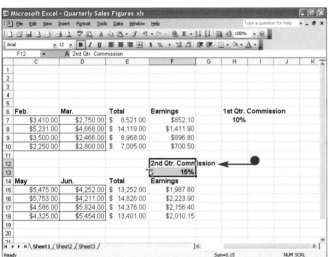

● The data appears in the new location.

Did You Know?

If you cut or copy multiple pieces of data in your Excel worksheet, the Office Clipboard task pane opens. The Office Clipboard holds up to 24 items. You can paste them in whatever order you choose, or you can opt to paste them all at once. The Office Clipboard is just one of many task panes available in Excel.

Did You Know?

You can also use keyboard shortcuts to cut, copy, and paste data. To copy data, press Ctrl+C. To cut data, press Ctrl+X. To paste data, press Ctrl+V. You can also right-click data to access a shortcut menu that displays the Cut, Copy, and Paste commands.

DATA:
Enter Dates and Times

You can use dates and times as values in Excel, allowing you to perform various calculations and use the data in your worksheet formulas and functions. For example, you can calculate the difference between two dates or calculate elapsed time.

When you type recognizable dates or times in Excel, the program converts the data into serial data format. Dates are converted into whole numbers that count the number of days elapsed since January 1, 1900. For example, if you type **01/01/2006**, Excel stores the value as 38718. Times are converted to fractional decimal values. For example, if you type **10:00 AM**, Excel stores the value as 0.416667. To view the data as a value, change the cell's number

format to General or Number. You do not need to view the serial date format unless you really want to.

When entering dates, you can use either dashes or slashes with your dates, and you can choose to abbreviate or spell out the month or year. When entering times, Excel assumes you are using 24-hour military values. If you type **8:20**, Excel views the value as 8:20 AM. If you want the time to be 8:20 PM, add 12 to the number: 20:20.

See also>>

1. Type the date or time data you want to appear in the cell.

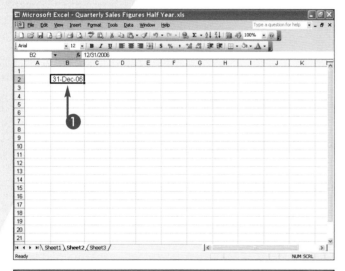

2. Click Format.
3. Click Cells.

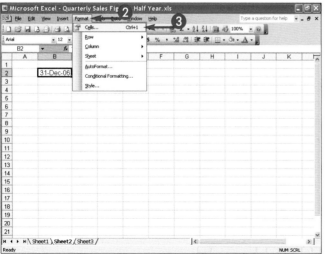

The Format Cells dialog box opens.

④ Click the Number tab.

⑤ Click the General or Number category.

⑥ Click OK.

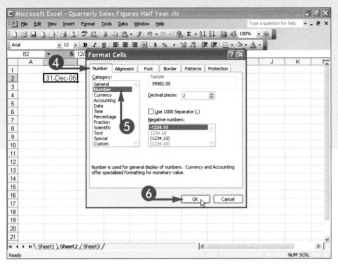

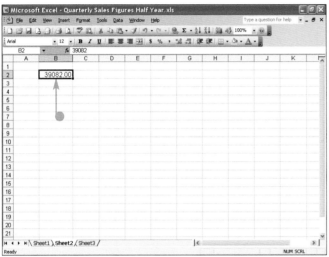

● Excel displays the true value of the date or time data.

You can perform various calculations on the data regardless of what format you assign to the cell.

TIPS

Did You Know?

To enter fractions into worksheet cells, type the integer, followed by a space, and then the fraction, such as **2 1/4**. If you leave out the space, Excel assumes the value is a text entry rather than a number entry. If you want only the fractional part, such as 1/4, you must type a zero, a space, and then the fraction; otherwise Excel assumes the value is a date.

Did You Know?

To enter the current date into any cell, simply press the Ctrl key and press the semicolon key (;). To enter the current time, press Ctrl+Shift+;. Excel fills in the date and time from your computer clock. To make sure your computer's clock is accurate, open the Control Panel and activate the Date, Time, Language, and Regional Options link.

DATA:
Rotate Data

You can rotate cell data to flip text sideways or print it from top to bottom as opposed to from left to right. For example, for long column headers, you may want to rotate them to keep your column widths shorter, making it easier to fit data horizontally on a printed page.

You can find Excel's rotation settings among the formatting options in the Format Cells dialog box. The Alignment tab includes options for setting the horizontal and vertical positioning of data in cells, as well as orientation controls for rotating text. You can specify a degree of rotation, or drag the orientation slider to the desired position. For completely vertical text, you can select the vertical text box and make

the text read vertically instead of horizontally in a cell.

With any rotation you apply to your data, the depth of the row increases to fit the text. For example, if you rotate your text by 45 degrees, Excel increases the size of the cell and entire row to fit the rotated text.

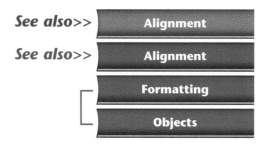

See also>> Alignment

See also>> Alignment

Formatting

Objects

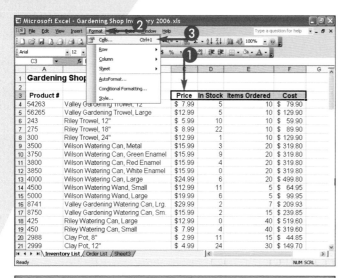

① Select the cells you want to rotate.

② Click Format.

③ Click Cells.

The Format Cells dialog box opens.

④ Click the Alignment tab.

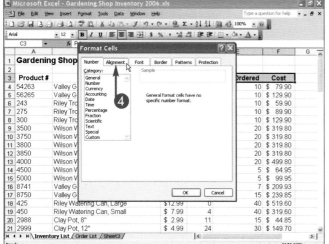

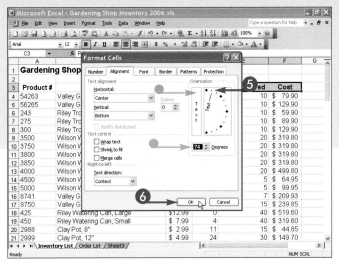

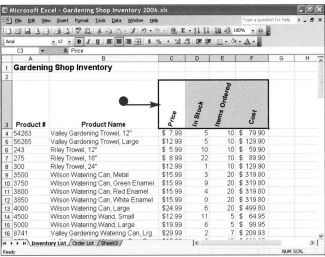

⑤ Click the degree of orientation you want to apply.

● You can also type the degree of rotation you want to set here or click the arrow buttons to set a value.

● To display data from top to bottom, as opposed to left to right, click this box.

⑥ Click OK.

● Excel applies the orientation alignment to the cells.

TIPS

Did You Know?

You can also rotate objects you draw or place in your Excel worksheets. For example, you can rotate a shape or rotate a clip art image. To access an object's rotation command, first select the object and display the Drawing toolbar. Click the Draw button, click Rotate or Flip, and then click a rotation command. With objects you draw, such as shapes, a tiny green rotation icon (⊙) automatically appears at the top of the selected object. You can click and drag the icon to rotate the object.

Caution

If you share your workbooks with other users, particularly users that do not have Excel installed, the rotated text may not display properly. Although most file formats support rotation up to the full 180 degrees, or 90 degrees in either direction, other file formats may not support the effect.

DATA VALIDATION:
Set Data Validation Rules

You can set up your database list to control exactly what kinds of data are allowed in the cells. This is handy if other people use your list to enter records. You can make sure that they type the right kind of data in a cell by assigning a data validation rule. If they type the wrong data, such as text data instead of numerical data, Excel displays an error box to prompt them about what data can be entered into the cell.

For example, in a contact list, you can prevent users from entering anything less than a 5-digit number in the zip code field. Or you might limit a text entry to

a specified number of characters, such as allowing only two characters in the field for entering the name of the contact's state.

You can restrict data entry to whole numbers or positive numbers, and limit choices to a list of choices or a range of dates, and more. You can add an input message that appears as soon as the field is clicked and instruct the user how to enter data for that particular field. You can also create a custom error message to appear when invalid data is entered.

See also>> **Database: Create**

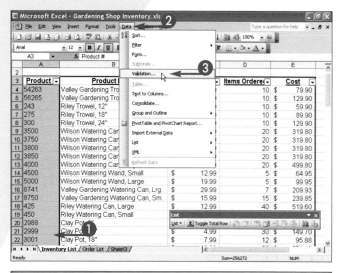

1 Select the range to which you want to apply a data validation rule.

2 Click Data.

3 Click Validation.

The Data Validation dialog box opens.

4 Click the Settings tab.

5 Set the Allow option to the type of data you want the cell to allow.

6 Define the data type parameters, if needed.

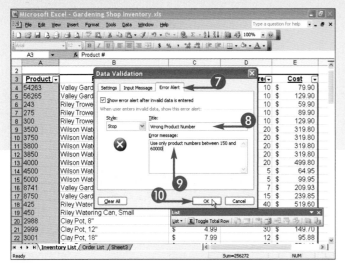

7 Click the Error Alert tab.

8 Type a title for the error message.

9 Type instructions for the user to help them remedy the mistake.

10 Click OK.

D

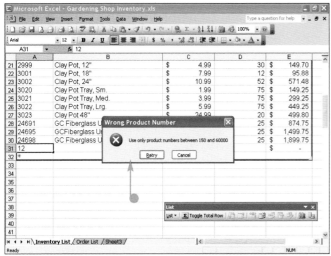

● If you or another user types the wrong data in the table's cells, an error alert box appears.

TIPS

Options
You can include an input box that helps users know what data to type when they select a cell. For example, you might create an input box to instruct users about text character limitations for a particular field, or instruct the user to type only numbers in a field. The input box appears as soon as a user selects a cell in the table. To add an input box, click the Input Message tab in the Data Validation dialog box and enter an input title and message.

Remove It
To remove data validation from a field, select the range containing the data validation rule and reopen the Data Validation dialog box. Click the Clear All button. This turns off the data validation rules.

DATABASE:
Add Records Using a Data Form

When using Excel to create database tables, you can use Excel's Data Form to enter database records more easily. The Data Form is a handy dialog box you can use to type the data for each field in your table, one record at a time. You can also use data forms to locate and edit records in your table.

Database forms are an easy way to populate your tables and lists with data. You are less likely to enter wrong information into a field when using a form than if you directly enter data into your worksheet cells. Trying to directly enter data can be a tedious process, especially if your database table is large and

filled with many records. Save yourself from scrolling through the worksheet by using a form instead.

A data form can display a maximum of 32 fields. The data form also contains navigational buttons for moving between records in your list as well as buttons for searching for a particular record.

See also>>

Database: Create

Database: Edit

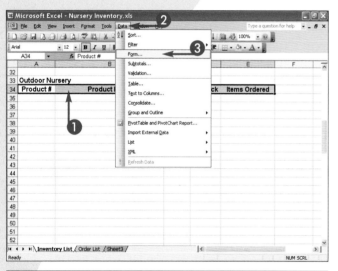

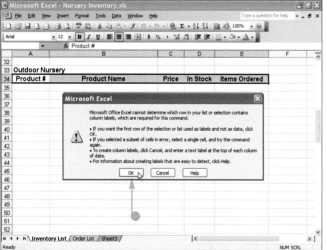

1. Select the field labels you want to use in your form.

2. Click Data.

3. Click Form.

● If your database has no records yet, a prompt box appears. Click OK to continue.

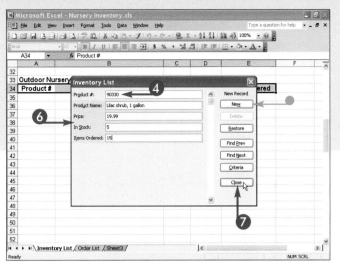

The data entry dialog box opens.

4 Type the data for the first field.

5 Press the Tab key to move to the next field.

6 Repeat Steps 4 and 5 to continue filling in form fields.

● You can click New to enter another record.

7 When finished, click Close.

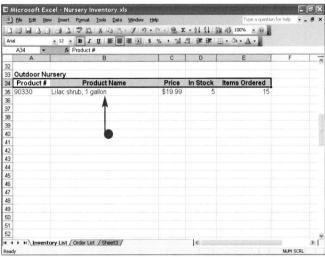

● Excel adds the record or records to the database list.

You can reopen the form to add more records at any time.

TIPS

Apply It

You can use the Data Form dialog box to navigate between all the records in your table. Click the Find Prev button to move backward through the table, or click the Find Next button to move forward. Any time you want to add a new record, click the New button and fill out the fields.

Did You Know?

You can customize your Excel program and add a toolbar button to the Standard or Formatting toolbars to quickly activate the Data Form dialog box. By adding a button, you can access the dialog box with a click rather than going through the Data menu. To learn more about customizing Excel toolbars, see the "Customize" techniques.

D

DATABASE:
Add a Subtotal

With many types of database tables, you end up with long columns of data that need to be totaled. You can use the Subtotals command to quickly add a subtotal to any column in your table. For example, you can add a subtotal to a column of prices or add a subtotal to a column of order quantities.

When you apply the Subtotals command, Excel outlines the list of records. The outline feature allows you to display and hide detail rows, which is helpful if your table has subgroups within the table. For example, perhaps your database table tracks the

sales of several different product groups. You can use the Subtotal command to add a subtotal to each group of products within the table. In addition, the Subtotal command gives you the option of adding a grand total at the bottom of the table and page breaks between subgroups.

See also>>

- Database: Add Records
- Database: Sort

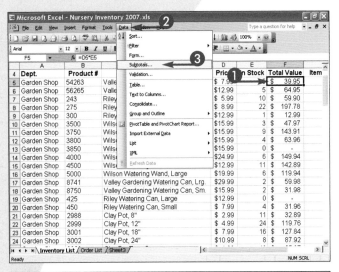

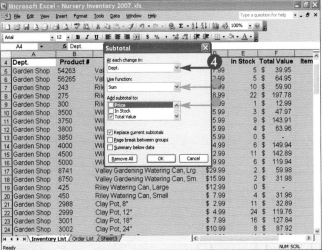

① Click anywhere in the column you want to total.

Note: If your records are not sorted, you can perform a sort first to organize the records before subtotaling columns.

② Click Data.

③ Click Subtotals.

The Subtotal dialog box opens.

④ Click here to set where each subtotal should occur in the table.

- If you prefer another function besides the SUM function, click here and change the function.

- To add more columns to be subtotaled, click here to choose which columns to use.

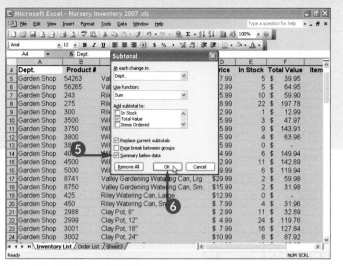

5 Click which display options you want to assign.

6 Click OK.

● Excel displays the subtotals and outline view of the table.

◐ You can click here to expand or collapse a subgroup in the table.

TIPS

Remove It

To remove subtotals from a database column, first click a cell in the list and then click the Data menu, Subtotals, and Remove All. This removes all the subtotals in the list. You can also reopen the Subtotal dialog box and click the Remove All button to delete all subtotals in the table.

More Options

If you turned your database table into a list using the Create List command, you can add a subtotal row to the bottom of your list. Click View, Toolbars, and then List to display the List toolbar. Next, click the Toggle Total Row button (Σ). Excel immediately totals the last column in the list.

DATABASE:
Create an Excel Database Table

You can use an Excel worksheet to build a database to manage large lists of data. A database is simply a collection of related records, such as a phone directory, address list, inventory, and so on. After creating a list, you can perform a variety of analysis, sorting, and filtering techniques on the data.

All database lists, also called tables, are built of fields and records. To start a database table in Excel, first determine what sort of fields you need for your entries. For example, when creating a table of contacts, such as clients or vendors, the table would include fields for first name, last name, address, city, state, zip code, phone number, and e-mail information. An inventory table might include different fields, such as product ID numbers, product

names, and cost. Databases commonly use field names as column labels, or headings, across the top of the table.

After determining fields and adding field labels to the top of the table, you can start entering records for the table. A record is a single entry in the table in which you fill out the information for each field. In the Excel structure, a record comprises a row in the worksheet. Each cell in the record contains information for the corresponding field.

See also>>

Database: Add Records

Database: Edit

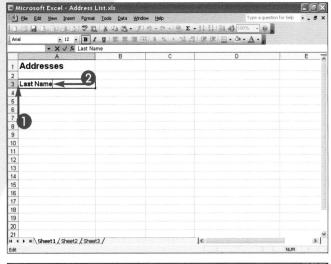

Type Field Labels

① Click where you want to insert the first column of your table.

② Type a field label.

③ Press Tab.

④ Type the next field label.

⑤ Repeat Steps 3 and 4 to continue entering as many field labels as your list requires.

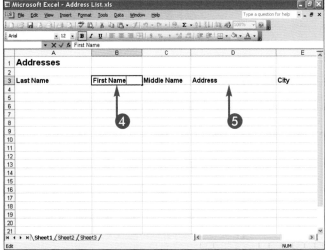

172

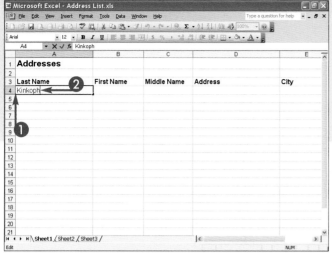

Enter Records

1 Click the first row beneath the field labels.

2 Type the data for the first field.

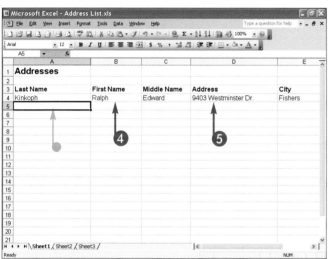

3 Press Tab.

4 Type the next field data.

5 Repeat Steps 3 and 4 to continue filling in a complete record.

6 Press Enter.

● Excel starts a new record for the table by moving automatically to the next row.

Did You Know?

Entering data into a list can be tedious. To speed up the task, you can use Excel's PickList feature. PickList is activated as soon as you create the first record in your table. It remembers the previous field entries so you can repeat them, if necessary. To use PickList, first right-click the cell in the new record. Next, click Pick From Drop-Down List. Excel displays a list of previous entries. Click an entry to repeat it in the current cell. You can also press Enter or Tab to accept the entry, or press Esc to cancel.

Did You Know?

If you use Microsoft Windows SharePoint Services, you can publish your Excel database list to a server to share the information with other users. To do so, you must have permissions to create the list on the server. After it is published, other users with permissions settings can view or edit the data, depending on their permissions level. To publish a list, click Data, List, and then Publish List.

D

DATABASE:
Create an Excel Database Table (Continued)

After entering records into your table, you can turn the data into a database list using the Create List command. Excel automatically adds filter arrow buttons, called *AutoFilter* arrows, to each field label in your table, allowing for quick filtering tasks. For example, you can filter all the records in a client table to show only the clients from a particular zip code, or filter all the records in an inventory to show all the products of a particular price point. You cannot create a list in a shared workbook.

When you activate the Create List command, Excel surrounds the list with a dark blue border. This

indicates the table is active, and allows you to easily see which cells comprise the database. When you click outside the list, the border changes to a light blue color.

Excel also displays the List toolbar when you create a database list. You can use the toolbar to perform different tasks, such as quickly adding a total to the bottom of a column.

See also>>

Database: Filter

Database: Sort

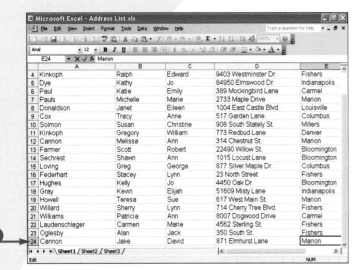

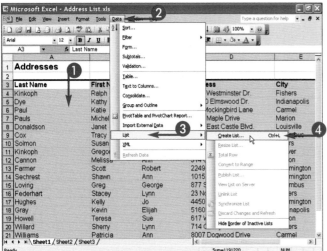

7 Repeat Steps 2 to 6 to continue entering records for your list.

Create a List

1 Select the data you want to turn into a database list.

2 Click Data.

3 Click List.

4 Click Create List.

Note: You do not have to turn your database into a list to use Excel's database features.

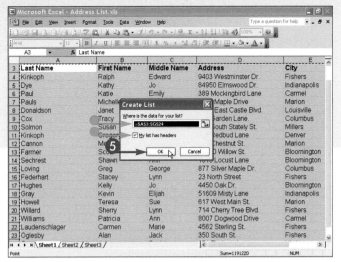

The Create List dialog box opens.

● By default, the selected range appears here. If the range is not correct, you can select the correct cell references.

● Leave this option activated to include the field labels in your list.

5 Click OK.

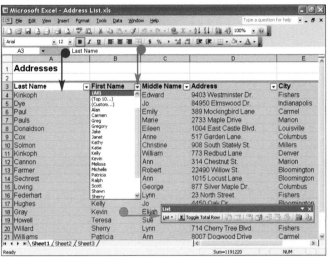

● Excel turns the data into a list, surrounds the list with a blue border, and displays filter drop-down arrows for each field.

● The List toolbar also appears on-screen.

Note: If the List toolbar does not appear, you can click View, Toolbars, and then List to display the toolbar.

● To filter a list, click a drop-down arrow and click the data.

TIPS

Options

You do not have to turn your Excel table into a list. You can still treat your data as a database list without having to turn it into an official Excel list. The advantage to the Create List command is that it automatically adds AutoFilter arrows to your field labels and displays a blue asterisk marking the next new record in the table. You can also sort by ascending or descending order from the AutoFilter drop-down lists. To learn more about filtering data, see the technique "Database: Filter Records."

Remove It

You can convert a list back to a regular Excel range by clicking the Data menu and then clicking List and Convert to Range. Click Yes when prompted. Excel removes the AutoFilter arrows from the field labels. You can still treat the data as a database and perform sorts and filters, even without the official list status.

DATABASE:
Edit Records

You can edit your database list by making changes to the records. A record is a single entry in a table. For example, you may need to change a record's details or delete a record you no longer need. You can edit cells, columns, and rows directly in a table, or you can use the Data Form dialog box to make changes.

If your database list is particularly long, it may not be easy to make changes to cells. Picking out the cell to edit from among the many cells populating the screen can strain your eyes. You may find it easier to

make your changes using a form instead. A form allows you to concentrate on one record at a time.

Excel's Data Form feature creates a dialog box containing all the fields in your list. You can navigate between fields in the form using the Tab key, or you can click in the field you want to edit.

See also>> Database: Add Records

Database: Create

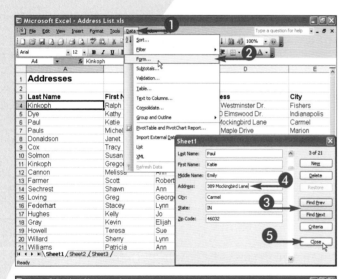

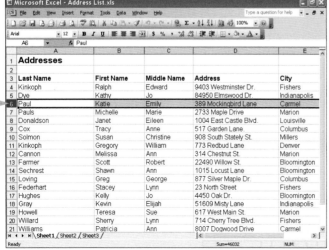

Change a Record

① Click Data.

② Click Form.

③ Click Find Next or Find Prev to navigate to the record you want to change.

④ Click in the field you want to edit and make your changes.

You can double-click a field to highlight all the data.

⑤ Click Close.

● The record is changed.

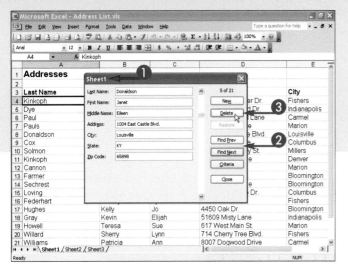

① Open the Data Form dialog box.

Note: See the previous steps to learn how to open the dialog box.

② Click Find Next or Find Prev to navigate to the record you want to remove.

③ Click Delete.

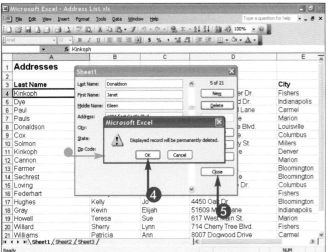

● A prompt box appears warning about the deletion.

④ Click OK.

⑤ Click Close.

The record is deleted.

More Options

To add a new record at any time, you can click the New button in the Data Form dialog box. The Data Form dialog box immediately displays a new record where you can start typing new data into the fields. You can click the Restore button to undo the previous action. For example, if you just typed data into a field, clicking Restore immediately removes the data.

More Options

You can also use the Data Form dialog box to locate a particular record in your list. Click the Criteria button to open a blank form and then type the criteria you are searching for in the appropriate field. You can use wildcards to help you with the search. For example, you can type a question mark character to find a single character; typing **b?ll** finds "bill," "ball," and "bull." You can type an asterisk to find any number of characters; typing ***west** finds "northwest" and "southwest."

DATABASE:
Filter Records

You can use a filter to view only portions of your Excel database table. Unlike a sort, which sorts the entire table, a filter selects certain records to display based on your criteria, while hiding the other records that do not match the criteria.

For example, if you are working with a product inventory list, you may want to filter the list to show only the products of a certain price point, or only the products on backorder. If you are working with a client list, you might want to filter the list to show only clients from the same zip code area.

When you apply Excel's AutoFilter feature, filter arrow buttons are automatically added to each field label in your list. You can click an arrow to reveal the filter criteria for a particular field. As soon as you select a criteria, Excel immediately filters the table for you, showing only the records that match the selected criteria.

See also>>

Database: Create

Database: Sort

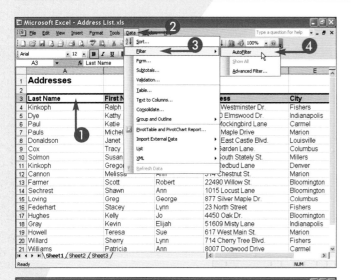

① Select the field labels for the data you want to sort.

② Click Data.

③ Click Filter.

④ Click AutoFilter.

If you used the Create List command to create a database list, your table already displays the AutoFilter buttons.

Excel adds drop-down arrow buttons to your field labels.

⑤ Click an AutoFilter arrow.

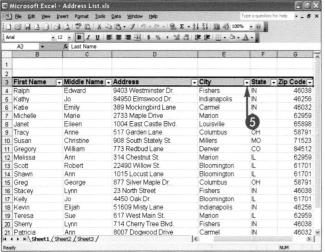

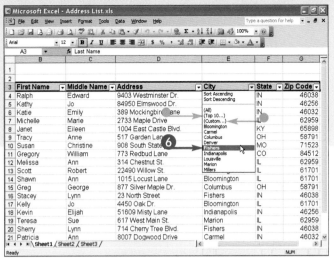

6 Click a filter type.

You can filter the table based on a particular field.

- To display the 10 most-repeated items for this field, you can click the Top 10 option.

- To customize your filter, you can click this option.

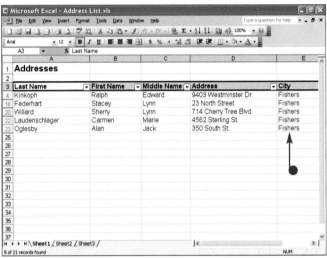

- Excel filters the table.

To view all the records again, display the filter list and click All.

Options

AutoFilter lists a Top 10 option for every field. You can use the option to quickly filter for the top or bottom 10 items in your table. For example, you might want to view the top 10 salespeople, or the bottom 10 sellers from your product list.

Options

You can activate the Custom command in the filter drop-down list to open the Custom AutoFilter dialog box. Here you can further customize the filter by selecting operators and values to apply on the filtered data. For example, you might filter a product list to show only the products with prices equal to or greater than $100. To learn more about customizing AutoFilters, see Excel's Help files.

D

DATABASE:
Sort Records

You can sort your database tables to reorganize information. For example, you might want to sort a client table to list the names alphabetically. An ascending sort lists records from A to Z, and a descending sort lists records from Z to A.

You can also sort your list based on criteria. You can choose up to four criteria for a sort. For example, if you are working with an inventory list, you might want to sort the list by price, by product type, and then by quantity available. If you are working with a contact list, you might sort the table by state, by city, and then by last names.

When you perform a sort, Excel saves the newly sorted record order in the list. If you do not want to keep the new order, you can apply the Undo command after the sort to return the table to its original record order.

See also>>

Database: Create

Database: Filter

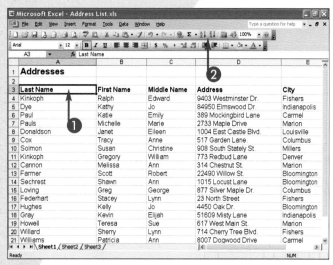

Perform a Quick Sort

1 Click in the field name you want to sort.

2 Click the Sort Ascending or Sort Descending button on the Formatting toolbar.

If your table already displays filter buttons, you can also click the filter arrow button and click a sort option.

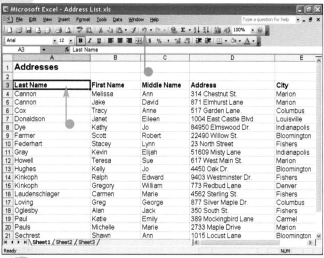

● Excel sorts the records based on the field you specified.

● If you do not want the records sorted permanently, click the Undo button to return the list to its original state.

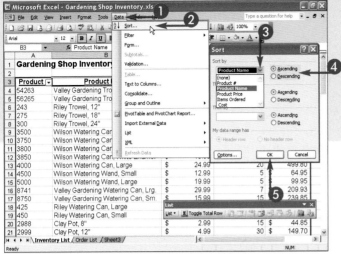

D

① Click Data.

② Click Sort.

The Sort dialog box opens.

③ Click the first Sort By box and select the primary field to sort by.

④ Click whether you want to sort the field in ascending or descending order.

To specify additional fields for the sort, repeat Steps 3 to 4 to select other sort fields.

⑤ Click OK.

● Excel sorts the data.

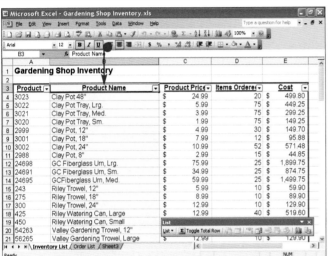

TIPS

More Options

If the listed data is across a row instead of down a column, you can activate the Sort Left to Right option in the Sort dialog box. Click Data and then Sort to open the Sort dialog box. Click Options. The Sort Options dialog box opens. Click the Sort Left to Right option (○ changes to ●) and then click OK to sort the list.

Caution

If a sort does not produce the results you were expecting, you may need to check your cell values to make sure they are formatted correctly. For example, if a cell's data is formatted as text and not a number, Excel may not sort the cell correctly. If a column contains both numbers and numbers including text, such as 10a or 10b, be sure to format the data as text instead of numbers.

DECIMAL:
Increase or Decrease Decimal Points

You can use Excel's Increase Decimal and Decrease Decimal commands to control the number of decimals that appear with numeric data in your worksheet. For example, you may want to increase the number of decimals shown in a cell, or reduce the number of decimals in a formula result.

The quickest way to add or subtract decimals is to use the Increase Decimal or Decrease Decimal buttons found on the Formatting toolbar. If you click the Increase Decimal button, Excel adds one decimal point to the selected cell or range. Click the button

again to insert another decimal point. You can continue clicking the decimal buttons as many times as needed to achieve the desired results.

You can control decimal points through the Format Cells dialog box. By applying the Number category as the format style, you can specify the number of decimals, add a thousands separator, and designate how negative numbers appear in a worksheet.

See also>> | **Decimal**

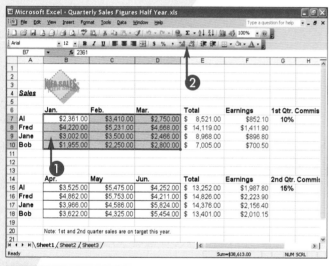

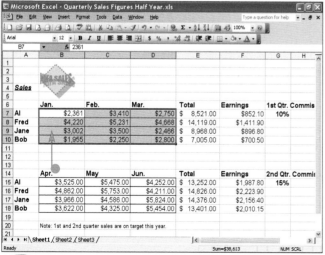

Use the Decimal Buttons

① Select the cell or range you want to edit.

② Click a decimal button.

Click the Increase Decimal button ( ) to increase the number of decimals.

Click the Decrease Decimal button ( ) to decrease the number of decimals.

● Excel adjusts the number of decimals showing in the cell or cells.

In this example, the Decrease Decimal button was clicked twice to remove two decimal points in the selected range.

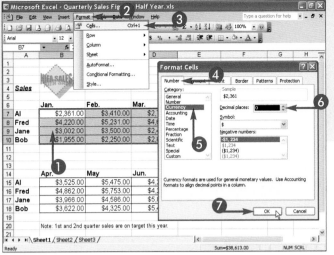

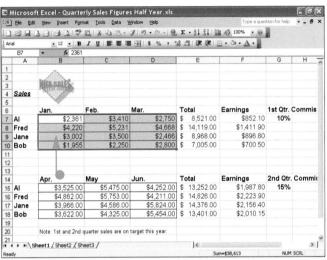

1 Select the cell or range you want to edit.

2 Click Format.

3 Click Cells.

The Format Cells dialog box opens.

4 Click the Number tab.

5 Click the Currency, Accounting, Percentage, or Scientific category.

6 Type the number of decimal places you want to display, or use the arrow buttons to set a value.

7 Click OK.

● Excel assigns the decimal formatting.

TIPS

Did You Know?

You can use the ROUNDUP, EVEN, or ODD functions to round a number up to avoid decimal places. For example, if your formula results or cell data reads 20.3, you can use the ROUNDUP function to round the number to the nearest whole number (21). The formula might look like this: =ROUNDUP(B2,0). To round up to the nearest hundredth and leave two decimal places, your formula might look like this: =ROUNDUP(B2,2). In both examples, the value following the comma controls the number of decimals.

More Options

By default, Excel displays a period as a decimal separator. If you need to use a different separator, such as a different character to display for international users, you can change the default setting. To do so, click Tools and then Options to open the Options dialog box. Click the International tab and type a new character in the Decimal Separator box. To return to the default settings later, select the Use System Separators check box (☐ changes to ☑) to activate the defaults again.

DELETE:
Delete Cell Contents or Formatting

Excel offers you several ways to perform deletions in your worksheet cells. You can choose to delete everything and leave an empty cell, or you can choose to remove just the formatting or any comments assigned to a cell. You can also choose to delete the cell entirely.

You can use the Clear command to clear a cell of its contents, its formatting, or any assigned comments. You can also use the Clear command to remove all three. You can also press the Delete key on the keyboard to clear a cell of its contents. When you use the keyboard key, Excel does not remove comments or formats.

You can use the Delete command to remove the cell from the worksheet. When you remove the cell, Excel shifts the other cells up or over to fill the void. Use the Delete command when you want to reposition remaining cells in a worksheet. Use the Delete key when you merely want to clear a cell of its contents.

See also>>

Comment

Formatting

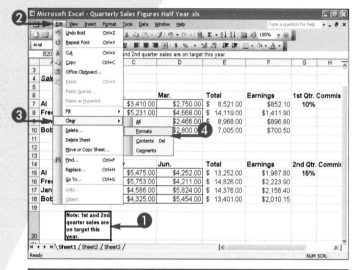

Clear Contents

1. Click the cell or range you want to clear.

2. Click Edit.

3. Click Clear.

4. Click an option.

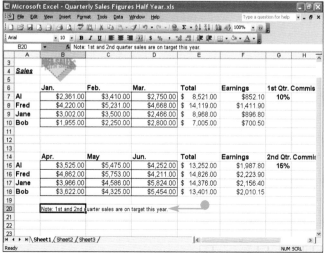

● Excel applies the changes to the cell.

In this example, only the formatting is removed from the cell.

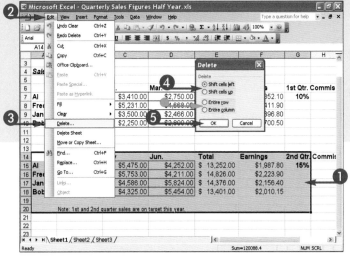

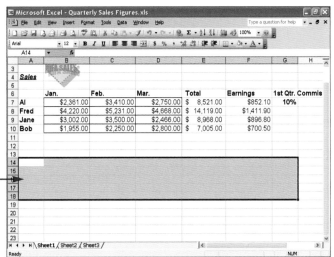

Delete Cells

① Click the cell or range you want to delete.

② Click Edit.

③ Click Delete.

The Delete dialog box opens.

④ Click Shift cells left or Shift cells up.

● To delete a row or column instead, choose from these options.

⑤ Click OK.

● Excel applies the changes to the worksheet.

D

 TIPS

Did You Know?

You can delete objects you place on your worksheets. You can delete shapes, WordArt objects, clip art, pictures, charts, and any other objects you add to a worksheet. To do so, simply click the object and then press the Delete key on the keyboard. Excel immediately removes the object.

Did You Know?

You can easily delete a sheet or workbook file in Excel. To delete a sheet from the workbook, first activate the sheet, click the Edit menu, and then click Delete Sheet. A prompt box may appear warning you that you are about to delete data. You can click the Delete button in the prompt to finalize the deletion. To delete a workbook, open the Open dialog box and navigate to the file you want to remove. Right-click the filename and click Delete from the shortcut menu.

DIAGRAM:
Insert a Diagram

You can use the Microsoft Office diagram feature included in Excel to create all kinds of diagrams to illustrate concepts and processes on your worksheets. Diagrams are much like charts, but composed of individual shapes that link to form a hierarchical tree or flow diagram. You can use diagrams to explain how something works or illustrate the relationship between parts of a whole.

The Diagram feature offers several different types of diagrams you can create, including Cycle, Target, Radial, Venn, and Pyramid diagrams. You might insert a cycle diagram to show workflow in your department, or you might use a radial diagram to compare related items.

To create a diagram, you can use a drawing space, called a *canvas*, and add shapes to create the diagram elements. You can add as many shapes as you need to complete your diagram. Within each shape, you can add the name of a process or concept you want to illustrate and format the text any way you like. You can use the Diagram toolbar to help you format and add to your diagram.

See also>>   **Diagram**

           Organization Chart

See also>>   **Organization Chart**

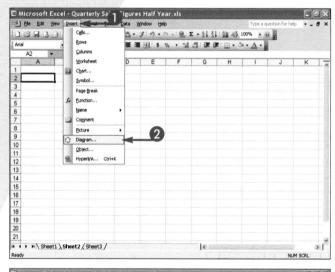

① Click Insert.

② Click Diagram.

You can also click the Insert Diagram button (▨) on the Drawing toolbar.

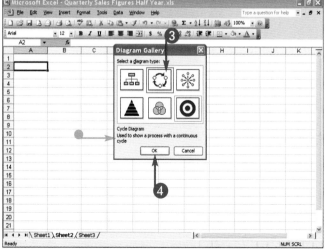

The Diagram Gallery dialog box opens.

③ Click the type of diagram you want to create.

● You can view a description of the diagram type here.

④ Click OK.

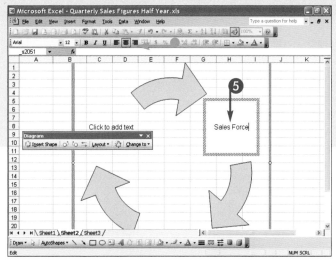

The diagram and placeholder text boxes appear, along with the Diagram and Drawing toolbars.

5 Click a text box and type the diagram text.

● You can apply any of the text formatting options to change the appearance of the text.

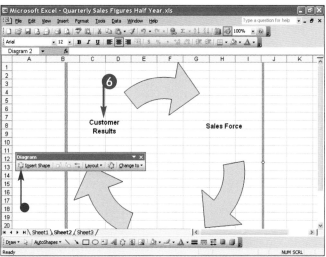

6 Continue filling in each diagram text box as needed.

● To add another text box and element to the diagram, click the Insert Shape button on the Diagram toolbar.

To deselect the diagram object, click anywhere outside the diagram.

TIPS

More Options

Each diagram type has a different use. The table below explains each type:

Type	Use
Cycle	Use to show a continuous cycle process
Target	Use to step toward a goal
Radial	Use to show relationships between elements of a core element
Venn	Use to show overlapping between elements
Pyramid	Use to show foundation-based relationships

Did You Know?

You can create a flowchart diagram using the flowchart shapes and connectors available among Excel's AutoShapes. Click the AutoShapes button on the Drawing toolbar, click the Flowchart category, and then click the type of flowchart shape you want to add. You can continue adding shapes to build the flowchart. You can find connector shapes in another category on the AutoShapes palette and use the connectors to connect the flowchart shapes. To learn more about AutoShapes, see the technique "AutoShapes: Draw AutoShapes."

D

DRAW:
Draw Objects

You can use Excel's drawing tools to draw your own shapes and graphics for your worksheets. You can choose to draw lines, arrows, ovals, or rectangles. For example, you might draw an arrow to draw attention to a particular range or cell in a worksheet. You might draw an oval or rectangle to create your own logos for your worksheets.

You can also combine the drawn objects to create all kinds of illustrations. For example, you might draw a shape and add an arrow object over the shape.

After you select an object to draw, you can control the size and position of the object as you draw on

the worksheet. After completing the object, you can continue to move it and resize it as needed. You can also add formatting to the object, such as changing the fill color, line color, line style, or adding shadow or 3-D effects. You can apply formatting to objects after you draw them on the worksheet. You can also layer and group objects.

See also>> 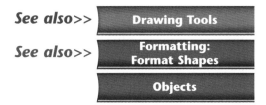 Drawing Tools

See also>> Formatting:
Format Shapes

Objects

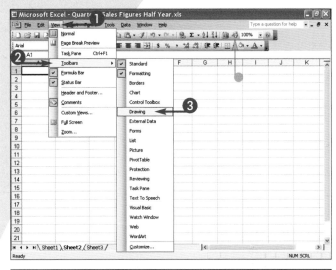

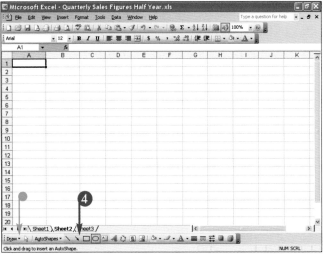

① Click View.

② Click Toolbars.

③ Click Drawing.

● You can also click the Drawing button on the Standard toolbar.

● The Drawing toolbar appears at the bottom of the program window.

④ Click the button for the type of object you want to draw.

Click the Line button (◻) to draw a line.

Click the Arrow button (◻) to draw an arrow.

Click the Rectangle button (◻) to draw a rectangle.

Click the Oval button (◻) to draw an oval.

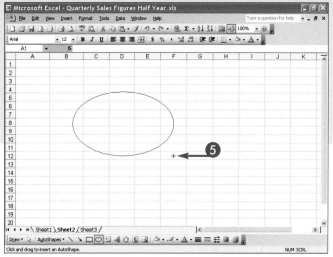

⑤ Click and drag on the worksheet to draw the desired shape or object.

D

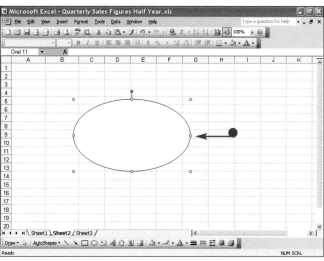

● When you release the mouse, Excel completes the object.

Note: *You can move and resize the object or edit it with the Drawing toolbar buttons.*

More Options

If you want to draw a freeform shape, you can use Excel's AutoShapes. Click the AutoShapes button on the Drawing toolbar, click the Lines category, and then click Freeform or Scribble. You can use either tool to draw your own shapes on the worksheet. After you complete the shape, you can use any of the formatting tools on the Drawing toolbar to change the line thickness, fill color, line style, and more.

Try This

You can retain a shape's proportions by holding down the Shift key while dragging the shape on a worksheet. This same technique also works for any objects you draw using AutoShapes. For example, if you click the Oval tool (▢) and hold the Shift key while drawing, Excel maintains a perfect circle shape.

DRAW:
Draw a Text Box

You can add a text box to your worksheet to use as a receptacle for blocks of text or for other objects. For example, if you use the drawing tools on the Drawing toolbar to create shapes on your worksheet, you can add text boxes to appear layered over the shapes to create logos and other types of graphic effects.

After you draw the size of the text box you want to add, you can start typing text into the box. You can use a text box to hold a single word, or several paragraphs, depending on your needs. After typing the text, you can format it using any of Excel's text formatting tools. For example, you can change the font and size, add color to the text, adjust alignment, and more.

You can also use a text box as a container for other objects you add to Excel, such as shapes and clip art. You can also add text boxes to your Excel charts and diagrams.

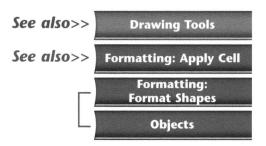

See also>>   **Drawing Tools**

See also>>   **Formatting: Apply Cell**

Formatting: Format Shapes

Objects

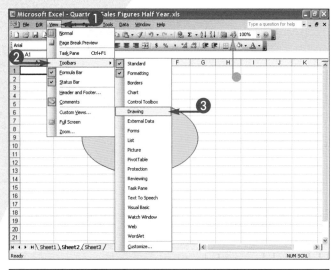

1. Click View.
2. Click Toolbars.
3. Click Drawing.

● You can also click the Drawing button on the Standard toolbar.

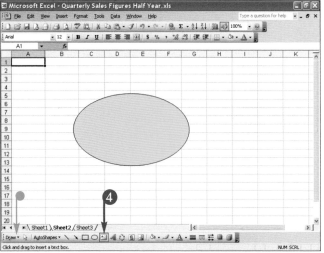

● The Drawing toolbar appears at the bottom of the program window.

4. Click the Text Box button.

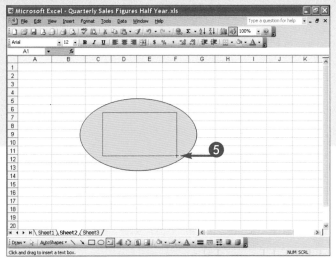

5 Click and drag on the worksheet to draw the text box.

Excel creates an empty text box.

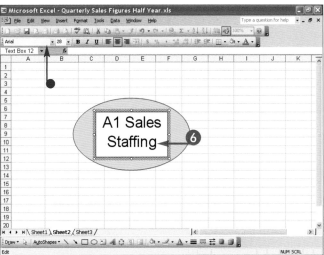

6 Type the text.

● When you finish typing the text, you can format the text as needed.

You can click outside the text box to deselect the box.

TIPS

More Options

You can control the margins inside a text box using the Format Text Box dialog box. For example, you may want to increase the left and right margins to allow more space between the text and the outer edges of the box. To adjust the margins, right-click the text box border and click Format Text Box. This opens the Format Text Box dialog box. Click the Margins tab and make your adjustments to the internal margins of the box. Click OK to apply your changes.

Did You Know?

If you click the Text Box tool (⌷) on the Drawing toolbar and then click the worksheet, you can immediately start typing and the box adjusts itself to fit the text you type. When you employ this method of text box creation, Excel does not assign a default border to the text box.

E-MAIL:
E-mail a Worksheet

You can e-mail a workbook without leaving the Excel program window. For example, you might want to send the workbook to a colleague for review or send a sales report to your corporate headquarters. When e-mailing Excel data, you can choose to send the entire workbook as a file attachment, or send the selected range or worksheet as a message.

When you send an attachment, the data is sent as a separate workbook file which the user can save and open. When you send the data as a message, the information appears in the message body text.

If you use Microsoft Outlook or Outlook Express as your e-mail editor, you can tap into the program's features to insert e-mail addresses and send your Excel data. You can send e-mails to multiple addresses as well as access the CC (carbon copy) or BCC (blind carbon copy) features to send copies of the data to people in addition to the main recipients.

You may need to log on to your Internet account before sending an e-mail message from Excel.

See also>>   **E-mail**

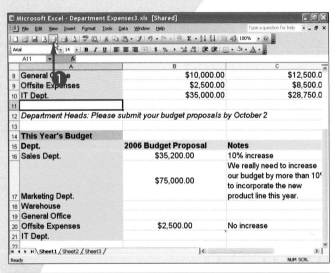

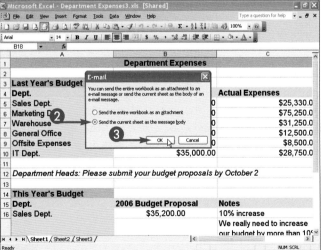

1 Click the E-mail button on the standard toolbar.

> *Note: The E-mail button is not available if Outlook or Outlook Express is not your default mail program.*

> *Note: You can also click the File menu, Send To, and then Mail Recipient.*

If e-mailing a shared workbook, the E-mail dialog box appears.

2 Choose whether you want to send the workbook as an attachment or in the message body.

If you send the file as an attachment, Outlook opens a new window for addressing and sending the message.

3 Click OK.

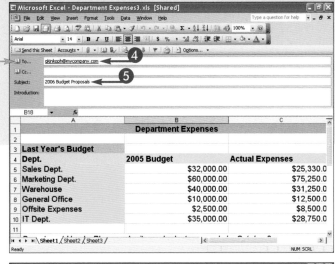

In this example, the worksheet data appears as the message text.

④ Type the recipient's e-mail address.

● You can click the To button to access the Outlook Address Book and retrieve an address.

If typing more than one e-mail address, use a semicolon (;) to separate them.

⑤ Type a subject title for the message.

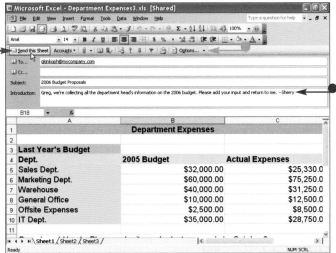

● You can use the Outlook program controls to assign any additional options to your message.

● Optionally, you can type a brief intro about the message here.

⑥ Click the Send This Sheet button.

The message is sent to Outlook's Outbox ready for e-mailing.

TIPS

Did You Know?

If you send the workbook as a review attachment, the recipient can make changes and send it back. When the user receives the attachment, they can review the file, add their own changes, and e-mail the file back to you. Click the File menu, click Send To, and then click Mail Recipient (for Review). Outlook opens the mail message with the workbook as a file attachment. You can address and e-mail the message.

Change It

If Outlook or Outlook Express is not your default mail program, you can easily change the setting to display the e-mail options in Excel. From Outlook Express, click the Tools menu and then click Options. This opens the Options dialog box. Under the Default Messaging Programs options, look for the This Application Is the Default Mail Handler setting and click the Make Default button. From Outlook, click Tools, Options, and then click the Other tab and make sure the Make Outlook the Default Program setting is selected.

E

EMBED:
Embed Objects in a Worksheet

You can use embedded objects to share data between Excel files or between other programs. For example, you might embed a Word document or a PowerPoint slide in your Excel worksheet. Excel's embedding feature is based on the OLE (Object Linking and Embedding) data-sharing protocol. The OLE protocol began with Microsoft Windows 3.1, and most programs support OLE today.

With embedded data, you can make edits to the embedded object without leaving the destination program. Unlike linked data, which retains a direct link with the source data, embedded objects only retain a connection with the source program, not the source data. If the source object changes, the embedded object remains the same.

For example, you can embed a PowerPoint slide in your worksheet to illustrate your data. Any time you need to make changes to the slide, you can do so without opening the PowerPoint program directly. With OLE, you can access the PowerPoint controls to make your edits from within the Excel program window.

You can also embed or link to another Excel workbook file in order to use its macros.

See also>>
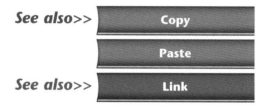

Copy

Paste

See also>>

Link

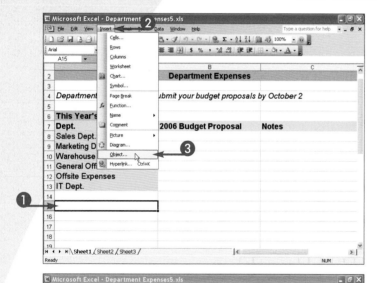

1. Click where you want to insert the embedded object.
2. Click Insert.
3. Click Object.

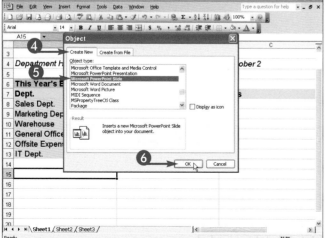

The Object dialog box opens.

4. Click the Create New tab.
5. Click the object type you want to embed.
6. Click OK.

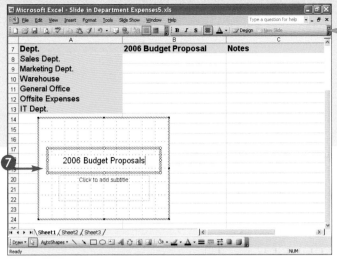

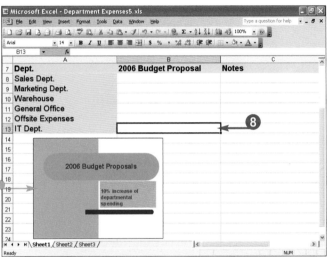

● Excel embeds the object and displays the source program's controls for you to create the new object.

In this example, PowerPoint's toolbars appear.

⑦ Create the new object using the source program's controls.

⑧ Click anywhere outside the object.

Excel's program controls reappear.

● To edit the object at any time, simply double-click the object and use the source program's controls to make changes.

E

TIPS

Change It

If you already have an object you want to embed in a worksheet, you can use the Object dialog box to locate and embed the object. Open the Object dialog box and display the Create from File tab. Click the Browse button to navigate to the file you want to embed. Double-click the filename and then click OK to embed the object and exit the Object dialog box.

Did You Know?

Object linking and embedding is not quite the same as copying, cutting, or pasting data. When you activate the Cut, Copy, or Paste commands, you are moving or copying and then pasting data without retaining any connection to the original data. Use the Cut, Copy, and Paste commands when you do not require any relationship to the original data.

ERRORS:
Fix Errors

To check your worksheet for formula errors, you can activate the Error Checking tool. Excel's Error Checking feature searches through your worksheet for formula errors, highlighting each error it encounters. The Error Check tool looks for common formula errors, such as problematic cell references, formula punctuation problems, incorrect function arguments, and more.

When Error Checking finds an error, you can choose to fix the error yourself by making corrections in the Formula bar, ignore the error, or access additional help information to correct the error. The Error Checking dialog box also offers navigational buttons to move back and forth between worksheet errors.

After you correct an error, you can move on to the next problem in the worksheet until the error check is complete.

The Error Checking tool is just one of several worksheet auditing tools you can apply to diagnose and correct formula errors. Error checking is particularly helpful in larger worksheets that require you to scroll through screens of cells and data to view formula problems. By using the Error Checking tool, you can quickly locate and fix formula errors.

See also>>

Audit

Errors: Trace

---

① Click cell A1 or another cell at the top of the worksheet.

② Click Tools.

③ Click Error Checking.

You can also activate the Error Checking tool (⚡) on the Formula Auditing toolbar.

● Excel highlights the first error and displays the Error Checking dialog box.

④ To fix the error, click Edit in Formula Bar and make your corrections.

● To find help with an error, click here to open the Help files.

● You can use the Previous and Next buttons to scroll through all the errors on the sheet.

When the error check is complete, click OK when prompted.

ERRORS:
Trace Errors

If a worksheet cell displays an error, you can use the Trace Error command to quickly view the relationship between the referenced cell and the cell containing the formula. The Trace Error command is just one of several worksheet auditing tools you can apply to help you diagnose and correct formula errors.

When you fill your worksheet cells with data and formulas, it is not always easy to see how the cells relate to each other, particularly when building formulas. By using the Trace Error command, you can graphically view how each cell reference relates to the formula and determine which cell is creating a formula error.

Excel displays a variety of error messages in a cell based on the type of formula error. For example, if you leave out a comma to separate cell ranges that do not intersect, Excel displays the #NULL message. If you try to divide a cell value by zero, Excel displays the #DIV/0! message.

When you activate the Trace Error command, Excel displays trace lines, also called trace arrows, which show how each referenced cell contributes to the formula. When you determine the formula problem, you can make corrections to the cells to alleviate the formula error.

See also>>　　**Audit**

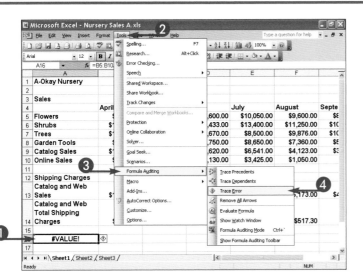

① Click the cell containing the formula error.

② Click Tools.

③ Click Formula Auditing.

④ Click Trace Error.

Note: You can trace precedents and dependents using the Formula Auditing toolbar. See the technique "Audit: Apply Error Checking to a Worksheet" to learn more.

● Excel displays trace lines from the current cell to the cells referenced in the formula.

You can make corrections to the formula as needed.

Note: To remove the trace lines without fixing the formula, click the Tools menu, Formula Auditing, and then Remove All Arrows.

FIND:
Find and Replace Worksheet Data

Excel's Find and Replace tools can help you with the drudgery of looking through your worksheet for data. You can use Excel's Find tool to search through your spreadsheets for a particular word or phrase, or to look for specific numeric data. You can use the Replace tool to replace instances of a word or data with other data. For example, you may need to look through a long spreadsheet for a particular product name and replace it with a new name. Or you may need to locate all the references to a particular sales number.

The Find and Replace dialog box offers a convenient way to utilize both tools. The dialog box features two

tabs, one for conducting a search for data, the other for searching and replacing data. You can click the Options button in either tab to view additional search options you can apply, such as searching by rows or columns, searching for formulas or comments, or searching for case-sensitive data.

After you start a search, the Find and Replace dialog box remains open so you can continue searching or replacing data.

See also>> **Find and Replace**

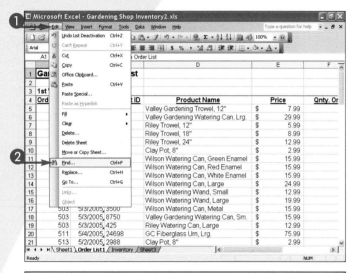

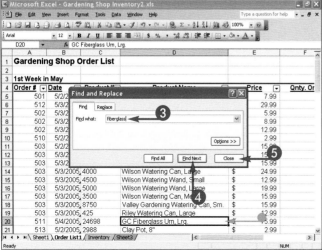

Find Data

1 Click Edit.

2 Click Find.

The Find and Replace dialog box opens with the Find tab displayed.

3 Type the data you want to find.

4 Click Find Next.

● Excel searches the worksheet and finds the first occurrence of the specified data.

You can click Find Next again to search for the next occurrence.

5 When finished, click Close or Cancel to close the dialog box.

Note: *Excel may display a prompt box when the last occurrence is found. Click OK.*

Replace Data

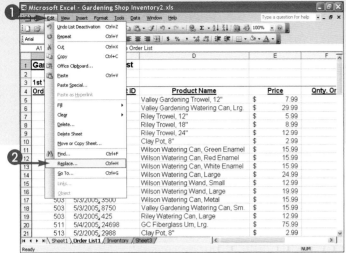

1. Click Edit.
2. Click Replace.

The Find and Replace dialog box opens with the Replace tab displayed.

3. Type the data you want to find.
4. Type the replacement data.
5. Click Find Next.

- Excel locates the first occurrence of the data.

6. Click Replace to replace the occurrence.
7. When finished, click Close.

Note: Excel may display a prompt box when the last occurrence is found. Click OK.

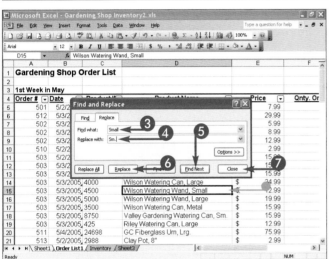

More Options

You can click the Options button in the Find and Replace dialog box to reveal additional search options you can apply. For example, you can search by rows or columns, matching data, and more. You can also search for specific formatting or special characters using the Format buttons. To hide the additional search options, click the Options button again.

Did You Know?

You can search for a particular word, number, or phrase using the Find and Replace dialog box and remove the data completely from the worksheet. Start by typing the text in the Find What text box. Leave the Replace With box empty. When you activate the search, Excel looks for the data, and replaces it without adding new data to the worksheet.

FORMATTING:
Apply Cell Formatting

You can use the Format Cells dialog box to apply a variety of formatting options to your worksheet data. The dialog box features six tabs of formatting attributes. You can find most of the data formatting options on the Number, Alignment, and Font tabs.

The Font tab features formatting options you can apply to text and numbers, including fonts, styles, sizes, colors, and other effects. For example, if you need to set subscript or superscript in your worksheet cells, you can assign the Subscript or Superscript effects. The Preview area displays a preview of any font formatting options you select so you can see what they look like before actually applying them to your data.

The Number tab features formatting options that apply directly to different number values you use in your worksheet. You can use number formats to add currency signs, percent signs, decimals, and other numeric formats to your data.

The Alignment tab displays options for controlling the horizontal and vertical positioning of data in the worksheet cells.

See also>>

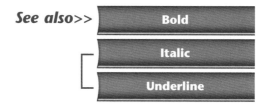

Bold

Italic

Underline

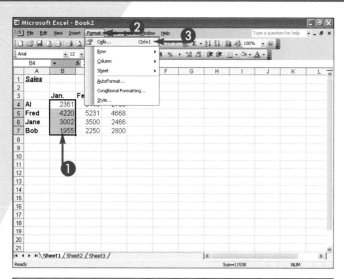

① Select the data you want to format, or click in the cell to which you want to apply formatting.

② Click Format.

③ Click Cells.

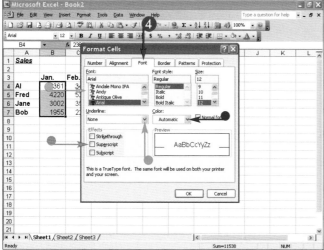

The Format Cells dialog box opens.

④ Click the Font tab.

● You can set the font, style, and size using these controls.

● You can click here to specify an underline style.

● Click here to change the data color.

● You can use these options to assign subscript, superscript, and other text effects.

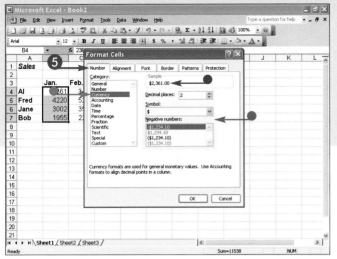

⑤ Click the Number tab.

● You can click a number format from the category list.

● You can preview the format here.

● You can set more options for the format using the additional settings that appear here after you select the number format.

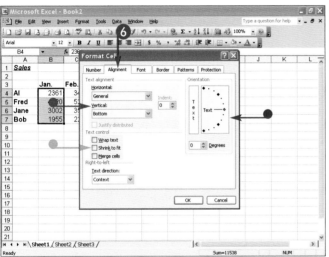

⑥ Click the Alignment tab.

● You can use the text alignment controls to specify horizontal and vertical positioning of text in a cell.

● You can use the orientation options to rotate text in a cell.

● You can use the text control options to specify how text fits into a cell.

TIPS

Options

Many of the common formatting choices you make in the Format Cells dialog box are available as toolbar buttons on the Formatting toolbar. For example, clicking the Font drop-down arrow displays the same list of available fonts found on the Font tab in the dialog box. Most users find it simpler to click a toolbar button to apply formatting rather than opening the Format Cells dialog box. However, if you need to apply numerous attributes, the dialog box allows you to do so all at once.

Did You Know?

You can use keyboard shortcuts to apply some of the basic formatting options in Excel. For example, if you press Ctrl+B, you can bold the current cell or selected data. If you press Ctrl+I, you can apply italics. If you press Ctrl+U, you can immediately apply underlining. If you press Ctrl+Shift+&, you can immediately apply an outside border to a cell. You can also press Ctrl+1 to open the Format Cells dialog box at any time.

FORMATTING:
Apply Cell Formatting (Continued)

You can use the Border tab in the Format Cells dialog box to select and customize any borders you want to apply to your worksheet cells. The tab features controls for specifying a line style and color for the borders.

The Patterns tab features a color palette you can use to assign a background color to your worksheet cells. You can choose from any color in the palette, or you can select a background pattern to apply. When applying any background to a cell, whether it is a color or a pattern, be careful not to make a selection that detracts from the readability of your worksheet data.

If you assign password protection to a sheet, you can use the Protection tab to lock cells from any changes or hide formulas. The Protection options only work if you assign worksheet protection.

See also>>

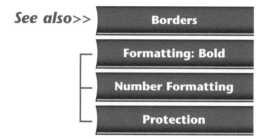

Borders

Formatting: Bold

Number Formatting

Protection

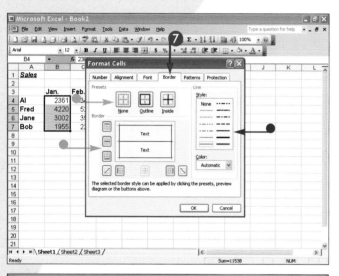

⑦ Click the Border tab.

● You can use the Presets to specify a preset border for a cell.

● You can customize cell borders using these options.

● You can use the Line options to choose a line style or color for the border.

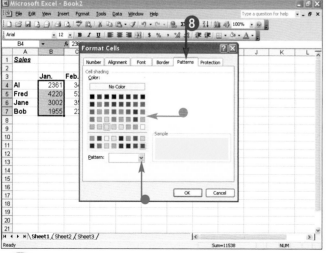

⑧ Click the Patterns tab.

● You can select a cell background color using the color palette.

● Click here to choose a pattern for the background.

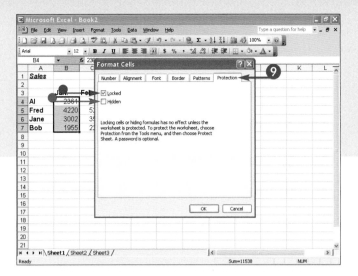

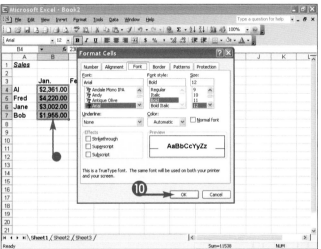

9 Click the Protection tab.

● You can select the Locked option to prevent cells from being changed.

Note: *Locking cells does not have any effect unless the worksheet is protected.*

● You can select the Hidden option to hide a formula from appearing in the cell or in the Formula bar.

Note: *Selecting the Hidden option has no effect unless the worksheet is protected.*

10 Click OK to exit the Format Cells dialog box.

● Excel applies the changes.

Did You Know?

If you are preparing a worksheet to share with others, and not feeling too confident about your formatting choices, consider using Excel's AutoFormat tool instead. With AutoFormat, you can choose from a variety of preset formatting designed especially for worksheet data. To activate the feature, select the cells you want to format and then click Format and AutoFormat. To learn more about AutoFormat, see the technique "AutoFormat: Apply Preset Formatting."

Apply It

When applying formatting to a worksheet, there are a few rules that can help you. Choose a font and stick to it. If you try to use too many fonts, the worksheet data looks too busy. Larger font sizes are easier to read, especially when trying to read numerous worksheet cells. Do not be afraid to leave blank rows and columns around your cells. Whitespace can actually help your data stand out and appear easier to read.

F

FORMATTING:
Apply Conditional Formatting

You can use Excel's conditional formatting feature to assign certain formatting only when the value of the cell meets the required condition. For example, perhaps your worksheet tracks weekly sales and compares them to last year's sales during the same week. You can set up conditional formatting to alert you if a sales figure falls below last year's level and make the cell data appear in red or bold. Or if you use a worksheet to track purchases, you can use conditional formatting to tell which clients owe you money.

Excel's conditional formatting allows you to specify up to three conditions and automatically change the cell's formatting if those conditions are met. You can choose what type of formatting to apply if the conditions are met, including a change in font, font color, cell borders, and more. If your worksheet is large, you can set conditional formatting in one cell and then copy it to all the other cells in a row or column.

See also>> **Formatting: Apply Cell**

Formatting: Bold

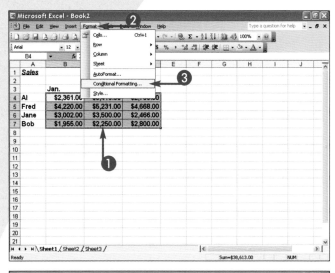

① Select the cell or range to which you want to apply conditional formatting.

② Click Format.

③ Click Conditional Formatting.

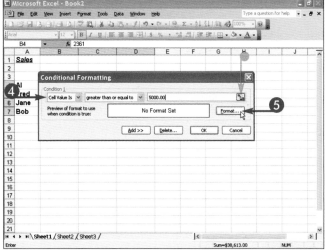

The Conditional Formatting dialog box opens.

④ Specify the operator and values you want to assign for Condition 1.

● If you need to select a cell or range, click the Collapse button to minimize the dialog box and view more of the worksheet.

⑤ Click Format.

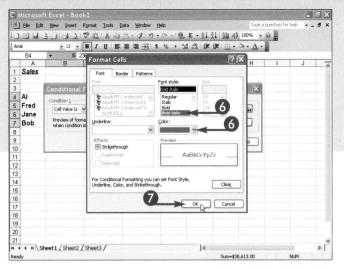

The Format Cells dialog box opens.

6 Apply all the formatting you want to set for the cell after it meets the condition.

7 Click OK.

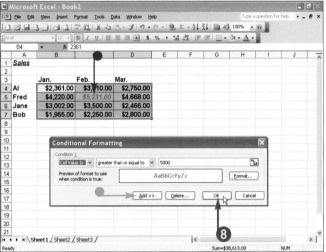

● To include additional conditions, click Add and repeat Steps 4 to 7.

8 Click OK.

● If the cell value changes to meet the condition, Excel applies the conditional formatting.

TIPS

Options

You can apply several formatting attributes when assigning conditional formatting. For many users, simply color coding the data is all the formatting required to bring attention to a cell that meets a condition. You might also format the cell in italics or bold. If your worksheet is exceptionally long, you might also consider applying a background color to the cell to help you highlight the cell when it meets a condition.

Delete It

To remove conditional formatting, first select the cell and then open the Conditional Formatting dialog box as shown in this section. After it is open, click the Delete button. If the cell has more than one condition assigned, an additional dialog box opens where you can choose which condition to remove.

FORMATTING:
Bold, Italic, and Underline

You can use basic formatting to change the appearance of your data. For example, you may want to bold a number in a range of sales figures, underline a department name to make it stand out from the rest of the data, or italicize the column labels for a table. You can assign basic formatting to a cell, or to data you select within the cell.

Basic formatting includes the Bold, Italic, and Underline commands. These basic formatting commands are common throughout most programs, including the Microsoft Office programs. The quickest way to utilize basic formatting is to click the formatting buttons on the Formatting toolbar. When activated, each formatting button remains on while you type in the cell until you deselect the formatting.

When you select another cell, the formatting is turned off unless you activate the command again.

You can also use the Format Cells dialog box to assign bold, italic, or underlining to your data. The Font tab displays bold formatting as a style you can apply, along with italics. You can also specify a particular type of underlining to apply.

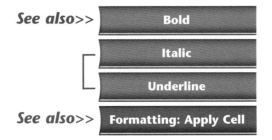

See also>>   **Bold**

   Italic

   Underline

See also>>   **Formatting: Apply Cell**

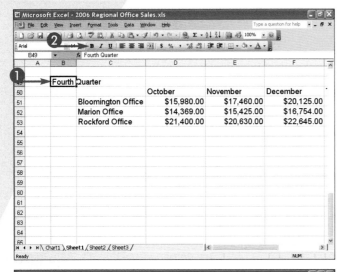

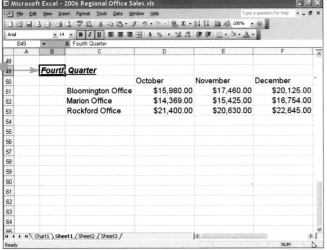

Apply Bold, Italic, or Underline with the Toolbar Buttons

① Select the data you want to format, or click in the cell to which you want to apply formatting.

Note: You can also select specific data to format in the Formula bar.

② Click a formatting button.

Click Bold (**B**) to assign bold formatting.

Click Italic (*I*) to assign italics.

Click Underline (U) to apply underlining.

● Excel immediately applies the formatting to the data.

In this example, all three formatting options are applied to the selected cell.

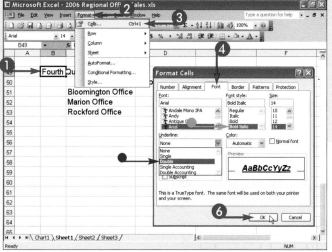

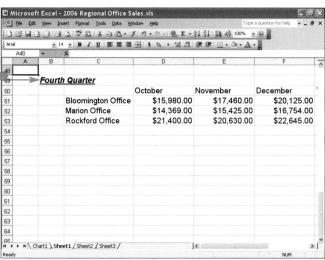

1. Select the data you want to format, or click in the cell to which you want to apply formatting.

2. Click Format.

3. Click Cells.

   The Format Cells dialog box opens.

4. Click the Font tab.

5. Click the basic formatting you want to apply.

● Click the bold or italic option to assign bold or italic formatting.

● Click the Underline drop-down arrow to select an underscore style to apply.

6. Click OK.

● Excel applies the formatting to the selected data or cell.

Did You Know?

You can also use basic formatting on text you add in a text box or text found in a chart. A text box is a special object you draw on a worksheet to hold text. For example, you might add a text box over a shape to create a logo. You can click any of the basic formatting buttons to apply formatting to selected text in a text box or chart. See the Draw or Objects techniques for more information.

Did You Know?

If you find yourself using the same formatting settings over and over again, you can save the formatting to a style and apply it all at once. This saves you from the time spent applying each formatting attribute separately. To learn more about creating styles in Excel, see the technique "Style: Create a Style."

FORMATTING:
Format Shapes, Lines, and Arrows

You can format the objects you draw in Excel to change their appearance. For example, if you draw an AutoShape on a worksheet, you can adjust the formatting to make the shape look the way you want. You might change the fill color, give the shape a thicker border, or add a three-dimensional effect. You can find numerous formatting controls for Excel objects on the Drawing toolbar.

You can change the fill, or background, color of an object using the Fill Color tool. When activated, this tool displays a palette of color choices you can apply. You can change the line or border of an object using the Line Style tool. For example, you can change the thickness of a line or border, measured in points, or change the dash style.

Excel objects include lines, arrows, and shapes you draw using the Drawing toolbar features. Objects also include WordArt objects, clip art, pictures, charts, and other objects you place on a worksheet.

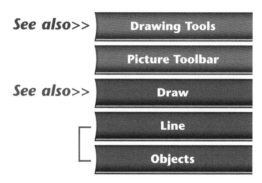

See also>> Drawing Tools

Picture Toolbar

See also>> Draw

Line

Objects

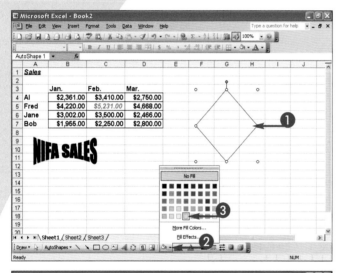

Change the Fill Color

1 Click the object you want to format.

2 Click the Fill Color drop-down arrow.

3 Click a color from the palette.

Excel immediately applies the fill color.

Change the Line Color

1 Click the object you want to format.

2 Click the Line Color drop-down arrow.

3 Click a color from the palette.

Excel immediately applies the color to the line.

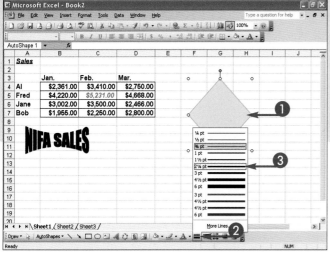

Change the Line Style

1 Click the object you want to format.

2 Click the Line Style drop-down arrow.

3 Click a line style from the menu.

Excel immediately applies the style to the line or border.

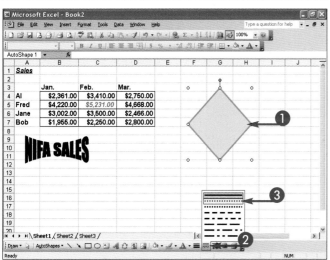

Change the Dash Style

1 Click the object you want to format.

2 Click the Dash Style drop-down arrow.

3 Click a dash style from the menu.

Excel immediately applies the style to the line or border.

Options

You can also find controls for positioning objects on a worksheet on the Drawing toolbar. You can click the Draw menu to display a variety of commands for grouping objects, layering, rotating, and aligning objects. For example, you can position two or more objects on top of each other to create a layered effect using the Order commands. To learn more about using various positioning tools, see the Objects techniques.

Did You Know?

The Picture toolbar includes commands for editing pictures; however, you can also use some commands to edit other objects on your worksheet. For example, you may want to use the Crop tool (⊞) to crop out part of a clip art object. Click View, Toolbars, and then Picture to open the Picture toolbar.

FORMATTING:
Format Shapes, Lines, and Arrows (Continued)

You can use the formatting tools on the Drawing toolbar to create a variety of different looks for your objects. For example, you can drastically change the appearance of a shape object by turning it into a three-dimensional shape using the 3-D Style tool. The 3-D Style palette offers 20 styles of varying positions.

You can also give your objects more depth on a worksheet by applying a shadow effect. For example, you can make a chart stand out on a page by applying a slight shadow around the edges. The

Shadow Style palette features 20 shadow effects you can apply.

Regardless of which formatting you apply to an object, you can always reverse the changes. For example, if you decide a shape no longer needs a fill color, you can click the Fill Color tool and select No Fill to remove the formatting effect. If you decide a line no longer requires a shadow, you can click the Shadow Style tool and click No Shadow to remove the effect.

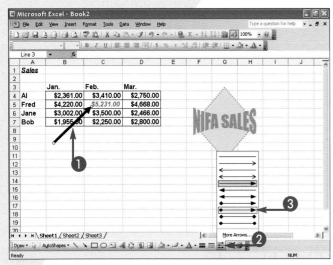

Change the Arrow Style

1. Click the arrow object you want to format.

2. Click the Arrow Style drop-down arrow.

3. Click an arrow style from the menu.

   Excel immediately applies the style to the arrow.

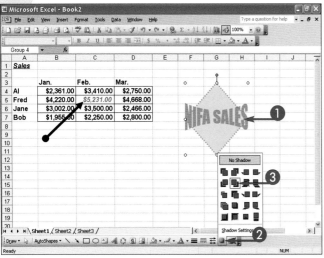

Assign a Shadow Effect

1. Click the object you want to format.

2. Click the Shadow Style drop-down arrow.

3. Click a style from the menu.

   Excel immediately applies the style to the object.

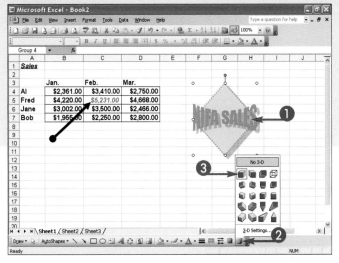

Assign a 3-D Effect

1. Click the object you want to format.

2. Click the 3-D Style drop-down arrow.

3. Click a style from the menu.

   Excel immediately applies the style to the object.

F

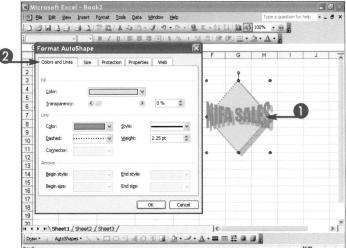

Use the Format Dialog Box

1. Double-click the object you want to format.

   Excel opens the Format dialog box. The name of the box changes based on the type of object you select.

2. Click the Colors and Lines tab for settings to control the color and style of lines and borders for your object.

3. Change a setting.

   Excel applies the settings to your object.

Caution
Not all the Drawing toolbar's formatting commands work on every part of an object. For example, you may add a fill color to a clip art's background, but Excel may not allow you to assign all the available 3-D styles to the clip art object. You can add a line or border around a picture, but you cannot change the fill color unless the picture has a transparent background.

Options
Many of the formatting tools on the Drawing toolbar offer additional settings you can use to fine-tune the appearance of an object. Depending on the formatting, you can access additional settings through a dialog box or through a toolbar. For example, if you need a color not shown on the Fill Color palette, you can click the More Fill Colors option and open the Colors dialog box. If you want to fine-tune a shadow effect, you can click the Shadow Settings option and open the Shadow Settings toolbar.

FORMULAS:
Absolute and Relative Cell Addressing

By default, Excel treats the cells you include in formulas as relative locations rather than set locations in the worksheet. This is called *relative cell referencing*. For example, when you copy a formula to a new location, the formula automatically adjusts using relative cell addresses. If cell D5 contains the formula =B5*C5, and you copy the formula to cell D6, Excel automatically changes the formula referencing to =B6*C6 for you.

If you want to address a particular cell location no matter where the formula appears, you can assign an *absolute cell reference*. Absolute references are preceded with a $ in the formula, such as =$D$2+E2. If cell D5 contains the formula

=$B$5*$C$5, and you copy the formula to cell D6, Excel keeps the formula referencing as originally entered.

You can type in the dollar sign needed for absolute cell references, or you can use the F4 key to add the dollar signs. When you press F4, Excel cycles through absolute and relative cell references. You can continue pressing the key until you see the reference you want to apply.

See also>> **Formulas: Construct**

Appendix B

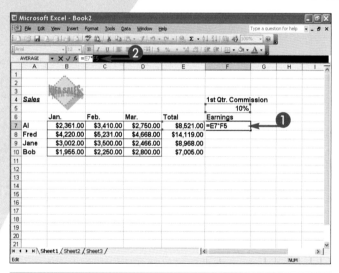

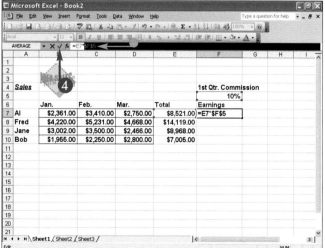

Assign Absolute References

① Click the cell containing the formula you want to change.

② Select the cell reference.

③ Press F4.

   Note: You can also type the dollar signs to make a reference absolute.

● Excel enters dollar signs ($) before each part of the cell reference, making the cell reference absolute.

   Note: You can continue pressing F4 to cycle through mixed, relative, and absolute references.

④ Press Enter or click here.

   Excel assigns the changes to the formula.

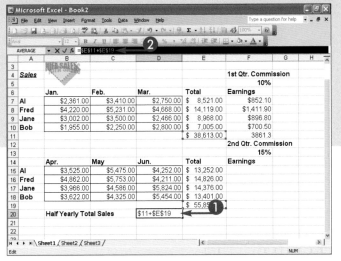

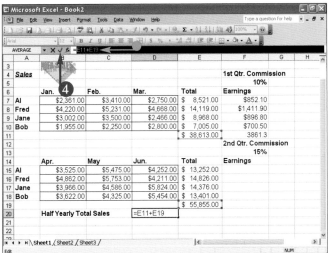

1 Click the cell containing the formula you want to change.

2 Select the cell reference.

3 Press F4 to cycle to relative addressing.

Note: You can press F4 multiple times to cycle through mixed, relative, and absolute references.

Note: You can also type the dollar signs to make a reference absolute.

4 Press Enter or click the Enter button on the Formula bar.

● Excel assigns the changes to the formula.

Apply It

You can use absolute referencing to always refer to the same cell in the worksheet. For example, perhaps your worksheet contains several columns of pricing information that refer to one discount rate disclosed in cell G10. When you create a formula based on the discount rate, you want to make sure the formula always refers to cell G10, even if the formula is moved or copied to another cell. By making cell G10 absolute instead of relative, you can always count on an accurate value for the success of your formula.

Did You Know?

You can use mixed referencing to reference the same row or column — but different relative cells within — such as $C6, which keeps the column from changing, but the row remains relative. If the mixed reference is C$6, the column is relative but the row is absolute. You can use the F4 key while writing a formula to cycle through absolute, mixed, and relative cell referencing, or you can type in the dollar signs ($) as needed.

FORMULAS:
Construct a Basic Formula

You can write a formula to perform a calculation on data in your worksheet cells. With formulas, you can execute subtraction, addition, multiplication, and division using the values in various cells. You can use mathematical operators, such as + (addition), - (subtraction), * (multiplication), and / (division), to write your Excel formulas.

All formulas begin with an equal sign (=) in Excel. You can reference values in cells by entering the cell name, also called a *cell reference*. For example, if

you want to add the contents of cells C3 and C4 together, your formula would look like this: =C3+C4.

You can create a formula in the Formula bar at the top of the worksheet. Formula results always appear in the cell in which you assign a formula. Any time you select a cell containing a formula, the formula results appear in the cell while the formula itself appears in the Formula bar.

See also>>   **Appendix B**

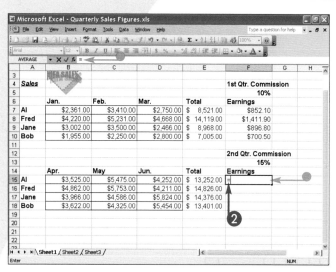

① Click the cell to which you want to assign a formula.

② Type =.

● Excel displays the formula in the Formula bar and in the active cell.

③ Click the first cell you want to reference in the formula.

● Excel inserts the cell reference into the formula.

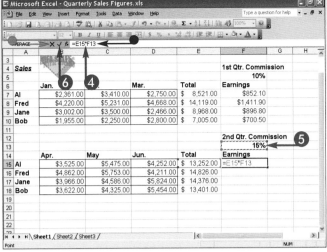

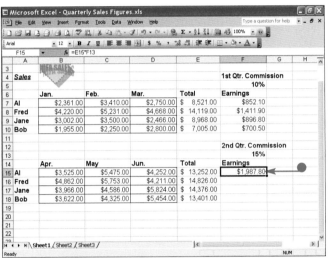

④ Type an operator for the formula.

⑤ Click the next cell you want to reference in the formula.

● Excel inserts the cell reference into the formula.

⑥ Press Enter or click the Enter button on the Formula bar.

● You can click Cancel to cancel the formula.

● The formula results appear in the cell.

To view the formula, simply click the cell. The Formula bar displays any formula assigned to the active cell.

Note: *If you change any of the values in the cells referenced in your formula, the formula results automatically update to reflect the changes.*

TIPS

Did You Know?

To edit a formula, simply click the cell containing the formula and make any corrections in the Formula bar. You can also double-click the cell to make edits directly to the formula within the cell rather than the Formula bar. You can use the Backspace and Delete keys to make changes to the formula and type new values or references as needed. When finished with the edits, press Enter or click the Enter button (☑) on the Formula bar.

Caution

If you see an error message, such as #DIV/0!, double-check your formula references, making sure you referenced the correct cells. Also make sure you did not attempt to divide by 0, which always produces an error. To learn more about fixing formula errors, see the technique "Errors: Fix Errors."

FORMULAS:
Copy a Formula

You can use Excel's AutoFill feature to quickly copy formulas across rows or columns in your worksheets. AutoFill is a handy tool you can use to copy cell data as well as copy formulas. You can also use the Copy and Paste commands to copy formulas; however, the AutoFill handle is much faster to use.

When copying formulas, it is important to note whether the cell references are relative or absolute. If the cell references in a formula are relative, Excel automatically adjusts the formula for the current cell. For example, if cell C3 contains the formula =A3+B3, and you copy the formula to cell C4, Excel

automatically changes the cell references for you and the formula reads =A4+B4.

If the cell references in a formula are absolute, Excel copies the formula exactly as written without making changes to the cell references.

See also>>

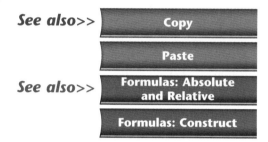

| Copy |
| Paste |
| Formulas: Absolute and Relative |
| Formulas: Construct |

See also>>

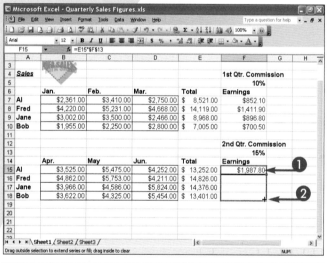

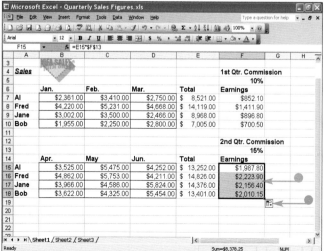

1 Click the cell containing the formula you want to copy.

2 Click and drag the cell's fill handle across or down the number of cells to which you want to copy the formula.

● Excel copies the formula into each cell you drag over.

● An AutoFill smart icon may appear.

In the case of relative cell referencing, Excel adjusts the formula relative to each cell you copy to.

With absolute cell referencing, Excel keeps the absolute cell reference the same no matter where the formula is copied to.

FORMULAS:
Reference Cells from Other Worksheets

You can reference cells in other worksheets in your Excel formulas. When referencing data from other worksheets, you must specify the sheet name, followed by an exclamation mark, and then the cell address, such as Sheet2!D12.

If the sheet has a specific name, such as Sales, you must use the name along with an exclamation mark, followed by the cell or range reference (Sales!D12). If the sheet name includes spaces, enclose the reference in single quote marks, such as 'Sales Totals!D12'.

You can use three-dimensional, or 3D references to designate a cell range that includes two or more sheets in a workbook. For example, you

might have a workbook containing four worksheets, one for each sales quarter. You can use a 3-D reference to reference the same cells in each sheet. To do so, you can use a colon to indicate the range, such as Sheet1:Sheet4!D5:G12.

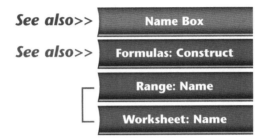

See also>> **Name Box**

See also>> **Formulas: Construct**

Range: Name

Worksheet: Name

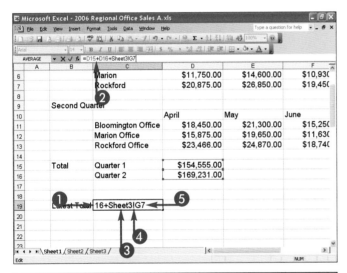

① Click the cell to which you want to assign a formula.

② Create the formula you want to apply.

③ When you are ready to insert a cell or range from another sheet into the formula, type the sheet name.

④ Type an exclamation mark.

⑤ Type the cell address or range.

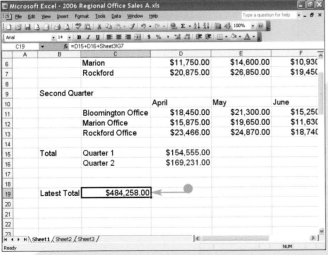

You can continue creating the formula as needed.

⑥ When finished, press Enter or click the Enter button on the Formula bar to complete the formula.

● The formula results appear in the cell.

FREEZE/UNFREEZE:
Freeze and Unfreeze Cells

You can freeze a column or row to keep the labels in view as you scroll through larger worksheets. The area you freeze is non-scrollable, while the unfrozen areas of the worksheet are still scrollable. The Freeze command essentially lets you split your worksheet into two panes. Unlike the Split command, however, the Freeze command freezes one of the panes, making it stay put on-screen.

The Freeze command is especially helpful for larger worksheets in which the columns or rows are not entirely viewable in one window. If your worksheet has a row of column labels at the top, and you are working at the bottom of the table, you can freeze

the labels so you know which column holds which type of entry. For example, if you are working on a product inventory list, you can freeze the labels at the top of each column and then as you scroll down the worksheet to add more entries, you can view what column contains what part of the inventory list.

After you finish freezing cells, you can unfreeze them using the Unfreeze command. This returns the worksheet to its full-screen status, making the entire sheet scrollable again.

See also>> **Worksheet: Split**

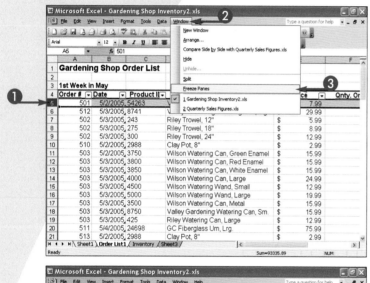

Freeze Panes

1. Click to the right of the column or below the row you want to freeze.

2. Click Window.

3. Click Freeze Panes.

● Excel freezes the areas above where you applied the Freeze Panes command.

● The area below the panes is scrollable.

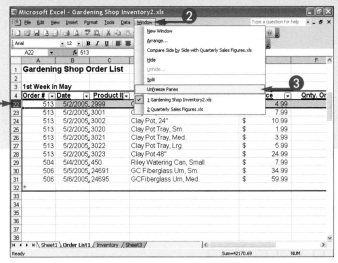

Unfreeze Panes

1. Click to the right of the column or below the row you want to unfreeze.
2. Click Window.
3. Click Unfreeze Panes.

Excel unfreezes the panes, making the entire worksheet scrollable again.

TIPS

Options

Excel freezes cells depending on where you click in a worksheet. To lock rows with the Freeze command, simply click the row below where you want to freeze the cells. To lock columns, click the column to the right of where you want to freeze cells. To lock both rows and columns, you can click the cell below and to the right of where you want to freeze cells.

Did You Know?

You can freeze a cell and its formula as a separate window and always keep it in view using a Watch Window. To create a Watch Window, click the cell you want to watch, click the Tools menu, click Formula Auditing, and then click Show Watch Window. You can also click the Add Watch button in the Watch Windows and then click Add. This adds the cell to the window. You can now view the cell no matter where you scroll. You can also move the window around on-screen as needed.

FUNCTIONS:
Build a Basic Function

You can use functions to speed up your Excel calculations. Functions are simply built-in formulas you can use to accomplish a variety of worksheet calculation tasks. Excel offers more than 300 functions covering a wide range of calculations. The functions are grouped into 10 distinct categories: Database & List Management, Date & Time, Engineering, Financial, Information, Logical, Lookup & Reference, Mathematical & Trigonometric, Statistical, and Text.

For example, you can find basic calculation functions in the Mathematical & Trigonometric category, including functions for rounding off, calculating

logarithms, square roots, and more. You can find functions for calculating probabilities, rankings, and trends in the Statistical category.

You can use the Insert Function dialog box to look for a particular function from among Excel's 10 function categories. Depending on the function you select, the dialog box offers a brief description of the function. The dialog box also keeps track of recently used functions so you can quickly apply them again.

See also>>

> **Formulas: Construct**

> **Appendix B**

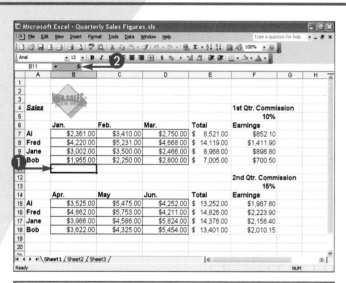

① Click the cell to which you want to assign a function.

② Click the Insert Function button on the Formula bar.

Note: You can also click the Insert menu and click Function.

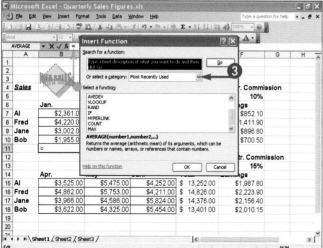

● Excel inserts an equal sign automatically to denote a formula and displays the Insert Function dialog box.

③ Click the Category drop-down arrow.

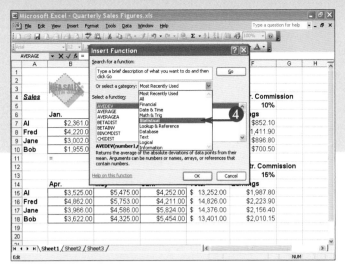

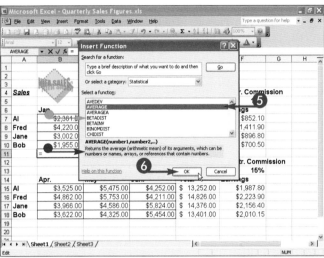

④ Click a category.

Excel's built-in functions are grouped into 10 categories.

● A list of functions appears here.

⑤ Click the function you want to apply.

● A description of the function appears here.

⑥ Click OK.

TIP

Did You Know?

Most of the time, the functions you create will produce number results. Because functions use different types of arguments, however, some functions produce different types of results. The following table describes several types of function results you can encounter:

Result	Description
Number	Number results can include any integer or decimal number.
Time and date	When applying time and date functions, you can expect time and date results.
Logical values	Logical arguments produce results such as TRUE, FALSE, YES, NO, 1, 0.
Text	Any text results always appear surrounded by quote marks.
Arrays	An array is a column or table of cells that are treated as a single value, and array formulas operate on multiple cells.
Cell references	Some function results display references to other cells rather than actual values.
Error values	If a function uses error values as arguments, the results appear as error values as well. Error values are not the same as error messages.

FUNCTIONS:
Build a Basic Function (Continued)

After selecting a function, you can then apply the function to a cell or range of cells in your worksheet. You can use the Function Arguments dialog box to help you construct all the necessary components of a function. The dialog box can help you determine what values you need to enter to build the formula.

Most functions have a particular syntax you must use to construct the formula. Syntax includes the order and format of the arguments, but also the punctuation and spacing required by the function. If you make a mistake typing syntax, Excel warns you about the error and offers a suggestion for fixing the problem.

Some functions do not require any arguments. For example, the function =NOW() returns the current date and time, but you must still type the parentheses to make the function work properly. Other functions may require several arguments to create the formula. The Function Arguments dialog box can help you determine what arguments you need to complete the function.

You can type cell references and values directly into the Function Arguments dialog box, or you can select the cells directly in the worksheet.

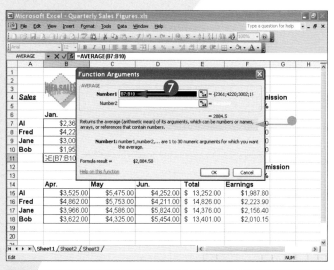

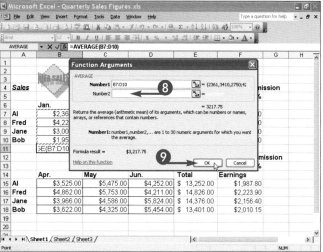

The Function Arguments dialog box appears.

⑦ Depending on the function's arguments, enter the desired cells for each argument required by the function.

You can select a cell or range of cells directly in the worksheet and Excel automatically adds the references to the argument.

You can also type a range or cell address directly into the Argument text box.

● The dialog box displays additional information about the function here.

⑧ If needed, continue adding necessary cell references to complete all the function's arguments.

⑨ When finished constructing the arguments, click OK.

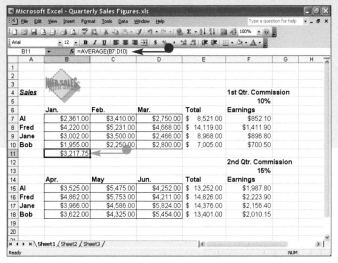

- Excel displays the function results in the cell.
- The function appears in the Formula bar.

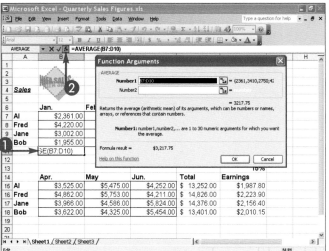

Edit a Function

1 Click the cell containing the function you want to edit.

2 Click the Insert Function button on the Formula bar.

Excel displays the Function Arguments dialog box where you can make changes to the cell references or values as needed.

Options

If you click the Help On This Function link in either the Insert Function or Function Arguments dialog boxes, you can access Excel's help files to find out more about the function. The function includes an example of the function in action and tips about how to use the function.

Did You Know?

If the Function Arguments dialog box covers the cells you need to select in the worksheet, you can move the dialog box out of the way. You can click the Collapse button (▦) at the end of the Argument text box to minimize the dialog box. You can then select any cells needed and click the Expand button (▦) to maximize the dialog box again. You can also click and drag the dialog box by its title bar to move it around the screen.

GO TO:
Navigate to a Cell or Range

ou can use a variety of techniques to navigate around your Excel worksheets. The longer the length of your worksheet, the more difficult it is to find the cell you are looking for. You can use the Go To command to quickly locate any cell in your worksheet. You can use the Go To dialog box to locate any cell or named range.

You can also use the Go To Special dialog box to locate and select cells that meet specific conditions. For example, you can quickly locate all the cells in

your worksheet that contain a specific type of data, such as cells containing comments or formulas. You can locate cells that meet criteria, such as locating the last cell in the worksheet that contains formatting, or else find all the cells that are blank.

You can start your cell search at any point in the worksheet, or you can activate the Go To command from the beginning of the worksheet.

See also>> **Range**

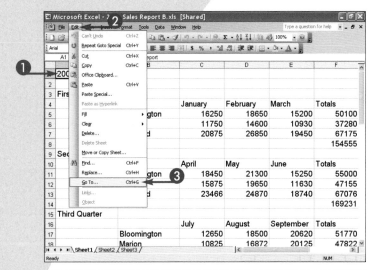

1 Click any cell in the worksheet.

To start your search from the top of the worksheet, click cell A1 or press Ctrl+Home.

2 Click Edit.

3 Click Go To.

You can also press Ctrl+G or F5 at any time to access the Go To dialog box.

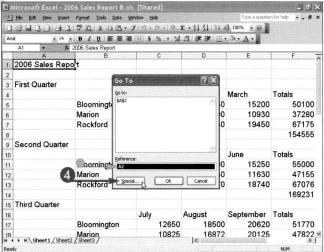

The Go To dialog box opens.

● To navigate to a particular cell reference or range name, type the reference here and click OK.

4 Click Special.

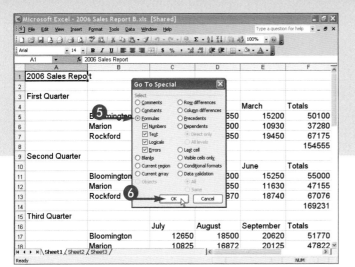

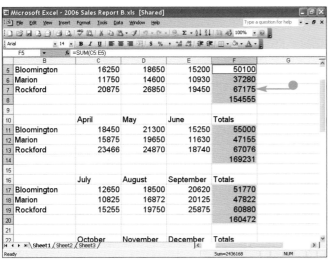

The Go To Special dialog box opens.

⑤ Select the criteria you want to apply.

⑥ Click OK.

● Excel navigates to the cell or cells and highlights the cells in the worksheet.

In this example, Excel highlighted all the cells containing formulas.

Did You Know?

You can also use the keyboard keys to quickly navigate around a worksheet. The following table lists a few keyboard shortcut keys you can use.

Shortcut Key	Action
Ctrl+Arrow key	Moves to the edge of the current data region
Home	Moves to the beginning of the row
Ctrl+Home	Moves to the first cell in a worksheet or list
Ctrl+End	Selects the last cell in a worksheet or list
Page Down	Moves down one screen
Page Up	Moves up one screen
Alt+Page Down	Moves one screen to the right
Alt+Page Up	Moves one screen to the left
Ctrl+Page Down	Moves to the next sheet in the workbook
Ctrl+Page Up	Moves to the previous sheet
Ctrl+Backspace	Scrolls to display the currently active cell

GOAL SEEK:
Analyze Values with Goal Seek

You can use Excel's Goal Seek tool to work backward to a desired result and analyze what happens when you change values along the way. Goal Seek is one of several "what if" analysis tools you can use in Excel. For example, if you want to calculate how much you can afford each month on a new car purchase, Goal Seek can help you determine the loan amount for just such a goal.

To use Goal Seek, you must have at least one input cell that affects the value of the cell containing your goal. This feature works by allowing you to make

adjustments to the data in the cells contributing to the goal value.

You can use Goal Seek to help you solve single variable equations of any kind. One of the most popular uses of Goal Seek is figuring out loan amounts and payments. You can also use Goal Seek to figure out how much you need to sell to reach a sales goal or to break even.

See also>>   Add-Ins

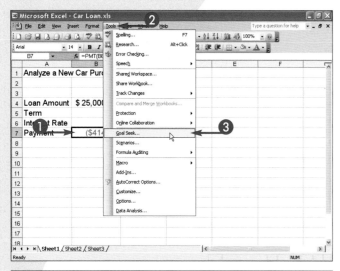

1 Click the cell containing the goal you want to change.

2 Click Tools.

3 Click Goal Seek.

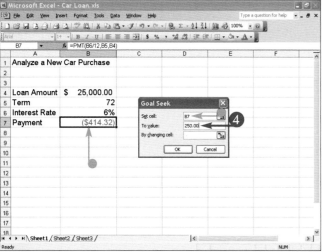

The Goal Seek dialog box opens.

● The Set cell value is already filled in with the cell contents you selected in Step 1.

4 Type in your goal value.

In this example, Goal Seek works backward from the desired monthly payment amount.

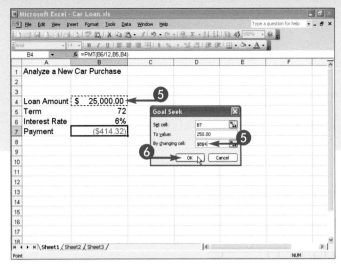

⑤ Select or type the cell reference you want to change to reach your goal value.

In this example, the loan amount is the amount that needs to change to reach the goal value.

⑥ Click OK.

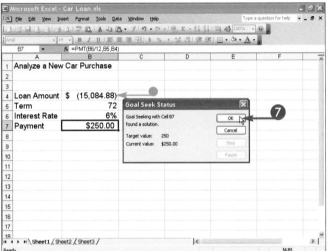

● Goal Seek produces a value change to meet your goal and displays the Goal Seek Status dialog box.

In this example, Goal Seek determines the needed loan amount in cell B4 to reach the monthly payment amount specified in cell B7.

⑦ Click OK.

Excel closes the Goal Seek Status dialog box.

Did You Know?

You can use another tool to figure out more complex goals in your Excel worksheets. Use Goal Seek when you want to produce a specific value by adjusting one input cell that influences the value. If you require more than one input cell, use Excel's Solver tool instead. Solver is an add-in you can use for complex problems that use multiple variables. Solver is very similar to Goal Seek. See the technique "Add-Ins: Use the Solver Add-In" to learn more about using Solver.

Attention

When using Goal Seek, it is important that the Set cell contains a formula, function, or cell reference in order to produce Goal Seek results. Also, when filling out the Goal Seek dialog box, the By Changing cell field must be a number or a blank cell. It cannot contain a formula, function, or cell reference. The By Changing cell field must reference the formula or function in the Set Cell field.

HELP:
Find Help with Excel

You can use the Excel Help tools to assist you when you run into a problem or need more explanation about a particular task. With an Internet connection, you can use Microsoft's online help files to quickly access information about an Excel feature. The Help pane offers tools for searching for topics you want to learn more about. You can choose to view the entire table of contents, or conduct a search for a particular keyword or Excel feature.

Excel's Help topics are arranged into categories, such as Printing and Workbooks and Worksheets, and numerous subtopics, such as Printer Setup. When you expand any particular category or subtopic, you can view individual Help topics. When you choose a specific topic, a separate Help window opens revealing information about the topic. You can click links within the Help window to view related information or print the information you need.

You must log on to your Internet connection to use the online help files.

See also>> **Help**

Task Pane

See also>> **Task Pane**

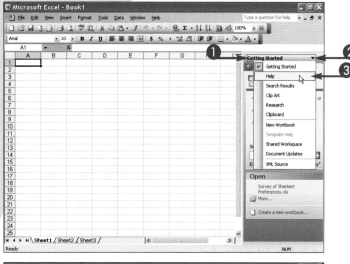

① Display the task pane.

② Click the Other Task Panes button.

③ Click Help.

The Excel Help pane opens.

④ Type a word or phrase you want to learn more about.

⑤ Click the Start Searching button.

You can also press Enter to start the search.

● You can click this link to look for topics in the table of contents.

Note: You will need to log on to your Internet connection to access Microsoft Excel's online help files.

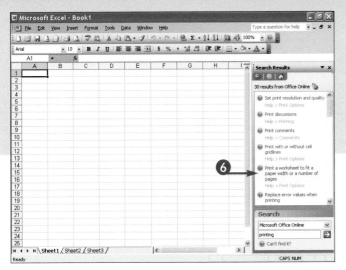

The Search Results pane opens, displaying a list of possible matches.

6 Click a link to learn more about a topic.

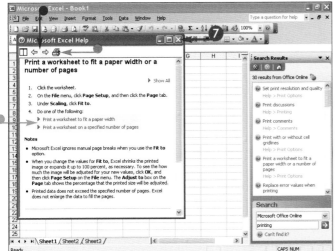

The Microsoft Excel Help window opens and you can read more about the topic.

● You can click links to learn more about a subject.

● You can use the Back and Forward buttons to move between help topics.

● You can click the Print button to print the information.

7 Click here to close the window.

TIPS

More Options

You can also use the Type a Question box on the menu bar to find help. Simply click inside the box and type the question, phrase, or word you want to know more about. Press Enter and the Search Results pane opens listing possible matches. You can click a topic to learn more about the subject.

Did You Know?

Many of the Excel help topics are accessed through the Microsoft Office Web site. You can also look up additional information on the Web site to learn more about how to use Excel. The site includes discussion groups where you can read messages posted by other Excel users, files you can download and use with Excel, and online demos to help you learn more about a technique or feature. To access the Web site directly, you can click the Microsoft Office Online graphic link in the task pane, or click the Help menu and then click Microsoft Office Online.

HYPERLINK:
Insert a Hyperlink

You can insert hyperlinks into your worksheets that, when clicked, open a Web page. When linking to a Web page, you must designate the URL or Uniform Resource Locator. Every page on the Web has a unique address. If you know a page's URL, you can view it over the Internet. You can also view pages using hyperlinks. Called links for short, hyperlinks connect pages through embedded URLs presented as text or images on a page. Users can jump from one page to another by clicking links.

In your Excel worksheet, you can designate data as a link, or turn a graphic object into a link. For example, you may turn a column heading into a link that,

when clicked, opens a Web page detailing information about the subject.

You can also use hyperlinks to link to other files on your computer. You must designate the address or path of the page you want to link to when adding links to a worksheet.

See also>> Hyperlink

See also>> Save: Save Worksheet as Web Page

Web Toolbar

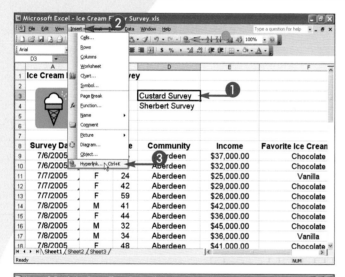

1 Select the cell, text, or image you want to use as a hyperlink.

2 Click Insert.

3 Click Hyperlink.

● You can also click the Insert Hyperlink button on the Standard toolbar.

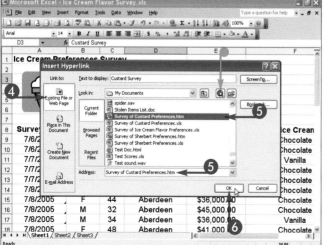

The Insert Hyperlink dialog box appears.

4 Click the type of document to which you want to link.

5 Select the page or type the address or URL of the page to which you want to link.

● To browse the Internet, you can click this button and open your default browser window.

6 Click OK.

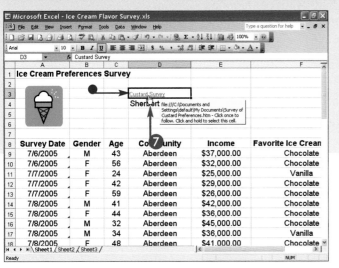

● Excel creates a hyperlink.

⑦ To test the link, click it.

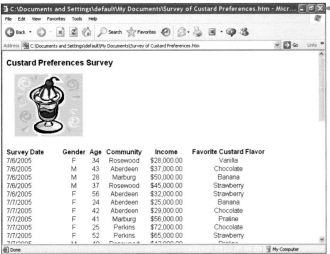

The default Web browser opens and displays the designated page.

● You can click here to close the browser window and return to Excel.

TIPS

Change It

To change a link, such as editing the Web page URL, you can reopen the Edit Hyperlink dialog box and make any necessary changes. Right-click the link and click Edit Hyperlink. The Edit Hyperlink dialog box appears. You can use the dialog box to change the hyperlink text, address, or the type of page you want to use in the link.

Delete It

You can remove a hyperlink from your worksheet just as easily as you created it. Right-click a link and click Remove Hyperlink from the shortcut menu that appears. Excel removes the associated link and leaves the text or image. To remove a hyperlink from the Edit Hyperlink dialog box, you can click the Remove Link button.

IMPORT AND EXPORT:
Import and Export Excel Data

You can input data from other sources into your Excel worksheet. For example, you can import text files and database and Web queries. If you want to analyze data you previously typed into another file type, you can import the data into Excel rather than retyping it. *External data* is considered any data stored outside of Excel.

You can use the Select Data Source dialog box to specify the type of data you want to import into Excel. If you need to import data from a remote location, such as a database on a Web server, you can activate the Data Connection Wizard to walk you through the import procedure.

You can also export your Excel data into different file types that other users can access. You can use the Save As dialog box to export your workbook data by saving the data as another file format. For example, you might save your workbook as a text file to send to someone who does not use Excel as their spreadsheet program.

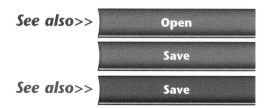

See also>> Open

Save

See also>> Save

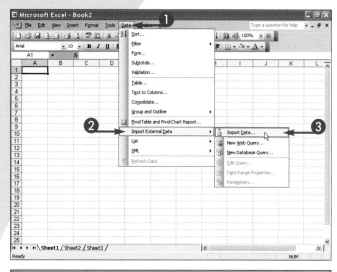

Import Data

❶ Click Data.

❷ Click Import External Data.

❸ Click Import Data.

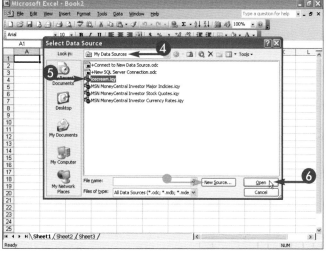

The Select Data Source dialog box opens.

❹ Navigate to the folder containing the file you want to import.

● To import other types of external data, you can activate the Data Connection Wizard by clicking New Source.

❺ Click the filename.

❻ Click Open.

Excel imports the data.

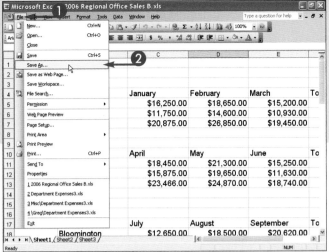

1 Click File.

2 Click Save As.

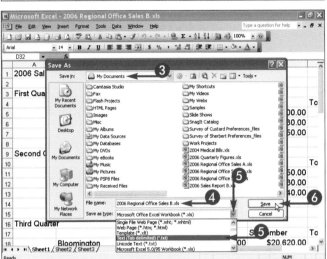

The Save As dialog box opens.

3 Navigate to the folder to which you want to save the file.

4 Type a filename.

5 Click here and select a file type.

6 Click Save.

Excel saves the data to the new format.

TIPS

More Options

If you import a text file, the Text Import Wizard opens to help you control how text is split into worksheet columns and rows. In text files, text is split using *delimiters* — characters that separate each field of text, such as commas or tabs. For example, with .txt file types, tabs are delimiters, and in .csv files, commas are delimiters. The Text Import Wizard walks you through three steps for defining how text fields are imported into worksheet cells. You also have the option of placing the imported text on the current sheet or in a new worksheet.

More Options

Different database management systems use different types of connections to export data. The Data Connection Wizard can help you specify the type of connection you need to make. The Data Connection Wizard can help you import Microsoft SQL Server, Microsoft Access, dBase, FoxPro, Oracle, and Paradox data. If you are unsure of which connection type to use, contact your system administrator.

INDENT:
Indent Data

You can indent data within your worksheet cells to help improve the appearance of your data. You can use the Increase Indent and Decrease Indent commands to quickly change the positioning of data from the left and right edges of the cell. For example, if a cell contains a paragraph of text, you can indent the entire block of text to help set it apart from surrounding cells.

The Increase Indent command inserts the width of one character to create the indent. When you activate the command more than once, you can increase the amount of indent. The same is true of

the Decrease Indent command, except it decreases the indent by one character width.

You can use the Increase Indent and Decrease Indent buttons on the Formatting toolbar to quickly set an indent for a cell or range. You can also control horizontal indents using the Format Cells dialog box.

See also>>   Indent

See also>>   Margins

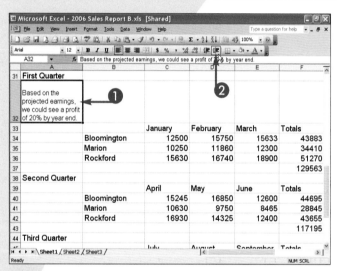

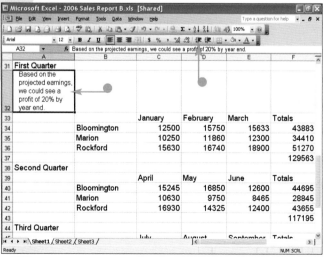

Create a Quick Indent

① Click the cell or range you want to indent.

You can also indent a single line by first clicking in front of the line.

② Click the Increase Indent button on the Formatting toolbar.

● Excel indents the data.

● To decrease an indent, click the Decrease Indent button.

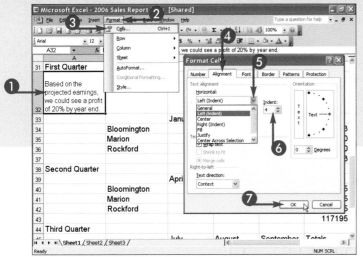

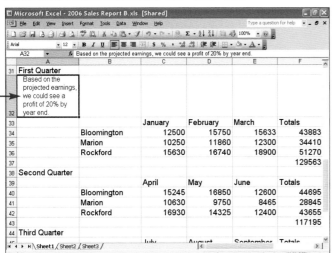

Indent with the Format Cells Dialog Box

1 Click the cell or range you want to indent.

2 Click Format.

3 Click Cells.

The Format Cells dialog box opens.

4 Click the Alignment tab.

5 Click here and then click a left or right indent.

6 Type an indent value or click the arrows to set a value.

The value 1 indents the data by the width of one character.

7 Click OK.

● Excel applies the new indent.

LINE COLOR:
Set a Line Color

When using Excel's drawing tools, you can control the color assigned to any line you draw. For example, when drawing a basic shape, such as an oval, you can specify a color for the line defining the oval shape. If the shape includes an inner fill color, the line color only affects the outer edge or outline of the shape. You can also change the line color for clip art borders and borders around pictures and WordArt objects.

When drawing arrows and lines using the Arrow and Line tools, you can specify a line color after you draw the object on the worksheet. The color palette lists 40 colors, including basic black and white. The default Automatic setting assigns the color black to any new shapes or lines you draw. You can also open the Colors dialog box to choose from more colors or

set a custom color by adjusting the color channels. You can also use the Colors dialog box to make a color appear more transparent.

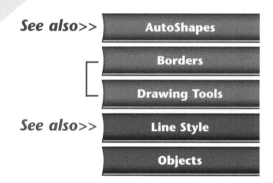

See also>>

See also>>

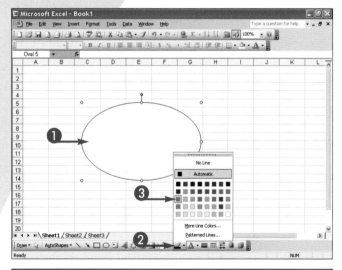

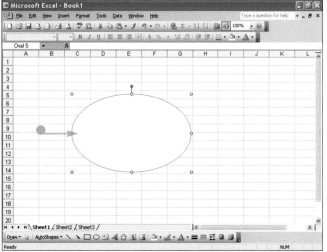

Assign a Line Color

① Using the Excel drawing tools, create an object on the worksheet.

You can assign a line color to shapes, AutoShapes, lines, arrows, and more.

② Click the Line Color button on the Drawing toolbar.

Note: If the Drawing toolbar is not displayed, click the Drawing button ( ) on the Standard toolbar or click the View menu and then click Toolbars and Drawing.

③ Click a color.

● Excel immediately changes the object's line color.

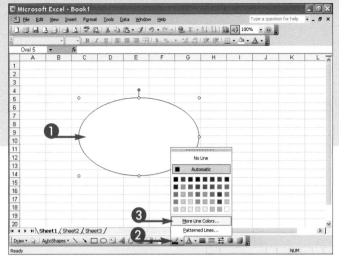

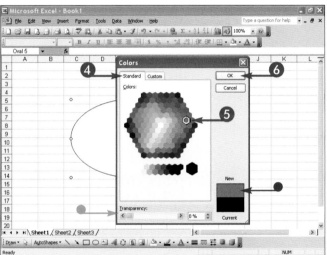

Assign a Color with the Colors Dialog Box

① Using the Excel drawing tools, create an object on the worksheet.

② Click the Line Color button on the Drawing toolbar.

③ Click More Line Colors.

The Colors dialog box opens.

④ Click the Standard tab.

⑤ Click a color.

● You can drag the transparency slider or type a percentage to control the transparency of the line color.

● The sample area displays both the new color and the current color.

⑥ Click OK.

Excel assigns the new line color.

TIPS

Customize It

You can create a custom color by making adjustments to the color channels. Computers use color channels to create the wide range of colors used on the monitor screen. To set a custom color for a line, open the Colors dialog box and click the Custom tab. Click a color in the palette and fine tune the color using the Red, Green, and Blue color settings.

Change It

You can return a line's color to the default color assignment, which is black. To do so, click the Line Color button on the Drawing toolbar and choose Automatic from the palette. To remove the line color entirely, click the Line Color button and click No Line from the palette list. The No Line command removes all color, but the line object remains.

LINE STYLE:
Set a Line Style

You can use Excel's Line Style and Dash Style tools to control the style of any line you draw with the drawing tools. For example, when drawing lines and arrows on a worksheet, you can choose a specific style for the line, such as a dotted or dashed line, or you can specify a different thickness for the line. You can also control the line style for any shapes, AutoShapes, WordArt objects, or clip art borders you add to a worksheet.

You can specify a line style after you draw the object on the worksheet. The Line Style tool palette lists a wide variety of line thicknesses you can apply, including double lines. The Dash Style tool palette lists a variety of dash styles, ranging in width.

You can also open the Format dialog box and use the settings to create a custom line style for an object. Depending on the type of object you edit, the Format dialog box uses different names. When you edit a shape, for example, it is called the Format AutoShape dialog box. When you edit a clip art object, it is called the Format Picture dialog box.

See also>>

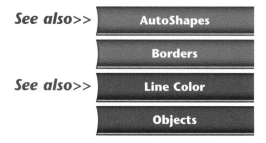

- AutoShapes
- Borders
- Line Color
- Objects

See also>>

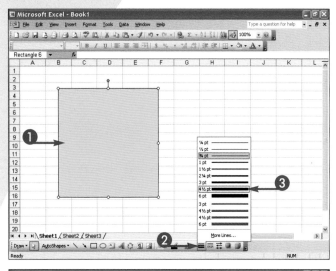

Assign a Line Style

① Using the Excel drawing tools, create an object on the worksheet.

You can assign a line color to shapes, AutoShapes, lines, arrows, and more.

② Click the Line Style button on the Drawing toolbar.

Note: If the Drawing toolbar is not displayed, click the Drawing button ( ) on the Standard toolbar or click the View menu and then click Toolbars and Drawing.

③ Click a style.

- Excel immediately changes the object's line style.

- To set a dash style, click the Dash Style button and click a dash style.

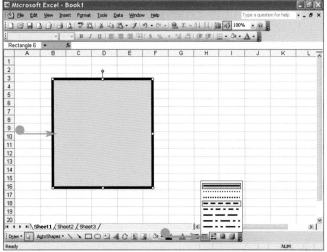

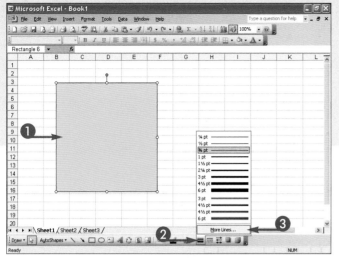

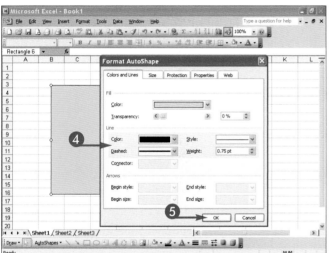

Customize a Line Style

L

1. Using the Excel drawing tools, create an object on the worksheet.

2. Click the Line Style button on the Drawing toolbar.

3. Click More Lines.

The Format dialog box opens.

4. With the Colors and Lines tab selected, change the line style setting you want to edit.

   You can use the Color setting to change the line color.

   Use the Style setting to set a new line style.

   Use the Dashed setting to assign dashed lines.

   Use the Weight setting to assign a specific line thickness.

5. Click OK.

   Excel assigns the new line style.

TIPS

More Options

To control the line styles in Excel charts, you can double-click the chart element and make changes to the line styles using the available options. For example, if you double-click the axis, the Format Axis dialog box opens and you can change the line thickness and color for the axis using the Patterns tab. If you double-click the chart gridlines, the Format Gridlines dialog box opens and you can change the line style.

Did You Know?

Line thickness for any objects you draw on a worksheet is measured in points. Points are a unit of measurement from the printing industry. Commonly used in font sizing, points control the height of a character. In the case of line styles, points control the thickness of the line. The smaller the point size, the smaller the height of the line, which creates a thinner-looking line. A larger point size creates a thicker-looking line.

LINK:
Link Excel Data

You can link data between cells, worksheets, and workbooks using Excel's OLE data-sharing protocol. *OLE*, which stands for *Object Linking and Embedding*, began with Microsoft Windows 3.1 and is a common way to share data between programs today, including Excel and the other Microsoft applications.

Ordinarily when you copy data, the data does not retain any connection to its source. With linking, the data retains a connection to its source, and any changes you make to the source data are immediately reflected in the linked data. You can use linking to share data between Excel files or between other programs. For example, you might link to another workbook or to a Word document or

PowerPoint slide. You can also link data between worksheets or cells. In the case of linked cells in the same worksheet, any changes you make to the source cells are immediately reflected in the destination cells.

You can use the Paste Special dialog box to create links. When linking between workbooks, you can use the Edit Links dialog box to maintain and edit links.

See also>>

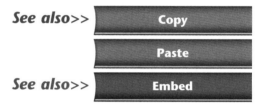

See also>>

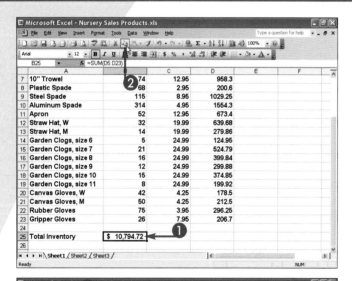

① In the source file, select the data you want to link.

② Click the Copy button.

Note: You can also click the Edit menu and then click Copy.

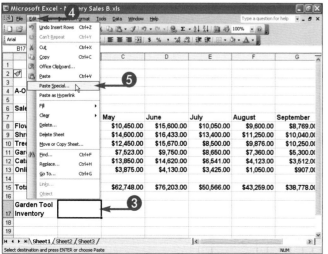

③ Open the destination file and click where you want to insert the copied data.

④ Click Edit.

⑤ Click Paste Special.

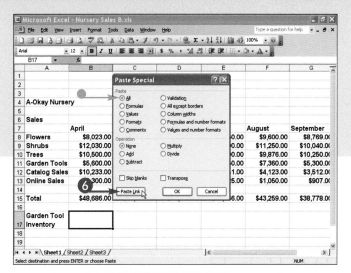

The Paste Special dialog box opens.

● By default, the All option is selected.

6 Click Paste Link.

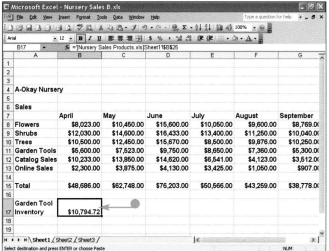

● Excel pastes the data into the worksheet.

Any changes you make to the source data are now reflected in the destination file.

TIPS

Attention

If you move the source file to a new location, or delete the source file, any links you have to the source data are broken. Broken links can also occur if you move the worksheet within the workbook. You can fix a link using the Edit Links dialog box. In the destination file, click Edit and then click Links to open the Edit Links dialog box. This dialog box keeps track of all the links in a destination file, and allows you to check link status, break links, and to view the source data. You can click the link you want to edit and select from the link options available.

More Options

You can link data between sheets using the Paste Options Smart Tag (▣). When you create a link between sheets, any time you make changes to the source cells, the linked cells automatically reflect the new changes. The Paste Options Smart Tag appears immediately after you paste data. Simply click the icon to display the paste options.

MACRO:
Create a Macro

You can use macros to automate the tasks you perform in Excel. For example, you can create a macro to apply formatting, assign a formula, or print sheets. Any sort of repetitive task you perform in Excel is a good candidate for a macro. After you record a macro, Excel saves the actions so you can reuse the macro again.

A macro is simply a set of instructions — much like a computer program — that Excel follows in the sequence you designate. The easiest way to create a macro in Excel is to use the macro recorder. When you use the recorder, Excel records each action you take, including menu commands and keyboard presses.

You can assign a keyboard shortcut key to your macro and activate the macro at any time using the keyboard.

You can also choose to store macros in the workbook with which you used to create the macro, or you can store the macro in the personal macro workbook file. Labeled Personal.xls, it is a special workbook file that only contains macros and remains open all the time, yet hidden.

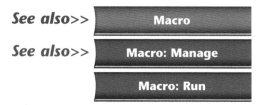

See also>> **Macro**

See also>> **Macro: Manage**

Macro: Run

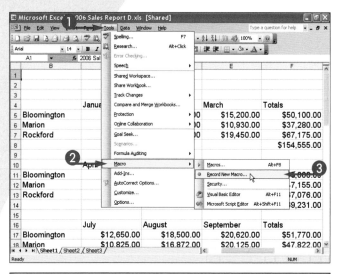

① Click Tools.

② Click Macro.

③ Click Record New Macro.

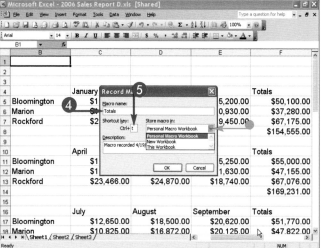

The Record Macro dialog box opens.

④ Type a name for the macro.

⑤ Assign a shortcut key for the macro.

Note: *A shortcut key is a combination of two keyboard keys you can use to activate a command.*

● You can click here to store the macro in a different workbook rather than the default location.

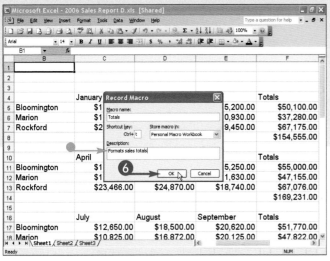

● Optionally, you can type a description of the macro here. By default, Excel enters generic data about the macro.

⑥ Click OK.

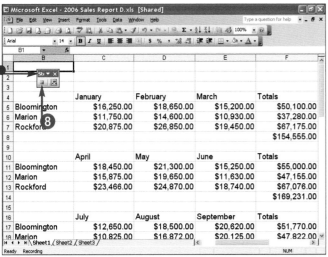

● The Stop Recording toolbar appears.

⑦ Execute each command or task you want to record as a macro.

⑧ When finished, click the Stop Recording button.

Excel saves your actions.

To execute the macro at any time, press the keyboard shortcut you assigned.

TIPS

Caution

Macros are often carriers of computer viruses. Excel has safeguards in place to protect against malicious macros. When you attempt to run a macro from a source other than your own computer, Excel displays a prompt box that warns you about the macro execution. This allows you to verify their source before attempting to run macros. If your macro security setting is set to High, the macro is disabled. To set macro security levels, click Tools, Macro and then Security to open the Security dialog box. In the Security tab, click a security level and then click OK to apply the new setting.

Did You Know?

You can also use Excel's Visual Basic Editor to create and manage macros if you know how to write macro code. Visual Basic Editor is a separate program built into Excel. To activate the feature, click Tools, Macro and then Visual Basic Editor. The Visual Basic Editor opens a separate window you can use to write and edit macro coding. You can use the program's online Help feature to assist you with the task.

MACRO:
Manage Macros

You can use the Macro dialog box to manage your Excel macros. A macro is simply a series of prerecorded instructions Excel carries out to complete a worksheet task. The Macro dialog box lists all the macros assigned to a workbook. For example, you can remove a macro you no longer need from your worksheet or macro library. When you remove a macro, it is permanently deleted.

You can also choose to execute any macro in the list. For example, you may need to run two or three macros to make changes to your worksheet data or formatting.

You can use the Options command to make changes to the shortcut key assigned to the macro as well as edit the macro description. If you know how to write macro code, you can also edit a macro using the Visual Basic Editor window. All these settings and features are available through the Macro dialog box.

See also>>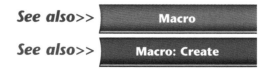

See also>> Macro: Create

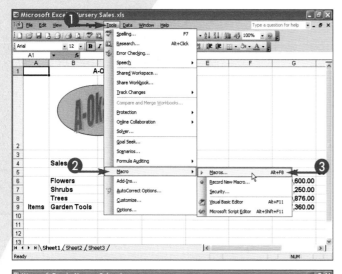

① Click Tools.

② Click Macro.

③ Click Macros.

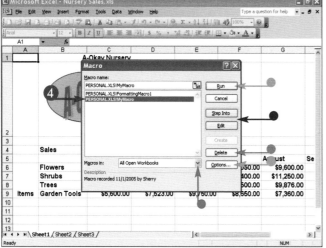

The Macro dialog box opens.

④ Click a macro.

● Click here to execute the macro.

● To assign a new shortcut key or description, click here.

● Click these options to open the Visual Basic Editor window and edit macro coding.

● Click here to delete the macro.

● You can click here to open macros in a different location.

MACRO:
Run a Macro

You can execute a macro to help speed up the Excel tasks and actions you perform on your worksheet data. When you save and store a macro, you can run it at any time. A macro is simply a mini-program of recorded actions, such as formatting commands you can apply to your data, or instructions for checking a formula.

If the macro has a keyboard shortcut key assigned, you can easily activate the macro with the press of a key. You can also use the Macro dialog box to manage and run your recorded macros. You can also associate macros with toolbar buttons.

If you know how to use Visual Basic programming, you can also use Excel's Visual Basic Editor to create, manage, and run macros.

Not all macros are safe to run. Some may contain viruses. Always be sure of a macro's source before attempting to run that macro.

See also>> **Select: Select Worksheet Cells**

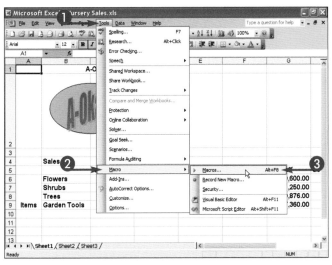

1 Click Tools.

2 Click Macro.

3 Click Macros.

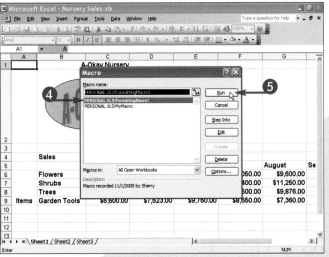

The Macro dialog box opens.

4 Click the macro you want to run.

5 Click Run.

Excel executes the macro.

MARGINS:
Set Page Margins

You can control how your worksheet data fits onto a printed page by assigning page margins. Unlike other types of documents, printing spreadsheets can often cause problems when determining how much data fits onto a page. The larger the worksheet, the more difficult it is to fit onto a page.

You can use margins to help you adjust how your data fits and insure your printouts appear professional and easy to read. For example, if you want to print the data using portrait mode and the data does not fit properly, you can adjust the page margins to create a better fit. Or if your printout needs more white space along a particular edge of

the paper, you can adjust that particular margin for the page.

You can find page margin controls in the Page Setup dialog box. By default, Excel assigns a 1-inch margin at the top and bottom of a page and a .75-inch margin at the left and right sides of a page. You can override these values with your own preferences.

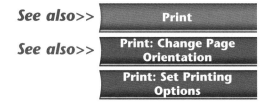

See also>> Print

See also>> Print: Change Page Orientation

Print: Set Printing Options

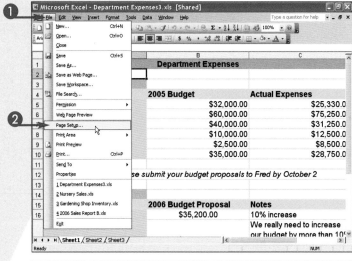

1 Click File.

2 Click Page Setup.

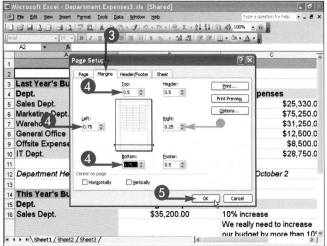

The Page Setup dialog box opens.

3 Click the Margins tab.

4 Set the left, top, right, or bottom margins as needed.

● You can type a margin value or click the arrow buttons to set a value.

5 Click OK.

Excel applies the new settings.

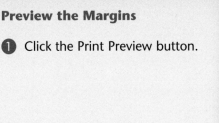

Preview the Margins

1 Click the Print Preview button.

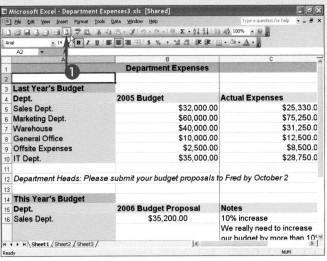

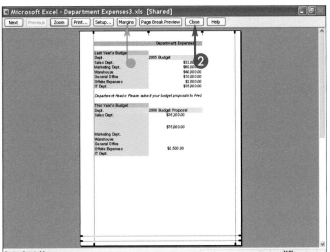

Excel displays the workbook in Print Preview mode showing the page margins.

● If margins do not appear, click the Margins button.

2 Click Close.

Excel closes Print Preview mode.

TIPS

Did You Know?

You can also adjust page margins using Print Preview mode. Click the Print Preview button (📄) on the Standard toolbar to open Print Preview. Click the Margin button in the Print Preview toolbar to turn on margin lines. You can drag a margin line to adjust a margin.

More Options

The Margins tab in the Page Setup dialog box also has options for centering a page horizontally or vertically in the printout, and controls for setting margins for any headers or footers you add to the page. To learn more about headers and footers, see the technique "Print: Add Headers and Footers."

MERGE AND CENTER:
Center Data Across Cells

You can center a title or heading across a range of cells in your worksheet. For example, you may want to include a title across multiple columns of labels. You can use the Merge and Center command to quickly create a merged cell to hold the title text.

You can use merged cells in a variety of ways. For example, you may want to merge a cell across several rows and format the text to read from top to bottom or rotate the text. You might create a larger merged cell to hold a small chart in the middle of your worksheet without affecting the surrounding

cells. Merged Cells allow you to create a larger cell in the midst of the other cells. You can use the larger cell to contain labels, titles, images, and other data you want to set apart in your worksheet.

You can use the Merge and Center command on the Formatting toolbar, or you can activate the Merge Cells option in the Format Cells dialog box.

See also>>
Merge and Center

See also>>
Select: Select Worksheet Cells

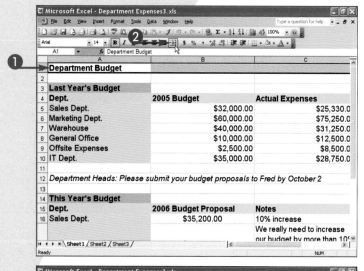

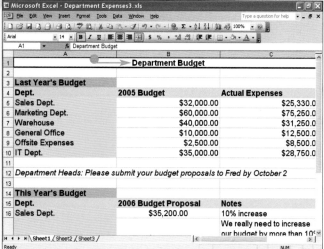

Apply the Merge and Center Button

① Select the cells you want to merge.

② Click the Merge and Center button on the Formatting toolbar.

● Excel merges the cells.

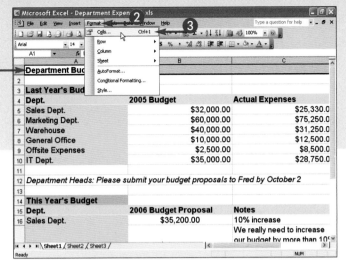

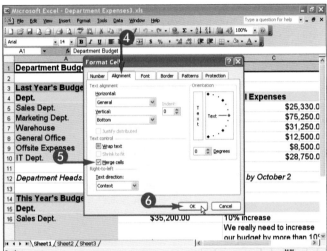

Merge Cells with the Format Cells Dialog Box

1 Select the cells you want to merge.

2 Click Format.

3 Click Cells.

The Format Cells dialog box opens.

4 Click the Alignment tab.

5 Select the Merge Cells check box.

6 Click OK.

Excel merges the cells.

TIPS

Did You Know?

You can also find the Center Across Selection command as a horizontal alignment option in the Format Cells dialog box. Unlike the Merge Cells command, the Center Across Selection does not create a merged cell, but merely centers text across several selected cells.

Did You Know?

When you create a merged cell, the cell reference takes the first cell in the selected group as the cell name. For example, if you merge cells B1, C1, and D1, the newly merged cell reference is B1. Cells C1 and D1 are no longer references in the worksheet. For this reason, you may want to make sure the cells you merge are not used in any formula references.

NUMBER FORMATTING:
Change the Number Format Style

You can use number formatting to control the appearance of numerical data in your worksheet. For example, if you have a column of prices, you can apply currency formatting to the data to format the numbers with dollar signs and decimal points. If you have a range of percentages, you can apply the percent formatting to the numbers to add percent signs to the data.

When you apply number formatting to data, the formatting only affects numeric values in the cell or range. Text data remains unaffected.

Excel offers 12 different number categories, or styles, from which to choose. With some of the number styles, you can fine-tune the formatting to suit your

worksheet needs. For example, you may only want to show one decimal place instead of two, or you might prefer to show more than one digit for fractions. You can use the Format Cells dialog box to assign any of the number styles and make adjustments to the appearance of the numeric formatting.

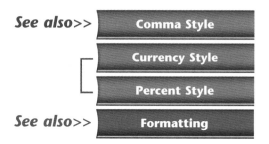

See also>> Comma Style

Currency Style

Percent Style

See also>> Formatting

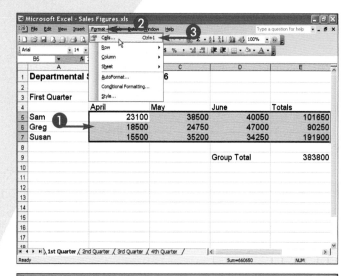

① Select the cell, range, or data you want to format.

② Click Format.

③ Click Cells.

Note: You can apply number formatting to single cells, ranges, columns, rows, or an entire worksheet.

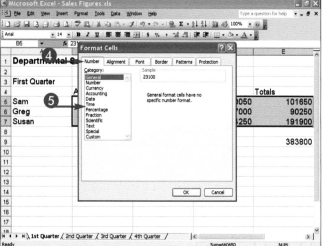

The Format Cells dialog box opens.

④ Click the Number tab.

⑤ Click a number category.

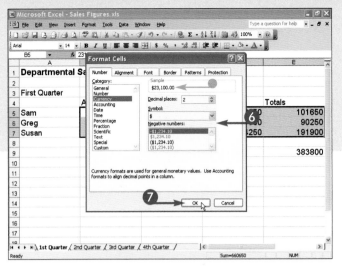

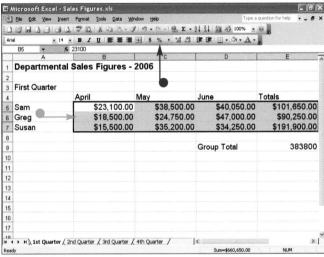

6 Specify any additional options, if desired.

● The Sample area displays a sample of the selected number style and options.

7 Click OK.

● Excel applies the number formatting to the numerical data in the cell or range.

● To quickly apply a number format to your data, click one of these buttons.

To apply dollar signs to your data, click Currency Style.

To apply percent signs to your data, click Percent Style.

To apply commas to your number data, click Comma Style.

Did You Know?

Each number format style is designed for a specific use. The table below explains each number category.

Style	Description
General	The default category; no specific formatting is applied.
Number	A general number display with two default decimal points.
Currency	Adds dollar signs and decimal points to display monetary values.
Accounting	Lines up currency symbols and decimal points in a column.
Date	You can use this to display date values.
Time	You can use this to display time values.
Percentage	Multiples a cell value by 100 and displays a percent sign.
Fraction	Displays a value as a specified fraction.
Scientific	You can use this for a scientific or exponential notation.
Text	Treats values as text.
Special	Works with list and database values.
Custom	Enables you to create your own custom format.

OBJECTS:
Add Shadow and 3-D Effects

You can add shadow and 3-D effects to your AutoShapes, lines, arrows, and any other shapes you draw with the drawing tools. You can also add shadows and 3-D effects to other objects on your worksheet, such as clip art, pictures, WordArt objects, charts, and more. Adding shadow and 3-D effects can give an object the illusion of depth on the worksheet page.

When adding shadow effects, you can control which side of the object to place the shadow. For example, you can add a shadow effect that makes it look as though directional lighting is shining on the object.

When adding 3-D effects, you can control the positioning of the dimensional effect.

As with any formatting you add to enhance your data, you may need to experiment with the formatting to get just the right look for your worksheet. The result of the effect should not detract from the data, so try not to add too many special effects at once.

See also>>   Drawing Tools

See also>>   Draw

   Objects

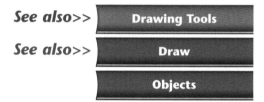

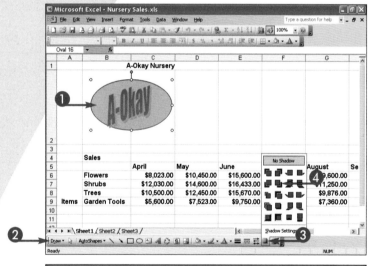

Add a Shadow

1 Select the object to which you want to add shadow effects.

2 Display the Drawing toolbar.

3 Click the Shadow Style button.

4 Click a shadow style.

Excel applies the shadow to the object.

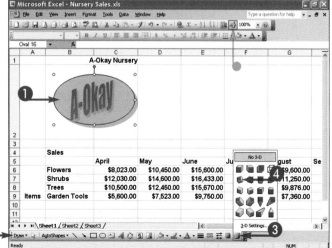

Add a 3-D Effect

1 Select the object to which you want to add 3-D effects.

2 Display the Drawing toolbar.

● If the Drawing toolbar is not displayed, you can click the Drawing button on the Standard toolbar.

3 Click the 3-D Style button.

4 Click a 3-D style.

Excel applies the 3-D style to the object.

OBJECTS:
Align Objects

You can use the alignment options on the Drawing toolbar to control the positioning of objects in a worksheet. For example, if your worksheet contains multiple objects, you can choose to align all the objects in the same position. You might make all your shape objects line up on the left, or make a row of objects line up along the bottom edge of each object.

You can apply the alignment options to lines, shapes, arrows, clip art, pictures, WordArt objects, and more. The Align and Distribute options offer horizontal alignments, including Align Left, Align Right, Align Center, and vertical alignments, including Align Top, Align Middle, and Align Bottom. You can also apply the Distribute

Horizontally or Distribute Vertically commands to spread out the objects evenly in a horizontal or vertical fashion.

The key to aligning multiple objects is to first select all the objects you want to align. Although you can apply the alignment options to a single object, the results are not as noticeable as when you align multiple objects.

See also>> **Drawing Tools**

See also>> **Draw**

Objects

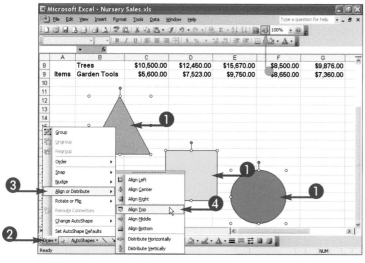

1 Select the objects you want to align.

You can press and hold the Ctrl key while clicking multiple objects.

2 Click the Draw button.

● If the Drawing toolbar is not displayed, you can click the Drawing button on the Standard toolbar.

3 Click Align or Distribute.

4 Click an alignment option.

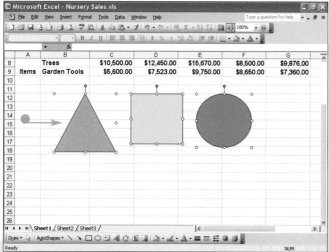

● Excel aligns the objects.

In this example, the shape objects are all top aligned.

OBJECTS:
Change an Object's Position

Excel offers several tools you can use to help you place objects in your worksheets. These tools are especially handy when trying to position an object just so in the midst of your worksheet data. You can use the Nudge and Snap commands to control the positioning of all kinds of objects in Excel, including clip art, shapes, charts, and more.

You can use the Nudge command to make slight adjustments to an object's position. For example, if you need to reposition an object closer to another object or data, you can move the selected object in small increments using the Nudge command.

You can use the Snap command to apply two different snap options: To Grid or To Shape. You

can use the To Grid command to automatically line up an object to the edges of the worksheet cells as you move or draw an object. With the command activated, any time you move the object, Excel automatically positions it so the object lines up with the nearest cell border. You can use the To Shape command to align an object to the nearest shape.

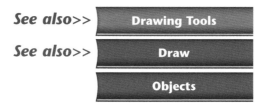

See also>> Drawing Tools

See also>> Draw

Objects

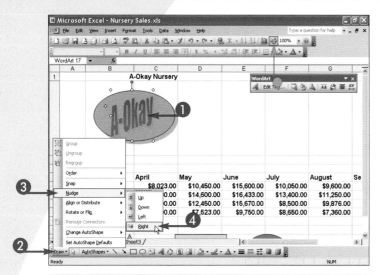

Nudge an Object

① Click the object you want to adjust.

② Click the Draw button on the Drawing toolbar.

● If the Drawing toolbar is not displayed, you can click the Drawing button on the Standard toolbar.

③ Click Nudge.

④ Click a direction.

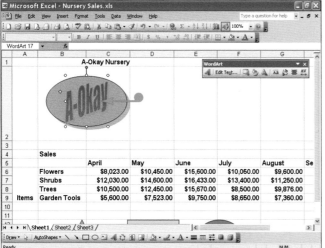

● Excel immediately nudges the object slightly in the specified direction.

In this example, the WordArt object is nudged to the right to better center the text over the shape.

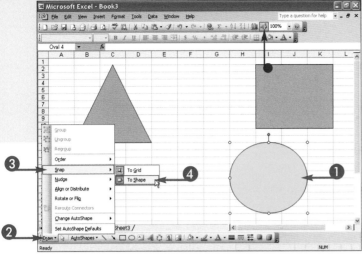

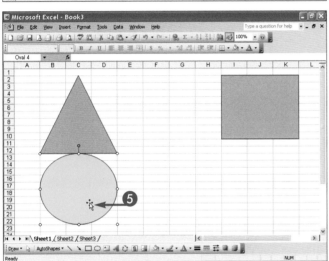

Snap to Grid

① Click the object you want to adjust.

② Click the Draw button on the Drawing toolbar.

● If the Drawing toolbar is not displayed, you can click the Drawing button on the Standard toolbar.

③ Click Snap.

④ Click a snap option.

⑤ Move the object to the designated area.

Excel immediately aligns the object to the nearest cell gridline or aligns the object to the adjacent shape.

Note: The Snap command remains activated until you turn it off again. Repeat the steps shown in this technique to toggle the Snap command off again.

In this example, the selected shape aligns with the triangle shape.

TIPS

Did You Know?

You can use the alignment and distribution commands to line up all types of objects on a worksheet. For example, if you need to line up several shapes horizontally or vertically in a sheet, you can apply the alignment commands using the Draw button on the Drawing toolbar. To learn more about aligning objects, see the technique "Objects: Align Objects."

More Options

If you prefer to place an object in a single worksheet cell, you can resize the cell to fit any object. The quickest way to resize a cell is to drag the row or column border to the desired size. This creates a row or column of the same size cells. You can also merge several cells to create one large cell. Simply select the cells you want to merge and click Format and then Cells to open the Format Cells dialog box. Click the Alignment tab and select the Merge Cells check box (☐ changes to ☑).

OBJECTS:
Delete an Object

You can remove an object you no longer want on your Excel worksheet. For example, you may decide you no longer need a clip art object to illustrate the data, or you may want to remove an outdated chart or an AutoShape you no longer require.

In Excel, objects include shapes, pictures, diagrams, WordArt, clip art, charts, text boxes, lines, and arrows. Objects can also include object types from other programs. Although the objects differ in type, you can apply the same sorts of commands to

manipulate objects in your worksheets, including the Delete command.

When you remove an object, it is permanently deleted from the worksheet. If you accidentally remove an object you prefer to keep, simply apply the Undo command immediately to return the object to the worksheet.

See also>> **Objects**

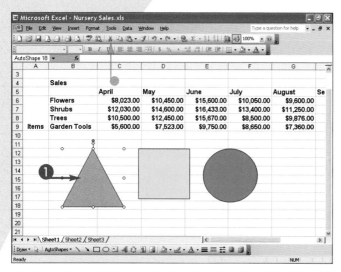

1 Select the object you want to delete.

2 Press the Delete key.

● You can also click the Cut button on the Standard toolbar to delete objects.

Excel deletes the object.

OBJECTS:
Format an Object

You can edit the objects you add to a worksheet by accessing the Format dialog box. For example, for an AutoShape, you can make adjustments to the shape's fill color, alignment, and line thickness. For a clip art object, you can make changes to the border, size, and cropping of the object.

You can use the Format dialog box to fine-tune an object to your worksheet. Depending on the object, the Format dialog box may display a slight variation in the dialog box name. For example, if you edit clip art or an image, the dialog box is named Format Picture. If you edit a shape, the dialog box is named Format AutoShape.

The dialog box displays different tabs depending on the object type. If you edit a text box object, the Format dialog box includes tabs for changing the font and alignment. If you edit a shape, the Format dialog box includes tabs for editing lines and colors as well as shape size.

See also>>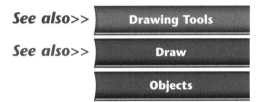

See also>>

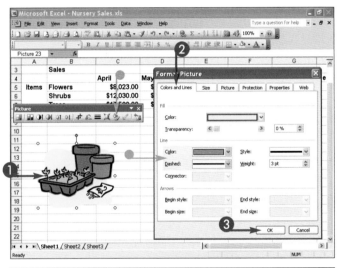

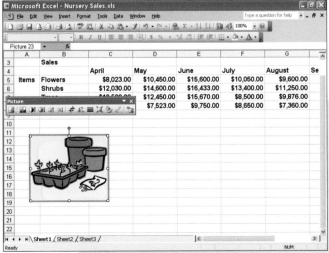

① Double-click the object you want to edit.

You can also right-click the object and activate the Format command.

● If you are editing clip art or an image, you can click the Format Picture button on the Pictures toolbar.

The Format Picture dialog box opens.

② Click a tab and make any changes you want to apply.

Use the Colors and Lines tab to make changes to the fill color or line or arrow colors.

Use the Size tab to make changes to the size and scale of the object.

Use the Picture tab to make changes to cropping and appearance.

● In this example, a border is added.

③ Click OK.

Excel applies any new settings to the object.

OBJECTS:
Group Objects

If you add multiple objects to a worksheet, such as multiple shapes you draw with Excel's drawing tools, you can turn them into a single group. Grouping objects allows you to move the objects as a unit rather than as separate pieces. You might also group objects to perform edits all at once.

For example, you might group a chart, a clip art image, and a WordArt object into one group in the worksheet and move the items to another area at the bottom of the sheet. This saves you time from having to move each object individually. You can also use this same technique to apply the same edits to all the objects in a group. For example, if you group

three AutoShapes together, you can apply the same fill color and line styles to the shapes all at once.

You can group all kinds of objects, including shapes, lines, arrows, charts, clip art, WordArt, and more. After you create a group, you can move, resize, or edit the objects as needed. You can ungroup the objects again to edit them individually.

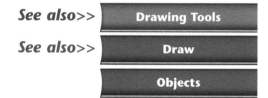

See also>> **Drawing Tools**

See also>> **Draw**

Objects

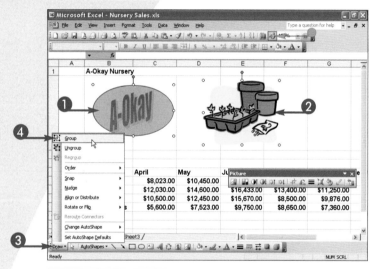

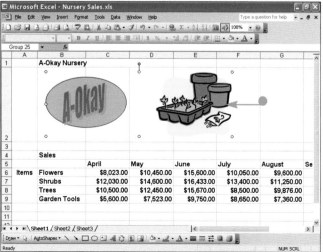

① Click the first object you want to include in a group.

Handles surround the selected object.

② Press and hold the Shift key and click the next object you want to include in the group.

Another set of handles surround the selected object.

You can repeat Step 2 to select any additional objects you want to group.

③ Click the Draw button on the Drawing toolbar.

● If the Drawing toolbar is not displayed, you can click the Drawing button on the standard toolbar.

④ Click Group.

● Excel groups the objects as one unit and replaces the multiple selection handles with a single set of handles around the entire group.

Note: To ungroup, select the group, click the Draw button, and then click Ungroup.

OBJECTS:
Layer Objects

You can layer objects in your Excel worksheets to create the appearance of depth or to create different types of artwork. For example, you might layer a text box over an AutoShape to create a logo, or move a WordArt object over a chart to create a new chart title.

When you layer objects in Excel, you can create a stack and position the objects at different layers in the stack. For example, when creating a logo using WordArt and an AutoShape, you can place the WordArt object on top of the AutoShape, making the WordArt appear at the top of the layered stack. If layering three or more objects, you can control each object's position in the stack. You

can move an object forward or backward in the layered stack to change its position.

You can use the layering commands on the Draw menu, found on the Drawing toolbar, to move objects forward and backward in the stack. You can use the Bring to Front or Send to Back commands to move an object to the very front or back of the stack. You can use the Bring Forward or Send Backward commands to move the object one layer up or back in the stack.

See also>> **Drawing Tools**

See also>> **Draw**

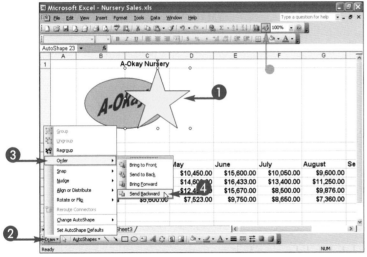

① Click the object you want to layer.

② Click the Draw button on the Drawing toolbar.

● If the Drawing toolbar is not displayed, you can click the Drawing button on the Standard toolbar.

③ Click Order.

④ Click a stacking order for the object.

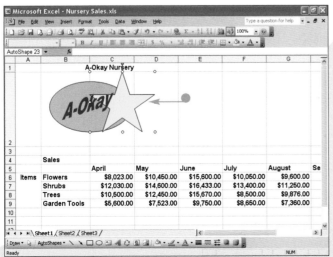

● Excel applies the new layer order to the object.

In this example, the star shape moves back one layer in the stack.

OBJECTS:
Move an Object

You can move any object you place on an Excel worksheet. Objects include clip art, AutoShapes, lines, arrows, WordArt, charts, photos, and text boxes. When you select an object, it is surrounded by handles. You must first select an object to move it.

You can move objects wherever you please on a worksheet. For example, you may prefer to place a chart at the top of a worksheet, or move a clip art object into a specific cell. When you reposition objects, any data you place the object over remains covered. For example, if you move an AutoShape object on top of a range of cells, any data in the

range is no longer viewable beneath the shape. For that reason, you may want to make room for the object before moving it. For example, you may need to move a range of cells to make room for the object you want to place in that particular area of the worksheet.

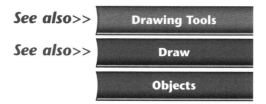

See also>> Drawing Tools

See also>> Draw

Objects

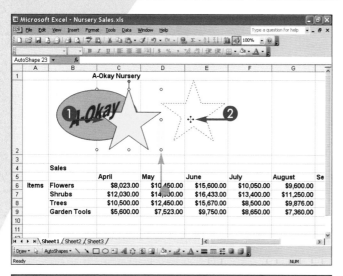

① Click the object you want to move.

● Excel surrounds the selected object with handles.

② Drag the object to a new location on the worksheet.

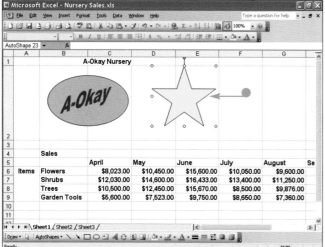

● As soon as you stop dragging, Excel moves the object.

OBJECTS:
Resize an Object

You can resize any clip art, image, or shape — called *objects* in Excel — you place on an Excel worksheet. For example, you may need to make a photograph appear smaller to fit into an area of the worksheet, or you might want to enlarge a clip art object to fill a large cell. You can also resize other types of objects, such as charts, WordArt, text boxes, and more. When you select an object, it is surrounded by handles which you can, in turn, use to resize the object.

Normally, when you resize an object, it increases or decreases in size based on the handle you drag. If you drag a corner handle in an outward direction, the object enlarges. If you drag the

same handle to the left or right, the object resizes horizontally and not vertically. To maintain an object's height-to-width ratio when resizing, you can press and hold the Shift key while dragging a resizing corner handle. To resize from the center of the object in two dimensions at once, you can press and hold the Ctrl key while dragging a corner handle.

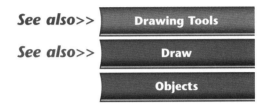

See also>> Drawing Tools

See also>> Draw

Objects

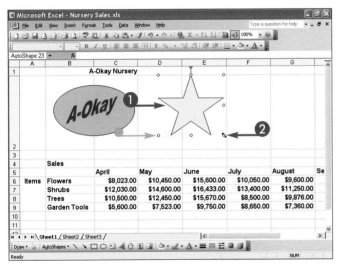

① Click the object you want to resize.

● Excel surrounds the selected object with handles.

② Move the mouse pointer over a selection handle.

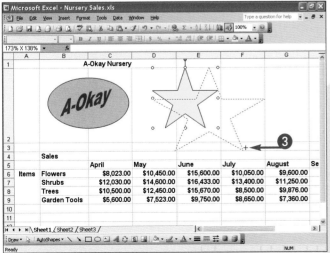

③ Drag the handle to resize the object.

Excel resizes the object.

OBJECTS:
Rotate and Flip Objects

You can rotate and flip objects on your worksheets to change their appearance. For example, you might flip a clip art image to face another direction, or rotate an arrow object to point elsewhere on the page.

You can rotate objects to change their position on a worksheet. For example, you might tilt a clip art object to make it more aesthetically pleasing, or turn a WordArt object sideways to line up with a column of data. You can rotate an object using 90-degree angles, or you can use the Free Rotate command to freely rotate an object in any direction you like.

You can flip objects on your worksheets as a simple way to change their appearance. You might flip a

photo image to face another direction or flip a clip art object vertically to reverse the top and bottom of the image. You can flip an object horizontally or vertically in a worksheet.

You can rotate and flip objects using the Draw menu on the Drawing toolbar.

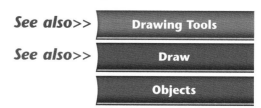

See also>> Drawing Tools

See also>> Draw

Objects

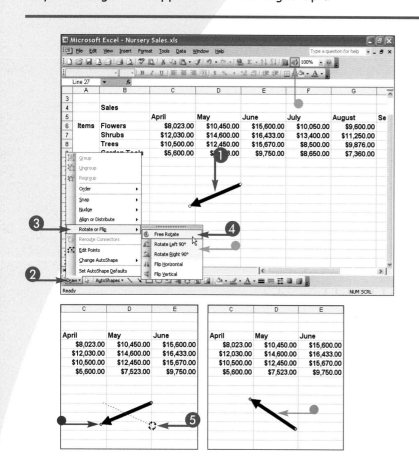

Rotate an Object

① Click the object you want to rotate.

② Click the Draw button on the Drawing toolbar.

● If the Drawing toolbar is not displayed, you can click the Drawing button on the Standard toolbar.

③ Click Rotate or Flip.

④ Click Free Rotate.

● You can also rotate an object 90 degrees left or right.

● A rotation handle appears on the selected object.

Note: Many objects automatically display the rotation handle when you select an object.

⑤ Click and drag the handle to rotate the object.

Note: To constrain the rotation to 15-degree angles, press and hold the Shift key while rotating the object.

● Excel rotates the object.

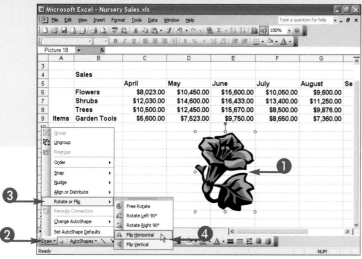

1. Click the object you want to flip.

2. Click the Draw button on the Drawing toolbar.

3. Click Rotate or Flip.

4. Click Flip Horizontal or Flip Vertical.

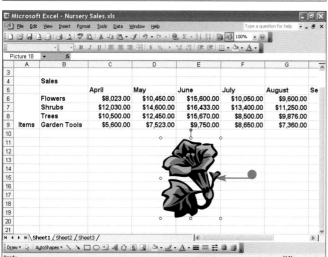

● Excel flips the object.

Did You Know?

You can rotate text in a cell, or you can create a WordArt object to rotate. You can use the Alignment tab in the Format Cells dialog box to control the vertical orientation of text in a cell. Click Format and then Cells to display the dialog box. In the case of WordArt text, after you create the WordArt object, you can rotate it using the steps shown in this task. You can also choose from several vertical text styles from the WordArt Gallery.

Caution

When you position an object just the way you want it on the worksheet, other users who have access to your file can make changes to the data, including changes to the objects in your worksheets. The only way to prevent someone from making changes to your worksheet is to assign a password or apply the read-only option. To learn more about protecting Excel workbooks with passwords, see the techniques "Protection: Assign a Workbook Password," "Protection: Assign a Password to a Sheet," and "Worksheet: Protect a Sheet."

ORGANIZATION CHART:
Insert an Organization Chart

You can use the Microsoft Office diagram feature to create all kinds of diagrams to illustrate concepts and processes. For example, you might insert an organizational diagram in a worksheet to show the hierarchy in your company, or you might use a cycle diagram to show workflow in your department.

Organization charts are composed of individual shapes that inhabit a drawing space, called a canvas. The shapes define the chart tree for the organization you illustrate. There are four types of shapes: superior, assistant, subordinate, and coworker. The

superior shape appears at the top of the chart. You can add as many shapes as you need to complete your chart.

Within each shape, you can add the name or title of a person or process and format the text any way you like. You can also control the formatting of the shape itself, including the border and fill color. You can use the Organization Chart toolbar to help you format and add to your diagram.

See also>> | **Chart**

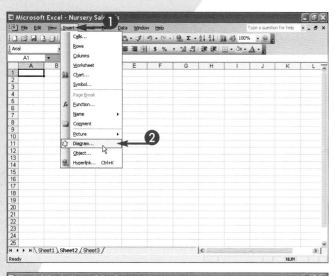

① Click Insert.

② Click Diagram.

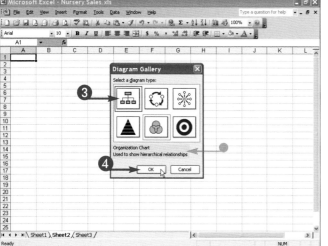

The Diagram Gallery dialog box opens.

③ Click the type of diagram you want to create.

● You can view a description of the diagram type here.

④ Click OK.

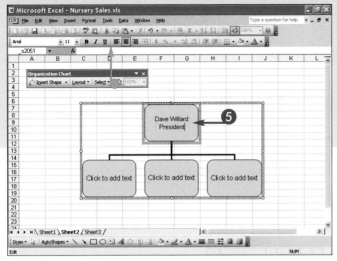

The diagram and placeholder text boxes appear, along with the Diagram toolbar.

⑤ Click a text box and type the diagram text.

● You can apply any of the text formatting options to change the appearance of the text.

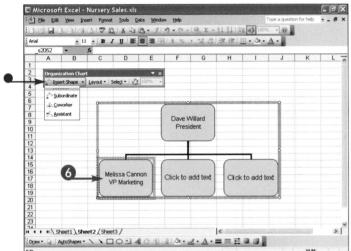

⑥ Continue filling in each diagram text box as needed.

● To add another text box and element to the diagram, click the Insert Shape button.

To deselect the diagram object, click anywhere outside the diagram.

Did You Know?

The diagram is an object which you can move and resize just like other objects in the Microsoft Office programs. To move or resize a diagram, see the techniques "Objects: Move an Object" and "Objects: Resize an Object." You can also use the Layout button on the Diagram toolbar to change the sizing of the diagram layout, such as fitting the diagram to the contents or expanding the chart. Click the Layout button to view resizing options.

More Options

Click the Change To button on the Diagram toolbar to view a list of other diagram types. To change the diagram style, simply click the one you want to assign from the drop-down list. Any existing text you entered is immediately plugged into the new diagram design.

PASTE:
Copy Attributes with the Paste Special Command

You can use the Paste Special command to copy composite attributes in a worksheet, along with the actual data you want to copy, and paste them into another worksheet or the same worksheet. For example, you might copy a range of formulas along with all the number formatting assigned to the range and paste them into another sheet.

The Paste Special command displays a dialog box of paste actions. You can choose to copy all or some of the attributes assigned to the data you are copying, specify whether any mathematical operations are included in the paste, include the column width along with the pasted data, and more. The Paste Special dialog box offers 10 Paste options for controlling how data is copied, as well as options for controlling the

copied mathematical operations. The dialog box also features a setting for transposing copied columns to rows and vice versa. If the copy area has blank cells, you can activate the Skip blanks feature to avoid replacing data in the paste area with blanks.

The Paste Special dialog box is also used to link data between cells, worksheets, and workbooks. You can activate the Paste Link feature to link data.

See also>>

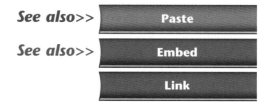

See also>> **Paste**

See also>> **Embed**

Link

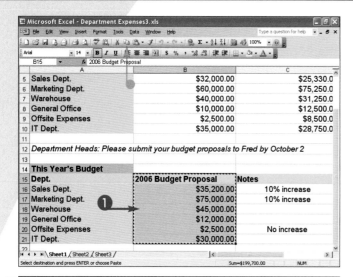

① Copy the data you want to paste.

● You can press Ctrl+C to copy data, or click the Copy button on the Standard toolbar.

Note: *You can also copy data from another program to paste into your Excel worksheet.*

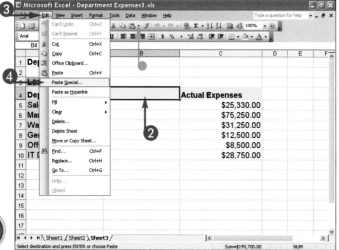

② Open the worksheet or workbook and click where you want to paste the data.

You can also copy and paste data within the same sheet.

③ Click Edit.

④ Click Paste Special.

● You can also click the Paste drop-down arrow and click Paste Special.

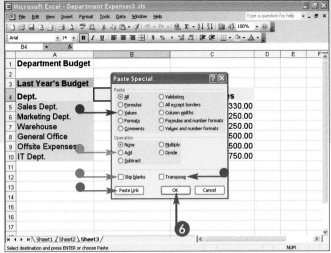

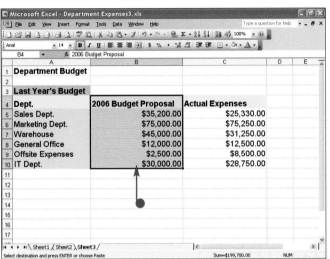

The Paste Special dialog box opens.

⑤ Click the Paste options you want to apply.

● Use the Paste options to control what attributes are pasted along with the data.

● Use the Operation options to control what mathematical operations are pasted along with the data.

● Select this option to skip blanks.

● Select this option to transpose data in the paste area.

● Click here to link the data.

⑥ Click OK.

● Excel pastes the data along with any attributes you specify.

Caution

If you use the Paste Special dialog box to link data and you move the source file to a new location, or delete the source file, any links you have to the source data are broken. Broken links can also occur if you move the worksheet within the workbook. You can fix a link using the Edit Links dialog box. In the destination file, click Edit and then click Links to open the Edit Links dialog box. This dialog box keeps track of all the links in a destination file, and allows you to check link status, break links, and view the source data.

Did You Know?

You can also link data between sheets using the Paste Options smart tag (📋). The Paste Options smart tag appears immediately after you paste data into a worksheet. Simply click the icon to display the Paste options. When you create a link between sheets, any time you make changes to the source cells, the linked cells automatically reflect the new changes.

PICTURE:
Crop a Picture

You can crop a picture you add to an Excel worksheet to create a better fit or to focus on an important area of an image. Cropping simply means discarding an area of the picture you do not want to keep. For example, you might crop out a distracting part of the image background, or crop out a group of people to focus on just one person.

The Crop tool, located on the Picture toolbar, can help you crop out edges of an image you do not need. You can also use the Crop tool to crop clip art images. When cropping a picture, you can crop as many sides of the image as you need. For example, you might crop all four sides to focus on the object in the center of the picture, or you might crop out a

single side of a picture to remove unwanted background.

Excel's cropping feature does not affect the original image file, just the copy of the image you place in a worksheet.

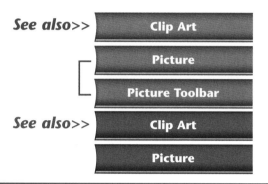

See also>> Clip Art

Picture

Picture Toolbar

See also>> Clip Art

Picture

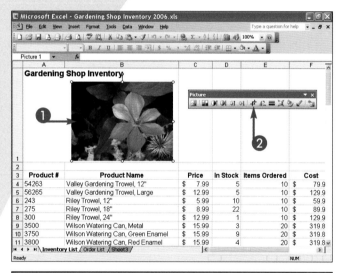

① Click the image you want to edit.

② Click the Crop button on the Picture toolbar.

Note: *If the Picture toolbar is not displayed, click View, Toolbars, and then Picture. You can also right-click the image and click Picture Toolbar.*

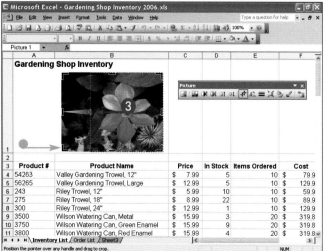

Excel surrounds the image with crop handles.

③ Click and drag a crop handle to crop out an area of the image.

● You can drag a crop border handle to crop two sides at once.

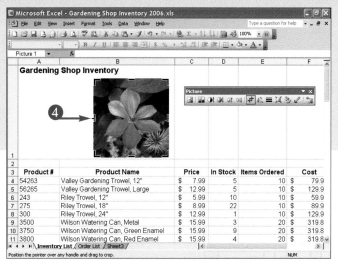

④ Release the mouse button.

Excel crops the image.

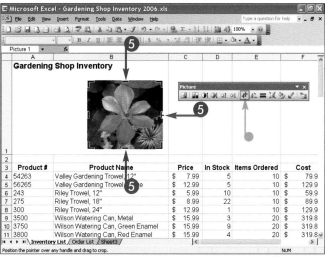

⑤ Continue cropping other edges of the image, as needed.

● You can click the Crop button again to turn off the Crop tool.

More Options

You can click the Reset Picture button ( ) on the Picture toolbar to reset the image to the size it originally appeared on your worksheet. Any cropping or other edits made to the image are discarded. You can also click the Undo button ( ) on the Standard toolbar to undo each edit you made to the image.

More Options

You can use the sizing options in the Format Picture dialog box to control different aspects of the picture size in your worksheet, including cropping. You can double-click the picture to open the Format Picture dialog box, and then click the Size tab to view all the sizing options. For example, you can scale a picture to change the image size, or you can return the picture to its original size before your edits. Click the Picture tab to find the cropping controls.

PICTURE:
Format a Picture

You can edit the picture objects you add to a worksheet by accessing the Format Picture dialog box. For example, using the dialog box you can make adjustments to the picture's color and border. Although the Format Picture dialog box does not offer as many varied tools as a graphics editor program, you can find a few tools to tweak the appearance of a picture in a worksheet.

For example, you can make subtle changes to a picture by adding a border around the image. You can use the Colors and Lines tab in the Format Picture dialog box to add a border, or you can use the Line Style (▤) and Line Color buttons (▨) on the Drawing toolbar to add a border. You can control the color and thickness of any border you add to a picture.

Depending on the picture's background, you can also make changes to the fill color or transparency setting. You can also use the Format Picture dialog box to make adjustments to the picture's size and scale.

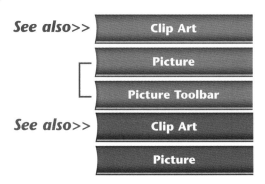

See also>>   Clip Art

      Picture

      Picture Toolbar

See also>>   Clip Art

      Picture

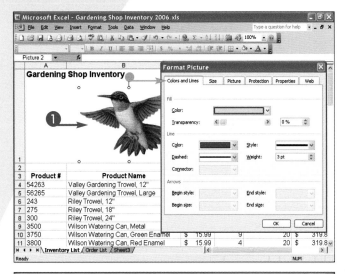

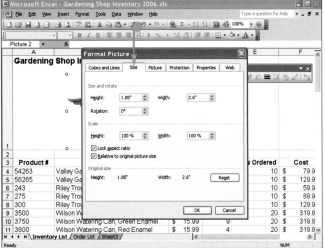

① Double-click the clip art you want to edit.

Note: You can also click Format and then Picture, or right-click the object and activate the Format Picture command.

If you are editing clip art or an image, you can click the Format Picture button (▨) on the Picture toolbar.

The Format Picture dialog box opens.

● You can use the Colors and Lines tab to make changes to the fill color or line or arrow colors of the picture using these settings.

● You can use the Size tab to make changes to the size and scale of the picture.

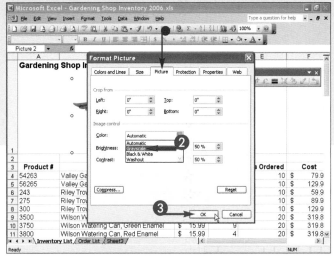

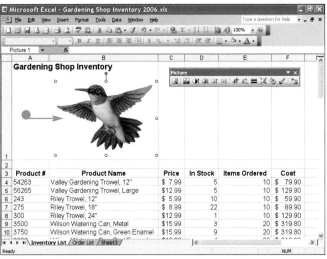

● You can use the Picture tab to make changes to cropping and the appearance of the picture.

② Change any formatting options you want to assign to the picture object.

③ Click OK.

In this example, click the Color drop-down arrow and then Grayscale.

● Excel applies any new settings to the picture.

More Options

You can make portions of your picture background transparent, allowing you to view the worksheet cells beneath the image or assign a fill color to the image. Click the Set Transparent Color tool (🖉) on the Picture toolbar and then click a background area of the picture. Excel makes the area transparent. Not all pictures may allow for transparent backgrounds. You can also find a transparency setting on the Colors and Lines tab of the Format Picture dialog box.

Try This

Image files are notorious for consuming large amounts of file space, and when you insert a large image into a worksheet, it adds to the size of the Excel file. You can apply the Compress Pictures tool (🖼) on the Pictures toolbar to reduce the resolution of an image or discard extra information from cropping the image. You can also find the Compress feature on the Picture tab in the Format Picture dialog box. When activated, the Compress Pictures tool opens the Compress Pictures dialog box and offers several options for controlling the overall file size of an image.

PICTURE:
Insert a Picture File

You can illustrate your Excel worksheets with pictures stored on your computer. For example, if you have a photo or graphic file from another program that relates to your Excel data, you can insert it into the worksheet. You might use a photograph of the latest product to illustrate a sales data sheet, or add a picture of your company headquarters to illustrate a financial report.

Image or picture files, also called *objects* in Excel, come in a variety of file formats, such as GIF, JPEG or JPG, and PNG. You can use the Insert Picture dialog box to locate and insert a picture file into a worksheet. After you insert a picture, you can resize and reposition it as well as perform other types of edits on the image. For example, image files from a

digital camera may be too large to fit into your worksheet. You can resize the picture object just as you resize other types of objects in Excel, such as shapes and charts.

See also>>

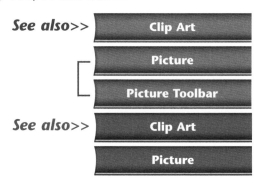

See also>>

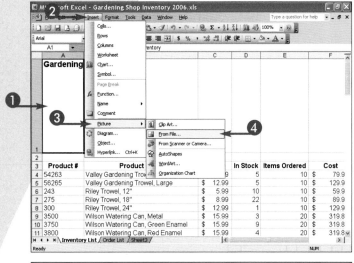

① Click the cell in the worksheet where you want to add an image.

You can also move the image to a particular location after inserting it onto the worksheet.

② Click Insert.

③ Click Picture.

④ Click From File.

You can also click the Insert Picture button (⊡) on the Drawing toolbar.

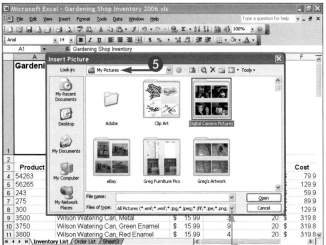

The Insert Picture dialog box opens.

⑤ Navigate to the folder or drive containing the image file you want to use.

● To browse for a particular file type, click here and choose a file format.

⑥ Click the file.

⑦ Click Insert.

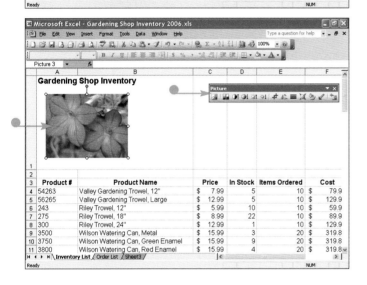

● Excel adds the image to the worksheet and displays the Picture toolbar.

You may need to resize or reposition the image to fit with your data, or resize the cell in which you want the image to appear.

Note: *If the Picture toolbar is not displayed, click View, Toolbars, and Picture.*

To remove an image you no longer want, click the image and press the Delete key.

TIPS

More Options
In addition to picture files, you can also insert other types of objects, such as Word tables, scanned images, digital photographs, or another Excel worksheet. Click Insert and then Object to open the Insert Object dialog box. Click the Create From File tab and click the Browse button. This opens the Browse dialog box. Navigate to the file you want to use, click the file, and then click Insert. Excel returns you to the Insert Object dialog box. Click OK and the object is inserted into your worksheet.

Did You Know?
You can insert most of the popular graphics file types into your Excel worksheets. You can insert Enhanced Metafiles (.emf), Joint Photographic Experts Group (.jpg), Portable Network Graphics (.png), Microsoft Windows Bitmap (.bmp), Windows Metafile (.wmf), and Graphics Interchange Format (.gif), to list a few. Depending on the type of file format, you may need to install a separate graphics filter. Excel prompts you to do so when encountering a specific file type.

PIVOTTABLE:
Create a PivotTable

You can use Excel's PivotTables to gauge different viewpoints of your data. PivotTables allow you to ask certain questions of your data to help you see beyond the obvious. Rather than examining the data for answers yourself, a PivotTable makes short work of the task.

For example, perhaps you have a sales order table that describes products, quantities ordered, dates, amounts, buyers, and salespersons. You can use a PivotTable to find out which salesperson has the most sales, which buyer buys the most product, what items are top sellers, and who sold the most product on a given day. These are just a few analysis points you can determine with PivotTables.

A PivotTable is a dynamic table you can create using Excel's PivotTable Wizard. PivotTables offer a convenient way to build flexible summary tables and change data reflected in the tables to produce different viewpoints of the data. The beauty of PivotTables is the ability to rearrange the data shown in the table to view different aspects of the data.

See also>>   **PivotTable**

See also>>   **Database**

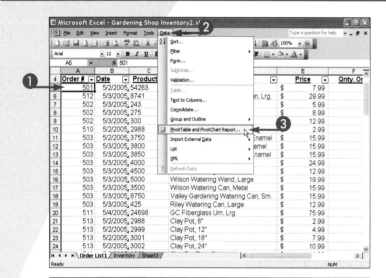

① Click inside the database list or range you want to evaluate.

② Click Data.

③ Click PivotTable and PivotChart Report.

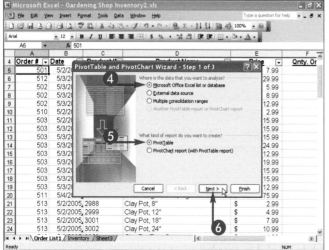

The first of three Wizard dialog boxes opens.

④ Click Microsoft Office Excel list or database.

⑤ Click PivotTable.

⑥ Click Next.

274

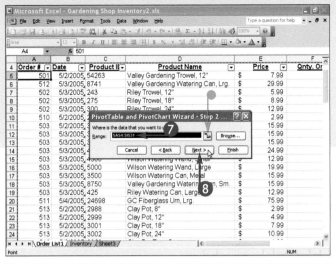

7. Verify the data range.

● If the range is incorrect, click the Collapse button and select the correct range.

8. Click Next.

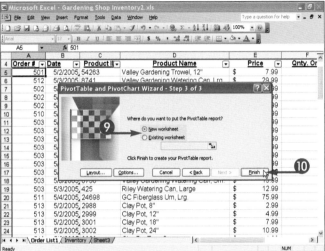

9. Click whether you want the PivotTable to appear in a new worksheet or an existing worksheet.

10. Click Finish.

TIPS

More Options

If you click the Layout button in the third PivotTable Wizard dialog box, you can change the layout of your PivotTable by rearranging how you want the field settings to appear in the table. Most users find it easier to rearrange the PivotTable after first creating the table. You can skip this option unless you really want to use a dialog box to set up the PivotTable instead of doing so on a worksheet.

More Options

The last PivotTable Wizard dialog box offers you the choice of placing the PivotTable in a new worksheet or in an existing worksheet. Because PivotTables are rather complex by nature, placing them in a separate worksheet makes it easier to manage the tables. If you do choose to place the table in an existing worksheet, you must specify the cell range where you want to insert the table.

PIVOTTABLE:
Create a PivotTable (Continued)

After you create a PivotTable, you can drag various fields into the table to perform analysis. It may take some experimenting to figure out how your data works within the PivotTable. PivotTables are made of row fields and column fields that summarize data across rows and fields respectively. As you add and subtract fields and change their position on the table, the data you examine *pivots*; hence the name *PivotTable*.

All the source data's columns are referred to as *fields* in the PivotTable. Any field you drag to the row area

of the table becomes a row, while any field you drag into the column area becomes a column in the table. The middle area of the table is where the actual analysis occurs for summarizing different fields of data pertaining to the row and column fields. You can place fields you want to subtotal in this region of the table, called the Data Items area. Any field you want to summarize you can drag into the data area of the table. You can add multiple fields to the analysis.

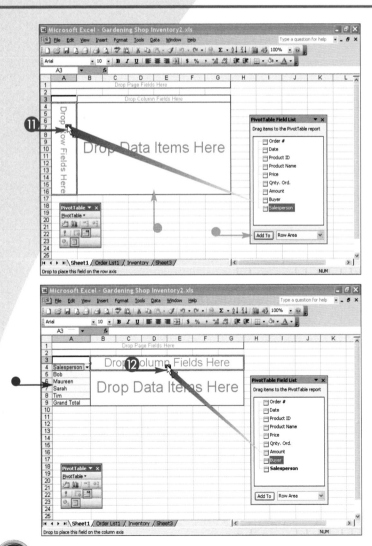

● Excel opens a new, empty PivotTable.

⓫ Click a field you want to analyze and drag it to the PivotTable's row area.

In this example, the PivotTable analyzes each salesperson.

● You can also click a field, click where you want to place it in the table, and then click the Add To button. Use this method if you do not want to drag fields onto the table.

● Excel adds the field data to the row area.

⓬ Click another field you want to analyze and drag it to the PivotTable's column area.

In this example, the PivotTable adds the buyer to the analysis.

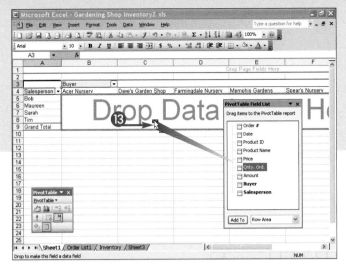

⑬ Click another field you want to analyze and drag it to the PivotTable's data item area.

In this example, the PivotTable analyzes the quantities ordered.

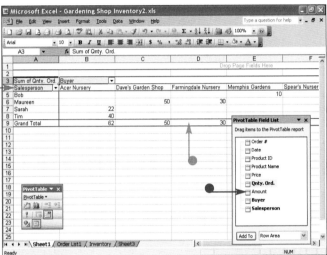

● Excel adds the field data and you can analyze the data.

In this example, the PivotTable shows which salesperson sold what quantity to a particular buyer.

● To remove a field from the table, drag it off the table.

● To add more fields to the mix, drag them onto the table. You can also drag the fields from one area of the table to another.

You can save the PivotTable when you save the workbook file.

Attention

Not all Excel data is suited for a PivotTable. To fully utilize the PivotTable features, your data range should include at least one column that has duplicate values, such as a Customer column with multiple records from the same customer. Secondly, your data range should include some numeric data, such as a simple count. A good example of a data range suited for a PivotTable is an order information table that includes columns listing product, category, customer, shipping city, shipping country, unit price, and quantity ordered.

More Options

While creating the PivotTable using the wizard dialog boxes, you can click the Options button in the final wizard to open the PivotTable Options dialog box. Use this dialog box to set formatting and data options for your table. For example, you can choose to display grand totals for columns and rows, turn off AutoFormat, and more. You can also access these options after creating the table; simply right-click the PivotTable and click Table Options.

PIVOTTABLE:
Remove Blank Cells and Error Messages

The default function setting for a PivotTable is to summarize all data. When summarizing a database table or list of data, it is not uncommon to see blank cells and error messages in the Data Items area of the PivotTable. This is especially true of long lists of data in which some items have no data.

For example, if your table is examining sales with regions by column and product categories by row, some regions may not have sales for a particular category. Rather than display a blank cell, you can display a value, such as 0, or a text value, such as NA (Not Applicable).

You can make your PivotTable easier to read by replacing blank cells or error messages with other values. For example, rather than viewing a #DIV/0 error, you might replace the error text with a label such as NA for Not Applicable. You can use the PivotTable Options dialog box to set up options for handling blank cells or cells with error messages.

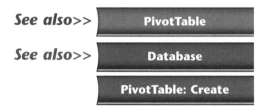

See also>> **PivotTable**

See also>> **Database**

PivotTable: Create

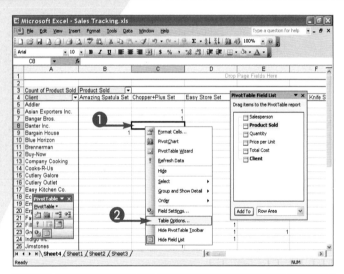

① Right-click the PivotTable.

② Click Table Options.

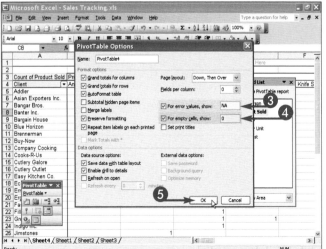

The PivotTable Options dialog box opens.

③ Select the For Error Values, Show check box and type another message, such as NA.

④ Select the For Empty Cells, Show check box and type another message, such as 0.

⑤ Click OK.

Excel saves the changes.

PIVOTTABLE:
Turn a PivotTable into a PivotChart

You can turn your Excel PivotTables into PivotCharts. A PivotChart is just as dynamic as a PivotTable, allowing you to rearrange fields by dragging field labels on the chart sheet. If you make any changes to the original PivotTable, the changes are automatically reflected in the PivotChart. Any changes you make in the PivotChart are also automatically reflected in the PivotTable.

When creating a PivotChart, row fields become category fields and column fields become series fields. You can drag fields from the Field List box and place them on the chart. You can drag category fields below the chart and drag series

fields to the right of the chart. You can also drag a page field to the top of the chart.

You can use the same formatting options you use with regular charts on the various elements of your PivotChart. For example, you can set a different chart type or format the plot area.

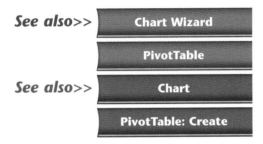

See also>> Chart Wizard

PivotTable

See also>> Chart

PivotTable: Create

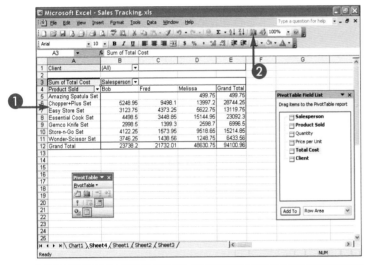

① Click anywhere in the PivotTable.

② Click the Chart Wizard button on the Standard toolbar.

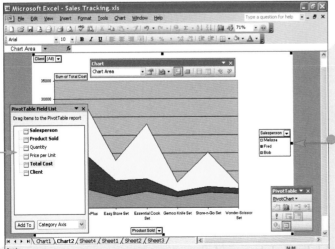

● Excel immediately creates a PivotChart on a new worksheet in the workbook.

● You can drag field buttons from the PivotTable toolbar and drop them anywhere on the chart.

PIVOTTABLE:
Update a PivotTable

After you create an Excel PivotTable, you can rearrange the fields and data items to change the table. For example, you can drag fields from one area to another in the table to change the data display and evaluate your information differently. You can remove fields and add new ones to perform more evaluation of the data.

You can also change the summary function assigned to the Data Items area to another function, such as AVERAGE or COUNT. For example, you may want to average sales numbers or perform a count.

You can use the tools on the PivotTable toolbar to edit a PivotTable. For example, you can refresh the table's data at any time using the Refresh button.

See also>>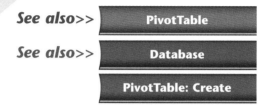

PivotTable

Database

PivotTable: Create

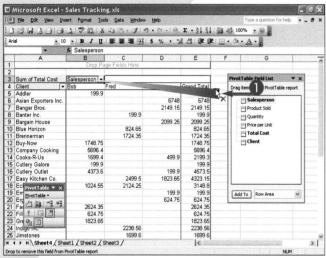

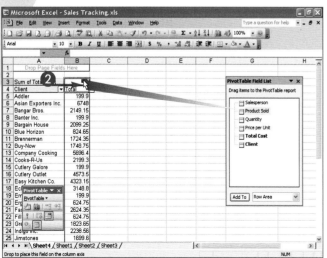

Change Fields

① Click the field you want to remove and drag it off the table.

You can also drag fields around on the table to rearrange how the data is presented.

② Click the field you want to add and drag it to the table.

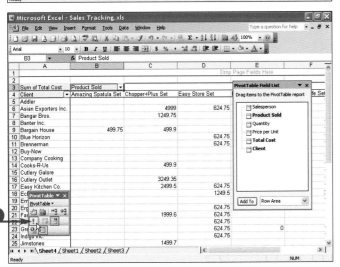

Change the Summary Function

1. Click the Field Settings button on the PivotTable toolbar.

   The PivotTable Field dialog box opens.

2. Click another summarize function.

3. Click OK.

   The PivotTable changes to reflect the new function.

Refresh the Data

1. Click here to refresh the data.

   Note: You can also click Data and then Refresh Data.

   Excel immediately updates the data to include any changes you made to the original list.

TIPS

Did You Know?

If you are not sure where to drop a field on the table, look for visual clues that appear as you drag across the table. As you move the mouse over areas of the table, different parts of the table are highlighted with a border as you drag. This can help you locate the area to drop the field. If you are still confused, use the bottom of the Field List box to move fields. You can click a field, click the drop-down arrow and select an area, and then click the Add button to add the field to the area.

More Options

You can apply Excel's AutoFormat feature to a PivotTable and format the information. Click the Format Report button ([icon]) on the PivotTable toolbar to open the AutoFormat dialog box. You can scroll through the list of AutoFormats and select the one you want to apply. Click OK to apply the formatting to your table.

PRINT:
Add Headers and Footers

You can use headers and footers to add text that appears at the top or bottom of every worksheet page you print. Headers and footers are useful for making sure every page prints with a page number, document title, author name, or date. Header text appears at the very top of a page outside the text margin. Footers appear at the very bottom of a page.

Headers and footers are built with *fields*, which are holding places for information that updates, such as page numbers or dates. To view header and footer text, switch to Page Break Layout view.

You can use the Page Setup dialog box to set up headers and footers for your workbooks. For example, you might want to add a header to your workbook that displays the name of the file as well as when it was prepared. Excel includes a variety of built-in header and footer fields you can choose from or you can create your own custom fields.

See also>>   **Print**

See also>>   **Print: Preview Worksheet**

Print: Print Workbook

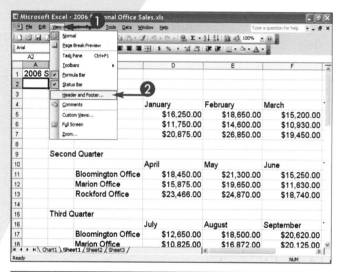

① Click View.

② Click Header and Footer.

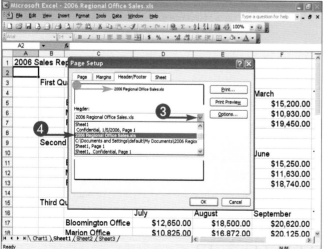

The Page Setup dialog box opens to the Header/Footer tab.

③ Click the Header drop-down arrow.

④ Click a header field.

● Excel adds the field to the header box.

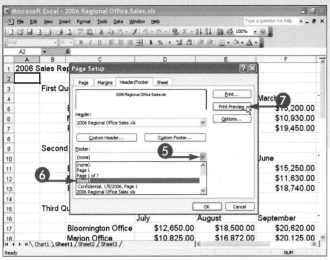

5 Click the Footer drop-down arrow.

6 Click a footer field.

Excel adds the field to the footer box.

7 Click Print Preview.

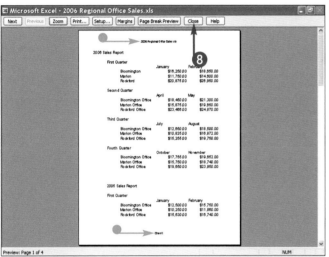

● Excel displays the header and footer text in Print Preview mode.

Note: You can only view headers and footers in Print Preview mode.

8 Click Close to return to the Excel worksheet.

 TIPS

Customize It

You can create custom headers or footers that include the date, filename, and any other information you want to add. To set a custom header or footer using the text you specify, open the Page Setup dialog box to the Header and Footer tab. Next, click the Custom Header or Custom Footer button. Click the section in which you want to add text and type your custom header or footer text. You can also click the buttons to add preset fields to the sections, such as the date or time. Click OK and the Page Setup dialog box displays the custom fields. Click OK to exit the dialog box and save your changes.

Did You Know?

You can assign a watermark to print faintly in the background of your printed spreadsheets. Click the Options button in any of the Page Setup dialog boxes tabs to open the printer's Properties dialog box. Click the Effects tab and click the Watermarks drop-down arrow and select the watermark you want to use. You can click the Edit button to create a custom watermark. Click OK to exit the printer's Properties dialog box and return to the Page Setup dialog box. Click OK to save your changes.

PRINT:
Change Page Orientation

The page orientation you choose depends on how you want to display the data on a page. It is not always easy to determine the correct page orientation for spreadsheets. Some worksheets are wider than they are long, and others may be longer than they are wide. You can use the Page Setup dialog box to specify a page orientation for the workbook you want to print.

For regular 8 1/2 × 11-inch paper, landscape orientation prints the page at 11" × 8 1/2", while portrait orientation prints 8 1/2" × 11". Select landscape orientation when you need to print lots of columns across the page. Choose portrait orientation to print more rows down a page.

To make sure the data fits properly on the pages you want to print, you can preview the orientation before committing the data to paper.

If you have any doubts about the way your printer handles page orientation, consult your printer's manual for more information.

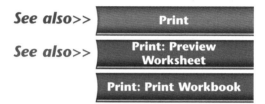

See also>> **Print**

See also>> **Print: Preview Worksheet**

Print: Print Workbook

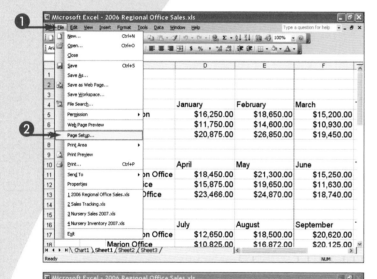

1 Click File.

2 Click Page Setup.

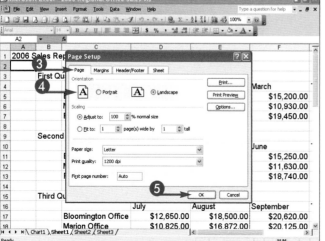

The Page Setup dialog box opens.

3 Click the Page tab.

4 Click an Orientation option.

5 Click OK to save the changes, or click Print to print the workbook.

PRINT:
Define a Print Area

You can assign a print area to print only a certain portion of a worksheet. For example, you may want to print only a range of cells. You can define the print area to prevent Excel from printing the entire worksheet every time you print. If your work involves continually updating the same range of cells in a worksheet and distributing the data to others, you can set the range up as a defined print area for the worksheet. This makes it easy to print just the data you need to share with other users.

After you define a print area, Excel prints only the defined area any time you click the Print button on the Standard toolbar or click Print in the Print

dialog box. The print area remains the only cell range you can print until you clear the print area.

The easiest way to define a print area is to use the Set Print Area command. You can also use the Page Setup dialog box to define a print area.

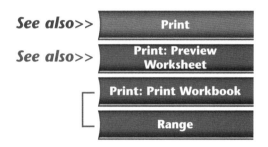

See also>> **Print**

See also>> **Print: Preview Worksheet**

Print: Print Workbook

Range

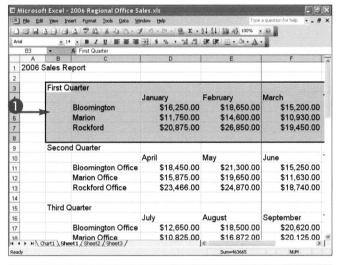

① Select the cells you want to include in the print area.

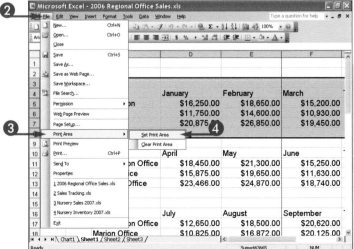

② Click File.

③ Click Print Area.

④ Click Set Print Area.

Excel saves the print area. The next time you print, Excel prints only the defined cells.

Note: *To clear a defined area, click File, Print Area, and then Clear Print Area.*

PRINT:
Insert a Page Break

You can insert page breaks to control what data appears on what page in a worksheet. By default, Excel breaks pages based on margins, column widths, and the amount of data that fits within the page parameters. You can add your own page breaks to suit the way you want to print or present the worksheet.

You can insert two types of page breaks in Excel: vertical and horizontal. Vertical page breaks divide the page at a particular column heading. Horizontal page breaks divide the page at a specific row. You can insert as many page breaks as you need in a worksheet.

After you insert page breaks, you can view them using Excel's Preview window, or you can view them using Page Break Preview mode. The Preview window only shows the different pages as they break, while Page Break Preview shows the pages with the breaks as blue lines on the page. You can also use Page Break Preview mode to insert and remove page breaks.

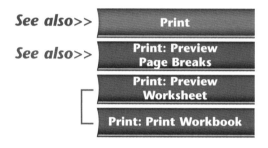

See also>> **Print**

See also>> **Print: Preview Page Breaks**

Print: Preview Worksheet

Print: Print Workbook

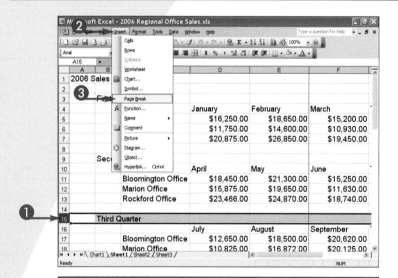

① Click the column heading to the right of where you want to break a page vertically or click the row label below where you want to break a page horizontally.

② Click Insert.

③ Click Page Break.

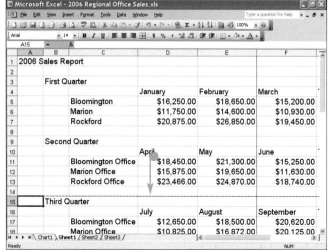

● Excel adds a page break, which appears as a dotted vertical or horizontal line on the worksheet.

Note: If the Page Break view option is turned off, you cannot see your page breaks. To turn the feature on, click Tools and then Options. Click the View tab and activate the Page Breaks check box.

Note: You can also view page breaks using Page Break Preview mode.

PRINT:
Preview Page Breaks

Page Break Preview is a view mode you can use to view and make adjustments to page breaks on your worksheets. You can also use the view to see the actual print area of your worksheet and define the area for printing.

The first time you use the feature, a Welcome prompt box appears. You can turn the dialog box off so it does not appear again.

When viewing worksheets in Page Break Preview, all manual page breaks appear as blue lines horizontally or vertically on the page. Automatic page breaks that Excel inserts appear as dotted blue lines. A large background page label

indicates which page you are viewing. You can use the Insert menu to insert more page breaks onto a page, and you can drag page breaks around to adjust their position. You can also drag a page break off a page to remove it.

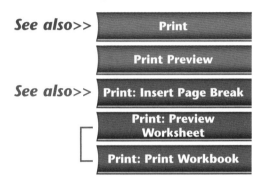

See also>> **Print**

Print Preview

See also>> **Print: Insert Page Break**

Print: Preview Worksheet

Print: Print Workbook

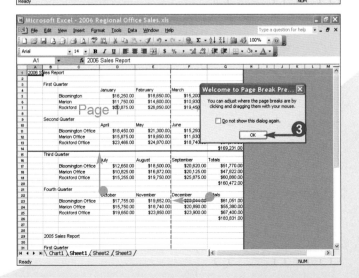

① Click View.

② Click Page Break Preview.

Excel switches to Page Break Preview mode and displays a Welcome prompt box.

③ Click OK.

● Default page breaks appear as blue dotted lines on the worksheet.

● Manual page breaks appear as solid blue lines.

To move a page break, click and drag the line to a new location on the page.

Note: To return to normal worksheet view, click View and then Normal.

287

PRINT:
Preview a Web Page

Before you turn a worksheet into Web content, you can preview how the data will look as a Web page. For example, you might want to see how a chart looks next to a range of cells, or view how your data's formatting appears in a browser window. You can use the Web Page Preview feature to see what your spreadsheet looks like in a browser window. This feature is especially helpful when you are determining what layout to use for your worksheet to make it easy to read online.

When you activate the Web Page Preview feature, your default Web browser window opens to display the current worksheet. After viewing your worksheet

as a Web page, you can turn the sheet into an HTML file that you can, in turn, publish to a Web server. This allows other users to view your Excel data online.

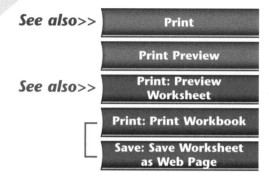

See also>> Print

Print Preview

See also>> Print: Preview Worksheet

Print: Print Workbook

Save: Save Worksheet as Web Page

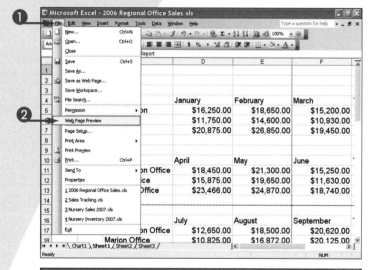

1 Click File.

2 Click Web Page Preview.

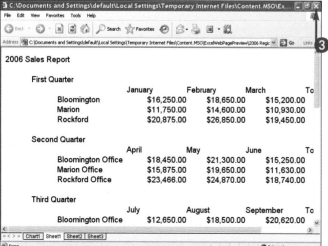

Your default Web browser opens and displays the worksheet as a Web page.

3 Click the Close button to close the browser window and return to Excel.

PRINT:
Preview a Worksheet

You can use Excel's Print Preview mode to preview worksheets before committing them to paper. In Print Preview, you can see how your worksheet looks when it is printed, including any headers, footers, and margins you have set. Previewing a worksheet is always a good idea before printing. It allows you to check the sheet for glaring errors and printing problems, such as discovering your worksheet data is too long to fit on a page.

Print Preview mode displays each page of a worksheet, along with a toolbar at the top of the preview window containing tools for zooming, viewing multiple pages, adding margins, and

more. When using Print Preview mode, you can move margins to make adjustments to the page.

You can also access the Page Setup and Print dialog boxes to further fine-tune your printer settings. When you finish previewing, you can exit the preview window.

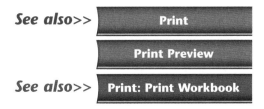

See also>> Print

Print Preview

See also>> Print: Print Workbook

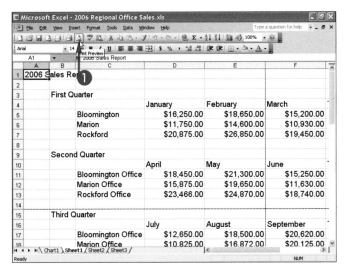

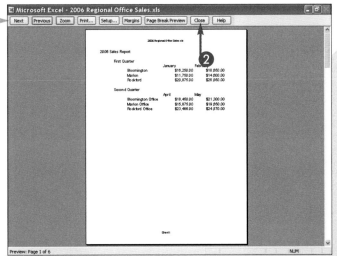

① Click the Print Preview button on the Standard toolbar.

Note: *You can also click File and then Print Preview to activate the feature.*

Excel opens the worksheet in Print Preview mode.

● You can use the toolbar buttons to make changes to your document.

You can click Zoom to change the magnification.

You can click Next and Previous to view multiple pages.

You can click Margins to hide or display margins on the page.

To view and edit page breaks, click Page Break Preview.

You can click Print to print the file.

② Click Close to exit Print Preview mode.

289

PRINT:
Print a Workbook or Worksheet

If you have a printer connected to your computer, you can print your Excel worksheets. You can send a file directly to the printer using the default printer settings, or you can open the Print dialog box and make changes to the printer settings.

If the worksheet appears exactly as you want it, you can activate the Print button on the Standard toolbar and print the current worksheet immediately. If you need to adjust a few printer settings first, you can open the Print dialog box, make your changes, and then print the worksheet.

The Print dialog box offers you the option of printing the active worksheet, the entire workbook, or just

the selected range of cells. You can also use the dialog box to select a particular printer to use, set the number of copies you want to print, and set a range of pages to print.

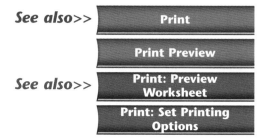

See also>> Print

Print Preview

See also>> Print: Preview Worksheet

Print: Set Printing Options

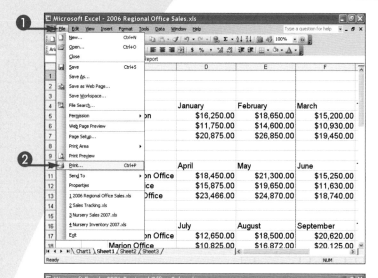

❶ Click File.

❷ Click Print.

To print a file without adjusting any printer settings, click the Print button (🖨) on the Standard toolbar.

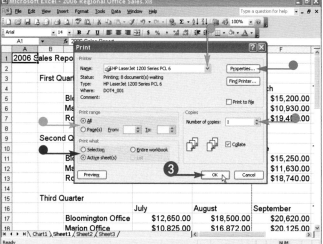

The Print dialog box opens.

● You can choose a printer from the Name drop-down list.

● You can print all the pages or a specific page using the Print Range settings.

● You can use the Print What options to print a selection, a worksheet, or the entire workbook.

● You can specify a number of copies to print.

● For more printer options, click Properties.

❸ Click OK.

Excel sends the file to the printer for printing.

PRINT:
Repeat Column or Row Headings

As your Excel worksheets get larger, the information is split across multiple pages, especially when you print the worksheet. Similar to the problem of not seeing headings when you scroll through the spreadsheet (see the technique "Freeze/Unfreeze"), when you print multiple pages, you do not see the column or row headings on each page. The headings appear only on the first page you print. You can solve this problem by selecting the Row and Column Headings option in the Page Setup dialog box. This adds the column labels to the top of each page or the row labels to repeat at the left.

Using the Sheet tab in the Page Setup dialog box, you can specify which rows or which columns you want to repeat on each printed page. You can collapse the dialog box to move it out of the way and select the rows or columns in the worksheet, or you can type the range for the row or column.

When you activate the Print command, Excel adds column or row headings to every printed page, making it easy for you or other users to continue following the data on each printout.

See also>>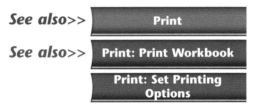

See also>> **Print**

Print: Print Workbook

Print: Set Printing Options

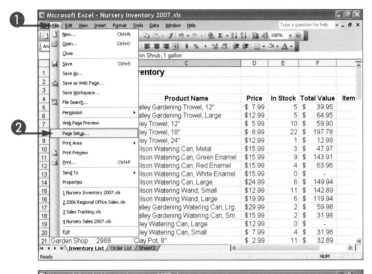

① Click File.

② Click Page Setup.

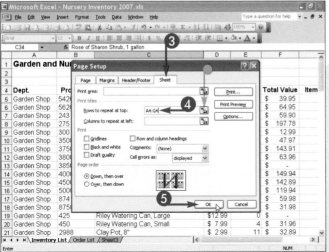

The Page Setup dialog box opens.

③ Click the Sheet tab.

④ Under the Print titles area, specify whether you want to print column or row labels.

● You can click the Collapse button to collapse the dialog box and select the cells directly on the worksheet.

⑤ Click OK.

Excel saves the settings.

PRINT:
Set Printing Options

You can use the Page Setup dialog box to control any printing options you want to assign to a worksheet. For example, you can set margins, change the page orientation, and control how various elements of your worksheet print, such as gridlines and row and column headings.

The Page Setup dialog box features four unique tabs, each offering a different set of options you can set for a page. You can use the Page tab to set a page orientation, choose a paper size, a print quality, and scale the worksheet data to fit the page. You can use the Margins tab to define margins for your printed worksheet. If you want to add header and footer text to your printed pages, you can do so using the options on the Header and Footer tab.

The Sheet tab offers options for defining a print area, printing repeating column or row labels, and setting the page order for printing. The tab also features various options you can turn on or off for printing, such as gridlines, column and row headings, and comments.

See also>>

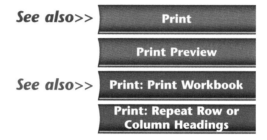

Print

Print Preview

See also>>

Print: Print Workbook

Print: Repeat Row or Column Headings

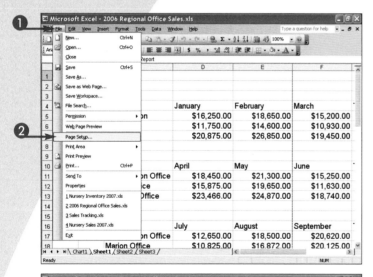

❶ Click File.

❷ Click Page Setup.

Note: *You can also access the page setup options through the Print Preview window; simply click the Setup button.*

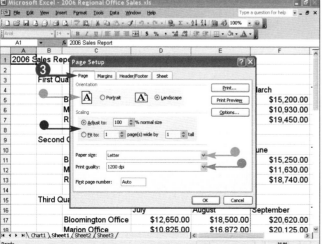

The Page Setup dialog box opens.

❸ Click the Page tab.

● To control the page orientation, click one of these options.

● To change the paper size, click here and choose a size.

● Use the Scaling options to fit data onto a page.

● To change the print quality, click here and select a quality setting.

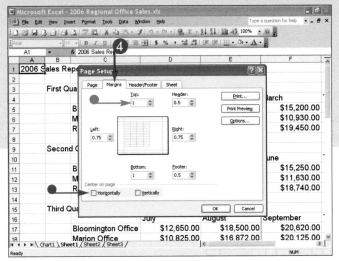

④ Click the Margins tab.

● You can make changes to the margins by typing an exact measurement or by clicking the buttons.

● You can also choose to center the data vertically or horizontally on the page.

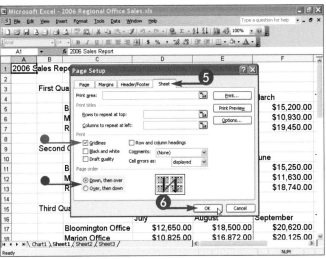

Note: See the technique "Print: Add Headers and Footers" for Header/Footer tab options.

⑤ Click the Sheet tab.

● To print the gridlines with your worksheet, activate this option.

● You can control the order in which the worksheets print by selecting one of these options.

⑥ Click OK.

Excel saves any changes you made and closes the Page Setup dialog box.

TIPS

More Options

You can use the Scaling options in the Page tab of the Page Setup dialog box to set up your data to fit on one page. You can accomplish this by shrinking or expanding the printed data image. After adjusting settings in the Scaling options, you can click the Print Preview button to preview what the printed worksheet will look like.

Did You Know?

You can print more than one worksheet at a time in Excel. To do so, press and hold the Ctrl key and click the tab of each sheet you want to print. Excel highlights each tab. Next, click File and then Print to open the Print dialog box. In the Print What section, select the Active Sheet(s) option (○ changes to ◉) and then click OK. This prints all the selected sheets.

PROPERTIES:
Assign File Properties

You can define the properties for a workbook file, such as assigning a title, subject, and author name. File properties are details about a file. File properties do not display with the file; rather, they are part of the unseen background information about the file. You can use the Properties dialog box to view properties for any workbook file in Excel. The Properties dialog box is also common with other programs, including all the Microsoft Office programs.

File properties include information about the file's origins, file size, and author. By default, Excel

automatically assigns some details about the file, such as the type, location, and size of the file. You can also add your own details to the file properties, such as your name and a title for the file.

You can use the Summary tab to enter property values such as title, author, subject, and company name. You can also assign a category and keywords to the file.

See also>> **Workbook**

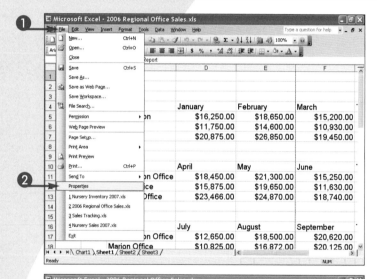

① Click File.

② Click Properties.

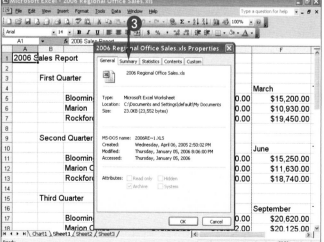

The Properties dialog box opens.

③ Click the Summary tab.

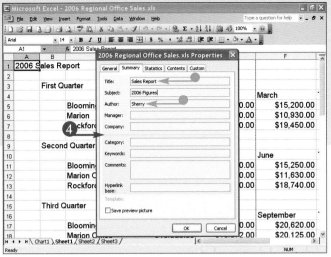

④ Fill in the Summary fields as needed.

● You can type a title for the file here.

● By default, Excel fills in the author information for you with the user name.

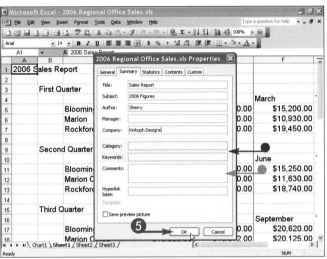

● You can assign a category and keywords using these fields.

● Add any comments about the file here.

⑤ Click OK.

Excel adds the information to the file.

TIPS

More Options

You can set custom properties for an Excel workbook file using the Custom tab in the Properties dialog box. You can click a field and then fill in the value with the data you want. For example, you can add a Project field and then define the project. Click the Add button and the field is added to the file's properties.

Try This

You can view file properties for any file on your computer using the Open dialog box in Excel. Click File and then Open to display the dialog box. Click the filename you want to view, click the Tools menu in the dialog box, and then click Properties. This opens the Properties dialog box and displays information about the current file.

PROTECTION:
Assign a Workbook Password

You can add security to your Excel data by assigning passwords to your workbooks. Assigning a password to the entire workbook is the best way to make the workbook secure and protect its contents. For additional protection of data within the workbook, you can assign passwords to individual worksheets.

You can assign a password to a workbook that makes the file inoperable unless the user knows the password. Or you can assign a password that allows other users to open the file but not make any changes to its data. You can use the Options dialog box to assign password protection to a workbook file.

When choosing a password, it is important to remember that the very best passwords contain a mix of upper- and lowercase letters, numbers, and symbols. For example, the password Bob32 is considered a weak password, but the password B6o!b9& is considered a stronger password and much more difficult to break.

See also>>

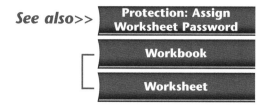

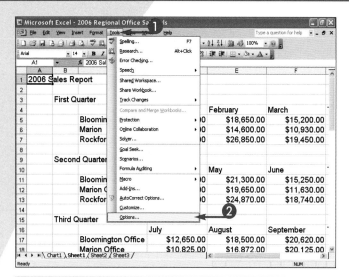

① Click Tools.

② Click Options.

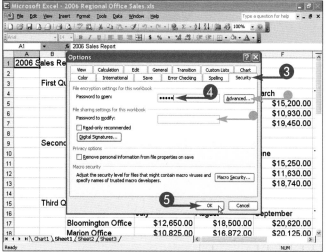

The Options dialog box appears.

③ Click the Security tab.

④ Type a password in the Password to Open box.

● Optionally, you can allow users to view the file but not make changes by typing a password here.

⑤ Click OK.

● If you want to set an encryption type, click the Advanced button and choose an encryption.

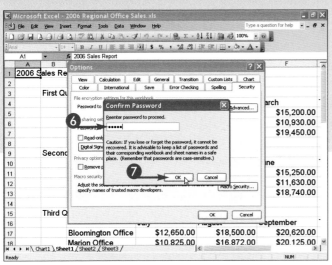

The Confirm Password dialog box opens.

6 Retype the password exactly as you typed it in Step 4.

7 Click OK.

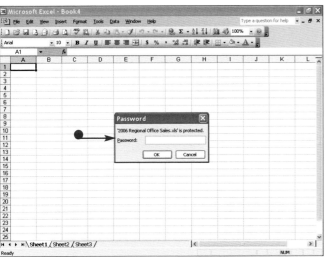

Excel assigns the password to the workbook.

● The next time you open the workbook, Excel prompts you for the password.

TIPS

Caution

It is crucial that you remember your Excel passwords. If you lose a password, you can no longer open the file. Lost passwords cannot be recovered. Consider writing the password down and keeping it in a safe place. Be sure to keep a record of which password goes with which workbook.

Remove It

To remove a password you no longer want, reopen the Options dialog box following the steps in this technique and click the Security tab. Delete the current password and click OK. You can also reset the password by typing and confirming a new password.

PROTECTION:
Assign a Worksheet Password

You can assign a password to any worksheet within a workbook to protect it from unauthorized use. Essentially, the password locks the worksheet from any changes. Other users can still view the worksheet, but the assigned password protection prevents them from making changes to the data.

Worksheet protection is helpful if you share your Excel workbooks with other users. You can use the Protect Sheet dialog box to assign a password to a sheet and protect all cell contents from changes or overwriting. This also prevents anyone from adding or removing columns and rows, cutting and pasting cell contents, or sorting the cell data.

Anyone given the password can make changes to the sheet.

The Protect Sheet dialog box also allows you to assign protection to parts of the worksheet. For example, you can choose to allow users to change certain aspects of a worksheet, such as inserting columns or changing the formatting in rows.

See also>>

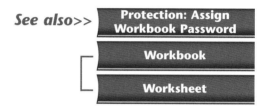

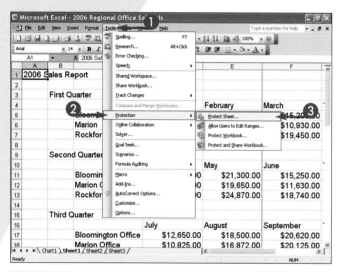

① Click Tools.

② Click Protection.

③ Click Protect Sheet.

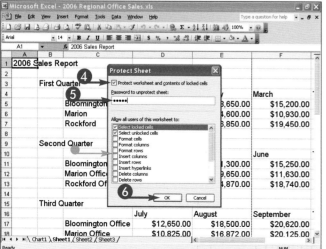

The Protect Sheet dialog box opens.

④ Click here to activate the worksheet protection, if it is not already selected.

⑤ Type a password for the worksheet.

● You can select which elements you want to allow for changes.

⑥ Click OK.

298

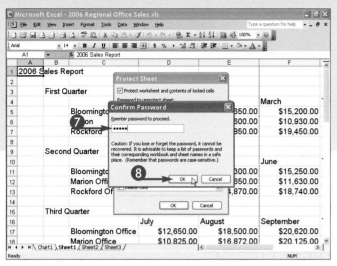

Excel prompts you to retype the password.

⑦ Retype the password exactly as you typed it in Step 5.

⑧ Click OK.

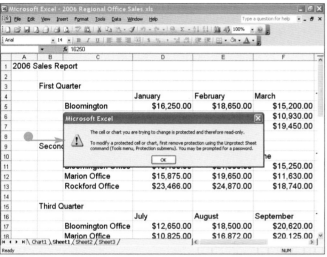

Excel locks the worksheet.

● The next time you or another user attempts to make changes to the worksheet data, Excel displays a warning prompt about the protected data.

TIPS

Remove It

You can turn off the password protection, hence unlocking the worksheet protection. Click Tools, Protection, and then Unprotect Sheet. This opens the Unprotect Sheet dialog box. Type the password and click OK. Excel unlocks the worksheet and you can now make changes to the data.

More Options

Excel's Protection menu offers three other protection commands you can assign to protect worksheet elements. You can click Tools, Protection, and then Allow Users to Edit Ranges command to grant permissions to different users to edit specific cells and ranges. You can click the Protect Workbook command to specify which items you want to protect, and assign a password to prevent changes to the items. You can click the Protect and Share Workbook command to turn tracking on and assign a password to turn the tracking off again.

RANGE:
Name a Range

You can assign distinctive names to the cells and ranges of cells you work with in a worksheet, making it easier to identify each cell's content. A *range* is simply a rectangular group of related cells, or a range can consist of a single cell. Normally when you select a range in Excel, the range name consists of the first cell in the group and the last cell in the group, separated by a colon — such as B24:E24. When you use the range in a formula, it is identified by the generic range name.

Generic range names are easy enough in simple formulas, but when you use complex formulas containing numerous ranges, keeping track of which data is in which range is challenging. To make formula-building easier, you can assign unique names

to your ranges. For example, a range name such as Sales_Totals is much easier to recognize than a generic reference.

Range names must start with a letter or an underscore (_). After that, you can use any character, uppercase or lowercase, and any punctuation or keyboard symbols, with the exception of a hyphen or a space. In place of a hyphen or space, substitute a period or underscore.

See also>> | Range

See also>> | Formulas

| Functions

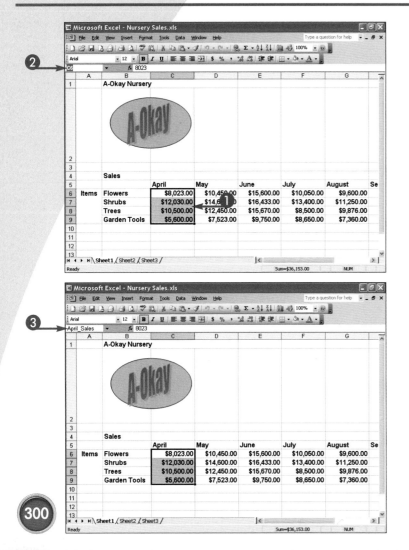

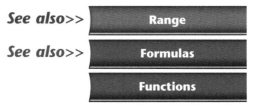

Assign a Range Name

1 Select the range you want to name.

2 Click inside the Name box on the Formula bar.

3 Type a name for the range.

4 Press Enter.

Excel assigns the name to the cells.

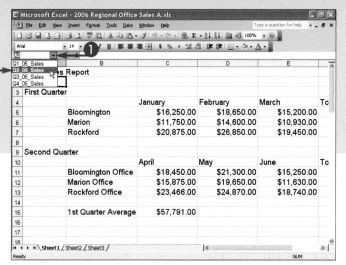

① Click the Name box down arrow.

② Click the range name you want to move to.

● Excel immediately activates the cells in the worksheet.

TIPS

Try This

You can reference cells in other worksheets in your Excel formulas. When referencing data from other worksheets, you must specify the sheet name followed by an exclamation mark and then the cell address, such as Sheet2!D12. If the sheet has a specific name, such as Sales, you must use the name along with an exclamation mark followed by the cell or range reference (Sales!D12). If the sheet name includes spaces, enclose the reference in single quote marks, such as 'Sales Totals!D12'.

More Options

You can use the Define Name dialog box to make changes to your range names. To display the dialog box, click Insert, Name, and then Define. You can edit existing range names, change the cells referenced by a range, or remove ranges you no longer need names assigned to in the worksheet.

RESEARCH:
Use the Research Task Pane

You can use the Research task pane to access a variety of research tools without leaving the Excel program window. You can search multiple sources of information, such as the Microsoft Encarta English dictionary, a built-in thesaurus, and the Microsoft Encarta online encyclopedia. You can also use the task pane to access translation tools, search for stock quotes, and tap into other third-party services.

For example, you can use the dictionary and thesaurus tools to help you look up words you type in Excel. If you share your workbooks with overseas users, you can tap into the translation tool to translate text.

When using the Research task pane, you can access several reference books, as well as access research, business, and financial Web sites. The Research task pane is just one of several task panes you can use in Excel to help you with common tasks. You can close the task pane when finished to free up on-screen workspace.

See also>>  Task Pane

See also>> Task Pane

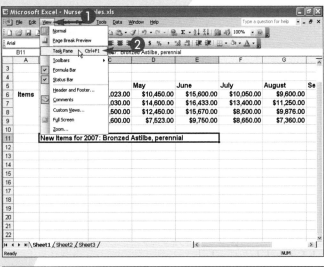

① Click View.

② Click Task Pane.

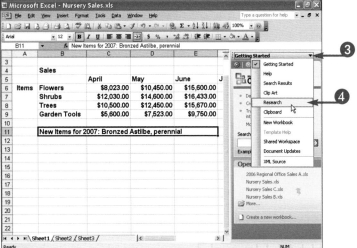

The task pane opens.

③ Click the Other Task Panes button.

④ Click Research.

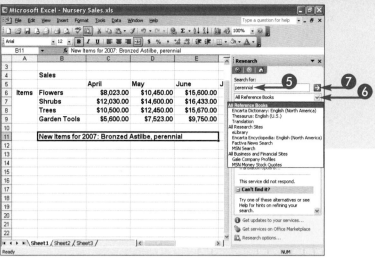

⑤ Type the word you want to look up.

⑥ Click here and click the reference sources you want to apply.

⑦ Click the Start Searching button.

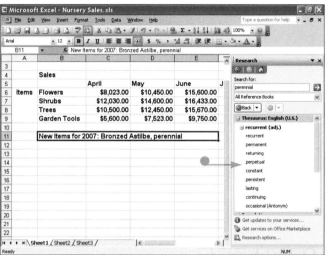

● The Research pane displays any results.

In this example, the pane displays the Thesaurus results for a term.

R

TIPS

More Options
You can control which reference books are used in your Research task pane searches. To do so, click the Research Options link at the bottom of the Research task pane to open the Research Options dialog box. You can use this dialog box to select or deselect which reference books and research sites are used. Simply check or uncheck the sources you want to apply.

Check It Out
You can add third-party premium resources to the Research task pane. For example, you can add services such as Factiva, a news service; eLibrary, a service for news and periodicals; Gale, a service for gleaning company information; and WorldLingo, a translation provider. Premium services cost a small fee to use. To access such services and view a complete list of resources available, click the Get Services on Office Marketplace link at the bottom of the Research task pane.

ROW:
Add a Row

You can add rows to your worksheets to add more data or add more space around existing data. For example, you may need to add a row in the middle of several existing rows for data you left out when you created the workbook. Or you might add a row to create a title area for the top of your worksheet.

The fastest way to add a row is to use the shortcut menu. You can also use the Insert menu to add rows and columns to your worksheets. When you add a row, Excel automatically shifts the existing rows down in the worksheet to make room for the new row.

By default, Excel displays a smart tag icon any time you add a new row. You can choose to ignore the smart tag or click the smart tag icon to view additional formatting options you can apply to the new row.

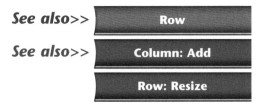

See also>> **Row**

See also>> **Column: Add**

Row: Resize

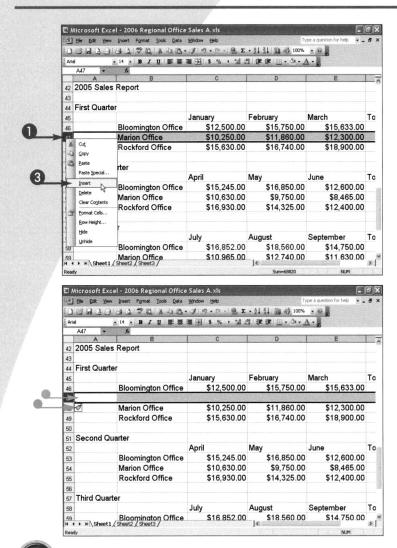

1 Click the row below where you want to insert a new row.

2 Right-click the selected row.

3 Click Insert.

● Excel adds a row.

● A smart tag may appear when you insert a row. You can click the icon to view a list of options you can assign.

Note: You can also use the Insert menu to add rows. Click Insert and then click Rows.

ROW:
Delete a Row

You can remove columns or rows you no longer need in the worksheet. For example, you might remove a row of out-of-date data or delete a row to cut down on extra space surrounding other data in the worksheet.

When you delete an entire column or row, Excel also deletes any existing data within the selected cells. For this reason, you need to double-check your cell data before deleting a row. If you accidentally delete a row you needed to keep in the worksheet, you can immediately apply the Undo command to reinsert the row.

When you delete a row, Excel moves the other rows up to fill the space left by the deletion. You can delete a single row or multiple rows in your worksheet. To remove more than one row, first select all the rows you want to delete before applying the Delete command.

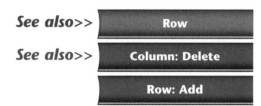

See also>> Row

See also>> Column: Delete

Row: Add

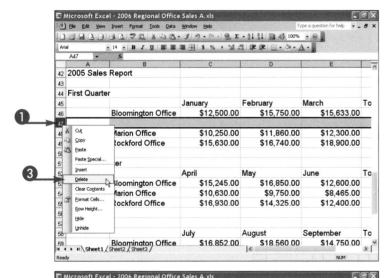

① Click the row you want to delete.

② Right-click the selected row.

③ Click Delete.

Note: *If you press the Delete key instead, Excel deletes the row's content but not the entire row.*

● Excel deletes the row.

Note: *You can also use the Edit menu to remove a row. Click Edit and then click Delete.*

ROW:
Hide a Row

You can hide rows in your worksheets to help you with a variety of scenarios. For example, if you work in a visible area, you can hide rows to keep confidential information out of view. You might hide a row to prevent the data from appearing on a printout. You can also hide data to eliminate distractions while you concentrate on other areas of the worksheet. For example, you might hide a group of rows between the top and bottom of a worksheet to allow you to focus on the data at either end.

When you hide a row, Excel simply collapses it in the worksheet so the data is no longer in view. When you are ready to view the data again, you can activate the Unhide command and expand the row again. You can hide a single row or multiple rows in a worksheet. You know a row is hidden by the row numbers along the left edge of the worksheet.

See also>>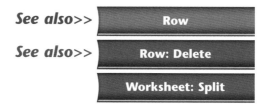

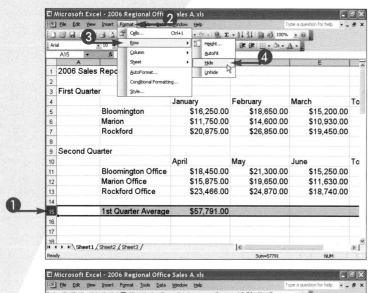

① Click the row you want to hide.

You can also select multiple rows to hide.

② Click Format.

③ Click Row.

④ Click Hide.

● Excel hides the row by shifting the other rows up.

Note: You can also hide an entire sheet in your workbook. Click Format, Sheet, Hide.

Note: To unhide a row, select the rows above and below the hidden row and then click Format, Row, and Unhide.

ROW:
Resize a Row

You can resize your worksheet's rows to accommodate text or make the worksheet more aesthetically appealing. When you resize a row, you are resizing the overall height or depth of the row. For example, you might make a row taller to fit a piece of clip art or to insert another visual element — such as a shape or picture. You can also change the row height to include multiple lines of data, such as a paragraph of text.

One of the easiest methods for resizing a row is to simply drag the row edge to a new position. Using this method, you can control exactly how

tall or short to make the row height. You can also use the Format menu to control row height.

You can adjust the row height of a single row or a group of multiple rows. To apply the adjustment to multiple rows, first select the rows before performing the resizing action.

See also>> Row

See also>> Column: Resize

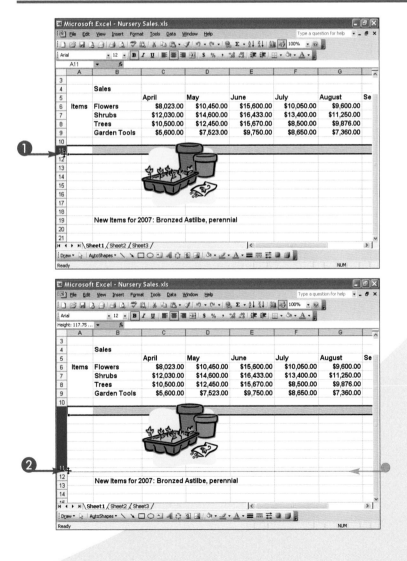

① Move the mouse pointer over the border of the row you want to resize.

② Click and drag the border to the desired size.

● A dotted line marks the new border of the row as you drag.

③ Release the mouse button and the row is resized.

SAVE:
Save a File to a Default Location

By default, Excel's Open and Save As dialog boxes are automatically set up to display and store your files in the My Documents folder. You may prefer to keep your workbooks in a different folder. For example, you may want to store your saved workbooks in a work-related folder or in a special project folder. You can specify another folder as the default working folder and save yourself time otherwise spent navigating to the folder containing your Excel files. By making a new default folder, the Save As dialog box is always set up to store your files in the designated location.

You can use Excel's Options dialog box to set up a new default folder to store your workbook files. You must first create the folder, and you need to know the exact path to the folder to create a new folder reference. For example, c:\work or c:\myprojects. You can change the default folder at any time.

See also>>

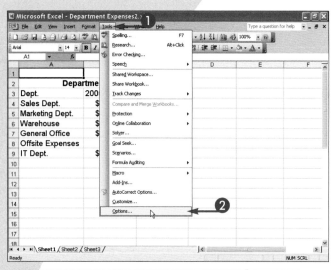

① Click Tools.

② Click Options.

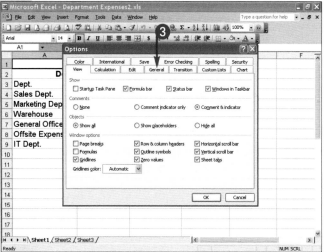

The Options dialog box opens.

③ Click the General tab.

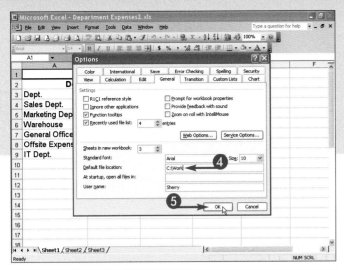

④ Click inside the Default File Location box and type the new path to which you want to save your Excel files.

⑤ Click OK to apply the changes.

Note: You must close the Excel program window before the changes are applied.

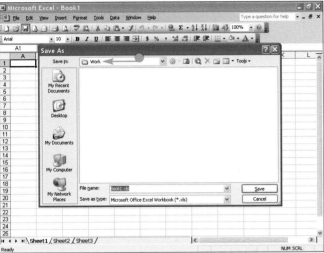

● The next time you open Excel and save a file with the Save As dialog box, Excel automatically assigns the default file location for you.

Try This

You can also change the default file type if you need to save your Excel workbook files in another format, such as a Lotus 1-2-3 file format or a template file format. You can also choose to save files in file formats supported in older versions of Excel. To do so, click the Tools menu and click Options to open the Options dialog box. Click the Transition tab and click the Save Excel Files As drop-down arrow and choose a format. Click OK to save the new setting. The next time you save a workbook, Excel automatically applies the default format.

More Options

You can use the Save tab in the Options dialog box to control how often Excel automatically saves your work. By default, Excel is set to save your work every 10 minutes in case you experience any sort of power interruption to your computer. You can change the number of minutes for the AutoRecover setting, or you can turn off the feature entirely.

SAVE:
Save a Workbook

You can save your data as a workbook file to reuse it again or share it with others. You can use the Save As dialog box to save a file. By default, Excel workbooks are saved in the Excel file format, which uses the XLS file extension. If you want to share your workbook with a Lotus 1-2-3 user, you can save your file in the 1-2-3 format. You can also save to other file formats, such as XML spreadsheet, text (tab delimited), CSV (Mac), DBF (dBASE), and HTML.

You can also save your workbooks in file formats read by earlier versions of Excel, such as 2.1 or 4.0.

You may need to do this if you want your file read by someone using an older version of Excel.

When you save a workbook, you can specify a folder or drive to save to, as well as a unique filename. After you save a workbook, the new filename appears in the program window's Title bar.

See also>>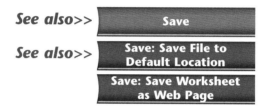

Save

Save: Save File to Default Location

Save: Save Worksheet as Web Page

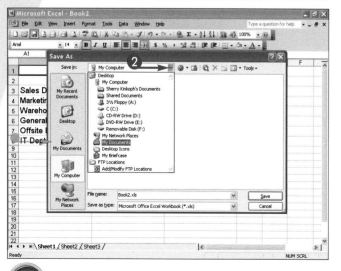

① Click the Save button on the Standard toolbar.

Note: You can also click the File menu and click Save or Save As.

The Save As dialog box opens.

② Click here to navigate and select the folder or drive to which you want to save the file.

● You can also click a folder listed here.

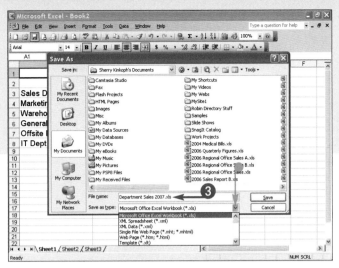

③ Type a name for the workbook file.

● To save the file as another format, click here and choose a format.

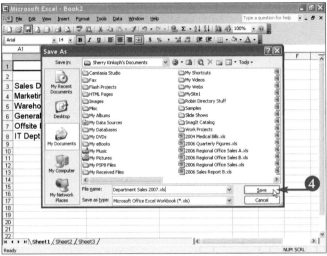

④ Click Save.

Excel saves the workbook and the new filename appears on the program window's Title bar.

Caution

If you try and save a workbook and receive the error message saying the file is read-only, you cannot save the file. You can, however, copy it as another filename to save the data. Simply save the file using the Save As dialog box, but assign the workbook a different name or folder location.

More Options

You can save a workbook file to a Web server if you have the correct administration permissions to do so. You can type the URL of the server you want to save to in the File name text box in the Save As dialog box. You can type the full path to the file or enter an Internet or intranet address, such as http://myworkbook.

SAVE:
Save a Worksheet as a Web Page

You can turn an Excel workbook into an HTML file that you can post on the Web. When you activate the Save As Web page command, Excel creates a file containing all the necessary HTML coding required to create a Web page that can be read by other Web browsers.

You can save the entire workbook as a Web page, a sheet, or a range of cells on a worksheet. If your workbook only consists of one worksheet, the HTML file you create only contains the single sheet.

You can use the Save As Web Page dialog box to save your work as a Web page. The dialog box features options for selecting which portion of the file to save — either the entire workbook or a single sheet — as well as an option for assigning the page a unique name. The page name is the title that appears in the title bar of the user's Web browser window.

See also>> **Save**

See also>> **Save: Save Workbook**

Web Toolbar

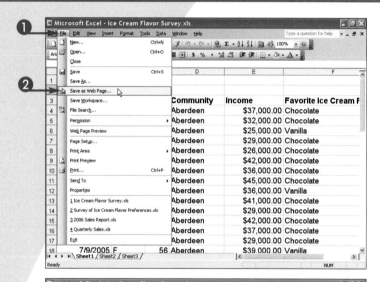

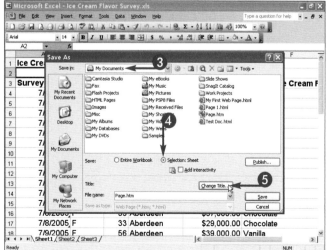

1 Click File.

2 Click Save As Web Page.

Note: The Save As dialog box only displays the Web page options when you activate the Save As Web Page command.

To save a range as a Web page, first select the range.

The Save As dialog box opens.

3 Navigate to the folder where you want to save the file.

4 Click whether you want to save the entire workbook or just the current sheet or selection.

5 Click Change Title.

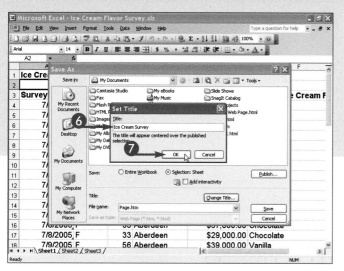

The Set Title dialog box opens.

6 Type a title.

7 Click OK.

8 Type a name for the file.

9 Click Save.

Excel saves the file as a Web page.

TIPS

More Options

If you are ready to publish the Web page to a server, you can click the Publish button in the Save As dialog box to open the Publish as Web Page dialog box. You can then use the Publish as Web Page dialog box to add spreadsheet functionality to the page and designate a server path and filename. When you activate the Publish command, Excel publishes the page and opens it in your default browser to display the Excel data.

Did You Know?

You can add interactivity to your Excel Web page. If you want to allow others to interact with your Excel data on a Web page, select the Add Interactivity check box (☐ changes to ☑) in the Save As dialog box. When this feature is activated, Excel saves the data and adds interactivity to the page. Other users who have Office Web components can view the page and make changes to the data.

S

SCENARIO:
Create a What-If Scenario

You can use Excel's Scenarios to perform "what if" speculations on your data. For example, you might use a scenario to examine the effects of increasing shipping prices or raising product prices on your inventory worksheet. When you create a scenario, you make changes to the worksheet data without affecting the original data.

Scenarios are a part of Excel's analysis tools. Specifically, a scenario is a set of values you can save and substitute in your worksheet to forecast different outcomes. A scenario includes variable cells linked together by a formula or several formulas.

To create a scenario, you first need to create worksheet data containing at least one formula that is dependent on variable cell data. Be sure to include all the data and formulas you want to use in your comparison before creating a scenario. The next step is to determine which cells you want to change in the scenario. The last step is to create and name scenarios and enter the data you want to change.

See also>> **Add-Ins**

See also>> **Add-Ins**

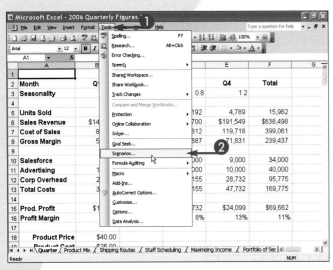

Create a Scenario

1. Click **Tools**.
2. Click **Scenarios**.

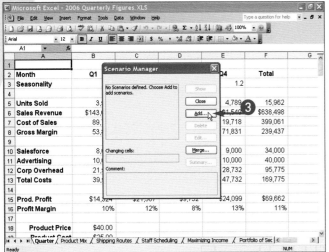

The Scenario Manager dialog box opens.

3. Click **Add**.

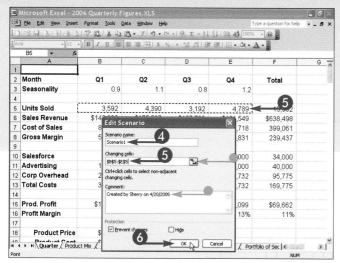

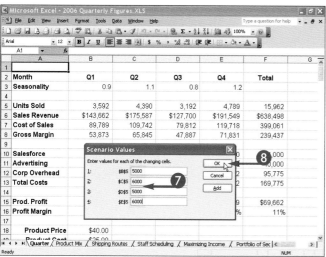

The Add Scenario dialog box opens.

4. Type a name for the scenario.

Excel changes the dialog box name to Edit Scenario.

5. Select the cells you want to change or type the cell references.

● You can click here to collapse and expand the dialog box while clicking cells in the worksheet.

● Optionally, you can type a note about the scenario here.

6. Click OK.

The Scenario Values dialog box opens.

7. Type values for each of the changing cells.

You can perform all kinds of changes to the data to create a scenario.

8. Click OK.

Caution

You need to save the original worksheet data before creating scenarios using Excel's Scenario Manager. Because the Scenario Manager works by entering new values, any existing formulas are overwritten by new values you record in a scenario. You might also consider saving the original workbook using a new filename to further prevent any problems.

Did You Know?

The Scenario Manager does not store formulas along with cell contents. Although the Scenario Manager does not save formulas, you can type them into the Scenario Values dialog box. For example, if you want to enter a value for cell G10 as 10 percent higher than the value in cell F10, you can enter the formula =F10*1.10 for the changing cell information for cell G10. Any results that are calculated are stored along with the scenario.

SCENARIO:
Create a What-If Scenario (Continued)

When you create scenarios, you can save the scenario data to reuse again at a later time. You can store multiple scenarios in a single workbook. The Scenario Manager dialog box keeps track of the workbook's scenarios, allowing you to revisit and make changes to the scenarios as needed.

You can assign each scenario a unique name and description. It is a good idea to keep your scenario names short and to the point, such as "Best Case"

and "Worst Case." The Comment box includes your name and the date you created the scenario. You can add more text to the box to add a description about the scenario. This is helpful if other users view and work with your workbook and the scenarios you create.

You can use the Scenario Manager dialog box to manage your scenarios as well as add, delete, or change each scenario as needed.

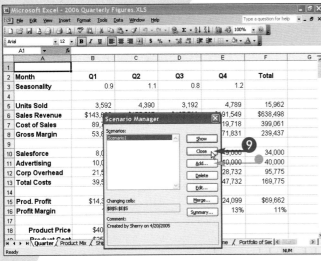

To view the newly created scenario, see the next set of steps and skip to Step 4.

● You can continue adding more scenarios to Scenario Manager by repeating Steps 3 to 8.

⑨ Click Close.

Excel closes the Scenario Manager dialog box.

View Scenarios

① Click Tools.

② Click Scenarios.

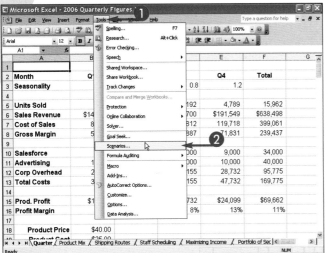

The Scenario Manager dialog box opens.

3 Click the scenario you want to view.

4 Click Show.

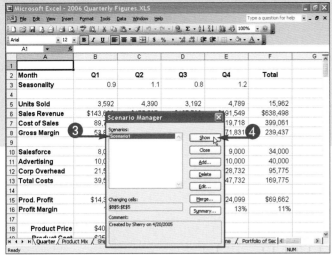

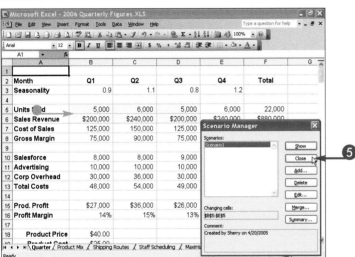

● Excel displays the scenario on the worksheet.

In this example, the scenario shows how sales revenue increases when units sold values increase.

5 When finished viewing the scenario, click Close.

Excel closes the scenario.

TIPS

More Options

To remove a scenario you no longer want, reopen the Scenario Manager dialog box by clicking the Tools menu and clicking Scenarios. In the dialog box, click the scenario you want to remove and click Delete. Scenario Manager permanently removes the scenario from the list.

Did You Know?

You can use the Summary button in the Scenario Manager to generate a summarization of your various scenarios. When activated, the Summary button opens the Scenario Summary dialog box where you can create a report to list all the inputs and results for all the scenarios.

SEARCH:
Conduct a File Search

You can use the Basic File Search task pane to search for an Excel file. This pane is only available through the File Search command. You can use the pane to look for a particular filename as well as search through specific folders or drives on your computer.

You can use the Basic File Search features to look for files containing specified text in the filename or specific text found in the contents of the file. You type the keyword or words you want to look for, and the search feature looks for the keywords in the body of the file, in the file properties, and in the filename.

You can also search for specific types of Microsoft Office files, including Word documents, PowerPoint slides, or even Web pages.

When the task pane displays any matching results, you can open a file, view it in a Web browser, view the file's properties, and more.

See also>>  Track Changes

See also>> Find

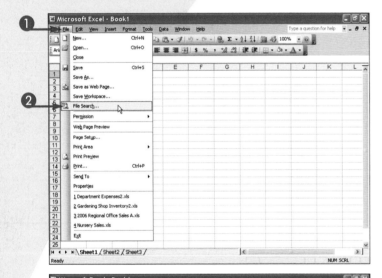

① Click File.

② Click File Search.

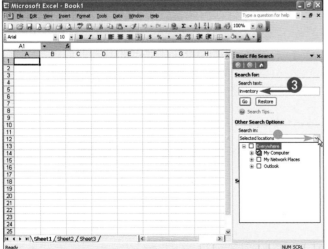

The Basic File Search pane appears.

③ Type a search keyword or filename.

● To search a particular folder or drive, click the Search In drop-down arrow and choose a folder or drive.

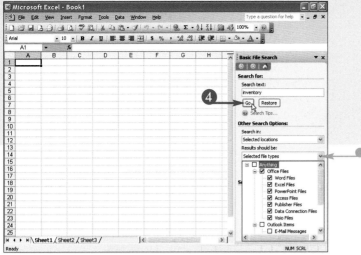

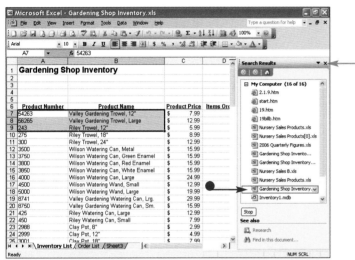

- To search for a specific file type, click the Results Should Be drop-down arrow and choose a file format.

④ Click Go.

Note: *If this is the first time using this feature, Excel may prompt you to install it first.*

Basic File Search conducts a search for the file and displays any matching results in the task pane.

- To open a file, click the filename.
- Click here to close the task pane when finished.

More Options

You can use advanced search techniques to locate files. For example, you can type wildcard characters if you are not quite sure of the full text you are looking for. Type a question mark to represent a single character, such as "workbook?" and Excel produces results such as workbook1, workbook2, and so on. Type an asterisk to look for a group of characters, such as "sales*" to return results such as salesreport1, salessheet, salespeople, and so on.

Did You Know?

If you are looking for a file you recently worked on, the Getting Started task pane and the File menu lists recently used files. The File menu lists the last four workbooks you opened. You can click any filename on the menu to open the workbook. You can also change the option so the File menu displays more or less workbook names. To do so, click Tools and then Options to open the Options dialog box. Click the General tab and change the Recently Used File List value.

SELECT:
Select Worksheet Cells

You can select cells in Excel to perform editing, mathematical, and formatting tasks. Selecting a single cell is quite simple: You just click the cell. A selected cell is highlighted in the worksheet by a bold black outline. After you select a cell, you can perform a variety of tasks on the cell or data within.

To select a group of cells, called a *range*, you can use your mouse or keyboard. For example, you might apply formatting to a range of cells rather than format each cell individually. You can also apply functions and formulas to a range of cells or a single cell in the worksheet.

In addition to cells and ranges, you can select entire columns and rows in your worksheet, or multiple columns and rows. You can also select data within a cell the same way in which you select data in a word processing program. You can select a single character, a word, or a string of text.

See also>>

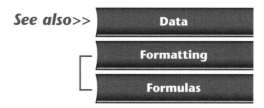

Data

Formatting

Formulas

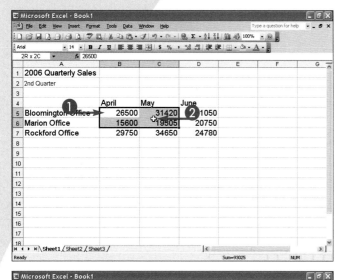

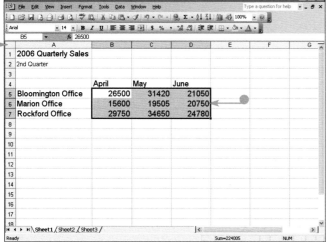

Select a Range

① Click the first cell in the range of cells you want to select.

② Click and drag across the cells you want to include in the range.

Excel highlights cells you select as you drag.

③ Release the mouse button.

⬤ The cells are selected.

⬤ To select all the cells in the worksheet, click here.

You can select multiple noncontiguous cells by pressing and holding the Ctrl key while clicking cells.

320

Select a Column or Row

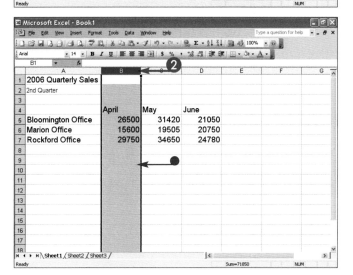

① Move the mouse over the header of the column or row you want to select.

② Click the column or row.

● Excel selects the entire column or row.

To select multiple columns or rows, drag across the column or row headings.

You can select multiple noncontiguous columns or rows by pressing and holding the Ctrl key while clicking column or row headings.

TIPS

More Options

To select a word or number inside a cell, you can click in front of the text and then drag over the characters or numbers you want to select. If a cell contains several words, you can double-click a specific word to select it.

Did You Know?

You can use the arrow keys to navigate to the first cell in a range. Next, press and hold the Shift key while using an arrow key to select the range, such as the Down Arrow and Right Arrow keys. Excel selects any cells you move over using the keyboard navigation keys.

S

SMART TAGS:
Work with Smart Tags

You can use Excel's smart tags to help you save time in your work. Smart tags are little icons that appear when Excel recognizes data and associates it with a task. Depending on the data, Excel may display smart tags for AutoCorrect options, paste options, and AutoFill options.

For example, when you type a person's name, a smart tag might prompt you to add the name to the Microsoft Office Outlook contact folder. If you type a stock symbol in a cell, a smart tag may appear offering you instant access to the latest stock quotes.

When a smart tag icon appears, you can choose to respond to the tag or ignore it. If you proceed with other Excel tasks, the smart tag disappears. Smart tags are turned on by default in Excel. You can turn them off if you no longer find them helpful.

See also>> **Smart Tags**

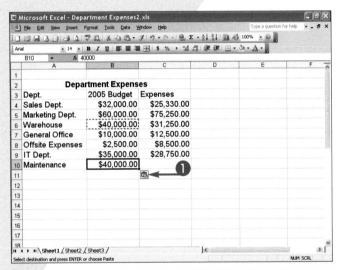

View a Smart Tag Icon

① To view a smart tag, click the smart tag icon.

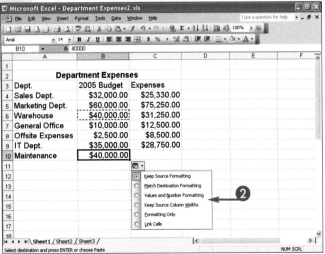

The smart tag displays a menu of actions you can perform with the data.

② Click an item from the list to perform an action.

To ignore the smart tag, simply continue working with your worksheet data.

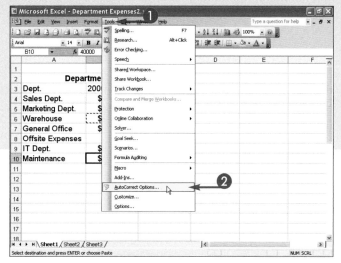

① Click Tools.

② Click AutoCorrect Options.

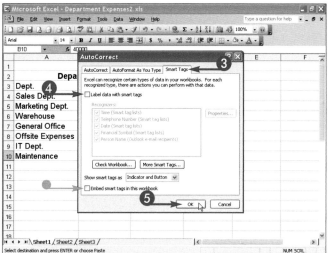

The AutoCorrect dialog box opens.

③ Click the Smart Tags tab.

④ Deselect the Label Data with Smart Tags check box.

● If you are embedding smart tags with your workbooks, also deselect the Embed smart tags in this workbook check box.

⑤ Click OK.

TIPS

More Options

You can add more smart tags to your Excel work. You can download additional smart tags from the Microsoft Office Web site, or download tags from third-party vendors to use with Excel. To add more smart tags, click Tools and then AutoCorrect Options to open the AutoCorrect dialog box. Click the Smart Tags tab and click More Smart Tags. Your default Web browser opens to the available smart tags Web page where you can pick and choose tags to suit your use of Excel.

More Options

You can customize which kinds of smart tag icons appear in your workbooks. Click Tools and then AutoCorrect Options to open the AutoCorrect dialog box. Click the Smart Tags tab and select or deselect the recognizers you want Excel to display. Click OK to apply your changes.

SORT:
Perform a Sort

If you are using Excel to create database lists, you can sort your database table to reorganize the information. For example, you might want to sort a client table to list the names alphabetically.

You can choose from two types of simple sorts using the sort buttons on the Standard toolbar. You can perform an ascending sort to list records from A to Z. You can perform a descending sort to list records from Z to A.

You can also use the Sort dialog box to sort your data. For example, you can sort by four criteria

based on your list columns. You can also sort a single column or multiple columns in your list. If you are sorting related columns — such as one column of student names and a second column of student scores — be sure to use both columns in the sort to keep the data related. Otherwise, Excel sorts just one column and leaves the other unaltered.

See also>> **Database**

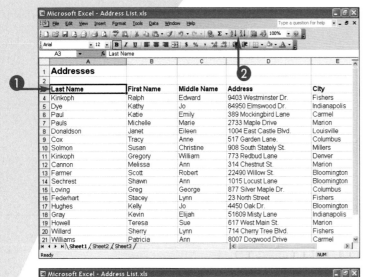

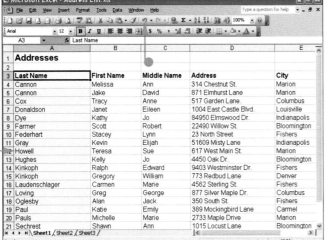

Perform a Quick Sort

1 Click in the field name you want to sort.

2 Click the Sort Ascending or Sort Descending button on the Formatting toolbar.

If your table already displays filter buttons, you can also click a filter drop-down arrow and click a sort option.

● Excel sorts the records based on the field you specified.

● If you do not want the records sorted permanently, click the Undo button to return the list to its original state.

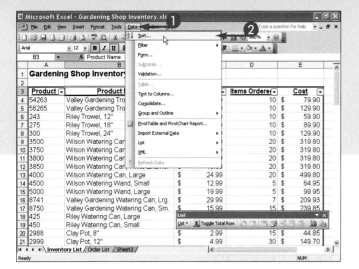

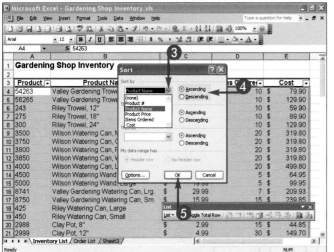

① Click Data.

② Click Sort.

The Sort dialog box opens.

③ Click the first Sort By box and select the primary field to sort by.

④ Select whether you want to sort the field in ascending or descending order.

To specify additional fields for the sort, repeat Steps 3 and 4 to select other sort fields.

⑤ Click OK.

Excel sorts the data.

TIPS

Did You Know?

Ordinarily Excel does not distinguish between lowercase and capital letters during a sort. You can change this by activating the case sensitive option. In the Sort dialog box, click the Options button to open the Sort Options dialog box. Select the Case Sensitive check box (☐ changes to ☑) and click OK. With this option turned on, Excel sorts lowercase letters first before capital letters.

More Options

If the listed data is across a row instead of down a column, you can activate the Sort Left to Right option in the Sort dialog box. Open the Sort dialog box and click Options. The Sort Options dialog box opens. Select the Sort Left to Right option (○ changes to ◉). Click OK.

SPELLING:
Spell Check a Worksheet

You can use Excel's spell check feature to check your worksheets for spelling errors. This tool is especially important if you plan to share your workbook or printouts of your data with others. Poor spelling can actually detract from the importance of your worksheet data and makes the worksheet author look unprofessional.

If you use the spell check feature in other Microsoft Office programs, such as Word, you may be used to seeing the program check your spelling as you type and underline any misspellings. Excel does not check spelling automatically. You can, however, activate the spell check at any time to check your worksheet for spelling mistakes.

When the spell check feature finds an error, it highlights it in the worksheet and offers suggestions for fixing the error. Depending on the word, you can replace it with a suggestion or ignore it and move on to the next error.

Although the spell check is a helpful feature, it is never a substitute for a good proofreading with your own eyes. Spell check can catch some errors, but not all, so take time to read over your workbooks for misspellings.

See also>> **Spelling**

See also>> **AutoCorrect**

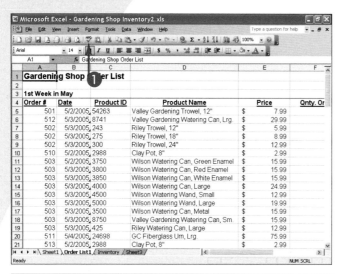

1 Click the Spelling button on the Standard toolbar.

To check only a section of your worksheet, select the section before activating the spell check.

Note: *You can also click the Tools menu and click Spelling.*

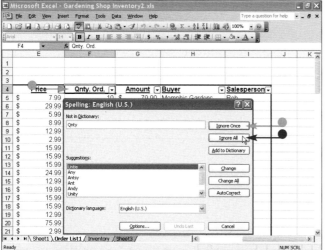

● Excel searches the worksheet for any mistakes, highlights any problems, and displays the Spelling dialog box if it finds an error.

● To ignore the error one time, click Ignore Once.

● To ignore every occurrence, click Ignore All or Ignore Rule.

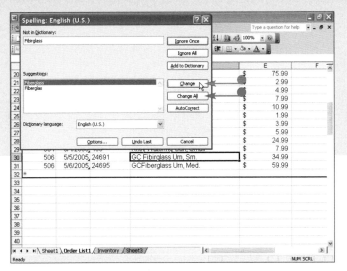

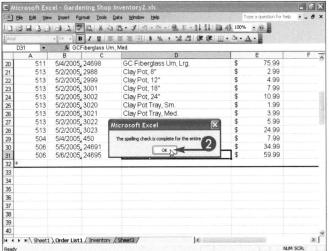

● Click Change to make a correction.

● To correct all the misspellings of the same word, click Change All.

When the spell check is complete, a prompt box appears.

② Click OK.

TIPS

Did You Know?

By default, Excel's AutoCorrect feature is turned on to fix common typing mistakes as you enter data into your cells. For example, if you type *adn*, AutoCorrect changes the text to *and* automatically. AutoCorrect operates with a library of common misspellings and you can view them through the AutoCorrect dialog box. Click Tools and then AutoCorrect Options to display the dialog box, and click the AutoCorrect tab to view the features. To turn off AutoCorrect, deselect the Replace Text As You Type check box (☑ changes to ☐).

More Options

If you have other languages enabled in your Microsoft Office programs, you can check the spelling of words in other languages using the Dictionary language menu in the Spelling dialog box. To activate other languages, click Start, Programs, Microsoft Office, Microsoft Office Tools, and then Microsoft Office 2003 Language Settings. This opens the Microsoft Office 2003 Language Settings dialog box. Next, click the Enabled Languages tab and select which languages you want to enable. Click the Add button to add them to your list. Click OK to apply the new selections to your Office programs.

STYLE:
Create a Style

You can use a style to quickly assign formatting throughout a workbook. A style is simply a collection of formatting, whether you define a font and size or a background color. If you use a lot of formatting in your worksheet cells, you might find that styles can save you valuable time and effort. Rather than apply various formatting commands to each cell or range separately, you can group a collection of formatting characteristics into a style and apply a single style instead.

You can create your own styles in Excel, apply existing styles, or copy styles from other workbooks. By default, the generic Normal style is applied to every workbook you create. Other existing styles

include Comma, Percent, and Currency. You can modify existing styles to create new styles, or you can create your own styles from scratch and assign them unique names.

Styles are available from the Styles dialog box. You can use the dialog box to manage all the styles in a workbook, including deleting, modifying, and creating new styles.

See also>>

Style

Formatting

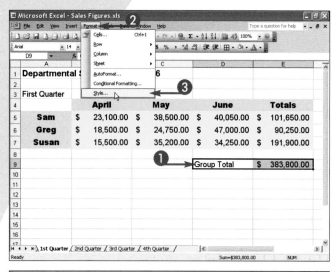

① Select the cell or cells to which you want to apply a style.

② Click Format.

③ Click Style.

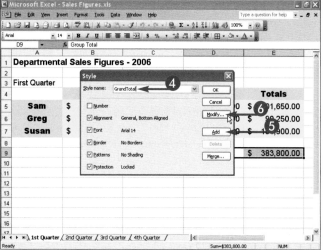

The Style dialog box opens.

④ Click the Style name text box and type a name for the style.

⑤ Click Add.

Excel adds the style name to the list of available styles.

⑥ Click Modify.

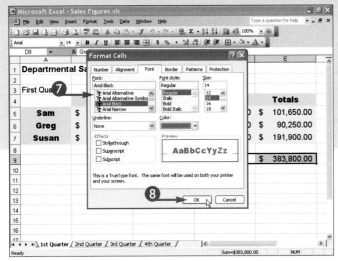

The Format Cells dialog box opens.

⑦ Apply all the formatting you want to set for the style.

You can use any of the tabs to set formatting options for the style.

⑧ Click OK.

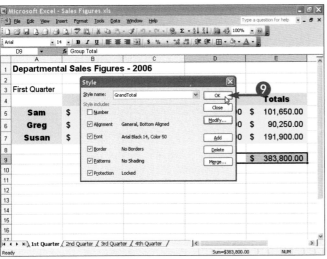

⑨ Click OK.

Excel applies the style.

Note: *To apply the style to other cells, simply open the Style dialog box and select the style to apply it.*

TIPS

More Options

To remove a style, first open the Style dialog box as shown in the steps in this technique. Then select the name of the style you want to delete from the Style Name drop-down list, and click the Delete button to remove the style.

Did You Know?

You can use the check boxes in the Style dialog box to specify which formatting you want to apply for a particular style. For example, if you want to apply everything but the alignment formatting for a style, simply deselect the Alignment check box (☑ changes to ☐) before applying the style to the selected cells.

SYMBOL:
Insert a Symbol

From time to time, you might need to insert a special symbol or character into an Excel worksheet that is not readily available using your keyboard, such as a registered trademark symbol, ornamental bullets, or an em dash character.

You can use the Symbol dialog box to access a wide range of special characters and symbols, including mathematical and Greek symbols, architectural symbols, and more. For example, you can access ASCII and Unicode characters using the Symbol dialog box. You can also access Wingding characters, including smiley faces and other decorative characters.

The Symbol dialog box is divided into two tabs. The Symbols tab gives you access to your installed fonts

and the various symbols. You can select a font and then view the available symbols. The Recently Used Symbols box lists all the recently used symbols you inserted into your workbooks, giving you quick access to the same symbols again. The Special Characters tab displays common characters, such as proofreading symbols.

After selecting a symbol to insert, the Symbol dialog box remains open so you can continue inserting symbols into your worksheet cells.

See also>>   **AutoCorrect**

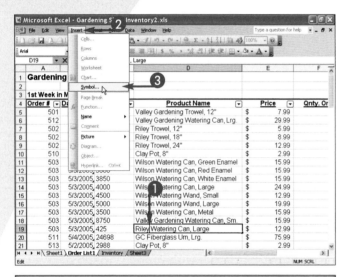

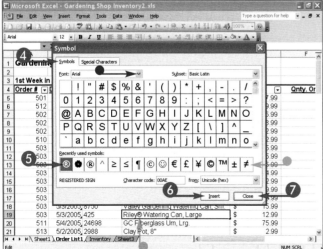

Insert a Symbol

1 Click where you want to insert a symbol.

2 Click Insert.

3 Click Symbol.

The Symbol dialog box opens.

4 To add a symbol, click the Symbols tab.

5 Click a symbol.

6 Click Insert.

● Excel inserts the symbol.

  The dialog box remains open so you can add more symbols to your text.

● This area displays recently used symbols you can quickly click to insert again.

● You can click here to change the font.

7 When finished, click Close.

Insert a Special Character

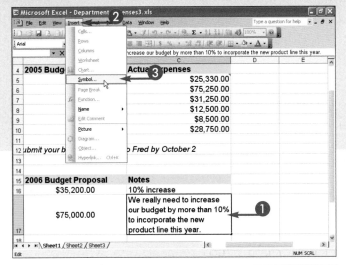

1. Click where you want to insert a character.
2. Click Insert.
3. Click Symbol.

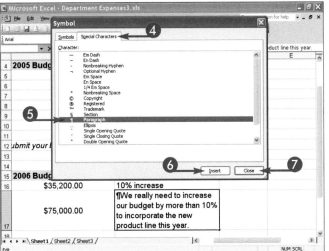

The Symbol dialog box opens.

4. To add a character, click the Special Characters tab.
5. Click the character you want to insert.
6. Click Insert.

Excel adds the character to the current cursor location in the worksheet.

The dialog box remains open so you can add more characters to your text.

7. When finished, click Close.

TIPS

Apply It

If you know you are going to insert a specific symbol over and over again, you can add it to the AutoCorrect library and assign a shortcut to insert the symbol. Insert and copy the symbol in the worksheet and then click Tools and AutoCorrect Options. In the AutoCorrect tab, paste the symbol in the With box and type a shortcut for the symbol in the Replace box. The next time you type the shortcut, AutoCorrect replaces it with the actual symbol.

Did You Know?

When you type some special characters on the keyboard, Excel inserts a symbol automatically. This is Excel's AutoCorrect feature at work. It inserts common symbols for certain keyboard combinations. For example, if you type (c), AutoCorrect immediately changes it to the copyright symbol, ©. To undo the occurrence, simply click the Undo button (🔄) immediately to return to (c).

TASK PANE:
Work with Task Panes

You can use Excel's task panes to access common commands and controls. You can display more than one pane in the task pane area, and you can use the navigation buttons to view open panes. New to Excel 2003, the task pane is displayed on the right side of the program window by default. You can close the task pane at any time to free up workspace on-screen.

Excel offers 11 different task panes you can use, each focusing on a specific area or group of related tasks. For example, the Getting Started task pane, which appears by default when you first use Excel, gives you quick access to common tasks such as

opening existing files, starting new files, accessing the Microsoft Office Online Web site, and using search tools to look up specific information. The Clip Art task pane features tools for searching clip art and adding artwork to your worksheets.

Some of the commands you can select in Excel open a task pane automatically. For example, when you create a new workbook, the New Workbook pane opens. When you finish using a pane, you can close it.

See also>>   **Task Pane**

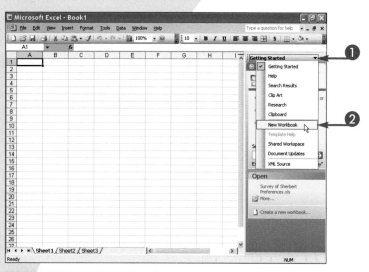

Display Panes

1. Click here to display a list of available panes.

2. Click a pane.

   The pane is displayed.

- If two or more panes are displayed, you can click the navigation buttons to move between panes.

- You can click a link to activate a feature.

- You can click here to return to the default task pane, Getting Started.

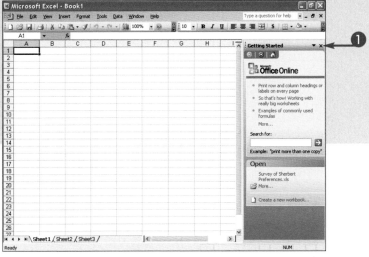

Close the Task Pane

1 Click here.

The task pane closes.

Reopen the Task Pane

1 Click the View menu.

2 Click Task Pane.

The task pane opens.

TIPS

Customize It

The task pane appears every time you open Excel, unless you choose to change the task pane startup mode. To turn off the pane when you open the program window, click the Tools menu and then click Options. This opens the Options dialog box. Click the View tab and deselect the Startup Task Pane check box (☑ changes to ☐). Click OK to save the changes. The next time you open Excel, the task pane will not appear.

Did You Know?

You can resize the task pane to make it wider or narrower in the window. To resize the pane, move the mouse pointer over the left edge of the pane's border until the pointer becomes a double-sided arrow pointer (↔). Click and drag the border to resize the pane. Drag to the left to make the pane wider, or drag to the right to make the pane narrower.

TEMPLATE:
Apply a Template

You can use Excel templates to speed up your workbook creation. Templates are ready-made documents you can use to quickly assemble spreadsheets. Excel includes several pre-made templates you can use containing preformatted placeholder text. All you have to do is add your own text. For example, you can apply the Balance Sheet template and add your own data to create a balance sheet for your company or department. You can use the Loan Amortization template to view loan payments over the course of a designated time.

You can also turn any existing worksheet into a template, or customize one of Excel's pre-made templates to suit your own needs. For example, you

might take the pre-made Sales Invoice template, and add or subtract various elements to create a workbook unique to your sales force.

By default, Excel stores pre-made templates in the Templates folder, a subfolder of the Documents and Settings folder. You can access the templates using the Templates dialog box. Excel templates use the .xlt file extension.

See also>>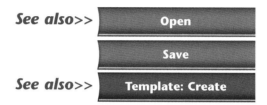

Open

Save

See also>> Template: Create

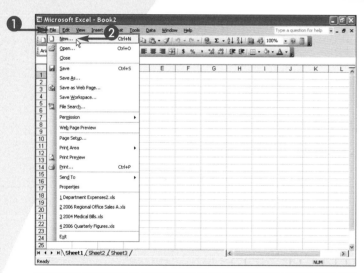

1 Click File.

2 Click New.

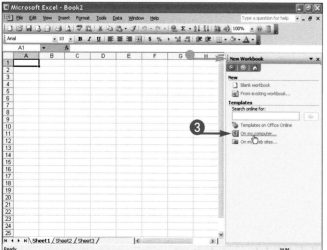

● The New Workbook task pane opens.

3 Click the On my computer link.

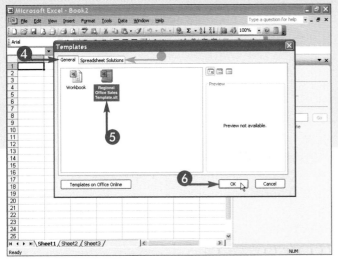

The Templates dialog box opens.

④ Click the General tab.

Excel displays any saved templates you create in the General tab.

● To choose a pre-made template, click the Spreadsheet Solutions tab.

⑤ Click the template you want to use.

⑥ Click OK.

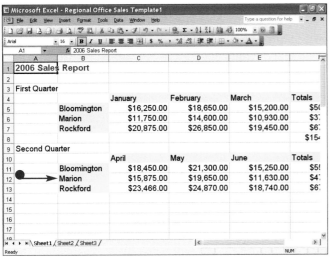

Excel opens the template file.

● You can make changes to the data and formatting as needed.

TIPS

Did You Know?

You can find five pre-made templates in the Spreadsheet Solutions tab of the Templates dialog box: Balance Sheet, Expense Statement, Loan Amortization, Sales Invoice, and Timecard. The template names describe the focus of each template. If the preview feature is activated in the Templates dialog box, you can also preview what a template looks like before assigning it to a workbook.

Caution

If the template you want to apply is not listed in the Templates dialog box, you may have to look for the file in another location. You cannot conduct a search from the Templates dialog box. Instead, consider relocating the template file to the Templates folder. You can find the folder using the following path: C:\Documents and Settings*user_name*\ Application Data\Microsoft\Templates (substitute your user name for *user_name* in the path).

TEMPLATE:
Create a Workbook Template

If you find yourself using the same formatting and worksheet elements over and over again, you can turn the information into a template file to reuse with other workbooks. For example, you can create templates for specific tasks and projects. If you use a worksheet for tracking monthly sales information and distribute it to other users, you can reuse it each month by simply plugging in new data as needed.

Templates include formatting, styles, and standardized data, such as text labels and formulas. When you create a template file, Excel stores not only the formatting and data information, but also the number of worksheets in the workbook, protected and hidden data, page formats and defined print areas, graphics, charts, data validation settings, and custom toolbars.

Excel templates are saved in the .xlt file format. You can store your templates in the Templates folder for handy application later. The Templates folder is a subfolder of the Documents and Settings folder. By storing templates in the default Templates folder, you make them easily accessible in the Templates dialog box when you are ready to apply a template.

See also>>

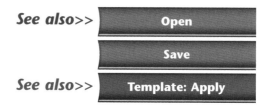

See also>> Template: Apply

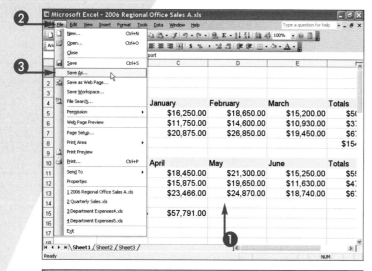

① Create a workbook containing all the elements and formatting you want to use as a template.

To create a worksheet template, create a workbook with only one sheet.

② Click File.

③ Click Save As.

The Save As dialog box opens.

④ Click the Save as type drop-down arrow.

⑤ Click Template.

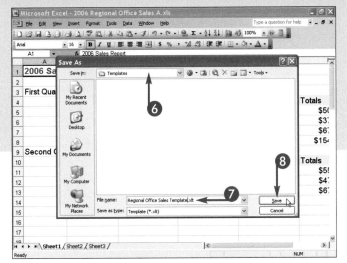

6 Navigate to the folder in which you want to store the template.

To keep your templates manageable, store them in the default Templates folder, which appears automatically when you activate the Template file type.

7 Type a filename for the template.

8 Click Save.

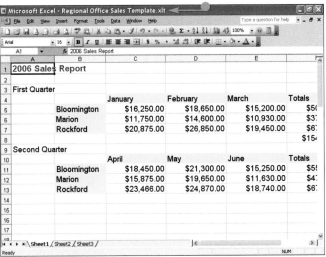

Excel saves the template file.

● The .xlt extension is added to the filename in the Title bar.

TIPS

Attention

The default Templates folder works best for templates you want to access through Excel's Templates dialog box. Any template you place in the default Templates folder appears in the Templates dialog box. The full path to the Templates folder is C:\Documents and Settings*user_name*\Application Data\Microsoft\Templates (substitute your user name for *user_name* in the path).

Attention

When creating a template file in the Save As dialog box, always click the Save as Type drop-down arrow and click the template file type. Simply typing **.xlt** after the filename does not save the file in the template format.

TEXT TO SPEECH:
Read Back Worksheet Cells

You can use the Text to Speech tool to read back the data in your worksheet cells. This is particularly helpful if you need to proofread your work or compare spreadsheet data between two spreadsheets. The Text to Speech tool reads the data in each cell of one worksheet while you compare it to another. If you hear an error, you can stop the procedure and make any necessary corrections.

To use the Text to Speech tool, you must have a sound card and speakers installed with your

computer. If this is the first time you have ever used the feature, Excel may first prompt you to install it.

The Text to Speech toolbar includes several buttons for controlling how Excel reads back your data. For example, you can choose to play back the data by columns or rows. As the feature reads the data in a cell, Excel highlights that cell in the worksheet.

See also>> **Text to Speech**

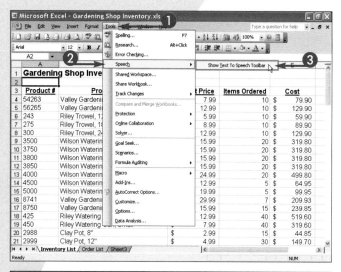

① Click Tools.

② Click Speech.

③ Click Show Text To Speech Toolbar.

The Text To Speech toolbar appears.

④ Select the cells that you want Excel to read back.

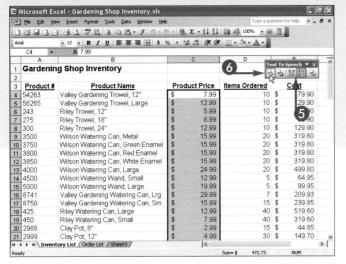

5️⃣ Click either the By Rows or By Columns button to specify the order in which you want Excel to read the cells.

6️⃣ Click the Speak Cells button.

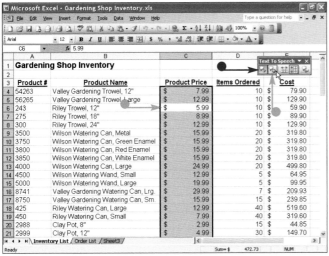

🔴 Excel begins reading the data in each cell, highlighting the cells as it reads them.

🔴 To stop and make a correction, click the Stop Speaking button.

⚫ To continue again, click the Speak Cells button.

TIPS

Did You Know?

You can have the cells read back to you as you type in data. Click the Speak On Enter button (🔲) on the Text to Speech toolbar. Any time you type data and press Enter, the Text to Speech feature reads back the contents of the cell. To turn the option off again, click the Speak On Enter button again.

Customize It

You can set up the Text to Speech feature to utilize another voice besides the default voice. To do this, click the Tools menu, click Speech, and then click Speech Recognition. This opens the Language bar. Click the Tools button, and then click Options to open the Speech Input dialog box. Click the Advanced Speech button to open the Speech Properties dialog box. Click the Text to Speech tab and click the Voice Selection drop-down arrow to choose another voice.

TOOLBARS:
Display and Hide Toolbars

You can use the Excel toolbars to quickly activate common tasks and commands with a click of a button. By default, the Standard and Formatting toolbars appear side by side at the top of the program window. Because of the shared space, lesser-used buttons may not appear on the toolbars but remain hidden from view in the Toolbar Options drop-down list.

You can turn on the full toolbar display and view each of the default toolbars entirely. You may prefer to keep the toolbars fully displayed if you find yourself frequently looking for specific toolbar buttons to activate.

You can also choose which toolbars to display at any given time while working in Excel. For example, you may want to hide all the toolbars to free up on-screen workspace, or you may prefer to turn on just the ones you use the most. You can control which toolbars appear on-screen using the View menu.

See also>> **Customize**

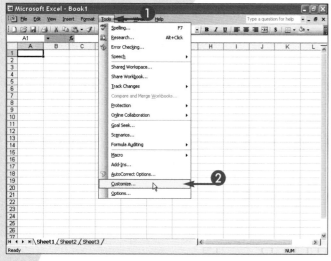

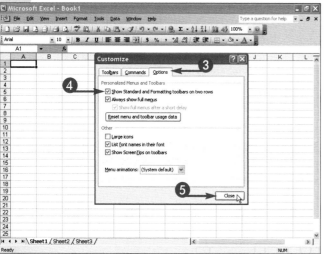

Display Full Toolbars

① Click Tools.

② Click Customize.

The Customize dialog box opens.

③ Click the Options tab if it does not already appear in front.

④ Select Show Standard and Formatting Toolbars on Two Rows.

⑤ Click Close.

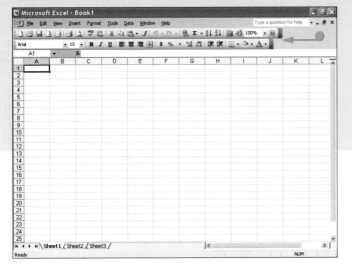

● The toolbars appear on separate rows, displaying all the available buttons.

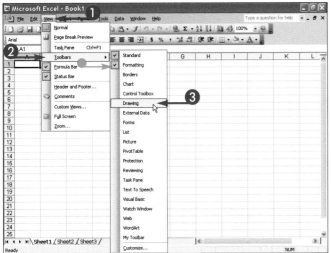

Hide or Display a Toolbar

① Click View.

② Click Toolbars.

③ Click the toolbar you want to display or hide.

● A checkmark next to the toolbar name indicates the toolbar is displayed.

Did You Know?

If two toolbars appear side by side, you can view the hidden buttons using the Toolbar Options button — the arrow button at the far right of any toolbar. Click the Toolbar Options button to display a menu of buttons that are not currently visible on the toolbar. Then click the button you want to activate. By default, the toolbars show only the most recently used buttons. You can also click Show Buttons on Two Rows to turn on the full toolbar display.

Customize It

You can find out what a particular button does in Excel by using ScreenTips. If you move your mouse pointer over a button on any Excel toolbar, a ScreenTip box appears identifying the button's name. By default, the ScreenTips feature is turned on in Excel 2003. To turn the feature on or off, click the Tools menu and then click Customize to open the Customize dialog box. Click the Options tab and then select the Show ScreenTips on Toolbars check box (□ changes to ✓) to turn the feature on or off.

TRACK AND REVIEW:
Keep Track of Workbook Changes

If you work in an environment in which you share your Excel workbooks with others, you can use the tracking and reviewing features to help you keep track of who adds changes to the file. For example, you can see what edits others have made, including formatting changes and data additions or deletions.

The tracking feature changes the color for each person's edits, making it easy to see who changed what in the workbook. As each person works with the file, Excel highlights each change in the workbook by surrounding the changed cell in a colored border. You can see details about the change when you move the mouse pointer over the cell. A comment box appears with a description of the change. When you review

the workbook, you can choose to accept or reject the changes.

When you activate the tracking feature, Excel automatically enables the workbook sharing feature, allowing you to share the file over a network with other users, if needed. In a network scenario, two or more users can access the file at the same time.

See also>>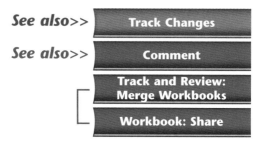

Track Changes

See also>> **Comment**

Track and Review: Merge Workbooks

Workbook: Share

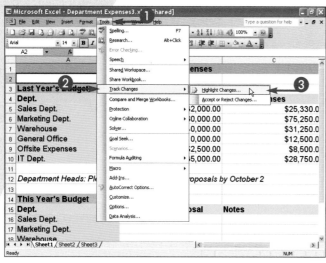

Turn On Tracking

1 Click Tools.

2 Click Track Changes.

3 Click Highlight Changes.

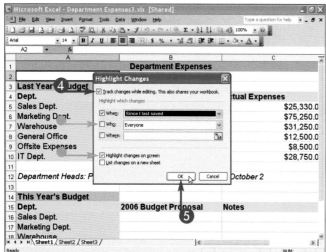

The Highlight Changes dialog box opens.

4 Select Track Changes While Editing.

This option automatically creates a shared workbook file if you have not already activated the share workbook feature.

● You can choose when, who, or where you track changes using these options.

● Leave this option selected to view changes in the file.

5 Click OK.

342

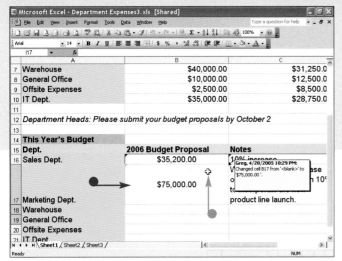

Excel's tracking feature is activated.

● Excel highlights any changes in the worksheet.

● To view details about a change and the author, move the mouse pointer over the highlighted cell.

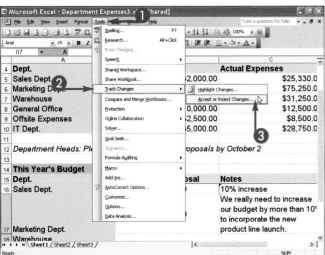

Review Changes

① Click Tools.

② Click Track Changes.

③ Click Accept or Reject Changes.

TIPS

Did You Know?

When you display the Highlight Changes dialog box by clicking Tools, Track Changes, and then Highlight Changes, you can activate the List Changes on a New Sheet option. This opens a special History sheet in the workbook for viewing each edit. The History sheet breaks out the details of each edit, including the author, date, and time. You can use the filters to change the list of edits. When you save the workbook, the History sheet is deleted.

Did You Know?

If sharing a workbook for review through e-mail, you can use the Reviewing toolbar to help you track and review changes in the file. To view the toolbar, click View, Toolbars, and then Reviewing. The toolbar features buttons for adding and viewing comments, adding annotations, e-mailing, and creating a Microsoft Outlook task.

TRACK AND REVIEW:
Keep Track of Workbook Changes (Continued)

After you activate the reviewing process, Excel goes through each change in the worksheet and allows you to accept or reject the edit using the Accept or Reject Changes dialog box. You can choose to accept a single change, accept all the changes in the file, reject a change, or reject all the changes.

As you review the file, Excel moves through each edit on the workbook, displaying details about the change. This includes who made the change, the

date and time of the edit, and what sort of change occurred in the cell. The affected cell is highlighted in the workbook as well as described in the Accept or Reject Changes dialog box.

When the review is complete, you can turn the tracking feature off. Turning off the tracking feature returns the file to its original status. This removes the [Shared] notation in the title bar next to the filename.

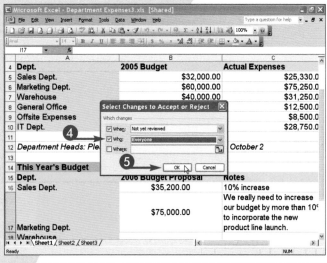

The Select Changes to Accept or Reject dialog box opens.

④ Select which changes you want to view.

⑤ Click OK.

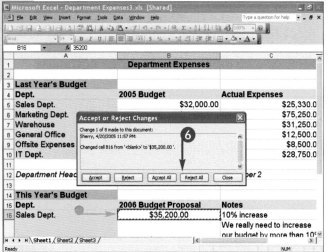

The Accept or Reject Changes dialog box opens.

● Excel highlights the first change in the worksheet.

⑥ Specify an action for each edit.

Click the Accept button to add the change to the final worksheet.

To reject the change, click the Reject button.

Click the Accept All or Reject All buttons to accept or reject all the changes at once.

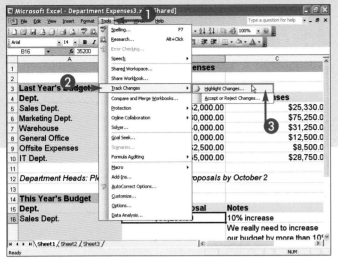

① Click Tools.

② Click Track Changes.

③ Click Highlight Changes.

The Highlight Changes dialog box opens.

④ Deselect Track Changes While Editing.

⑤ Click OK.

Excel's tracking feature is turned off.

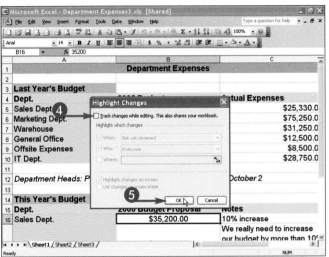

Did You Know?

There are certain edits Excel does not track or highlight. Excel's tracking feature does not keep track of changes in sheet names, inserted or deleted sheets, or hidden rows and columns. In addition, some of Excel's features do not work with shared workbooks, such as grouping data, recording and assigning macros, or inserting pictures and hyperlinks. For a complete list of changes and features supported with shared workbooks, see Excel's help files.

Customize It

You can remove a user from a shared workbook. You can open the Share Workbook dialog box and view which users are using the file. See the technique "Workbook: Share Workbooks" to learn how to access the dialog box. You can then remove a user by clicking his name and clicking the Remove button.

TRACK AND REVIEW:
Merge Workbooks

You can merge shared workbooks to create a single final file incorporating every user's input. For example, if each user saves the same file with a different name, you can incorporate all the versions of the file into one workbook to include everyone's edits to the data.

To merge workbooks, make sure all the workbooks are stored in the same folder. To do this, each version of the shared workbook needs a unique name. For example, you can simply add a character or number to the end of the filename to create different versions of the same file.

When distributing a workbook for review, you must enable workbook sharing. After workbook sharing is enabled, you can put the file on a network to share with colleagues. The workbook sharing feature does not work on a Web server.

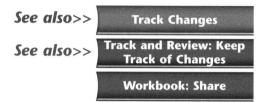

See also>> Track Changes

See also>> Track and Review: Keep Track of Changes

Workbook: Share

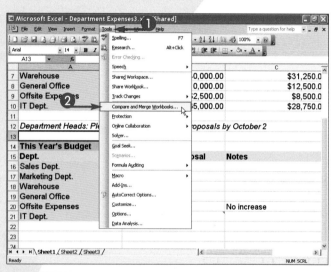

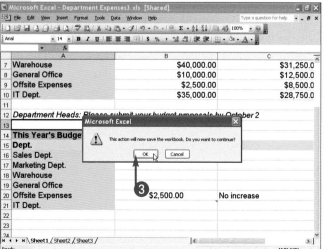

1 Click Tools.

2 Click Compare and Merge Workbooks.

Note: This feature is only available in shared workbooks.

Excel may prompt you to save the workbook.

3 Click OK.

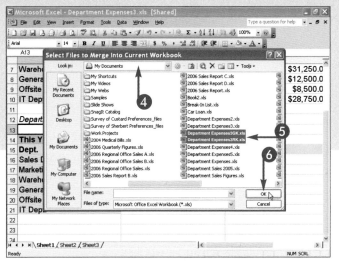

The Select Files to Merge Into Current Workbook dialog box opens.

④ Navigate to the folder containing the workbooks you want to merge.

⑤ Click the filenames you want to merge.

To click multiple files, press and hold the Ctrl key while clicking filenames.

⑥ Click OK.

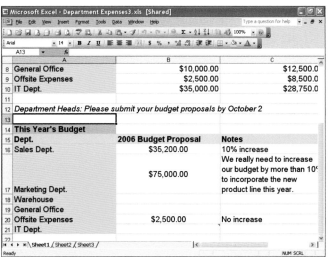

Excel merges all the workbooks into one.

In this example, other users' input is incorporated into the workbook.

TIPS

Change It

To turn off workbook sharing, open the Share Workbook dialog box by clicking Tools and then Share Workbook. Deselect the Allow Changes by More Than One User at the Same Time check box (☑ changes to ☐). Click OK and Excel turns off the sharing feature. If you plan on using the same file to collaborate again, you must turn the workbook sharing feature back on before distributing the file. To learn more about workbook sharing, see the technique "Workbook: Share Workbooks."

Caution

When two or more users are working on a shared workbook at the same time and attempt to make changes to the same cell, the Resolve Conflicts dialog box appears. You can choose to accept your own changes over the other user's changes. You may need to consult with the other user before determining which changes to keep or disregard.

UNDO AND REDO:
Use the Undo and Redo Commands

You can use Excel's Undo and Redo commands to make quick fixes of your edits and Excel actions. For example, if you accidentally delete a cell's contents, you can undo the deletion using the Undo command. If you prefer to keep the deletion instead, you can Redo the deletion action again.

When using Undo and Redo, Excel keeps track of your actions and edits. You can undo and redo up to 16 actions. For example, you can use the Undo command to undo the previous action, or the last four actions. You cannot, however, choose to undo the fourth action down the list without undoing the

other three recent actions as well. The same is true with the Redo command.

You can easily access the Undo and Redo commands using the buttons on the Standard toolbar. Both buttons also feature a drop-down arrow that, when clicked, reveals a list of previous actions. You can also use the keyboard shortcut keys to activate the commands, or you can find the commands on the Edit menu.

See also>>   Undo and Redo

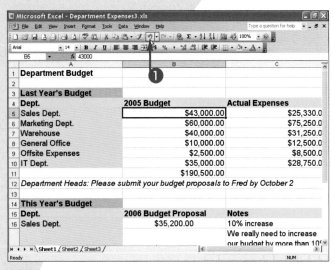

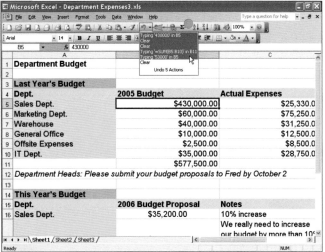

Use Undo

① Click the Undo button.

Excel immediately undoes the previous action.

Note: You can also click the Edit menu and then Undo or press Ctrl+Z to undo an action.

● To view a list of actions, click the Undo button's drop-down arrow, and then click the actions to undo.

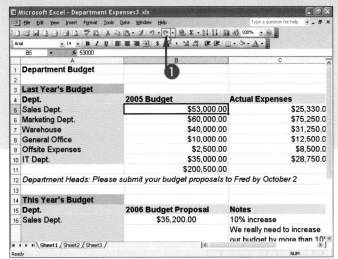

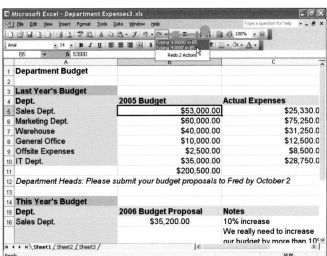

Use Redo

1 Click the Redo button.

Excel immediately reapplies the previous action.

Note: *You can also click the Edit menu and then Redo or press Ctrl+Y to redo the action.*

● To view a list of actions, click the Redo button's drop-down arrow, and then click the actions to redo.

Did You Know?

When you redo all the actions that were undone, Excel changes the Redo command on the Edit menu to the Repeat command. This allows you to repeat the actions again, if needed. Some actions cannot be repeated, such as applying a function in a cell. For any actions that cannot be repeated, Excel displays the command as Can't Repeat on the Edit menu.

More Options

You cannot use the Undo command to undo a worksheet deletion. If you delete a sheet, it is permanently removed from the workbook. To retrieve it, you must exit the workbook without saving your changes.

U

VIEW:
Change Worksheet Views

You can change the way in which you view your worksheet data in Excel. Excel offers several view modes you can use to zoom in and view your data, preview it for printing, or display the worksheet without a lot of program elements surrounding it. You can use Normal view and Full Screen view modes to toggle your overall view of a worksheet. You can use Page Break Preview to see how page breaks affect your worksheets.

By default, Normal view displays your worksheet along with all the program control elements, such as the toolbars. You can switch to Full Screen view to see only the worksheet without all the toolbars and title bar. Instead, you view the worksheet with only

the scroll bars and menu bar available. Full Screen view allows you to see more of your worksheet data, while Normal view includes all the tools you need to work with your worksheet.

Page Break Preview displays all the page breaks occurring in your worksheet. You can also use this view to make adjustments to page breaks.

See also>>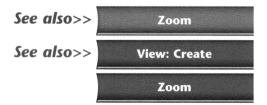

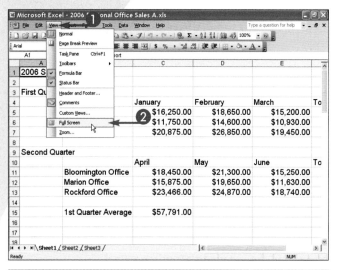

View Full Screen

① Click View.

② Click Full Screen.

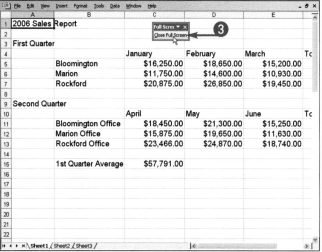

Excel switches to Full Screen view and displays the Full Screen toolbar.

③ When finished viewing your worksheet, click Close Full Screen.

Excel returns you to Normal view mode.

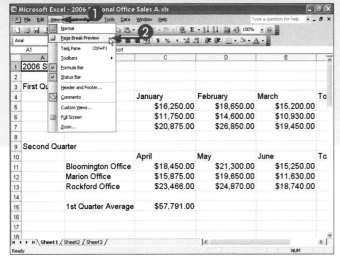

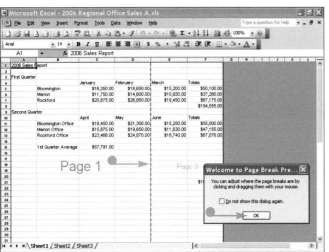

View Page Breaks

1 Click View.

2 Click Page Break Preview.

● A prompt box may appear when using Page Break Preview the first time. Click OK to continue.

Excel displays all the page breaks for the worksheet as dotted lines.

● You can drag a page break line to move the page break.

Note: *To return to Normal view again, click View and then Normal.*

Did You Know?
You can use Excel's Zoom command to magnify your view of worksheet cells, making data appear larger or smaller in the view. To quickly zoom your view, simply click the Zoom drop-down arrow on the Standard toolbar and click a zoom percentage. To learn more about using the Zoom command, see the technique "Zoom: Change the View Magnification."

More Options
You can also insert more page breaks in Page Break Preview, or delete breaks you do not want. To add a new page break, select the row or column below or to the right of where you want a new break, right-click, and then click Insert Page Break. To delete a page break, you can simply drag it off the view area. To remove all manual page breaks, you can right-click the worksheet and click Reset All Page Breaks.

VIEW:
Create a Custom View

You can use Excel's Custom View feature to save the appearance of a worksheet, including all the view and print settings assigned to the workbook. This feature is helpful if you have a large Excel spreadsheet and find yourself constantly scrolling around to view multiple cells.

For example, if you use AutoFilter to view portions of your Excel database list, you can save a filtered view as a custom view. If you filter the list in two or three ways, you can save each as a custom view, making it easy to return to the filtered data.

A custom view is similar to a style, but rather than save all the formatting you want to reuse, you save all the view attributes you want to apply into one

collection. You can use a custom view to store window attributes, including split screens and hidden rows and columns.

To create a custom view, first set up the worksheet to include all the view elements you want to save. For example, if you want to save an AutoFilter view, filter the database list first. Then you can assign the view a name and store it in the Custom View dialog box.

See also>>

View: Change

Zoom

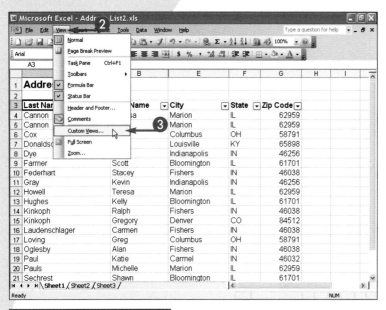

Create a Custom View

1 Set up the worksheet with the view attributes you want to store.

2 Click View.

3 Click Custom Views.

The Custom Views dialog box appears.

4 Click Add.

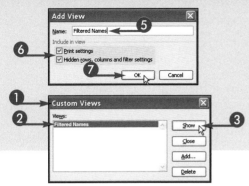

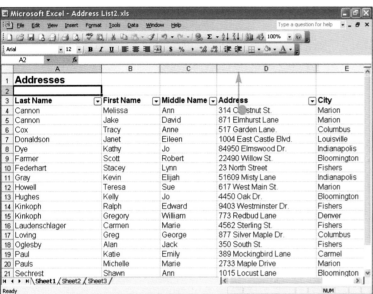

The Add View dialog box appears.

⑤ Type a name for the view.

⑥ Select which options you want to include.

⑦ Click OK.

Excel saves the view.

Display a Custom View

① Open the Custom Views dialog box.

Note: See the previous steps to learn how to open the dialog box.

② Click the view you want to display.

③ Click Show.

Excel displays the view.

● In this example, Excel displays the previously hidden rows.

Did You Know?

You can also use a custom view when you need to print a worksheet without certain columns showing, yet keep the same columns in view when working on the data. You can create two different custom views and use one for making printouts. For the printed view, simply hide the necessary columns and save the view as a custom view. For the other view, unhide the columns and save as another custom view, giving it a unique name.

More Options

To delete a custom view you no longer want to store with your workbook, open the Custom View dialog box (click View and then Custom Views). Click the view you want to delete and then click the Delete button. Excel permanently removes the saved view.

WATCH WINDOW:
Add a Watch Window

The longer your worksheet becomes, the more difficult it is to keep important cells and ranges in view as you scroll around the worksheet. For example, you may want to see the formula results in a cell at the very top of your worksheet while you make changes to the data referenced in the formula at the bottom of your worksheet. You can use a Watch Window to keep the cell containing the formula in view no matter how much you scroll.

You can also use the Watch Window to view cells in other worksheets or sheets in a linked workbook.

The Watch Window is simply a mini-window that floats on top of the worksheet regardless of where you scroll. When you no longer need to keep a

cell or range in view, you can close the Watch Window. The Watch Window behaves much like other Excel toolbars, which means you can move it around on-screen or dock it on any side of the program window. You can resize and move the window to suit your own work needs.

See also>>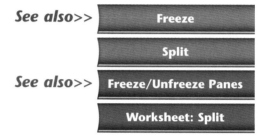

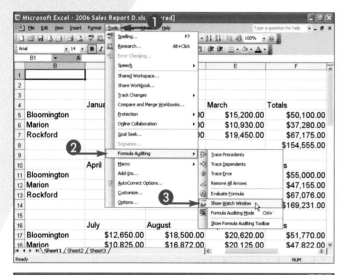

① Click Tools.

② Click Formula Auditing.

③ Click Show Watch Window.

The Watch Window opens.

④ Click Add Watch.

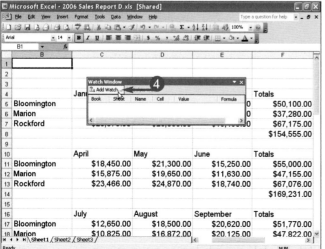

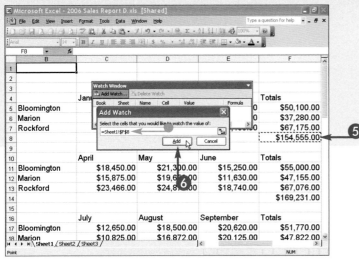

5 Select the cell or range you want to watch.

● You can also type the cell reference.

6 Click Add.

Note: You can add multiple cells to the Watch Window.

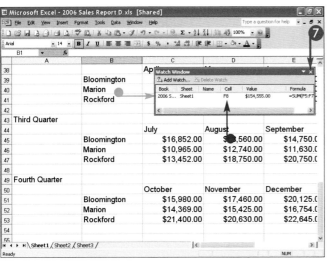

● Excel adds the cells to the Watch Window, including any values or formulas within the cells.

If you scroll away from the original cells, the Watch Window always displays the cell contents.

● To return to the original cell, double-click the cell name.

7 Click the Close button to close the Watch Window.

Remove It

To remove a cell from the Watch Window, click the cell name and then click the Delete Watch button. Excel immediately removes the cell from the window. You can add more cells by clicking the Add button and selecting the cell you want to add to the window.

More Options

To move the window, simply click and drag the window's title bar. You can reposition the window anywhere on-screen. You can also dock the window to appear with the toolbars at the top of the Excel program window. You can also resize the columns within the Watch Window. Move the mouse pointer over a column in the Watch Window and drag to resize the column.

WEB QUERY:
Run a Web Query

You can use a Web Query to import data from the Internet to use in your worksheets. A query is an action that retrieves data for analysis in Excel. Excel's Web Query feature is commonly used to extract live financial information off of Web sites to use in Excel. However, you can also use the feature to download other types of tabular information, such as class lists and schedules, timetables, inventory lists, and more.

To use Excel's Web Query, you must first know the hyperlink or Web address of the page containing the information you want to copy. Web Query works by

extracting table information from the Web page's HTML coding and importing it into your worksheet structure.

You must be connected to the Internet to perform a Web Query. Any time you copy data from someone's Web site, make sure you use it in compliance with the author's guidelines.

See also>>

Database

Web Toolbar

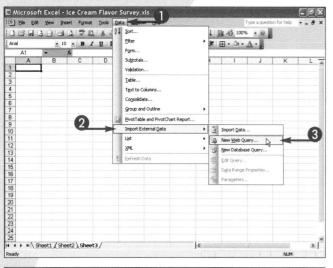

Run a Web Query

① Click Data.

② Click Import External Data.

③ Click New Web Query.

The New Web Query dialog box opens and displays your default browser home page.

④ Type the URL for the Web site you want to query.

⑤ Click Go or press Enter.

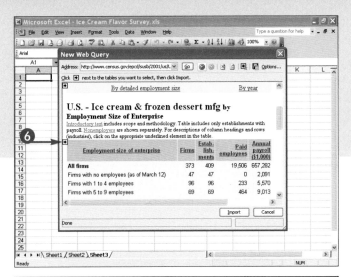

The New Web Query dialog box displays the page.

⑥ Click the arrow next to the table you want to select.

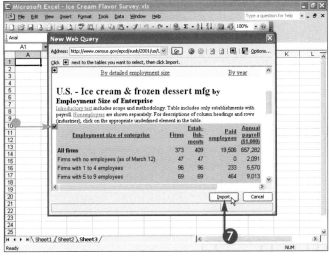

● The table is selected for importing, as indicated by the check mark.

You can continue selecting other tables, as needed.

⑦ Click Import.

More Options

You can use the Web Query Options dialog box to determine what formatting and other import settings are assigned to the data. When viewing the New Web Query dialog box, start by clicking the Options button to open the Web Query Options dialog box. Click any options you want to apply to the data you import. Click OK and Excel returns you to the New Web Query dialog box to finish importing the data.

Try This

You can also download stock quotes into Excel. You can use your Internet connection and Excel's Research task pane to look up stock quotes online. Click Tools and Research to open the pane, and then select MSN Money Stock Quotes. Type the stock ticker you want to look up and start the search. After the stock quote is located, you can click the Insert Price button to insert the data into your worksheet cell.

WEB QUERY:
Run a Web Query (Continued)

Viewing a Web page in the New Web Query window is very similar to a browser window. Each little yellow box with a black arrow indicates an area on the Web page that can be imported into Excel. You can select the arrows to designate which tables of information you want to import. You can import multiple tables, if needed.

After you make your selections, the Import Data dialog box prompts you to designate a location for the imported data. You can import the information into a new worksheet, or place it into the existing worksheet.

After you run a Web query, you can perform all kinds of analysis on the data you import, such as creating new formulas, changing the existing values, and so on. You can save the query to use again at a later time. Queries are saved with the IQY file extension. By default, Excel saves queries to the Queries folder unless specified otherwise.

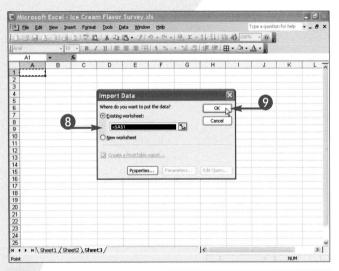

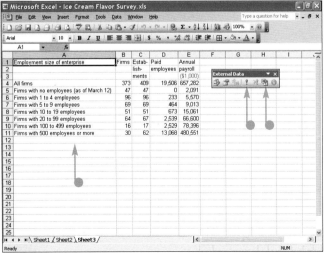

⑧ Designate where you want to insert the imported data.

You can import the data into the existing worksheet.

You can also import the data into a new sheet.

⑨ Click OK.

● Excel imports the data and displays the External Data toolbar.

You can make changes to the data to perform your own analysis, such as changing data and creating your own formulas.

● Any time you want to refresh the data, click the Refresh or Refresh All buttons.

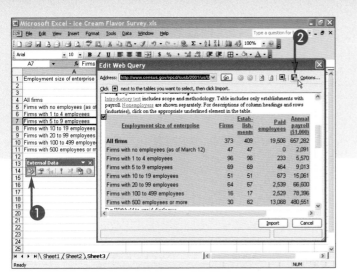

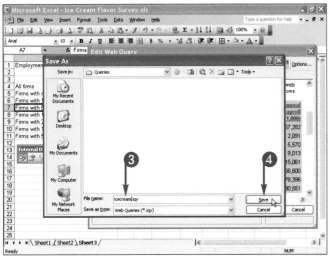

Save a Query

① Click the Edit Query button on the External Data toolbar.

Note: *If the External Data toolbar is not displayed, click View, Toolbars, and then External Data to display the toolbar.*

The Edit Web Query dialog box opens.

② Click the Save Query button.

The Save As dialog box opens.

③ Type a name for the query.

④ Click Save.

Excel saves the query.

TIPS

Did You Know?

When you save a query, you can access it again with other Excel files. To do so, first open the workbook where you want to run the saved query. Next, click Data and then Import Data. The Select Data Source dialog box opens. Click the query name and click the Open button. Designate where you want to insert the imported data and click OK. Excel runs the saved query in the new workbook.

More Options

You can change the query's refresh options and other properties using the External Data Range Properties dialog box. For example, you can set how often you want the data to refresh, as well as make adjustments to the data formatting and layout. You can also adjust column width or control whether you want to reserve formatting or not. To open the dialog box, click the Data Range Properties button ( ) on the External Data toolbar.

WEB TOOLBAR:
Use the Web Toolbar Tools

Using your Internet connection, you can access the Web directly from Excel using the Web toolbar features. The Web toolbar is just one of many helpful toolbars in Excel. When displayed, the Web toolbar appears by default directly below the Standard and Formatting toolbars. Like any Excel toolbar, you can turn the toolbar display on or off as needed.

You can use the Web toolbar to open a URL you type in, open your default home page, or display a page from your Favorites folder. When you activate any of the toolbar features, your default Web browser opens to display the actual Web page. You can use the

Copy and Paste commands to copy and paste Web page information into your Excel worksheets.

The toolbar also includes tools for conducting a Web search, refreshing a page, and stopping a page from loading. You must be connected to the Internet to use the Web toolbar features.

See also>> Web Toolbar

See also>> Save: Save Worksheet as Web Page

Web Query: Run

① Click View.

② Click Toolbars.

③ Click Web.

● The Web toolbar appears.

● To view your default home page, click the Start Page button.

● To perform a Web search, click the Search the Web button.

● To view your list of bookmarked pages, click the Favorites button and then click the page you want to view.

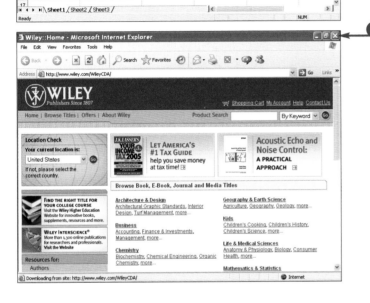

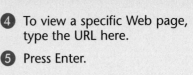

④ To view a specific Web page, type the URL here.

⑤ Press Enter.

Your default browser opens and displays the page.

⑥ Click the Close button to close the browser window and return to Excel.

More Options

You can click the Show Only Web Toolbar button () on the Web toolbar to hide all the other Excel toolbars but keep the Web toolbar in view. To display all the other toolbars again, simply click the Show Only Web Toolbar button again. The button toggles between hiding and displaying the other Excel toolbars.

More Options

You can customize any of the Excel toolbars to show just the buttons you use the most. For example, you might want to add buttons to the Web toolbar for previewing and publishing Web pages. To learn more about creating custom toolbars, see the technique "Customize: Customize a Toolbar."

WORDART:
Insert a WordArt Object

You can use the Microsoft Office WordArt feature to turn text into interesting graphic objects to use in your worksheets. For example, you can create arched text to appear over a range of data. You might also use WordArt text to create logos and other stylized graphics for your projects.

The WordArt Gallery dialog box offers 30 WordArt styles you can apply. You can create text graphics that bend and twist, or display subtle shadings of color. After choosing a style, you can type the text for the effect. You can use the default font suggested by the WordArt Editor, or you can change the font to meet your own project needs. You can also apply basic formatting and control the font size.

When you add the WordArt object to your worksheet, you can move and resize it. Like any other object you add to a worksheet, you can format and control the positioning of the WordArt.

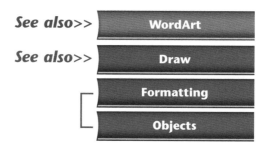

See also>>   **WordArt**

See also>>   **Draw**

Formatting

Objects

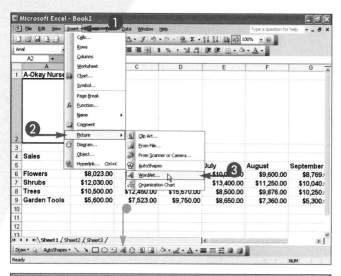

① Click Insert.

② Click Picture.

③ Click WordArt.

● You can also click the WordArt button on the Drawing toolbar.

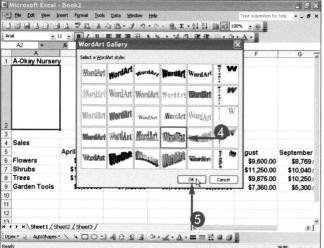

The WordArt Gallery dialog box opens.

④ Click a WordArt style.

⑤ Click OK.

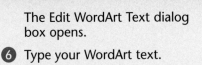

The Edit WordArt Text dialog box opens.

6 Type your WordArt text.

● You can change the font and size, and apply bold or italics using these settings.

7 Click OK.

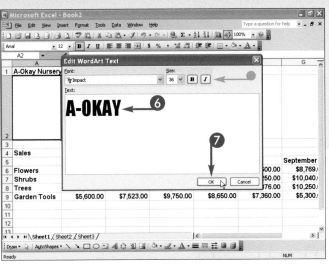

● The WordArt object is added to your worksheet and the WordArt toolbar is displayed.

You can resize or move the image, if needed.

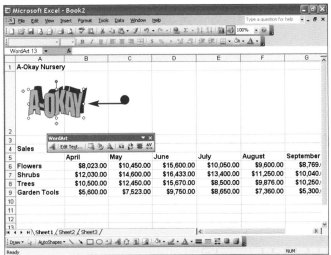

TIPS

More Options

To edit any portion of a WordArt object, whether it is the text, font, or font size, you must reopen the Edit WordArt Text dialog box. Simply double-click the WordArt object on your worksheet or click the Edit Text button on the WordArt toolbar. After you open the Edit WordArt Text dialog box, you can make changes to the existing text or type all new text for the effect.

More Options

You can click the WordArt Gallery button (⬚) on the WordArt toolbar to quickly access the Gallery dialog box and select another style to apply. You can also click the WordArt Shape button (⬚) and choose another shape for the text. For example, you may want to experiment with several styles and text shapes to find just the right one for your worksheet needs.

WORKBOOK:
Arrange Workbook Windows

You can open two or more workbooks and view them simultaneously on-screen using the Arrange Windows command. For example, you might want to view the data in three different workbooks to check your figures or formatting.

When using the Arrange Windows command, you can choose from four display modes for viewing two or more workbooks within the Excel program window: tiled, horizontal, vertical, or cascade. Tiled windows display the workbooks like a mosaic of tiles across the screen. Horizontal windows display the workbooks in horizontal panes on-screen, while vertical windows display the workbooks as vertical panes across the screen. Cascade windows display the workbooks in a stacked, cascading display, with overlapping windows.

Only one workbook can be active at a time in Excel. When viewing multiple workbooks, the current workbook's title bar always appears in a darker color than the other open workbooks.

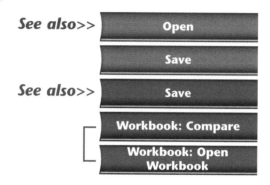

See also>> Open

Save

See also>> Save

Workbook: Compare

Workbook: Open Workbook

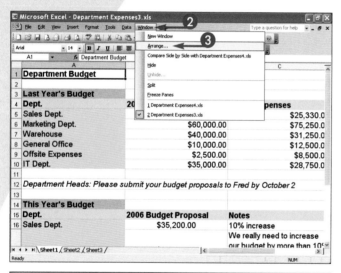

1 Open two or more workbooks.

2 Click Window.

3 Click Arrange.

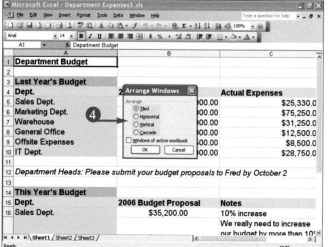

The Arrange Windows dialog box appears.

4 Click a display mode.

Tiled arranges the workbooks like mosaic tiles across the screen.

Horizontal arranges the workbooks stacked horizontally.

Vertical arranges the workbooks vertically.

Cascade arranges the workbooks stacked on top of each other in a cascading display.

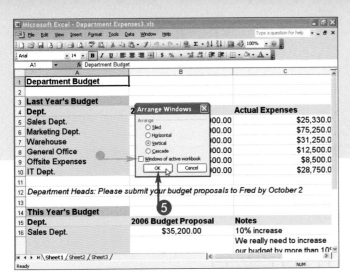

● You can select this option to display only the sheets in the active workbook.

⑤ Click OK.

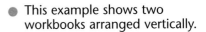

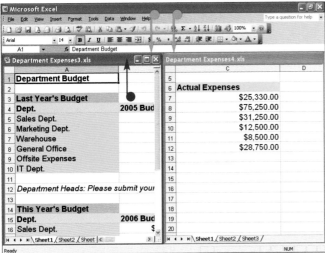

● This example shows two workbooks arranged vertically.

● The active workbook's title bar appears highlighted.

More Options

You can click a workbook to make it active, and then click the Maximize button on the workbook's toolbar to return the display to full screen mode. When you maximize one workbook to full display, all the open workbooks return to regular size as well.

Did You Know?

You can use the Split command to split a single worksheet into two panes and view them both on-screen at the same time. Both panes are scrollable, allowing you to see different portions of your worksheet. For example, you might split a long worksheet to keep the top portion in view while you scroll through the rest of the worksheet. To learn more about splitting worksheets, see the technique "Worksheet: Split a Sheet."

WORKBOOK:
Compare Workbooks

You can compare two workbooks side by side in Excel. For example, you might compare last year's sales data against the current year's figures. When you activate the Compare Side by Side command, Excel displays both workbooks stacked in the same program window.

When working with side by side workbooks, you can only make one workbook active at a time. The active workbook's title bar always appears darker blue in color. Each workbook's title bar also identifies which workbook is which, and you can use each workbook's scroll bar to move around in the active workbook.

When you activate the Compare Side by Side command, Excel also displays the Compare Side by Side toolbar. You can use the toolbar to help you

scroll simultaneously through two workbooks and view the data in each.

If more than two workbooks are open, the Compare Side by Side dialog box appears where you can choose which two open workbooks to compare.

See also>> Freeze

See also>> Open

Split

Freeze/Unfreeze

Worksheet: Split

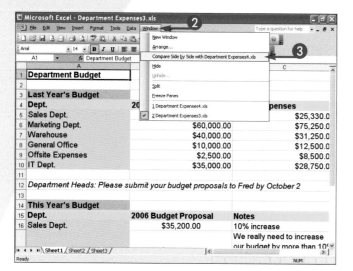

1 Open the two workbooks you want to compare.

2 Click Window.

3 Click Compare Side by Side.

The command displays the name of the second workbook.

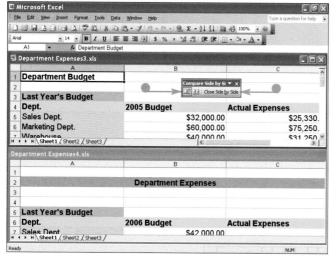

Excel displays both workbooks, along with the Compare Side by Side toolbar.

Note: *If the toolbar is not displayed, you can click Tools and Customize, and then select the Compare Side by Side check box on the Toolbars tab.*

● Click the Synchronous Scrolling button to scroll through both workbooks at the same time.

● Click here to restore the workbooks to their original window size.

WORKBOOK:
Create a New Workbook

You can start a new workbook any time you want to create a new file for your Excel data. Files you create in Excel are called *workbooks*. By default, every new workbook you open automatically contains three blank worksheets you can use to enter Excel data.

All Excel workbooks are based on a default template that contains basic formatting for creating new worksheets. For example, the default template assigns Arial as the font and 10-point as the font size. You can fine-tune any of the formatting settings to suit the way you work after you open the new workbook. You can also add and delete worksheets as needed.

The quickest way to create a new workbook is to activate the New toolbar button on the Standard toolbar. You can also use the New Workbook or Getting Started task panes to create a new workbook file.

See also>> | Open

| Save

See also>> | Save

Template

Workbook: Open Workbook

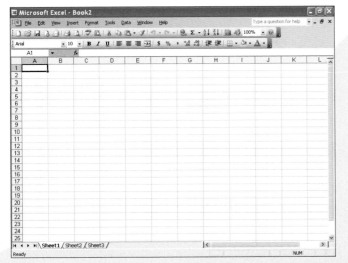

1 Click the New button on the Standard toolbar.

Note: You can also click the File menu and click New to use the New Workbook pane to start a new workbook file.

Excel opens a new, blank workbook containing three worksheets.

WORKBOOK:
Delete a Workbook

You can permanently remove any workbook you no longer use without exiting the Excel program window. For example, you may want to delete a temporary workbook you created for a quick calculation, or delete old workbooks containing outdated data.

Always open and double-check a workbook prior to removing it to be sure it does not contain important data. When you delete a workbook file, it is placed in the Windows Recycle Bin. If you accidentally delete a file you need, you can open the Recycle Bin and restore the file. If you have emptied the Recycle Bin, the file is permanently lost.

You can delete workbooks from the Open or Save As dialog boxes. After performing the deletion, you can exit the dialog boxes without opening or saving any files.

See also>>   Open
See also>>   Save
See also>>   Save

Workbook: Open Workbook

Worksheet: Delete

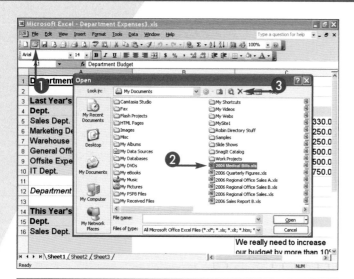

① Click the Open button on the Standard toolbar.

Note: You can also click the File menu and click Open or Save As.

The Open or Save As dialog box appears.

② Navigate to the Excel file you want to delete and click the filename.

③ Click the Delete button.

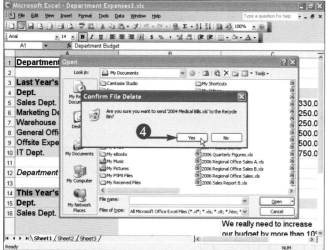

A Confirm File Delete dialog box appears.

④ Click Yes.

The workbook is deleted.

WORKBOOK:
Open a Workbook

You can open a workbook you previously worked on to continue adding or analyzing data. Regardless of whether you store a workbook in a folder on your computer's hard disk drive, or on a disk such as a CD, you can easily access files using the Open dialog box.

You can use the tools in the Open dialog box to navigate to the folder or drive where your file is stored. You can also change what type of files are displayed in the dialog box using the Files of type drop-down list. For example, you may want to list only template files or saved Web Query file types.

In addition to the Open dialog box, Excel automatically lists your most recent workbooks at the bottom of the File menu or in the Getting Started task pane. You can click any filename in the list of recent files to quickly open the workbook again.

See also>> **Open**

Save

See also>> **Save**

Workbook: Create New Workbook

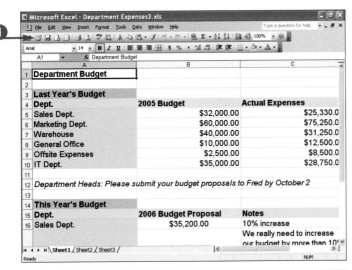

① Click the Open button on the Standard toolbar.

Note: You can also click the File menu and click Open. You can also use the Getting Started or New Workbook task panes to open existing files.

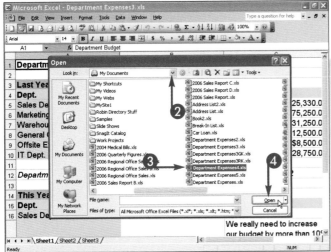

The Open dialog box appears.

② Click here to navigate and select the folder or drive where you stored the file.

③ Click the name of the file you want to open.

④ Click Open.

Excel opens the workbook.

369

WORKBOOK:
Open a Workbook Automatically

By default, Excel opens a new, blank spreadsheet every time you open the program window. If you work on the same spreadsheet every time you use Excel, you can tell the program to automatically open a particular workbook for you. This can save you the time you ordinarily spend activating the Open dialog box and looking for the workbook file or displaying the File menu to access the most recent files list.

To set up a workbook to open automatically, you must store the workbook file in the Xlstart folder. If you chose the default folders for storing Excel on your computer when you installed Excel, you can find the Xlstart folder within the Program Files folder. Look for a Microsoft Office folder within the Program Files folder. When it is opened, look for an Office11

folder. You can find the Xlstart folder within the Office11 folder. If you chose a different folder to store the Excel program files, look for the Xlstart folder in the folder you specified during installation.

You can also set up Excel to open all the workbooks in a particular folder. This is handy if you find yourself using the same two or three workbooks on a daily basis. You can use the Options dialog box to set up a folder to open at startup.

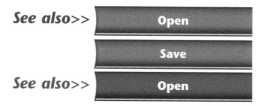

See also>>   Open

   Save

See also>>   Open

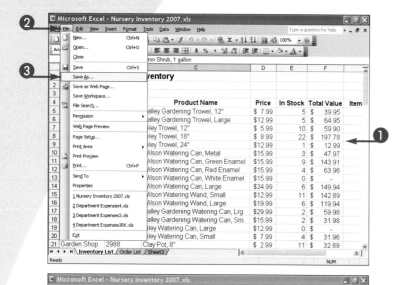

Open a File Automatically

1. Open the workbook you want to save as your default file.

2. Click File.

3. Click Save As.

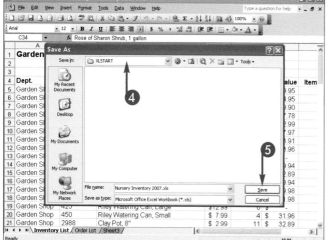

The Save As dialog box opens.

4. Navigate to the Xlstart folder.

5. Click Save.

The next time you open Excel, the specified workbook opens automatically.

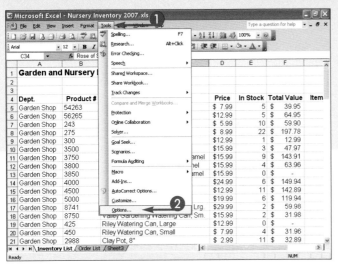

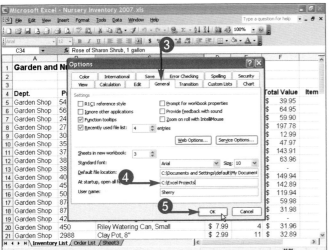

Open a Folder Automatically

1️⃣ Click Tools.

2️⃣ Click Options.

The Options dialog box opens.

3️⃣ Click the General tab.

4️⃣ Type the path to the folder containing the workbooks you want to open.

Note: Excel opens all the workbooks in the folder. Be sure to remove any unnecessary files from the folder before placing it in the startup folder.

5️⃣ Click OK.

The next time you open Excel, the specified workbooks open automatically.

Caution

Most users can find the Xlstart folder in the following location: C:\Progam Files\Microsoft Office\Office 11. If the folder is not there, you might also try locating it in the following path: C:\Documents and Settings*username*\ Application Data\Microsoft Excel. Substitute your own name for the *username* portion of the path.

More Options

You can also use the Options dialog box to assign a different default file location. When you installed Excel, the program set the My Documents folder as your default folder. Any time you open the Open or Save As dialog box, the My Documents folder and its contents are immediately displayed. If you prefer to view the contents of another folder, such as a work folder, you can change the setting in the Options dialog box. Simply type a path to the folder you want to use in the Default File Location text box.

WORKBOOK:
Share Workbooks

If you plan to share your workbooks with other users on a network, you can enable Excel's workbook sharing feature. Sharing workbooks allows multiple users to edit a workbook simultaneously. For example, you might pass along a departmental worksheet, such as an ongoing list, to two or more colleagues for additional input and edits. You might assign each colleague a different part of the worksheet to maintain.

With workbook sharing enabled, everyone who uses the workbook can change the data, change the formatting, add comments, and other editing changes. Excel can not only track the changes made to the workbook, but also keep note of which user

made which changes. Each user who works on the file must save their changes so other users can view all changes by all users. You can also use Excel's Track and Review feature to check changes made to shared workbooks.

When using shared workbooks, save the file to a network server or other location where all the users can access the file.

See also>> Track Changes

See also>> Comment

Track and Review

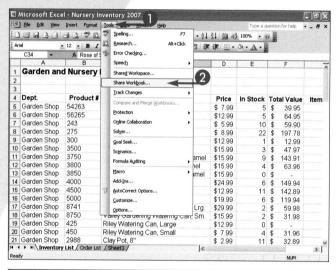

① Click Tools.

② Click Share Workbook.

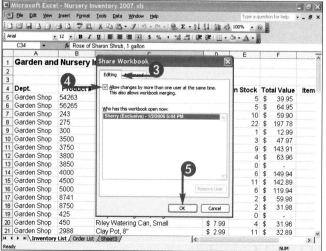

The Share Workbook dialog box opens.

③ Click the Editing tab.

④ Select the option to allow changes by more than one user at the same time.

⑤ Click OK.

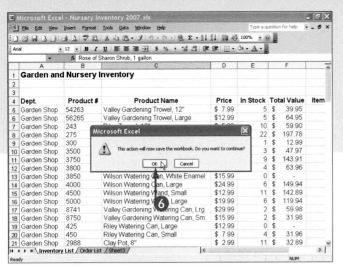

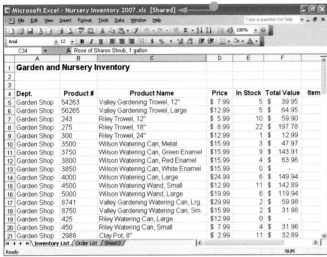

Excel prompts you to save the workbook.

Note: Be sure to save the workbook to a network location or a shared network folder so others can find and use the file.

6 Click OK.

If you have not previously saved the file, the Save As dialog box may appear. Save the file.

● Excel saves the workbook and adds the word [Shared] to the title bar.

You or other users can now make changes to the workbook.

More Options

You can use the Advanced tab in the Share Workbook dialog box to set controls for how long Excel keeps track of changes, how often the file updates, and what to do if conflicts arise between two users who change cells. Open the Share Workbook dialog box as shown in this task and click the Advanced tab. Next select any sharing options you want to apply. Click OK to exit the dialog box and apply your changes.

Caution

If two users try to save changes to the same worksheet cell at the same time, a Resolve Conflicts dialog box appears for one of the users. The person receiving the dialog box prompt must decide which change to keep in the workbook. With the shared workbook feature, all users have equal authority to resolve conflicts that occur while simultaneously using the file. To save a copy of your changes, click the Cancel button in the Resolve Conflicts dialog box, and then save the workbook under a new filename.

WORKSHEET:
Add a Sheet

You can add a worksheet to your workbook to create another sheet in which to enter data. For example, you might place quarterly data on four different worksheets in your workbook, one sheet for each quarter. If you are tracking an inventory list in Excel, you might use one sheet for the inventory list, and additional sheets for tracking invoices, customers, and vendors.

By default, every Excel workbook opens with three sheets. You can add more sheets as you need them. You can use Excel's Insert menu to add sheets to your workbook.

Depending on which worksheet is active, Excel adds a new worksheet immediately before the active worksheet. You can move worksheets to reposition their order in the workbook.

See also>>

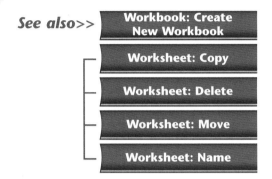

Workbook: Create New Workbook

Worksheet: Copy

Worksheet: Delete

Worksheet: Move

Worksheet: Name

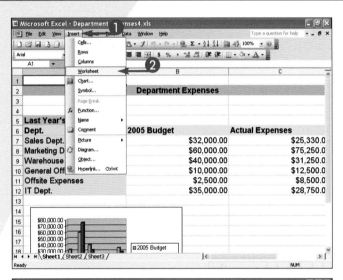

① Click Insert.

② Click Worksheet.

You can also right-click a sheet tab and click Insert. This opens the Insert dialog box where you can choose to insert a worksheet.

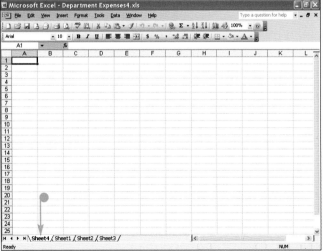

● Excel adds a new worksheet and a default worksheet name.

WORKSHEET:
Change Sheet Tab Colors

You can add color to your worksheet tabs to help distinguish one sheet from another. The color you add to a tab appears in the background, behind the worksheet tab name. When a sheet is active, the default tab color is white. When the sheet is not active, the tab color appears gray.

You can assign other colors to liven up the tabs or help you distinguish between one tab and another. For example, if you find yourself creating the same type of workbooks over and over again, you can assign tab colors to help you identify the contents of a sheet. You might assign green as the tab color for all sheets containing sales figures and red for all sheets containing budget data.

The quickest way to change the tab color is to access the sheet's shortcut menu. You can access shortcut menus in Excel by right-clicking over the feature you want to edit. You can also change tab colors by activating the Format menu and selecting the Sheet command.

See also>>

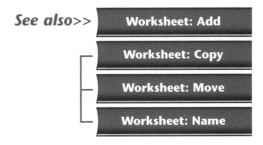

Worksheet: Add

Worksheet: Copy

Worksheet: Move

Worksheet: Name

---

① Right-click the worksheet tab you want to format.

② Click Tab Color.

Note: You can also click the Format menu, Sheet, and then Tab Color to access the Format Tab Color dialog box.

The Format Tab Color dialog box opens.

③ Click a color.

④ Click OK.

● Excel assigns the color to the tab.

To fully see the new tab color, click another worksheet tab.

Note: You can set the tab color to No Color to return it to the default state.

WORKSHEET:
Change the Worksheet Background

You can change the background of a worksheet in your Excel workbook. For example, you may want to add a picture of your latest product to the background of a sheet you use to track an inventory list, or you might insert the company logo into a worksheet tracking sales figures. You can use any picture file as a worksheet background.

When assigning an image as a worksheet background, any data the worksheet contains appears on the foreground of the image. For this reason, you must be careful that your worksheet data remains legible and easy to see on top of the background image. If you choose an image with a

busy background, your worksheet data may not be visible on top of the image.

You can make adjustments to the color of your worksheet data to make it appear more legible over a background image. For example, if the background image is very dark, you might change the data color to white or a light color that clearly shows up over the image.

See also>>

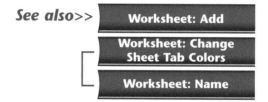

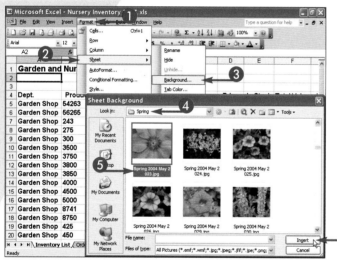

① Click Format.

② Click Sheet.

③ Click Background.

The Sheet Background dialog box opens.

④ Navigate to the drive or folder containing the image you want to use.

⑤ Click the image filename.

⑥ Click Insert.

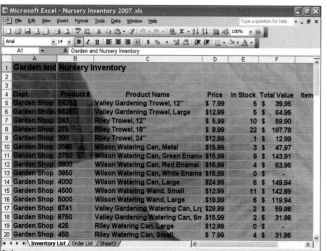

Excel adds the image to the background.

Note: If any worksheet cells have a fill color applied, the fill color covers over the background image.

Note: To remove the background, click the Format menu, Sheet, and then Delete Background.

WORKSHEET:
Copy a Sheet

You can copy a worksheet within a workbook. For example, you may want to copy a sheet to use as a starting point for new, yet similar data. If you use Excel to track quarterly sales, you might copy the worksheet that tracks the first quarter's sales figures and use it as a template for the second quarter's sales. You can then simply replace the existing data with new sales figures.

Although you can use the Copy command on the Edit menu to copy sheets, you may find it faster and easier to copy a sheet directly using the worksheet tabs. With a little help from your mouse and a keyboard press, you can quickly copy any sheet in your workbook.

You can also right-click a worksheet tab to display a shortcut menu that can access sheet-related commands and tasks.

See also>>

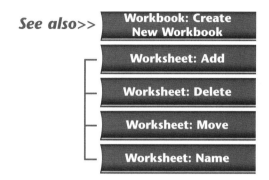

Workbook: Create New Workbook

Worksheet: Add

Worksheet: Delete

Worksheet: Move

Worksheet: Name

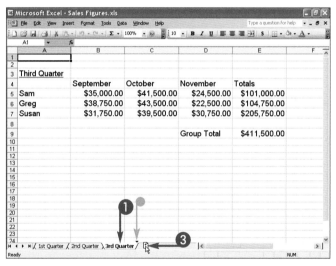

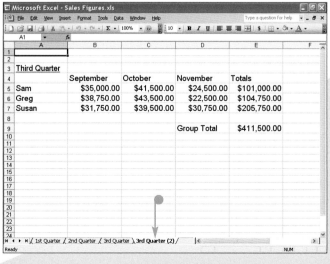

① Click the worksheet tab you want to copy.

② Press Ctrl.

The mouse pointer takes the shape of a paper sheet icon.

③ Drag the sheet to a new position in the list of sheets where you want the copy to appear.

● A small black triangle icon keeps track of the sheet's location in the group while you drag.

Note: *You can also use the Move or Copy command on the Edit menu to move or copy worksheets with the help of a dialog box.*

④ Release the mouse button.

● The worksheet is copied as a new sheet in the workbook and given a default name indicating it is a copy of another sheet.

Note: *Excel names sheet copies with a (2) after the sheet name.*

WORKSHEET:
Delete a Sheet

You can delete a worksheet you no longer need in your workbook. For example, you might want to delete an extra sheet you used for practice calculations or for holding charts and graphs you no longer need. You can delete blank sheets or sheets containing data. For example, you may want a workbook with only one worksheet. You can easily remove the other two default sheets Excel inserts into a workbook every time you start a new workbook file.

Always be sure to check the sheet's content before deleting to avoid removing important data. When you delete a worksheet, it is permanently removed from the workbook file.

The quickest and simplest way to delete a sheet is to use the sheet tab's shortcut menu. As with other

Excel shortcut menus, the sheet's shortcut menu appears when you right-click over a sheet tab. You can also use the Delete Sheet command found on the Edit menu to remove sheets.

See also>>

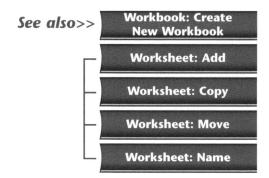

Workbook: Create New Workbook

Worksheet: Add

Worksheet: Copy

Worksheet: Move

Worksheet: Name

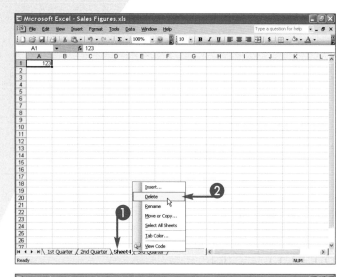

① Right-click the worksheet tab.

② Click Delete.

Note: You can also click the Edit menu and then Delete Sheet.

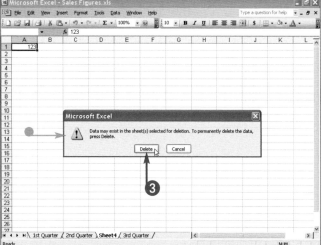

● If the worksheet is blank, Excel deletes it immediately.

● If the worksheet contains any data, Excel prompts you to confirm the deletion.

③ Click Delete.

The worksheet is deleted.

WORKSHEET:
Hide a Sheet

You can hide sheets in your workbook to help you with a variety of scenarios. For example, if you work in an area in which other people can view your computer screen, you can hide a sheet to keep confidential information out of view. You might hide a sheet to prevent the data from appearing on a printout.

If you share a workbook with other users and a sheet contains calculations other users will not find of use, you can hide the sheet in the workbook. If you use distinct names for your worksheets, no one will be able to tell whether a sheet is hidden or not.

You can apply the Hide command to hide the active worksheet. When you need to view the

sheet again, you can apply the Unhide command. If you do not want other users to unhide the worksheet, you can assign a password to the sheet to prevent changes.

See also>>

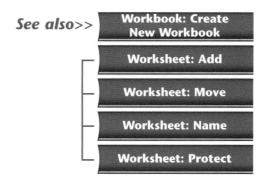

Workbook: Create New Workbook

Worksheet: Add

Worksheet: Move

Worksheet: Name

Worksheet: Protect

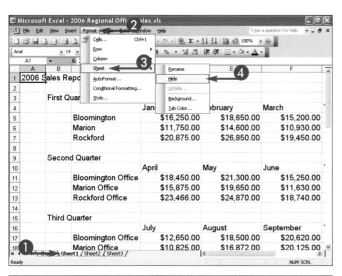

① Click the sheet you want to hide.

② Click Format.

③ Click Sheet.

④ Click Hide.

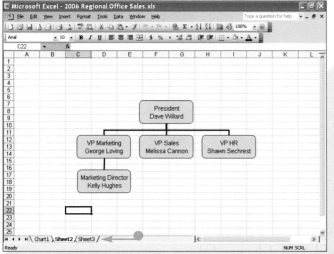

● Excel hides the worksheet.

Note: *To view the sheet again, click the Format menu, Sheet, and then Unhide.*

WORKSHEET:
Move a Sheet

You can move a worksheet within a workbook to rearrange the sheet order. For example, you may want to position the sheet you use the most as the first sheet in the workbook, or you might want to group related sheets in the workbook.

You might also move your sheets around in a particular order for printing. By default, Excel prints the sheets in the order displayed in the workbook. If you want a sheet to print first, move the sheet to the front of the tab list.

The quickest way to move a worksheet is to use the drag and drop method. You can use the mouse to

reposition sheets by dragging the worksheet tabs. You can also access the Move or Copy dialog box through the Edit menu to move sheets. You can also use this dialog box to move sheets to other workbooks.

See also>>

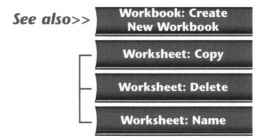

Workbook: Create New Workbook

Worksheet: Copy

Worksheet: Delete

Worksheet: Name

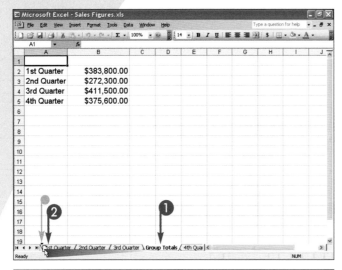

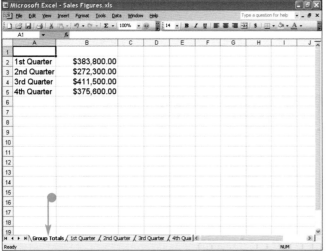

① Click the worksheet tab you want to move.

② Drag the sheet to a new position in the list of sheets.

The mouse pointer takes the shape of a paper sheet icon as you drag.

● A small black triangle icon keeps track of the sheet's location in the group while you drag.

Note: *You can also use the Move or Copy command on the Edit menu to move or copy worksheets with the help of a dialog box.*

③ Release the mouse button.

● The worksheet is moved.

WORKSHEET:
Name a Sheet

You can name your Excel worksheets to help identify their content. For example if your workbook contains four sheets, each detailing a different sales quarter, you can give each sheet a unique name, such as Quarter 1, Quarter 2, and so on. Or, if a worksheet tracks an inventory, you might type Inventory List as the sheet name.

A sheet's name appears on the sheet tab at the bottom of the workbook window. By default, Excel assigns the names Sheet 1, Sheet 2, and Sheet 3. If you add more sheets, Excel continues with the same naming process.

Giving your worksheets distinctive names can help you organize and keep track of your spreadsheet data. If you share your workbooks with other

users, naming a sheet can help everyone understand what sort of content you are entering into a sheet. Named sheets can also help you as you construct formulas in Excel. Sheet names can include up to 31 characters and spaces. You cannot use the following characters in a sheet name: [ ] * ; : ? / \.

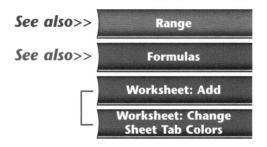

See also>> Range

See also>> Formulas

Worksheet: Add

Worksheet: Change Sheet Tab Colors

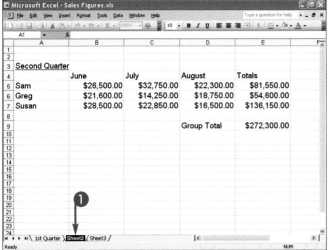

① Double-click the sheet tab you want to rename.

The current name is highlighted.

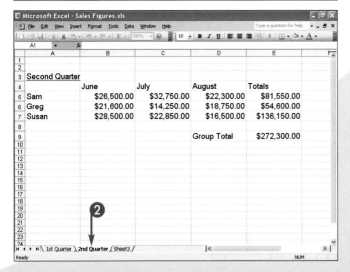

② Type a new name for the worksheet.

③ Press Enter.

Excel assigns the new worksheet name.

381

WORKSHEET:
Protect a Sheet

You can assign a password to any worksheet within a workbook to protect it from unauthorized use. Essentially, the password locks the worksheet from any changes. Other users can still view the worksheet, but the assigned password protection prevents them from making any changes to the data. For example, you might want to assign protection to prevent changes to a formula you carefully crafted or a scenario you painstakingly created.

You can use the Protect Sheet dialog box to protect a sheet's contents, objects, or scenarios. Excel's Protect Sheet options allow you to protect cell contents from any changes or overwriting, including cutting, pasting, and sorting. The feature also

protects columns and rows from being added or deleted from the sheet. It cannot prevent someone from copying and pasting the data into another workbook, however.

Whenever you assign a password to a worksheet or workbook, it is important to remember the password to use the file again or make changes to the data. Keep your Excel passwords in a safe place.

See also>>

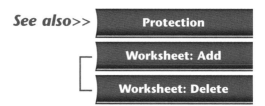

Protection

Worksheet: Add

Worksheet: Delete

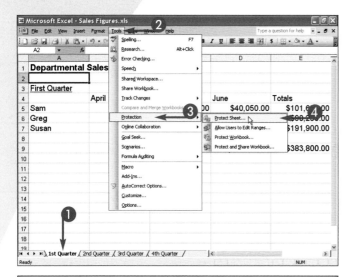

1. Click the sheet you want to protect.
2. Click Tools.
3. Click Protection.
4. Click Protect Sheet.

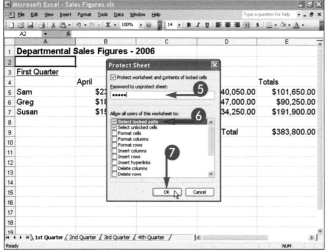

The Protect Sheet dialog box opens.

5. Type a password for the worksheet.
6. Select which elements you want to allow for changes.
7. Click OK.

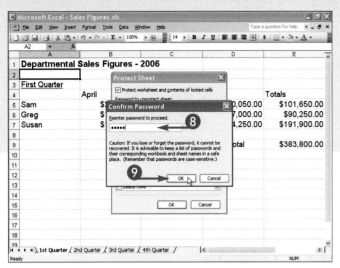

Excel prompts you to retype the password.

⑧ Retype the password exactly as you typed it in Step 5.

⑨ Click OK.

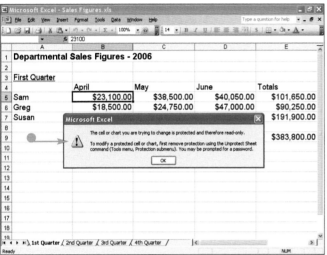

Excel locks the worksheet.

● The next time you or another user attempts to make any changes to the worksheet data, Excel displays a warning prompt about the protected data.

TIPS

Caution

If you have trouble typing in a password to reopen a protected worksheet, stop and make sure the keyboard's Caps Lock key is not on. Excel passwords are case-sensitive, so make sure you are not typing in all caps or all lowercase characters. Password protection can also inadvertently change if you save the workbook in a different file format. For example, if you save the workbook as a Web page, passwords are not saved along with the workbook data.

More Options

To assign worksheet protection, yet also allow changes to some cells, you must first unlock the cells before applying worksheet protection. To do so, select the cells and then click Format and Cells to open the Format Cells dialog box. Click the Protection tab and select the Locked check box (☐ changes to ☑) to clear the feature. You can now apply the Protect Sheet command and assign a password. In the Allow All Users of This Worksheet To list, select which elements you want users to be able to change.

WORKSHEET:
Show or Hide Gridlines

By default, every Excel worksheet you add includes gridlines. Gridlines help you differentiate between cells in your worksheets while creating a spreadsheet. However, gridlines may not be as important when sharing the worksheet with other users. For example, if you want to present your worksheet to your boss on-screen, you may prefer to view the data without the distracting gridlines. As more and more users share workbooks through networks and e-mail, controlling how data appears on-screen is an important part of presenting the spreadsheet information.

Gridlines are just one of several worksheet window formatting options you can control in Excel. You can turn the gridlines off for a particular sheet, and then turn them on again later when you need to add more data to your sheet. By default, gridlines do not print with your data unless you choose to print them.

See also>>

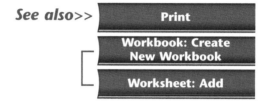

Print

Workbook: Create New Workbook

Worksheet: Add

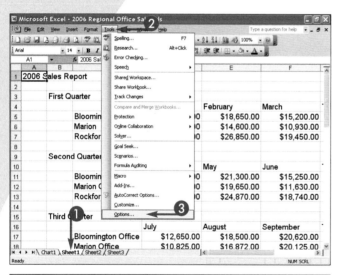

1 Click the sheet for which you want to hide gridlines.

2 Click Tools.

3 Click Options.

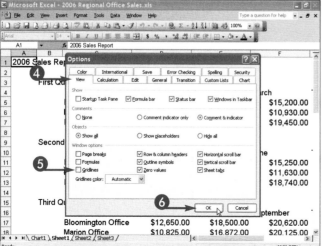

The Options dialog box opens.

4 Click the View tab.

5 Under Window options, deselect the Gridlines check box.

6 Click OK.

Excel turns off the worksheet gridlines.

To display the gridlines again, reopen the Options dialog box and select the Gridlines check box.

WORKSHEET:
Split a Sheet

You can view two different areas of a worksheet on-screen at the same time using the Split command. For example, you might want to view both the top and bottom of the worksheet to compare data. When you split panes in Excel, both areas of the split are scrollable.

You can split a sheet both vertically and horizontally in Excel. For example, if your worksheet is wider than it is long, splitting it into two vertical panes can help you view both sides of the sheet. If your worksheet is longer, you can use a horizontal split to view the top and bottom of the sheet at the same time.

Depending on where you click in the worksheet, you can split the sheet into two or four panes.

If you click a cell in the worksheet and apply the Split command, Excel splits the sheet into four panes. If you click a row or column, Excel splits the worksheet into two panes. Each pane is scrollable, allowing you to view different portions of the same worksheet. When you are ready to view the full sheet again, you can remove the feature.

See also>>

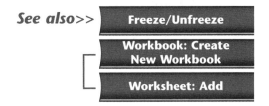

Freeze/Unfreeze

Workbook: Create
New Workbook

Worksheet: Add

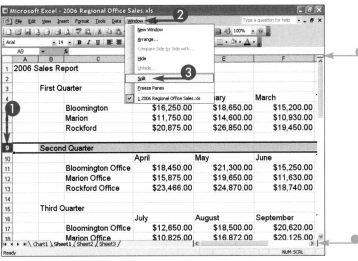

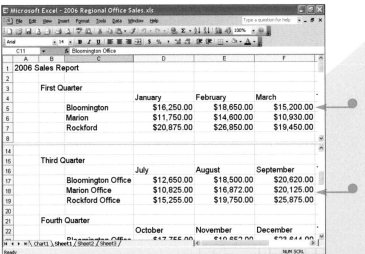

① Click to the right of the column or below the row you want to split.

If you want to split the sheet into four panes, click a cell.

② Click Window.

③ Click Split.

● You can also drag the split line on the scroll bar to split a sheet into two panes.

● Excel splits the worksheet into two scrollable areas.

Note: *To remove the split, click the Window menu and then Remove Split.*

ZOOM:
Change the View Magnification

The more data you add to a worksheet, the more difficult it may be to read the information in the cells. You can use Excel's Zoom controls to change how you view worksheet cells and data. For example, you may prefer to zoom in for a closer look, making the data easier to read on the computer screen. For a larger worksheet, you might want to zoom out to see more of the cells.

Excel's magnification settings are based on percentages. If you zoom your view to 50 percent, for example, you see much less detail and view more of the worksheet cells. If you zoom your view to 200 percent, you see your cell data close up. The

Zoom controls offer several preset magnification levels you can assign, or you can type in your own percentage to zoom.

When you zoom a view of your worksheet, the data does not print out at the magnified setting. Magnification does not affect printing.

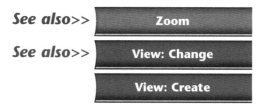

See also>> Zoom

See also>> View: Change

View: Create

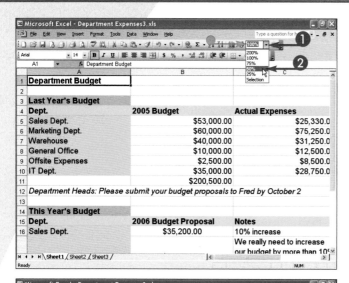

Magnify with the Zoom Button

1 Click the Zoom button's drop-down arrow.

2 Click a magnification setting.

● To enter a different percentage, type a value directly into the Zoom box.

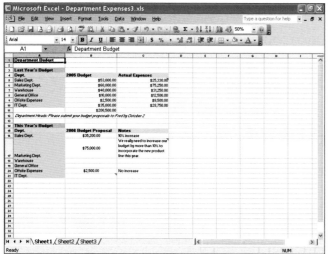

Excel immediately changes the magnification of the worksheet.

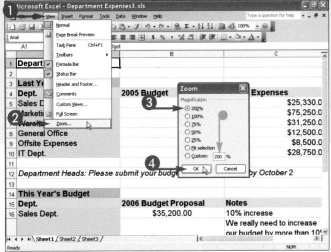

Magnify with the Zoom Dialog Box

1 Click View.

2 Click Zoom.

The Zoom dialog box appears.

3 Click a magnification setting.

● To enter a different percentage, type a value directly into the Custom box.

4 Click OK.

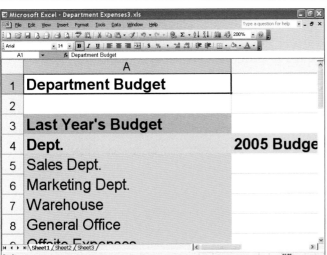

Excel immediately changes the magnification of the worksheet.

Did You Know?

If you want to print a worksheet showing a magnified view of the cells, you can use the scaling options located in the Page Setup dialog box. Click File and Page Setup to display the dialog box, and then click the Page tab to find the scaling options. If you scale the page to 150 percent, for example, you can enlarge the worksheet printout. To learn more about printing options, see the Print techniques.

More Options

If you use a mouse device with built-in scrolling and zooming, such as the Microsoft IntelliMouse, you can use the wheel to zoom in or out in your worksheet. To zoom in or out, press and hold the Ctrl key while rotating the wheel back and forth.

CHART:
Understanding Excel Charts

You can use charts to turn your Excel spreadsheet data into instant, persuasive visual presentations. A chart makes it easy for others to view patterns, trends, and comparisons in your spreadsheet data at a glance rather than reading the data in columns and rows. You can create dozens of different charts in Excel, from pie charts to bar charts, and more.

Any chart you create is linked to the data you used to build the chart. If you make changes to the original data, the chart updates to show the changes.

Data Series

The foundation of any chart is the worksheet data you use to create the chart. Called a *data series*, chart data is the content of a group of related cells, such as one row or column of data in your worksheet. For example, to make a pie chart of monthly household expenses, your worksheet data needs to consist of columns and rows tracking expenses such as electricity, gas, water, mortgage, groceries, and so on. You decide which cells to include in the chart and Excel's Chart Wizard can help you build a pie chart using the cells' content and labels.

Chart Plotting

Depending on the type of chart you create, a chart's plot area illustrates the data. Excel creates axis values and categories from the worksheet data you select for the chart. For example, perhaps you want to create a bar chart comparing the monthly sales of your company's sales staff. Your worksheet data shows a row of column labels for each month, and a column of names for each salesperson. Within the intersecting cells, your worksheet records the monthly sales for each person. When you turn that information into a bar chart, each salesperson's monthly sales are represented as a bar in the plot area of the chart. Data markers appear at major intervals on the axis, marking each value and comparing it with other salespeople.

In the example above, the X axis tracks each salesperson's monthly sales amounts, while the Y axis tracks each salesperson. The bar chart plot area displays each month's sales as a color bar on the chart, allowing you to compare the values between salespeople.

A chart's data marker represents a value from the worksheet cells you selected as the data series. The chart's major gridlines mark the major intervals on the axis.

Customize Charts

You can customize any chart you create in Excel. You can make changes to the formatting of the chart text, change the chart type, re-plot the data, and much more. You can angle text, change text color, or adjust the colors and patterns of the bars and lines displayed in a chart. You can also add new chart elements, such as callouts, labels, and titles.

Excel charts behave the same way as other objects you add to your worksheets, such as clip art, shapes, and WordArt objects. As such, you can move and resize charts as needed.

Chart Types

Excel offers 11 types of charts, and each type includes a variety of styles. You can use the table below to help choose the best chart for the type of data you want to present.

Chart Type	Description
Column charts	If you need to compare data in two or more categories, or show changes over time, column charts are a good choice.
Bar charts	Similar to column charts, bar charts display data horizontally instead of vertically.
Line charts	Line charts are similar to column charts, but instead of bars, the data series appears as dots on lines. This chart type is a good choice for showing changes across time.
Pie charts	If you need to show percentages of a whole, pie charts are a perfect way to present the data. You can also select from several pie chart styles, including 3-D.
Scatter charts	Use this chart type to show correlations between two value sets, one on the y-axis and the other on the x-axis.
Area charts	Another good choice for showing changes over time, an area chart emphasizes the individual contribution of each data part.
Doughnut	Use this chart type to compare multiple data series.
Radar	Radar charts allow you to depict separate axes for each data category radiating out from the center, like a spider web.
Surface	Use this chart type to show how three sets of data interact. This chart type is good for showing patterns in data.
Bubble	Similar to scatter charts, bubble charts use three columns of data; each data point indicates a third dimension.
Stock	This chart type is a good choice for tracking stock market activity.

Chart Elements

Charts are composed of a variety of elements. You can edit different elements to give you greater control of the visual representation.

Part	Description
Legend	Tells what each data series in your chart represents.
Chart title	Gives a headline to your chart.
Plot area	The background of your chart.
Value axis	The axis that lists values for the data series.
Value axis title	A headline identifying the value axis.
Category axis	The axis that lists categories for the data series.
Category axis title	A headline identifying the category axis.
Data series	The data you are plotting on a chart.

FORMULAS:
Operator Precedence

When you create equations in Excel, the order of operations determines the results. Excel performs a series of operations from left to right, giving some operators precedence over others. You can change the order of evaluation by enclosing any part of the formula you want Excel to calculate first in parentheses.

For example, if you want to determine the average of values in cells A2, B2, and C2, and you enter the equation =A2+B2+C2/3, you will calculate the wrong answer. This is because Excel divides the value in cell C2 by 3 and then adds that result to A2+B2. Following operator precedence, division takes precedence over addition. The correct way to write the formula is =(A2+B2+C2)/3. By enclosing the values in parentheses, Excel adds the cell values first before dividing them by 3. The following table lists the basic order of operator precedence.

Order	Description
First	All operations enclosed in parentheses
Second	Exponential equations
Third	Multiplication and division
Fourth	Addition and subtraction

If your formulas use nested parentheses, Excel tackles the calculations within the nested parentheses before the rest of the formula.

In the case of formulas that contain operators with the same precedence, such as both a multiplication and a division operator, Excel calculates the operators from left to right.

A common mistake Excel users make is forgetting to close a parenthetic term with a right parenthesis. Always check your formula for the correct number of parentheses.

The following table summarizes the complete order of precedence including all the operators:

Operator	Operation	Order of Precedence
:	Range	First
single space	Intersection	Second
,	Union	Third
-	Negation	Fourth
%	Percentage	Fifth
^	Exponentiation	Sixth
* and /	Multiplication and Division	Seventh
+ and -	Addition and Subtraction	Eighth
&	Concatenation	Ninth
= < > <= >= <>	Comparison	Tenth

FORMULAS:
Operators

You can use a variety of operators in Excel to write formulas and perform calculations. Operators simply specify the type of calculation you want to perform on the values and references in your formula. There are four types of operators you can use in Excel: arithmetic, comparison, text concatenation, and reference.

You can use arithmetic operators for basic operations, such as addition and subtraction. The following table lists the arithmetic operators:

Operator	Operation
+	Addition
-	Subtraction
*	Multiplication
/	Division
%	Percent
^	Exponentiation

You can use comparison operators to compare two values; the results are a logical value, TRUE or FALSE. For example, =C10>D10 or =E20<=F20. The following table lists comparison operators:

Operator	Operation
=	Equal to
<	Less than
<=	Less than or equal to
>	Greater than
>=	Greater than or equal to
<>	Not equal to

The ampersand (&) is the text concatenation operator. You can use it to join one or more text strings to produce a single piece of text. For example, if cell B5 contains the word "north," and cell H8 contains the word "pointe," the formula =B5&H8 would produce the result "northpointe."

You can use Excel's reference operators to control how a formula groups cells and ranges to perform calculations. For example, if your formula needs to include the cell range D2:D10 and the cell E10, you can instruct Excel to evaluate all the data contained in these cells using a reference operator. Your formula might look like this: =SUM(D2:D10,E10).

The table below lists reference operators:

Operator	Example	Operation
:	=SUM(D3:E12)	Range operator. Evaluates the reference as a single reference, including all the cells in the range from both corners of the reference.
,	=SUM(D3:E12,F3)	Union operator. Evaluates the two references as a single reference.
[space]	=SUM(D3:D20 D10:E15)	Intersect operator. Evaluates the cells common to both references.
[space]	=SUM(Totals Sales)	Intersect operator. Evaluates the intersecting cell(s) of the column labeled Totals and the row labeled Sales.

FORMULAS:
Understanding Formulas

Formulas are the backbone of Excel. You can use formulas to perform all kinds of calculations on your worksheet data. You can build formulas using mathematical operators, values, and cell references. For example, you can add the contents of a column of monthly sales figures to calculate the total number of sales, you can average a range of cells, or you can calculate the number of payments for a loan amount — all using formulas you write in Excel.

Formula Structure

Ordinarily, when you write a mathematical formula, you write out the values and the operators, followed by an equal sign, such as 5+5=. In Excel, formula structure works a bit differently. All Excel formulas begin with an equal sign (=), such as =5+5. The equal sign immediately tells Excel to recognize any subsequent data as a formula rather than as a regular cell entry. Any data following the equal sign becomes part of the formula's equation.

You can use Excel's Formula bar to enter and edit formulas. When you finish constructing a formula, Excel displays the final results in the cell, while displaying the formula itself in the Formula bar.

Operators

You can use operators to specify the types of calculations you want to execute in your formulas. You can perform basic mathematical operations using addition (+), subtraction (-), multiplication (*), and division (/) operators. For example, you can add two values together using a formula such as =5+9, or you can add the values in two cells using a formula such as =D4+E8.

In addition to arithmetic operators, you can also use comparative operators in Excel to compare values and evaluate results, such as =A5>B5 or =D12<=E12. You can also use reference operators to combine cells and ranges for calculations, such as =D6:D12,E12*2.

Excel performs a series of operations from left to right in a formula, which gives some operators precedence over others. To make sure Excel tackles your values in the order you want, you can group values in parentheses. Excel always calculates data within parentheses first. For example, if you want to multiply two cells and then add a value, your formula might look like this: =(A5*B5)+F5.

Reference Cells

Although you can enter specific values into your Excel formulas, you can also easily reference data in specific cells. For example, you can add two cells together or multiply the contents of one cell by a value. Every cell in a worksheet has a unique address, also called a cell reference.

By default, cells are identified by the specific column letter and then row number. For example, cell D5 identifies the fifth cell down in column D. To help make your worksheets easier to use, you can also assign your own unique names to cells. For example, if a cell contains a figure totaling weekly sales, you might name the cell Weekly_Sales.

A group of related cells in a worksheet is called a *range*. Cell ranges are identified by their anchor points, the upper-left corner of the range and the lower-right corner. The range reference includes both anchor points separated by a colon. For example, the range name A1:B3 includes cells A1, A2, A3, B1, B2, and B3. You can also assign unique names to your ranges to make it easier to identify their contents. Range names must start with a letter or underscore, and can include uppercase and lowercase letters. Spaces are not allowed in range names. Range names appear in the Name box, located to the left of the Formula bar.

You can also reference cells from other worksheets.

Absolute and Relative References

When you type a cell reference into a formula, Excel treats it as a relative reference rather than a set location in the worksheet. This makes it easy to copy the formula to other cells. For example, if you select cell A10 and type **=A8+A9**, and then copy the formula to cell B10, Excel adjusts the formula to read =B8+B9, keeping the references relative to the location of the formula.

You can use absolute referencing to always refer to a set location in the worksheet. For example, if you want the formula =A8+A9 to always refer to those cells, you can add dollar signs to the cell references to make them absolute, such as =$A$8+$A$9.

You can also use mixed references that contain both absolute and relative cell addresses in your formulas. For example, the reference $C6 keeps the column from changing, but the row is relative.

Formula Problems

If you enter any invalid information in a formula, such as the wrong operator or cell reference, Excel displays an error message. You can recheck the formula or use Excel's formula auditing tools to figure out how to fix a formula error.

Excel offers a wide variety of tools and techniques you can use to help monitor and correct problems you encounter with your formulas. For example, you can use the Formula Auditing toolbar to trace errors from the cell containing the formula to all the cells contributing values to the formula. You can use the Error Checking tool to locate and correct each formula problem in a worksheet.

FUNCTIONS:
Common Excel Functions

You can tap into a wide variety of built-in formulas in Excel, called *functions*. You can use functions as a speedier way to enter formulas. Functions are ready-made formulas that perform a series of operations on a specified range of values. Excel offers more than 300 functions you can use to perform mathematical calculations on your worksheet data.

Function Elements

Because functions are formulas, all functions must start with an equal sign (=). Functions are also distinct in that each one has a name. For example, the function that sums data is called the SUM function, while the function for averaging values is AVERAGE. You can type functions directly into your worksheet cells or use the Formula bar. You can also use the Insert Function dialog box to help construct functions. This dialog box offers help in selecting and applying functions to your data.

Construct Arguments

Functions typically use arguments to indicate the cell addresses upon which you want the function to calculate. Arguments are enclosed in parentheses. When applying a function to individual cells in a worksheet, you can use a comma to separate the cell addresses, such as =SUM(A5,B5,C5). When applying a function to a range of cells, you can use a colon to designate the first and last cells in the range, such as =SUM(B5:E12). If your range has a name, you can insert the name, such as =SUM(Sales).

Function Categories

You can choose functions for your worksheet calculations from 10 function categories. By grouping the functions, Excel makes it easier to track down the function you want to apply. The table below gives a description of each category.

Category	Description
Database & List Management	If you use Excel as a database program, you can use the database functions to count, add, and filter database items.
Date & Time	Includes functions for calculating dates, times, and minutes.
Engineering	This category offers all kinds of functions for engineering calculations.
Financial	Includes functions for calculating and tracking loans, principal, interest, yield, depreciation, and future values.
Information	Includes functions for testing your data.
Logical	Includes functions for logical conjectures, such as if-then statements.
Lookup & Reference	Use these functions to locate references or specific values in your worksheets.
Mathematical & Trigonometric	Includes a wide variety of functions for calculations of all types.
Statistical	This category includes functions for calculating averages, probabilities, rankings, trends, and more.
Text	Use these text-based functions to search and replace data and other text tasks.

Common Functions

Although Excel offers more than 300 functions to choose from, you may find yourself using several of the more common functions over and over again. Some functions, such as the SUM and AVERAGE function, prove quite handy with daily worksheet activities, while other functions may not be as popular with your spreadsheet needs.

The table below lists some of the more popular Excel functions you can use with your spreadsheet work.

Function	Category	Description	Syntax
SUM	Math & Trig	Adds up values	=SUM(number1,number2,...)
INT	Math & Trig	Rounds down to the nearest integer	=INT(number)
PI	Math & Trig	Finds the value of pi	=PI()
ABS	Math & Trig	Returns an absolute (positive) value of a number	=ABS(number)
ROUND	Math & Trig	Rounds a number specified by the number of digits	=ROUND(number,number_digits)
ROUNDDOWN	Math & Trig	Rounds a number down	=ROUNDDOWN(number,number_digits)
COUNT	Statistical	Returns a count of text or numbers in a range	=COUNT(value1,value2,...)
AVERAGE	Statistical	Averages a series of arguments	=AVERAGE(number1,number2,...)
MIN	Statistical	Returns the smallest value in a series	=MIN(number1,number2,...)
MAX	Statistical	Returns the largest value in a series	=MAX(number1,number2,...)
MEDIAN	Statistical	Returns the middle value in a series	=MEDIAN(number1,number2,...)
PMT	Financial	Finds the periodic payment for a fixed loan	=PMT(interest_rate,number_of_periods, present_value,future_value,type)
RATE	Financial	Returns an interest rate	=RATE(number_of_periods,payment, present_value,future_value,type,guess)
TODAY	Date & Time	Returns the current date	=TODAY()
DAYS360	Date & Time	Returns the number of days between two dates using a 360-day calendar	=DAYS360()
DCOUNT	Database	Counts the cells within a database field that match the criteria	=DCOUNT(database,field,criteria)
DGET	Database	Returns the records from a database that match the criteria	=DGET(database,field,criteria)
DSUM	Database	Finds the sum of a field's values that match the criteria	=DSUM(database,field,criteria)
CELL	Information	Returns information on the formatting, location, or contents of a cell	=CELL(infor_type,reference)
IF	Logical	Returns one of two results you specify based on whether the value is TRUE or FALSE	=IF(logical_text,value_if_true,value_if_false)
AND	Logical	Returns TRUE if all the arguments are true, FALSE if any are false	=AND(logical1,logical2,...)
OR	Logical	Returns TRUE if any argument is true, FALSE if all arguments are false	=OR(logical1,logical2,...)

KEYBOARD SHORTCUTS:
Apply Keyboard Shortcuts

You can use keyboard shortcuts in Excel to speed up your worksheet tasks. A *keyboard shortcut* is simply a key press or combination of key presses to activate a feature. Many shortcut keys involve pressing the Ctrl key while simultaneously pressing a designated shortcut key on the keyboard. You can also use the Function keys at the top of the keyboard to accomplish Excel tasks.

The table shown on these pages lists all the common keyboard shortcut keys you can use in Excel.

Keyboard Shortcut Keys	
Keys	**Action**
Ctrl+1	Displays the Format Cells dialog box
Ctrl+2	Applies or removes bold formatting
Ctrl+3	Applies or removes italic formatting
Ctrl+4	Applies or removes underlining
Ctrl+5	Applies or removes strikethrough
Ctrl+6	Alternates between hiding and displaying objects
Ctrl+7	Toggles the Standard toolbar display on and off
Ctrl+8	Displays or hides outline symbols
Ctrl+9	Hides a selected row
Ctrl+0	Hides a selected column
Ctrl+A	Selects an entire worksheet
Ctrl+B	Applies or removes bold formatting
Ctrl+C	Copies the selected data or cell
Ctrl+D	Applies the Fill Down command to copy the topmost cell in a range down the selected range
Ctrl+F	Displays the Find tab of the Find and Replace dialog box
Ctrl+G	Displays the Go To dialog box
Ctrl+H	Displays the Replace tab of the Find and Replace dialog box
Ctrl+I	Applies or removes italic formatting
Ctrl+K	Displays the Insert Hyperlink dialog box
Ctrl+L	Displays the Create List dialog box
Ctrl+N	Opens a new, blank workbook
Ctrl+O	Displays the Open dialog box
Ctrl+P	Displays the Print dialog box
Ctrl+R	Applies the Fill Right command to copy the leftmost cell in a range across the selected range
Ctrl+S	Saves a workbook file
Ctrl+U	Applies or removes underlining
Ctrl+V	Pastes cut or copied data, or inserts the contents of the Clipboard
Ctrl+W	Closes the current workbook
Ctrl+X	Cuts the selected cells or data
Ctrl+Y	Repeats the last command or action
Ctrl+Z	Applies the Undo command
Ctrl+(	Unhides hidden rows in the selected range

Keys	Action
Ctrl+)	Unhides hidden columns in the selected range
Ctrl+&	Applies an outline border
Ctrl+_	Removes an outline border
Ctrl+~	Applies the General number format
Ctrl+$	Applies the Currency number format
Ctrl+%	Applies the Percent number format
Ctrl+^	Applies the Exponential number format
Ctrl+#	Applies the Date format
Ctrl+@	Applies the Time format
Ctrl+!	Applies the Number format with two decimal places
Ctrl+-	Displays the Delete dialog box
Ctrl+*	Selects the data area around the active cell
Ctrl+:	Enters the current time
Ctrl+;	Enters the current date
Ctrl+`	Toggles between displaying and hiding formulas in cells
Ctrl+'	Copies a formula from the cell above to the active cell
Ctrl+Shift+"	Copies the formula results from the cell above to the active cell
Ctrl++	Displays the Insert dialog box
F1	Displays the Help task pane
Ctrl+F1	Displays and hides the current task pane
Alt+F1	Creates a chart using the current range
Alt+Shift+F1	Inserts a new worksheet
F2	Edits the active cell
Shift+F2	Edits a cell comment
F3	Pastes a defined name into a formula
Shift+F3	Displays the Insert Function dialog box
F4	Repeats the last command
Ctrl+F4	Closes the current workbook window
F5	Displays the Go To dialog box
Ctrl+F5	Restores the window size of the current workbook
F6	Switches to the next pane when viewing split panes
Shift+F6	Switches to the previous pane when viewing split panes
Ctrl+F6	Switches to the next workbook window
F7	Displays the Spelling dialog box
F8	Turns extend mode on or off for selecting a range
Alt+F8	Displays the Macro dialog box
F9	Calculates all worksheets in a workbook
F10	Selects the menu bar or closes an open menu
Shift+F10	Displays the shortcut menu for the selected item
F11	Creates a chart of the current range
Shift+F11	Inserts a new worksheet
F12	Displays the Save As dialog box

WORKSPACE:
Navigate the Excel Workspace

The Excel program window displays several common elements found in most programs, including a menu bar, toolbars, and scroll bars. In addition, the Excel window features a formula bar for entering mathematical formulas. The Excel worksheet itself appears in the center area of the program window. The intersecting columns and rows form cells which you can use to hold your worksheet data, including text, numbers, formulas, and more.

You can use several methods to move around an Excel worksheet. For example, you can move around using your mouse simply by clicking the cell in which you want to add or edit data. You can also use the keyboard arrows and Tab key to move from cell to cell or you can utilize a combination of both the mouse and keyboard. You can use the scroll bars to move around a large worksheet.

Title Bar and Menu Bar

The title bar appears at the very top of the program and displays the name of the open workbook file. Any time you save a workbook, the new filename appears in the title bar. The menu bar, located directly below the title bar, lists all the main menu groups found in Excel. When you click a menu, a drop-down list of commands appears.

Toolbars

Excel's toolbars display shortcut buttons to common Excel tasks. For example, you can click the Save toolbar button to quickly access the Save As dialog box, or click the Bold button to immediately assign bold formatting to a selected cell. By default, the Standard and Formatting toolbars share on-screen space at the top of the program window. You can choose to view each toolbar in full. In addition, Excel offers over a dozen other toolbars you can use for various tasks you perform in your worksheets.

Formula Bar

The formula bar is unique to Excel. You can use this bar to enter and edit formulas and perform calculations on your worksheet data. Whenever you click a cell in the worksheet, the formula bar displays the current cell contents or the formula associated with the cell. You can use the buttons on the bar to enter, cancel, or create functions.

Microsoft Excel - Book1

File   Edit   View   Insert   Format   Tools   Data   Window   Help

fx

Status Bar

The status bar appears at the very bottom of the Excel program window. The status bar displays information about the current worksheet or file, such as whether you are currently editing a cell.

Ready

Worksheet

The worksheet area appears in the middle of the program window. A worksheet consists of rows and columns that intersect to form cells. Cells hold your worksheet data, such as text and numbers, as well as any formula results. You can use the scroll bars located below and to the right of a worksheet to scroll through the worksheet cells.

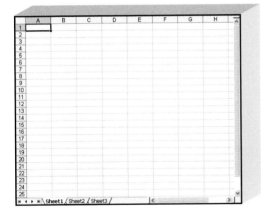

Task Pane

The task pane appears by default on the far right side of the program window. The task pane offers links to common program tasks. The task pane can display 11 panes of information or controls. For example, you can open a Help pane to look up information about using Excel, or you can open the Clip Art pane to search for clip art images. You can close the task pane to free up on-screen workspace.

Window Controls

You can use the window controls to control the appearance of the program window or the worksheet window. You can click any of the three buttons located in the top right corner of the title bar to minimize, maximize, or close the program window. You can use the worksheet window control buttons, located on the far right side of the menu bar, to minimize, maximize, or close the worksheet.

WORKSPACE:
Navigate the Excel Workspace (Continued)

Scroll Bars

You can use the worksheet scroll bars to navigate around a worksheet. Every worksheet includes both a vertical and a horizontal scroll bar. You can use the vertical scroll bar to scroll vertically up and down a worksheet. You can use the horizontal scroll bar to scroll left and right in a worksheet. You can click the scroll arrows located at either end of the bar to scroll, or you can drag the scroll box.

Worksheet Tabs

You can use worksheet tabs to view different worksheets in your workbook file. By default, every new workbook you create includes three worksheets. You can add and subtract sheets as needed. The current, or active, sheet's tab always appears highlighted.

\Sheet1 / Sheet2 / Sheet3 /

Worksheet Navigation Buttons

Worksheet Buttons	Action Performed
[I◄]	Scrolls to the first sheet in a workbook
[◄]	Scrolls to the previous sheet
[►]	Scrolls to the next sheet
[►I]	Scrolls to the last sheet in a workbook

Mouse Navigation

Mouse Action	Action Performed
Click a cell	Selects a cell
Click and drag across cells	Selects any cells you drag across
Double-click a cell	Selects a cell and inserts a cursor ready to enter or edit data
Double-click a cell border	Jumps to the corresponding cell
Click a row number	Selects the entire row
Click a column letter	Selects the entire column
Click and drag row numbers	Selects consecutive rows
Click and drag column letters	Selects consecutive columns

Keyboard Navigation

Keyboard Keys	Action Performed
→	Moves right one cell
←	Moves left one cell
↓	Moves down one cell
↑	Moves up one cell
Page Down	Moves down one screen
Page Up	Moves up one screen
Ctrl + End	Jumps to the lower-right corner of the working area
Ctrl + Home	Jumps to the first cell in a worksheet

Index

A

absolute references, formulas, 212, 393
Accept Changes dialog box, 67
active cells, 13
add
    3-D effect, objects, 252
    borders to cells, 114–115
    cells, 118–119
    columns, 17, 140
    comments, worksheets, 19
    decimals, 25
    footers, 282–283
    headers, 282–283
    misspellings, 102
    rows, 304
    shadows, 252
    subtotals, 170–171
    Watch Window, 354–355
    worksheets, 374
add-ins
    about, 2
    Analysis ToolPak, 90
    Data Analysis tools, 92–93
    find, 91
    install, 2, 90–91
    load, 90–91
    remove, 91
    Solver, 90, 94–95
    uninstall, 91
Add-Ins dialog box, 2, 90
advanced search, 319
Align Left command, 3
align objects, 253
alignment
    about, 3
    buttons, 3
    cell data, 96–97
    commands, 3
    Horizontal alignment, 3
Analysis ToolPak add-in, 90, 92–93
Applications tab, 379
apply
    cell formatting, 200–203
    conditional formatting, 204–205
    templates, 334–335
area charts, 389
arrange windows, workbooks, 364–365
arrow style, 210
arrows
    Drawing toolbar, 27
    formatting, 208–211
ASCII characters, 76
assign
    file properties, 294–295
    workbook passwords, 296–299
assistant shape, charts, 54
attachments, e-mail, 28
attributes, copy, 266–267
audit
    about, 4
    error checking, 98–101

AutoCalculate sum cells, 113
AutoCorrect
    about, 5, 72
    add misspelling, 102
    customize, 103
    delete words, 103
    spelling, 102–103, 327
AutoCorrect dictionary, 5
AutoFill
    about, 6
    customize, 105
    data series, 104
    number series, 105
AutoFill handle, 105
AutoFilter
    about, 7
    Custom View, 22
    filter database data, 106–107
AutoFormat
    about, 8
    customize, 109
    preset formatting, 108–109
AutoFormat dialog box, 8
AutoShapes
    about, 9
    customize, 111
    drawing, 110–111
AutoShapes palette, 9
AutoSum
    about, 10
    total data, 112–113
AutoSum function, 75
AVERAGE function, 39
axes titles, charts, 122

B

balloons, comment, 19
bar charts, 14, 389
Basic File Search task pane, 318–319
bold
    about, 11
    formatting, 206–207
Bold button, 11
borders
    about, 12
    add to cell, 114–115
    Custom Borders, 115
    draw on worksheets, 116–117
    erase border lines, 117
    Quick Borders, 114
Borders button, 12
bubble charts, 389
build functions, 220–223

C

canvas, 26, 54
CDs, install add-ins, 2

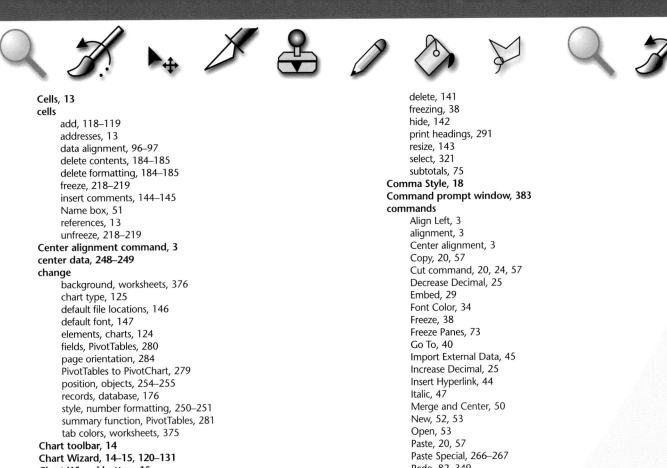

Cells, 13
cells
add, 118–119
addresses, 13
data alignment, 96–97
delete contents, 184–185
delete formatting, 184–185
freeze, 218–219
insert comments, 144–145
Name box, 51
references, 13
unfreeze, 218–219
Center alignment command, 3
center data, 248–249
change
background, worksheets, 376
chart type, 125
default file locations, 146
default font, 147
elements, charts, 124
fields, PivotTables, 280
page orientation, 284
PivotTables to PivotChart, 279
position, objects, 254–255
records, database, 176
style, number formatting, 250–251
summary function, PivotTables, 281
tab colors, worksheets, 375
Chart toolbar, 14
Chart Wizard, 14–15, 120–131
Chart Wizard button, 15
Chart Wizard dialog box, 15
charts
about, 120
axes scale, 120–121
axes titles, 122
change elements, 124
change type, 125
create, 126–129
customize, 388
data series, 123, 388
elements, 389
format elements, 130–131
plotting, 388
types, 389
X axis, 120
Y axis, 121
check errors, 98–101
clean cache, 387–389
clip art
about, 16
buying, 133
Clip Organizer, 138–139
download, 132–133
format, 134–135
insert, 136–137
view, 138–139
Clip Art task pane, 16, 77
close task panes, 33
Colors dialog box, 237
column charts, 389
columns
about, 17, 68
add, 140

delete, 141
freezing, 38
hide, 142
print headings, 291
resize, 143
select, 321
subtotals, 75
Comma Style, 18
Command prompt window, 383
commands
Align Left, 3
alignment, 3
Center alignment, 3
Copy, 20, 57
Cut command, 20, 24, 57
Decrease Decimal, 25
Embed, 29
Font Color, 34
Freeze, 38
Freeze Panes, 73
Go To, 40
Import External Data, 45
Increase Decimal, 25
Insert Hyperlink, 44
Italic, 47
Merge and Center, 50
New, 52, 53
Open, 53
Paste, 20, 57
Paste Special, 266–267
Redo, 82, 349
Remove Split, 73
Sort, 71
Split, 73
Toggle Total Row, 75
Undo, 82, 248
comments
about, 19
insert cell, 144–145
compare workbooks, 366
configure folders, 391–393
connect to server, Telnet client, 382–384
construct
arguments, 394
formulas, 214–215
Contents tab, 64
Contract button, 75
Control Panel, 394
control text wrap, 158–159
copy
attributes, 266–267
data, 160–161
formatting, 36
formulas, 216
worksheets, 377
Copy button, 20
Copy command, 20, 57
coworker shape, charts, 54
crop pictures, 268–269
Crop tool, 60
CSV file format, 69
Currency Style, 18, 21
Currency Style button, 21
Custom Borders, 115

Index

Custom tab, 64
Custom View, 22
Custom View dialog box, 22
custom views, 352–353
Custom Views dialog box, 353
Customize, 23
customize
    AutoCorrect, 103
    AutoFill, 105
    AutoShapes, 111
    cell comments, 144–145
    change default file locations, 146
    change default font, 147
    charts, 388
    create new menu, 148–149
    desktop themes, 389–391
    dialog box, 23
    menus, 152–153
    new toolbar, 150–151
    program windows, 154–155
    Taskbar, 380
    Text to Speech tool, 339
    toolbars, 156–157
    tracking, 345
Cut button, 24
Cut command, 20, 24, 57
cut data, 160–161

dash style formatting, 209
data
    alignment, 3
    center, 248–249
    control text wrap, 158–159
    copy, 160–161
    cut, 160–161
    dates, 162–163
    export, 233
    import, 232
    indent, 234–235
    link, 240–241
    merge, 248–249
    paste, 160–161
    rotate, 164–165
    shortcuts, 161
    times, 162–163
Data Analysis dialog box, 92
Data Analysis tools
    add-ins, 92–93
    functions, 92–93
    Help files, 93
Data Connection Wizard, 45
data entry tasks, 6
data series
    AutoFill, 104
    charts, 123, 388
data validation
    remove, 167
    set rules, 166–167
database
    add records, 168–169
    add subtotal, 170–171

    change records, 176
    create database table, 172–175
    data form, 168–169
    delete records, 177
    edit records, 176–177
    filter records, 178–179
    sort records, 180–181
database table, 172–175
dates, 162–163
dBASE, 30
DBF file format, 69
Decimal button, 182
decimals
    about, 25
    Decimal button, 182
    decrease decimal points, 182–183
    increase decimal points, 182–183
Decrease Decimal command, 25
decrease decimal points, 182–183
Decrease Indent button, 46
Default Messaging Programs options, 193
defaults
    location, save files, 308–309
    text alignment, 3
define print area, 285
delete
    cell contents, 184–185
    cell formatting, 184–185
    columns, 141
    database records, 177
    hyperlinks, 231
    objects, 256
    rows, 305
    Watch Window, 355
    words, AutoCorrect, 103
    workbook sheets, 378
    workbooks, 368
Delete Files dialog box, 388
desktop themes, 389–391
Device Manager window, 394
Diagram Gallery dialog box, 26, 54
diagrams
    about, 26
    insert, 186–187
dictionary, AutoCorrect, 5
Disk Cleanup, 386, 389
display
    task panes, 332
    toolbars, 340–341
Documents and Settings folder, 78
dollar signs, 21
doughnut charts, 389
downloads
    clip art, 132–133
    Microsoft Office Web site, 2
draw
    AutoShapes, 110–111
    borders on worksheets, 116–117
    objects, 188–189
    text boxes, 190–191
drawing space, 26
Drawing toolbar
    about, 9, 16, 27
    WordArt, 86

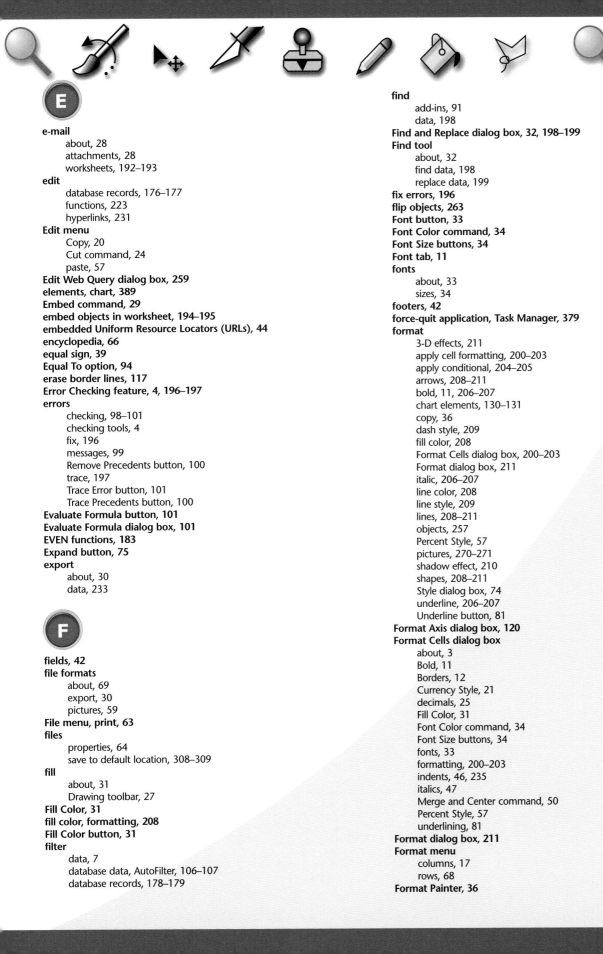

E

e-mail
    about, 28
    attachments, 28
    worksheets, 192–193
edit
    database records, 176–177
    functions, 223
    hyperlinks, 231
Edit menu
    Copy, 20
    Cut command, 24
    paste, 57
Edit Web Query dialog box, 259
elements, chart, 389
Embed command, 29
embed objects in worksheet, 194–195
embedded Uniform Resource Locators (URLs), 44
encyclopedia, 66
equal sign, 39
Equal To option, 94
erase border lines, 117
Error Checking feature, 4, 196–197
errors
    checking, 98–101
    checking tools, 4
    fix, 196
    messages, 99
    Remove Precedents button, 100
    trace, 197
    Trace Error button, 101
    Trace Precedents button, 100
Evaluate Formula button, 101
Evaluate Formula dialog box, 101
EVEN functions, 183
Expand button, 75
export
    about, 30
    data, 233

F

fields, 42
file formats
    about, 69
    export, 30
    pictures, 59
File menu, print, 63
files
    properties, 64
    save to default location, 308–309
fill
    about, 31
    Drawing toolbar, 27
Fill Color, 31
fill color, formatting, 208
Fill Color button, 31
filter
    data, 7
    database data, AutoFilter, 106–107
    database records, 178–179

find
    add-ins, 91
    data, 198
Find and Replace dialog box, 32, 198–199
Find tool
    about, 32
    find data, 198
    replace data, 199
fix errors, 196
flip objects, 263
Font button, 33
Font Color command, 34
Font Size buttons, 34
Font tab, 11
fonts
    about, 33
    sizes, 34
footers, 42
force-quit application, Task Manager, 379
format
    3-D effects, 211
    apply cell formatting, 200–203
    apply conditional, 204–205
    arrows, 208–211
    bold, 11, 206–207
    chart elements, 130–131
    copy, 36
    dash style, 209
    fill color, 208
    Format Cells dialog box, 200–203
    Format dialog box, 211
    italic, 206–207
    line color, 208
    line style, 209
    lines, 208–211
    objects, 257
    Percent Style, 57
    pictures, 270–271
    shadow effect, 210
    shapes, 208–211
    Style dialog box, 74
    underline, 206–207
    Underline button, 81
Format Axis dialog box, 120
Format Cells dialog box
    about, 3
    Bold, 11
    Borders, 12
    Currency Style, 21
    decimals, 25
    Fill Color, 31
    Font Color command, 34
    Font Size buttons, 34
    fonts, 33
    formatting, 200–203
    indents, 46, 235
    italics, 47
    Merge and Center command, 50
    Percent Style, 57
    underlining, 81
Format dialog box, 211
Format menu
    columns, 17
    rows, 68
Format Painter, 36

Index

Format Picture dialog box, 134
format styles, 8
Formatting toolbar, 50
Formula Auditing toolbar, 4, 37, 84
Formula bar, 65
formulas
    about, 392
    absolute references, 212, 393
    construct, 214–215
    construct arguments, 394
    copy, 216
    functions, 394–395
    operator precedence, 390
    operators, 391, 392
    problems, 393
    reference cells, 393
    reference cells from other worksheets, 217
    relative references, 213, 393
    structure, 392
freeze
    cells, 218–219
    panes, 218
Freeze command, 38
Freeze Panes, 38
Freeze Panes command, 73
Full Screen view, 83
full screen view, 350
functions
    about, 39
    build, 220–223
    Data Analysis tools, 92–93
    edit, 223
    formulas, 394–395

GIF files, 59
go to
    navigate cell or range, 224–225
    ranges, 301
Go To box, 51
Go To command, 40
Go To dialog box, 40
Go To Special dialog box, 40
Goal Seek tool, 41, 94, 226–227
Greek symbols, 76
group objects, 258

Header/Footer tab, 56
headers, 42
Help files, 93
Help pane, 43
Help tool, 228–229
Help tools, 43
hide
    columns, 17, 142
    rows, 306
    Taskbar, 380
    toolbars, 341
    worksheet gridlines, 384
    worksheets, 379
Highlight Changes dialog box, 80
Horizontal alignment, 3
hostname, 383
HTML file format, 69
hyperlinks
    about, 44
    delete, 231
    edit, 231
    insert, 230–231

import data, 232
Import External Data command, 45
Increase Decimal command, 25
increase decimal points, 182–183
Increase Indent button, 46
Indent, 46
indents
    data, 234–235
    Format Cells dialog box, 235
    Quick indent, 234
insert
    cell comments, 144–145
    diagrams, 186–187
    hyperlinks, 230–231
    organization charts, 264–265
    page break, print, 286
    picture files, 272–273
    special characters, 330–331
    symbols, 330–331
    WordArt, 362–363
Insert Clip Art button, 16
Insert Diagram button, 26, 54
Insert dialog box, 13
Insert Function dialog box, 39
Insert Hyperlink command, 44
Insert menu
    columns, 17
    rows, 68
Insert Object dialog box, 48
Insert Picture dialog box, 59
install add-ins, 2, 90–91
Internet Options dialog box, 387–388
Italic command, 47
italic formatting, 206–207

JPEG files, 59
JPG files, 59
justify cell data, 97

keyboard shortcuts, 396–397

L

languages, spelling, 327
layer objects, 259
Legend button, 14
line charts, 389
line color
    Drawing toolbar, 27
    formatting, 208
    set, 236–237
Line Color button, 134
line style
    formatting, 209
    set, 238–239
Line Style button, 134
line thickness, 27
linear charts, 14
lines
    Drawing toolbar, 27
    formatting, 208–211
link
    about, 48
    data, 240–241
load add-ins, 90–91
locate files, Temp folder, 384–387
lock
    columns, 38
    rows, 38

M

Macintosh, 30
Macro dialog box, 49
macros
    about, 49
    create, 242–243
    manage, 244
    run, 245
magnify, Zoom control, 386–387
manage
    files, Temp folder, 384–387
    macros, 244
margins, set page, 246–247
Margins tab, 56
menus, customize, 152–153
merge
    data, 248–249
    workbooks, 346–347
Merge and Center command, 50
messages, error, 99
Microsoft Encarta English dictionary, 66
MIcrosoft Office Online, 132
Microsoft Office Web site, 2
Microsoft online help files, 43
misspellings, 5
move
    objects, 260
    Taskbar, 381
    worksheets, 380
Move Items dialog box, 386

My Collections group, 138
My Computer, 78, 385

N

name
    ranges, 300
    worksheets, 381
Name box, 51, 65
navigate cell or range, 224–225
New button, 52
New command, 52, 53
new menu, 148–149
new toolbar, customize, 150–151
New Workbook task pane, 52, 53
Normal view, 83
number formatting
    change style, 250–251
    Comma Style, 18
    Currency Style, 21
number series, 105
numbers, subtotals, 75

O

Object dialog box, 29, 195
Object Linking and Embedding (OLE), 29, 48
objects
    about, 59
    add 3-D effect, 252
    add shadows, 252
    align, 253
    change position, 254–255
    delete, 256
    draw, 188–189
    flip, 263
    format, 257
    group, 258
    layer, 259
    move, 260
    resize, 261
    rotate, 262
    snap to grid, 255
ODD functions, 183
open
    folder automatically, 371
    workbooks, 369
    workbooks automatically, 370
Open command, 53
Open dialog box, 53
operator precedence formulas, 390
operators, formulas, 391, 392
Options dialog box, 23
Organization Chart toolbar, 26
organization charts
    about, 54
    insert, 264–265
    shapes, 54
Outlook, 193
ovals, 27

Index

P

Page Break Preview, 55
page breaks
    about, 55
    views, 351
page margins, set, 246–247
Page Setup dialog box, 42, 56
Page tab, 56
panes
    freeze, 218
    unfreeze, 219
passwords, assign workbook, 296–299
paste
    copy attributes, 266–267
    data, 160–161
    Paste Special command, 266–267
Paste button, 57
Paste command, 20, 57
Paste Special command, 266–267
Paste Special dialog box, 48
Patterns tab, 31
Percent Style, 18, 57
Picture toolbar, 60
pictures
    about, 59
    crop, 268–269
    format, 270–271
    insert files, 272–273
pie charts, 14, 389
PivotChart Report, 61
PivotTable Wizard, 61
PivotTables
    about, 61
    change fields, 280
    change summary function, 281
    change to PivotChart, 279
    create, 274–277
    refresh data, 281
    remove blank cells, 278
    remove error messages, 278
    update, 280–281
plotting charts, 388
PNG files, 59
positioning of data in cells, 3
Powerpoint, 194
preset formatting, AutoFormat, 108–109
preview
    page breaks, print, 287
    Web pages, print, 288
    worksheets, print, 289
print
    about, 62
    add footers, 282–283
    add headers, 282–283
    change page orientation, 284
    column headings, 291
    columns, 291
    define print area, 285
    insert page break, 286
    preview page breaks, 287
    preview Web pages, 288
    preview worksheets, 289
    row headings, 291
    set options, 292–293
    workbooks, 290
    worksheets, 290
Print button, 62
Print dialog box, 62
Print Preview, 63
Print Preview button, 63
problems, formulas, 393
program windows, customize, 154–155
properties, assign file, 294–295
Properties dialog box, 64
protect
    assign workbook password, 296–299
    worksheets, 382–383

Q

Quattro Pro, 30
Quick Borders, 114
Quick indent, 234
quick sort, 324

R

radar charts, 389
ranges
    about, 65
    cells, 13
    go to, 301
    Name box, 51
    naming, 300
    select, 320
Record Macro dialog box, 49, 242–243
rectangles, Drawing toolbar, 27
Recycle Bin, 387
Redo button, 82
Redo command, 82, 349
reference cells
    formulas, 393
    from other worksheets, 217
refresh data, PivotTables, 281
Reject Changes dialog box, 67
relative references, formulas, 213, 393
remove
    add-ins, 91
    blank cells, PivotTables, 278
    data validation, 167
    error messages, PivotTables, 278
    Taskbar, 382
Remove Precedents button, 100
Remove Split command, 73
reopen task panes, 333
replace data, Find tool, 199
Replace tool
    about, 32
    replace data, 199
Research task pane, 66, 302–303

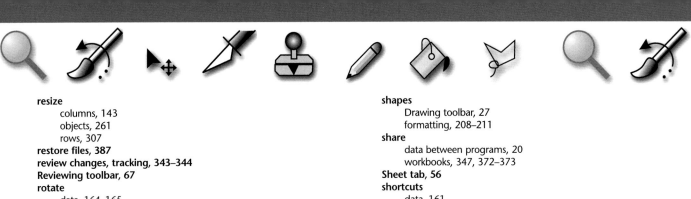

resize
    columns, 143
    objects, 261
    rows, 307
restore files, 387
review changes, tracking, 343–344
Reviewing toolbar, 67
rotate
    data, 164–165
    objects, 262
ROUNDUP functions, 183
rows
    about, 17, 68
    add, 304
    delete, 305
    freezing, 38
    hide, 306
    print headings, 291
    resize, 307
    select, 321
    subtotals, 75
run
    macros, 245
    Web Query, 356–359

save
    about, 69
    file to default location, 308–309
    Web Query, 359
    workbooks, 310–311
    worksheets as Web pages, 312–313
Save As dialog box, 30, 69
scatter charts, 121, 389
Scenario Manager dialog box, 317
Scenarios, 314–317
search
    Basic File Search task pane, 318–319
    Find and Replace, 32
    Research task pane, 66
select
    columns, 321
    ranges, 320
    rows, 321
    worksheet cells, 320–321
Select Data Source dialog box, 45
Selection zoom option, 87
selectors, cells, 13
set
    line color, 236–237
    line style, 238–239
    page margins, 246–247
    print options, 292–293
    rules, data validation, 166–167
Set Target Cell box, 94
Set Title dialog box, 313
Set Transparent Color tool, 60
shadow effects
    Drawing toolbar, 27
    formatting, 210

shapes
    Drawing toolbar, 27
    formatting, 208–211
share
    data between programs, 20
    workbooks, 347, 372–373
Sheet tab, 56
shortcuts
    data, 161
    Web toolbar, 85
show gridlines, worksheets, 384
Show Watch Window, 84
Shut Down menu, Task Manager, 379
Smart Tag icon, 101
smart tags
    about, 70
    turn off, 323
    view icon, 322
snap to grid, objects, 255
Solver add-in, 90, 94–95
Solver Parameters dialog box, 94
Solver Results dialog box, 94, 95
sort
    database records, 180–181
    quick sort, 324
    Sort dialog box, 325
Sort buttons, 71
Sort command, 71
Sort dialog box, 71, 325
special characters, insert, 330–331
Special Characters tab, 76
Spell Check tool, 72
spelling
    AutoCorrect, 102–103, 327
    languages, 327
    worksheets, 326
Spelling button, 72
Split command, 73
split worksheets, 385
Standard toolbar, 10
Statistics tab, 64
stock charts, 389
structure, formulas, 392
style, create, 328–329
Style dialog box, 74
subordinate shape, charts, 54
subtotals, 75
subtract decimals, 25
sum cells, 113
SUM function, 10, 39
superior shape, charts, 54
surface charts, 389
Symbol dialog box, 76, 330–331
symbols
    insert, 330–331
    insert special characters, 331
system, Task Manager, 378
System Properties dialog box, 394

Index

 T

Task Manager
about, 378
force-quit application, 379
Shut Down menu, 379
view system, 378
Task Pane, 77
task panes
close, 33
display panes, 332
reopen, 333
Taskbar
customize, 380
hide, 380
move, 381
remove, 382
Telnet client, 382–384
Temp folder
locate files, 384–387
manage files, 384–387
templates
about, 78
apply, 334–335
create, 336–337
Templates dialog box, 78, 335
Templates folder, 78
temporary Internet files, 387–389
text boxes, draw, 190–191
Text to Speech tool, 79, 338–339
Text to Speech toolbar, 79
themes, desktop, 389–391
thesaurus, 66
3-D Drawing toolbar, 27
3-D effects format, 211
thumbnails, 391–393
times, 162–163
Toggle Total Row command, 75
toolbars
customize, 156–157
display, 340–341
hide, 341
Web, 360–361
total data, AutoSum, 112–113
totaling cell contents, 10
Trace Error button, 101
trace errors, 197
Trace Precedents button, 100
track
merge workbooks, 346–347
review changes, 343–344
turn off, 345
turn on, 342–343
Track Changes, 80
troubleshooting wizards, 393–395
turn off
smart tags, 323
tracking, 345
turn on tracking, 342–343

 U

Underline button, 81
underline format, 206–207
Undo button, 82
Undo command, 82, 248
unfreeze
cells, 218–219
panes, 219
Unicode characters, 76
Uniform Resource Locators (URLs), 44
uninstall add-ins, 91
update PivotTables, 280–281

 V

view
clip art, 138–139
icon, smart tags, 322
Scenarios, 316–317
system, Task Manager, 378
views
custom, 352–353
Custom View, 22
full screen, 350
Full Screen view, 83
modes, 83
Normal view, 83
page breaks, 351
Task Pane, 77
Zoom tool, 87
Visual Basic Editor, 243

W

Watch Window
about, 38, 84
add, 354–355
delete, 355
Watch Window dialog box, 84
Web pages, save worksheets as, 312–313
Web Query
run, 356–359
save, 359
Web toolbar
about, 85
tools, 360–361
what-if analysis tools, 41
Windows Clipboard, 20
WordArt
about, 86
insert, 362–363
WordArt Gallery dialog box, 86
workbooks
arrange windows, 364–365
compare, 366

create, 367
delete, 368
delete sheet, 378
open, 369
open automatically, 370
open folder automatically, 371
print, 290
save, 310–311
sharing, 347, 372–373
worksheets
add, 374
adding comments, 19
change background, 376
change tab colors, 375
copy, 377
e-mail, 192–193
hide, 379
hide gridlines, 384
move, 380
name, 381
print, 290

protect, 382–383
save as Web pages, 312–313
select cells, 320–321
show gridlines, 384
spelling, 326
split, 385

XLS file extension, 69

Zoom button, 63, 87
Zoom dialog box, 87, 386–387
Zoom tool
about, 87
magnify, 386–387

Read Less–Learn More®

There's a Visual book for every learning level...

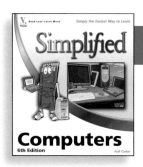

Simplified®

The place to start if you're new to computers. Full color.

- Computers
- Mac OS
- Office
- Windows

Teach Yourself VISUALLY™

Get beginning to intermediate-level training in a variety of topics. Full color.

- Computers
- Crocheting
- Digital Photography
- Dreamweaver
- Excel
- Guitar
- HTML
- Knitting
- Mac OS
- Office
- Photoshop
- Photoshop Elements
- PowerPoint
- Windows
- Word

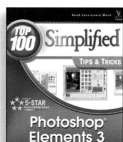

Top 100 Simplified® Tips & Tricks

Tips and techniques to take your skills beyond the basics. Full color.

- Digital Photography
- eBay
- Excel
- Google
- Internet
- Mac OS
- Photoshop
- Photoshop Elements
- PowerPoint
- Windows

Build It Yourself VISUALLY™

Do it yourself the visual way and without breaking the bank. Full color.

- Game PC
- Media Center PC